SATHER CLASSICAL LECTURES
Volume Forty-five

CHANGE AND DECLINE

CHANGE AND DECLINE

ROMAN LITERATURE
IN THE
EARLY EMPIRE

by GORDON WILLIAMS

UNIVERSITY OF CALIFORNIA PRESS

Berkeley · Los Angeles · London

PA6042
W54x

UNIVERSITY OF CALIFORNIA PRESS
BERKELEY AND LOS ANGELES, CALIFORNIA

UNIVERSITY OF CALIFORNIA PRESS, LTD.
LONDON, ENGLAND

Contents

vi   Contents

Preface

ONE of the most pleasurably memorable experiences
of my life was the delivery of the Sather Classical Lectures in
April, May, and June of 1973. Everything conspired to enjoyment: the physical surroundings, the climate, the friendly
hospitality of colleagues, and—by no means least—the large,
faithful audience that displayed its interest by many questions.
Those questions were both critically helpful and of such a kind
as to show that reflections on the problems I was discussing
prompted my listeners to see analogies not only in other cultures and periods, but, very emphatically, also in their own. I
very greatly profited from and enjoyed all such discussions; if
I have been careful to avoid analogies (even the now very popular
analogy with Mannerism) that is due to lack of knowledge and
confidence, not to lack of interest and stimulus.

I have taken the opportunity, in preparing the lectures for
the printer, to make some changes in format; in particular, I
have greatly extended the range of quotation, in the belief that
most of these writers are more talked of than read. I have translated all quotations into a prose that is designed to help with
understanding the Latin or Greek rather than to be read for its
own sake; this I did in the hope of making the subject as accessible as possible to students of other disciplines. Footnotes have
been kept to a bare minimum: they are less designed to acknowledge debts than to give the reader information. Some debts are

acknowledged in the Select Bibliography; but that is inadequate for my constant indebtedness to great books, like those, for instance, of Friedlaender, Eduard Norden, Ronald Syme, A. D. Leeman, or George Kennedy. Those (and others) are works that pass into the bloodstream of anyone who studies this period. The main intention of the Select Bibliography is to make it easy to trace works mentioned briefly in the notes; but I have also added—in an admittedly random fashion—works that I am conscious helped me, in one way or another, to reach a point of view. Study of the period has been greatly helped by scholars who have published surveys of the scholarly work done in various fields; I have tried to include most of these also. However, I have only been able to notice work published later than 1972 in a very restricted and random way.

My warm thanks must go to colleagues and friends in the Classics Department at Berkeley. Especially I thank Bill Anderson, who was chairman when I was there and who constantly helped me, with unfailing kindness. Those who have spent time at Berkeley will instantly understand the warmth of my gratitude to Kendrick and Betty Pritchett for their generous hospitality and for their constant thoughtful anticipation of difficulties that strangers in Berkeley might encounter. I acknowledge, too, the skilled and experienced help which I was most generously given by Bennett Price, who was my research assistant during my stay in Berkeley. His interest in, and knowledge of, rhetorical theory were invaluable to me. I am also greatly indebted to my old friend and colleague John Simon, who helped me in many ways and not least in correcting the proofs.

New Haven   G. W.
May 1976

Introduction

THE so-called Silver Age of Roman literature compels a critic's attention, and judgements on it have been increasingly favourable of late. This is not surprising, since the tastes and standards of our own time seem to have been changing in a way that has made them coincide more and more with those implicit in much of the literature of the early Empire. But it is worrying, since it suggests a highly subjective approach to the literature of the past. Has literary history any value under such conditions? Is it even possible?

Faced with the problem of characterizing and explaining the literary culture of a period, a critic may be tempted by two extreme positions: the one is permissive, in the sense that each writer is judged on his own terms and by reference to nothing outside his own work (it is almost a case of 'anything that is, is good'); the other is hierarchical, and clings to the ideal of objective criteria to be applied rigorously and impartially to all writers, with the aim of arranging them, like candidates in an examination, in an order of merit. From the latter point of view, the literature of the early Empire is 'silver' to the 'gold' of the previous period, and decline is obvious. To the former type of critic no qualitative judgement is possible; all writers have their own peculiar virtues, and if literary history has any function, it is to record a process of change in which the question of decline is simply irrelevant. But this latter extreme involves abdication of responsibility and leads to critical solipsism (which has almost become a characteristic of modern critical work on the period); the former is dictatorial and ultimately tends to reduce itself to meaningless labels. For in cultural history change involves growth and decay, and it is the predominance of particular types of growth or of decay that gives a period its cultural character. Neither critical procedure will serve to analyze that character. In what follows, I have not attempted an overall, unified portrait of the age. Instead, I have asked a series of questions which require different routes of approach into the literature of the period. Consequently, each of the six lectures is, to some extent, independent, and each approaches the problem of what happened to Roman literary culture in the early Empire from a different direction.

The writers of the period themselves expressed pessimistic views of a decadent culture. From the vantage of hindsight, I think that their pessimism was justified, but I have been concerned to examine their causal explanations to see if they have anything to contribute to modern understanding of the period. In general, I find that they relied too much on outworn and conventional categories of explanation (particularly on the insidiously attractive and rhetorically useful category of moral decline). There was, however, the very important exception of Tacitus; and a large part of the first lecture is therefore devoted to a detailed analysis of the *Dialogus de oratoribus*. Tacitus was not prone to simple exposition of a point of view, and in this he was only doing justice to the extreme complexity of historical explanation; but this makes it very difficult for the reader to discern and order the views that Tacitus was expressing, and a work like the *Dialogus* is a particularly subtle web of nuance and suggestion. The results of such an analysis cannot be simply tabulated; and there is much to be said for allowing the ideas to emerge from the sheer process of dialectical engagement with the work (as if it were a poem). But a limited optimism is clear in Tacitus in favour of literature that has two characteristics. The first is negative: literature cannot be like oratory; that is, it cannot depend on the capacity to persuade an audience *viva voce* on vital issues of the moment. The second is that it must be related to the type of imaginative literature that maintains a close link with real events in contemporary society. The model is the outmoded dramatic work of Maternus; the unstated example is probably Tacitus' own historiographical activity. What most strongly emerges from the *Dialogus*, however, is the vital nature of the link between literature and real life, a link that was missing in most of the literature of the early Empire.

Perhaps the most important new feature of the Augustan literary scene (and it is one which is implicitly represented in the *Dialogus* in the attractive figure of Curiatius Maternus) was the close integration of literature with society and politics, and the consequently inevitable confrontation with the personality of the emperor. This posed new and desperate problems for the writer, and these became acute in the early Empire. In the second lecture I have analyzed this increasingly tense dilemma of the literary artist in the paradigmatic figure of Ovid, who was not only a poet of enormous, even paramount, influence on the writers of the early Empire, but also one whose own career foreshadowed the perils of their situation. Essentially, all later writers up to the age of Trajan found themselves caught in Ovid's dilemma and fell back on the solutions he had devised—though he had devised them too late to save himself. His solutions were basically three modes of escapism: into Greek mythology, into a safe antiquarianism, and into ingenious panegyric of the emperor. All involved, almost inevitably, a retreat from reality. Most succeeding writers chose one, or a combination, of these modes.

In the third lecture I examine the problem of the relationship between Greek and Roman culture. As I see it, *Graecia capta ferum victorem cepit* is true in a sense that Horace probably did not intend: Greek culture came, during the early Empire, to dominate Roman culture and to induce a paralyzing sense of inferiority in Roman writers—to such an extent that they ended by actually preferring Greek as the language of literary composition. My view is that this increasing dominance of Greek culture was a powerful—and largely unrecognized—factor in Roman literary decline. But it was just one factor among many.

The fourth lecture is concerned to analyze a peculiar phenomenon in the literature of the period which was manifested in a range of ways: from failure of intellectual nerve and a consequent reliance on various forms of irrationality on the one hand to a widespread obsession with the macabre and the sensational on the other. The common feature in all of these related manifestations was a readiness in writers to favour emotion and appeals to the emotions over reason and rationality. I have tried to analyze various ways in which the intellectual strength that characterized writers of the Augustan age collapsed under new strains imposed by the imperial system no less than under that itch for novelty which itself grew up in response to social and political changes. Here cause and effect are particularly difficult to separate.

In the fifth lecture I have attempted an analysis of the more directly stylistic changes that distinguish the literature of the early Empire from that of the Augustan age; and in doing this I have tried to relate such changes to general changes in what writers regarded as, or assumed to be, the function of literature. It is my view that the changed conception of the function of literature was bound, in the end, to be self-defeating and to lead to frustration, and even to hysteria, in the effort to satisfy the demands (often self-imposed) which increased at each new literary attempt.

The approach of the sixth lecture is to pose the general question of the ways in which literature fulfilled a social function in the period. It becomes clear in the course of this analysis that the period was not homogeneous, and that at least three periods, each with different characteristics, can be distinguished. But, by asking social questions about the literature, it has been possible, to some extent, to draw in points of view derived from the earlier lectures. This I have tried to do; but it must be said that any attempt at a tabulation of results would be facile and false.

Each of the approaches, while to some extent enmeshed with all the others, opens up a point of view that needs to be considered in its own terms and that resists easy assimilation to the others—and that is a large part of the difficulty (and the fascination) of this type of literary enquiry. In pursuing it, I have come increasingly to admire and understand the methods, and even the evasions (as some critics would see them), of Tacitus in his *Dialogus de oratoribus*.

Still, in the end, values need to be asserted explicitly. A work may be made to seem perfectly adequate, even meritorious, if one sympathetically takes into account the intentions of the author, the literary conditions of the time, the demands that were made on him, and so on. But the more these factors are required to appreciate the work, the surer is the decline from an age when writers either ignored these factors or adapted them to suit themselves. Yet values are not divinely revealed and immutable: they change. In my view, however, the changes in values in the period of the early Empire were largely imposed by factors extraneous to literature. Writers adapted themselves and their values not only to fear, but also to the desire to impress, to a sense of the superiority of Greeks no less than to that of great Roman predecessors, to irrationality and sensationalism, and to a wistful romantic escapism. Writers were certainly subjected to all the controls of terror, but it was not just for that reason that they showed more interest in confronting audiences than issues. Some made adaptations with success; but, in general, the proportion of decline involved in the adjustment of values steadily increased until the sense of belonging to a living tradition was completely lost, and Roman writers, vainly imitating Greek predecessors, groped back into the most remote past to find, at any price, some shred of novelty. That is not just change: that is decline.

I

Contemporary
Analyses
of Decline

THERE is a powerful unanimity among Roman writers of the early Empire: most of them (including some of the greatest Roman writers) express the feeling that they live in a period of cultural decadence.[1] Theories of decline have a masochistic charm at most periods, but there are two special reasons —beyond the unanimity of their feelings—for taking these Roman writers seriously. The first lies in the curious fact that these diagnoses of decline began to be expressed very soon after the age of Augustus, which was a period of great cultural revival and optimism. It is surprising to find that confidence collapsing so soon. The second reason is that Roman literature did in fact run out into the sands of the so-called archaizing movement in the second century A.D.—this represented a relapse into admiration and imitation of the archaic period of Roman literature. Its beginnings can already be detected in the first century A.D., and it is a particularly peculiar phenomenon in that, unlike its contemporary Greek counterpart, it did not represent a return

1. A good general introduction to the topic is H. Caplan (1944). A useful collection of texts in translation with helpful comment is D. A. Russell and M. Winterbottom (1972).

to the great age of Roman literature but to its rough and primitive origins. There was, therefore, a complete collapse of the ideals and confidence that marked the great Classical age of Roman literature in the late Republic and the age of Augustus.

The most important document of this decline (though it is no document at all, but a highly artistic and difficult work) is the *Dialogus de oratoribus* of Tacitus. But first it is worthwhile considering the views of some other writers. Broadly speaking, there were three explanations of decline: there was the explanation in terms of morals; there was the explanation in terms of political change; and there was the explanation that posited a fundamental law of growth followed by inevitable decline. These explanations were differently formulated and treated by different writers.

1. The elder Seneca

Lucius Annaeus Seneca had been born in Corduba in Spain about 55 B.C.; he died between A.D. 37 and 41. In his old age he dedicated a remarkable book, entitled *Oratorum sententiae divisiones colores*,[2] to his three sons, Annaeus Novatus (later governor of Achaea), L. Annaeus Seneca (the philosopher), and M. Annaeus Mela (the father of Lucan). In it he recalls verbatim speeches which he had heard up to forty and fifty years previously (his memory used to be good, he says, and 'if two thousand names were read out I could repeat them in the exact order').[3] The tone of the book is nostalgic: 'I must confess that it is a pleasure for me to return to my old studies and look back to better years, and, when the three of you complain that you were not able yourselves to hear the famous men of that period, for me to clear away the destruction done by time'.[4] He goes on then to say:[5] 'Everything that Roman oratory has to match the arro-

---

2. References will be made to the Loeb edition by Michael Winterbottom (1974).

3. *controversiae* 1 *pr.* 2.   4. *contr.* 1 *pr.* 1.

5. *contr.* 1 *pr.* 6–7.

gant Greeks (or even outdo them) reached its peak in Cicero's day:[6] all the geniuses who have brought distinction to our subject were born then. Since that time things have got worse daily. Perhaps this is due to the luxury of our age (nothing is so fatal to talent as luxury). Perhaps, as this great art became less highly valued, competitiveness was transferred to sordid business that brings great prestige and profit. Perhaps it is just Fate, whose grim law is universal: things that reach the top sink back again to the bottom even faster than they rose'.[7] At this point the old man loses his temper and berates the younger generation for a page or so with sentiments like these:[8] 'Waving the hair, thinning the tone of the voice till it is as caressing as a woman's, competing in bodily softness with women, beautifying themselves with indecent cosmetics. . . . Which of your contemporaries is enough of a man? Born feeble and spineless, they stay like that all through their lives, destructive of others' chastity, careless of their own. . . '. He goes on to recall Cato's definition of the orator as *vir bonus dicendi peritus*, 'a man of high moral character who is a skilful speaker', and therefore to deny the title of 'orator' to any of the present generation.

Clearly Seneca the elder has, without explicitly saying so, opted for the moral explanation of decline. He puts it in the form that character has been undermined by the luxury-loving habits of the age. It was a common theme in Augustan writers that greed for wealth had caused the downfall of the last generation of the Republic and that Rome's hope of salvation lay in restraint and reform. But there had been no question of cultural decline, and, while the tone of these writers had indeed held warning, it had been optimistic. Yet here is Seneca the elder condemning the generation that had grown up in the last years of Augustus as decadent in character and deficient in literary culture. His view is of a steady decline beginning from

6. This idea was already expressed by Cicero in *Brutus* 254.
7. This idea too had already been expressed by Cicero, e.g., *Tusc. Disp.* 2. 5.
8. *contr.* 1 *pr.* 8–10.

Cicero's death in 43 B.C., continuing through the age of Augustus, and reaching a nadir in the time of Tiberius.

He tacitly rejects two other explanations: the idea of a universal law of growth and decline, and a political explanation, which is only given a vague outline.[9] Seneca says *sive, cum pretium pulcherrimae rei cecidisset, translatum est omne certamen ad turpia multo honore quaestuque vigentia*; literally 'perhaps, after the value of the most beautiful thing had dropped, all effort was transferred to disgraceful things that yet are highly esteemed and profitable'. By 'the most beautiful thing' he means oratory; and when he speaks of its value dropping he must refer to the fact that the value of oratory fell when control of the state passed into the hands of one man (Augustus, and then Tiberius), with the result that occasions on which a gift for oratory could be publicly exercised and could really influence decisions were greatly restricted. Cicero's whole career had been founded on his oratory. That could no longer happen. Both the vagueness of the language, however, and the brevity of treatment suggest that he attached as little importance to this explanation as to the concept of a universal law. It was, of course, a delicate subject, especially under Tiberius, and the very fact of his mentioning it at all suggests that bolder spirits had freely speculated that among disadvantages of the principate was an inevitable decline in oratory.[10]

2. *Velleius Paterculus*

This ex-army officer turned historian was not among the bolder spirits. Adulation of Tiberius and of adherents such as Sejanus mark his work,[11] a historical compendium called *His-*

---

9. For a similar point (also vaguely expressed) in Longinus, see below.

10. Seneca reports (*suas.* 7. 1) that Quintus Haterius (*cos.* 5 B.C.) advised Cicero in a *suasoria*: 'My advice, Cicero, would have been to rate your life highly if freedom is to hold its place in the state, if eloquence is to hold its place in a free state [literally: in freedom]. . .'. But this was in a private and highly artificial exercise. Haterius was no bold spirit, as appears from Tacitus *Annals* 1. 13.

11. See especially Syme (1939) 488–89.

toriae Romanae. Its style exhibits many of the faults condemned by the elder Seneca, and signs of hurried composition and triviality are everywhere. The work must have been published before the fall of Sejanus in A.D. 31 and belongs therefore more or less to the same period as that of the elder Seneca. Velleius had the novel idea of putting digressions on literary topics into his history: two deal with the early period of Roman literature (2. 9) and with the Ciceronian and Augustan periods (2. 36). He mentions Ovid, but the quality of his literary judgement is fairly indicated by his regarding Virgil and Rabirius as on the same literary level. In a third digression (1. 16–17) he ponders on the problem of decline. He has, it appears, constantly worried over the problem of why great geniuses come crowded together in brief periods. He decides that there is an inevitable law of decline in operation such that for each artistic form a brief period of greatness can be identified, associated with a galaxy of talent, and this is then followed by a period of decline. Velleius recognizes that he himself is living in a period of decline. This formulation of the problem, unlike that of the elder Seneca, who was thinking only of oratory, is applied by Velleius to all types of literature and indeed art—in fact to culture in general.

3. *Petronius*

Several passages in the novel of Petronius deal with the topic of cultural decline.[12] At the opening of the fragmentary text (1–4), Encolpius, the narrator, is found wildly declaiming against declaimers whose subject matter, he says, is sheer fantasy and whose style is windy, turgid, and loquacious. Agamemnon, a rhetor, agrees with him and makes more explicit the explanation underlying Encolpius' wild language: it is that morals have declined—parents are to blame and educationists. A more interesting passage on the question of cultural decline in general

---

12. For his identification and date, see chap. VI, sect. 4.

occurs later in the novel, where Encolpius questions a very odd
old poet, Eumolpus, about 'the decadence of the age' (88):

Stimulated by this conversation, I began to draw on his greater
knowledge about the age of the paintings and some of the legends
which were obscure to me and at the same time to examine the
cause of the present decadence when the fine arts had died out al-
together and painting had not left even the smallest trace of its
existence. 'Love of money', he replied, 'began this revolution. For
in olden times, when Virtue was still loved for her own sake, the
arts all flourished and men's greatest efforts were spent on discov-
ering anything that might be of benefit to future ages. So you find
that Democritus extracted the juice of every plant and spent his
whole life on experiments to reveal the special values of rocks and
plant life. Eudoxus, again, grew old on the top of the highest
mountain to find out the movements of the stars and the heavens,
and Chrysippus three times purged his mind with doses of helle-
bore just to maintain his inventive powers. But, to turn to sculp-
tors, Lysippus died of starvation as he brooded over the lines of
a single statue; and Myron, who pretty well caught the souls of
men and of animals in bronze, found no one to carry on his work.
We, on the other hand, are submerged in wine and women; we
do not deign to understand even the arts that have been discovered, but, slandering the past, ourselves learn and teach nothing
but vice. Where do you find dialectic now? Astronomy? Where is
that most civilized path of philosophy? Have you ever seen anyone
going into a temple and pledging an offering if only he may attain
to eloquence, or drink at the fountain of philosophy? They do not
even pray for sanity and good health, but, before even reaching the
Capitol's entrance, one is promising an offering if he can bury a
rich relative, another if he can dig up some treasure, another if he
can make a few millions and live. You find even the senate, that
exemplar of the Right and the Good, promising a thousand pounds
in gold to the Capitol, fixing Juppiter himself up with some cash—
an example designed to prevent anyone feeling shame at lusting
for money. So do not be surprised at the extinction of the art of
painting, when not only men but all the Gods too think an ingot
of gold more beautiful than anything that Apelles or Pheidias,
poor crazy Greeklings, produced'.

The poet's view is that decadence has affected science and all
the arts. His explanation is a version of the moral one: decad-

ence is due to greed for money and to excesses in wine and women. Since views expressed by characters in Petronius' novel often seem to be parodies of contemporary ideas,[13] it may be assumed that both the feeling of living in a decadent age and the moral explanation of its causation were hackneyed contemporary topics. In fact, the close coincidence of both passages in Petronius with the next couple of views to be examined underpins the case for detecting well-directed satire in Petronius.

4. *The younger Seneca*

The date of Petronius' novel is uncertain,[14] but the likeliest view is that it was written about A.D. 60. He was forced to commit suicide in A.D. 66 as a result of the same conspiracy against Nero that forced the suicide of the younger Seneca. The topic of decadence was of great interest to Seneca, and he treated it in many passages and from several points of view. In his *Natural Questions*, written about A.D. 60, he laments the decline of scientific research in terms somewhat similar to those of the elder Pliny, but in a much more plangently moralizing tone.[15] But his most important statement on the subject comes in the *Moral Epistles*, addressed to Lucilius and written probably in the years A.D. 62 to 65. In letter 114 he poses the problem in this form (1):

> Quare quibusdam temporibus provenerit corrupti generis oratio quaeris et quomodo in quaedam vitia inclinatio ingeniorum facta sit, ut aliquando inflata explicatio vigeret, aliquando infracta et in morem cantici ducta: quare alias sensus audaces et fidem egressi placuerint, alias abruptae sententiae et suspiciosae, in quibus plus intellegendum esset quam audiendum: quare aliqua aetas fuerit quae translationis iure uteretur inverecunde?

13. On this, see Index s.v. 'Petronius'.
14. See chap. VI, sect. 4.
15. Especially *Nat. Quaest.* 7. 31–32. The passage is close to Pliny in some respects, but it is much closer to what is parodied by Petronius (88). It is a much less sophisticated formulation than that in the *Epistles to Lucilius* and uses many of the details used by his father; in fact the passage is about halfway between Seneca the elder and *Epistle* 114.

You question why at certain periods there has appeared a corrupt literary style and how certain vices have become fashionable
with great writers—so that at one time expansive bombast has been
the custom, at another an emasculated, song-like style. Why at one
time have extravagantly incredible ideas found favour, at another
abrupt allusive sayings in which one had to understand more than
one heard? Why was there a time when there was a quite im-
moderate use of metaphor?

The very lengthy answer to this problem, supposed to have
been posed by Lucilius, takes the form of a sermon on the text
talis hominibus fuit oratio qualis vita 'as a man's life is, so is his
style'—originally a Greek proverb. Seneca starts with an attack
on Maecenas for effeminacy, for sloppiness in clothing, and for
immorality in general. He uses very much the same terms that
his father had used to attack the new generation.[16] He then goes
on very ingeniously to use the same terms that he had used to
criticize Maecenas' morals to criticize various quotations from
Maecenas' writings so that an almost exact correspondence is
asserted linguistically between life and literary style.

From Maecenas, Seneca generalizes the analysis to the whole
age (11):

> itaque ubicumque videris orationem corruptam placere, ibi
> mores quoque a recto descivisse non erit dubium. quomodo con-
> viviorum luxuria, quomodo vestium aegrae civitatis indicia sunt,
> sic orationis licentia, si modo frequens est, ostendit animos quoque,
> a quibus verba exeunt, procidisse.

> Accordingly wherever you find a corrupt literary style in favour,
> there you can be certain that morals too have deviated from the
> right path. Luxury in banqueting and in clothing is evidence of
> a sick society; so too a licentious literary style, once it is wide-
> spread, is evidence that the minds by which it is produced are
> decadent.

Seneca implies that there is a causal relationship between
moral decline and corrupt writing such that moral decline is
prior, but there is no real explanation either of the nature of

16. See sect. 1 above.

the relationship or of the basic cause of decline in the first place —other than that *felicitas* produces *luxuria* and so the itch for novelty (9–10). What is particularly important about Seneca's formulation is that he defines decadence in general terms of taste and style, so that his explanation, unlike his father's, is not confined to oratory, but can be extended to cover all forms of literary activity. Only by implication does he attribute decadence to his own age, but then he was writing under Nero with whom this would have been a particularly delicate subject.[17] Somewhat earlier (he died at the age of 28 in A.D. 62) Persius had given, in his first satire, a similar account of literary decadence in general, using the same basic connexion between morals and style; but Persius had quite explicitly identified the contemporary literary scene as decadent, and, like Petronius (in chapters 1 to 4), he had put much of the blame on the audience and on parents. But the two points of view are close enough to indicate dependence on a common pool of ideas. Seneca, following his father's lead, worked out the idea of a relationship between morals and style in an original way by tracing detailed correspondences between style and moral behaviour—the fantastic lengths to which he goes illustrate some of the faults that he himself condemns and that are related to a basic technique, characteristic of the first century A.D., in the literary handling of an idea.[18]

5. *The elder Pliny*

The *Natural History* of the elder Pliny was dedicated to the emperor Titus in A.D. 77; he died two years later, taking too close a scientific interest in the great eruption of Vesuvius in A.D. 79.[19] In book 14, about to discourse on fruit-bearing trees, he pauses to complain (2–6)

17. For the literary renaissance under Nero, see Index s.v. 'Nero'.
18. See chap. V, sect. 2.
19. Pliny *Letters* 6. 16.

illud satis mirari non queo, interisse quarundam memoriam
atque etiam nominum quae auctores prodidere notitiam. quis
enim non communicato orbe terrarum maiestate Romani imperii
profecisse vitam putet commercio rerum ac societate festae pacis,
omniaque etiam quae ante occulta fuerant in promiscuo usu facta?
at, Hercules, non reperiuntur qui norint multa ab antiquis prodi-
ta: tanto priscorum cura fertilior aut industria felicior fuit, ante
milia annorum inter principia litterarum Hesiodo praecepta agri-
colis pandere orso subsecutisque non paucis hanc curam eius; unde
nobis crevit labor, quippe cum requirenda iam sint non solum
postea inventa, verum etiam ea quae invenerant prisci, desidia
rerum internicione memoriae indicta. cuius vitii causas quis alias
quam publicas mundi invenerit? nimirum alii subiere ritus cir-
caque alia mentes hominum detinentur et avaritiae tantum artes
coluntur. antea inclusis gentium imperiis intra ipsas, ideoque et
ingeniis, quadam sterilitate fortunae necesse erat animi bona ex-
ercere, regesque innumeri honore artium colebantur et in ostenta-
tione has praeferebant opes, immortalitatem sibi per illas proro-
gari arbitrantes; quare abundabant et praemia et opera vitae.
posteris laxitas mundi et rerum amplitudo damno fuit. postquam
senator censu legi coeptus, iudex fieri censu, magistratum ducem-
que nihil exornare quam census, postquam coepere orbitas in
auctoritate summa et potentia esse, captatio in quaestu fertilissimo,
ac sola gaudia in possidendo, pessum iere vitae pretia, omnesque
a maximo bono liberales dictae artes in contrarium cecidere, ac
servitute sola profici coeptum. hanc alius alio modo et in aliis
adorare, eodem tamen habendique ad spes omnium tendente voto;
passim vero etiam egregii aliena vitia quam bona sua colere malle.
ergo, Hercules, voluptas vivere coepit, vita ipsa desiit.

I cannot adequately express my astonishment that the tradition
about some [trees] has perished and even the knowledge of their
names, handed on by earlier writers. For who can avoid thinking
that since intercommunication has now been established throughout the world by the majesty of the Roman Empire, life has progressed through the interchange of commodities and through the
general sharing in the blessings of peace, and that everything that
was previously unknown is now in common use. But, heavens, you
cannot now find men who know much of the science that was
handed down by earlier writers: so much richer in results was
their work and so much more successful their industry since, thou-
sands of years ago right at the beginning of literature, Hesiod un-

dertook to explain agricultural doctrine to farmers and many
followed him in this task. This has increased my work for me, for
I must now research not only into subsequent inventions, but also
into the discoveries of the ancients since destruction of the records
has been decreed by the laziness of men. One can find no causes for
this failing other than those that are common to the whole world.
The truth is that there are new ways now: men's minds are totally
occupied with other things, and only the arts of avarice are practised. Previously when races had to confine their empires within
their own boundaries, and for that reason their talents, there was
no scope for making fortunes, and they had to concentrate on
things of the spirit; thus endless kings had homage paid to them
in artistic tributes, and this was the wealth they put on display,
thinking that thus they were assured of immortality. So life's rewards and achievements were plentiful. To later generations the
openness of the world and the abundance of physical possessions
spelt ruin. Once you had senators being selected on income, judges
being appointed on income, magistrates and army commanders
finding honour in nothing so much as in income: once childless-
ness began to have the greatest influence and power, and will-
hunting was the richest source of profit, and the only pleasures were
in possessions—then the real values of life were lost, and the arts
called liberal from their greatest distinction (i.e., liberty) fell into
its opposite, and slavery began to be the sole means of progress.
This slavery took different forms of devotion and centred on different objects: what was common to all was the aim—the hope of gain.
Everywhere you found even outstanding men preferring to practise foreign vices rather than native virtues. So, by heaven, pleasure
began to live, life began to die.

Pliny is deadly serious, and it is this high moral seriousness
that is parodied by Petronius. Pliny's formulation of the moral
explanation is one of higher generality than any yet. He sees it
as a general disease over the whole world (this broadness of
view derives from the unifying effect of the Roman empire): the
widespread rise in the standard of living has not only made men
lazy but has caused them to devote what energies they have to
the avaricious acquisition of wealth. Wealth is now the index
of goodness in every sphere, and men are slaves to it. This formulation goes further than any other yet in another way: it ex-

plains moral decline in terms of politics and economics, and supplies the causal chain of explanation that was missing in the younger Seneca.

6. *Longinus*

The author of *On Sublimity*, probably the best work of literary criticism that has come from the ancient world, labours under two disadvantages: he is generally called pseudo-Longinus, and the date of his book is unknown. Interest here will concentrate on the somewhat unexpected final chapter (44) of the work,[20] in which Longinus discusses the causes of literary decline in the form of a dialogue between a philosopher and himself. The formulation of this discussion is of importance, and it would be very helpful in deciding the relationship between Longinus and Roman writers who dealt with this problem to have a reasonably firm date for the work. Unfortunately the evidence to decide the question does not exist. 'The received opinion of today is that we have to do with a book of the 1st century A.D.'[21] Some critics have dated the work to the time of Augustus and have identified the philosopher who appears in the last chapter with Philo of Alexandria (c. 30 B.C.–A.D. 45).[22] Others have dated the work to the reign of Tiberius, suggesting that it was written either between A.D. 20 and 50 or else about A.D. 40.[23] The latest editor (who dates the work 'in the 1st century A.D.') states the problem thus:[24] 'However, the main—I think incontrovertible—argument against the identification of L with Cassius Longinus [c. A.D. 213–273] rests on the discussion of *corrupta eloquentia* in 44. This whole topic is a commonplace in

20. For a good attempt to demonstrate the connexion of chap. 44 with the rest of the work, see C. P. Segal (1959).

21. D. A. Russell and M. Winterbottom (1972) p. 461.

22. See especially G. P. Goold (1961).

23. These were the formulations of Wilamowitz (1903), 378 and (1908), 223 respectively.

24. D. A. Russell (1964), xxv.

the first century, the mention of world peace is inconceivable in a writer of the middle of the third century (44. 6), and—a subordinate point—after the rise of the Second Sophistic, Greek literary men were no longer as modest as is L about the achievements of their own age'. All three points, however, admit of doubt. First, it is true that the topic is a commonplace in the first century—but in Roman writers who see literary decline in terms of a decline from the late Republic and age of Augustus to the time of Tiberius and later. When Greek writers consider the question of decline, they see it in terms of a decline that began in the fourth century B.C., and they contrast the literary scene of the later period with that of the great writers from Homer to Menander. For them, since they simply ignored the literature of the Hellenistic period, the significant political watershed was the conquest of Greece by Rome.[25] Greek writers do not seem to have been politically conscious of the change from republic to principate in the way that, for instance, Roman Stoics in the early Empire were. This point leads to the second because in Greek writers the connexion between Roman dominance and peace has become a cliché in the second century A.D., but they mean by it the imposed cessation of internecine warfare, endemic in Greece before the Roman conquest.[26] Consequently, a Greek writer could well use this cliché in the third century A.D., not in a directly descriptive way but in the traditional sense of an enforced blessing of Roman domination.[27] Third, even after the rise of the Second Sophistic, Greek writers were still modest about their achievements when they compared

25. On this whole question, see J. Palm (1959). For writers like Plutarch and Aristides, Rome is the guarantor of peace (Palm, 32, 61 f.).

26. Plutarch, e.g., *Flam.* 11–12 expresses the idea that the Romans saved the Greeks from tyrants (i.e., Macedonians) and Lucian *rhetorum praeceptor* 10 says 'he forgets that we are at peace now, with no invading Philip or hectoring Alexander to give temporary value to that kind of oratory [i.e., Demosthenic]'. The theme originates with Polybius 18. 46 and Livy 33. 33. 7.

27. There is (in principle) good reason, in any case, not to take such complaints about slavery as simple descriptive statements since they are used to set up the situation which the author wants to exploit and *ex hypothesi* are tailored to that purpose.

them with what really mattered—the Greek achievement from
Homer to Plato.[28] Such admiration for the great past was the
heart of the Second Sophistic.

So the case for positively dating Longinus to the first century
A.D. is weak. But it is time to look at his actual words (ch. 44):[29]

> I shall not hesitate, in adding this final point for your instruc-
> tion, to make clear, my dear Terentianus, a problem which one of
> our philosophers put to me.
>
> 'I am astonished', he said, 'as no doubt is everybody else, that
> in our age we have talents that are very persuasive and practical,
> both shrewd and quick and especially capable of giving pleasure
> with words, but, with scarcely any exception, there are none that
> are really sublime and grand. Such a worldwide dearth of literature
> characterizes our life. Must we believe', he said, 'the proverbial
> saying that democracy is a good nurse of great men, and with it
> and it alone coincided the flourishing of great writers and with it
> they died? For freedom (so the argument goes) has the power to
> nourish the thoughts of great minds and encourage them, as well
> as to arouse enthusiasm for rivalry with one another, and am-
> bition for prizes. Furthermore, the availability of political rewards
> sharpens and, as it were, polishes orators' talents by exercising
> them, and in action they naturally shine forth free. But nowadays
> we seem to be brought up from childhood in a just[30] slavery, pretty
> well swathed round from our first tender thoughts with the same
> habits and customs, never tasting the most beautiful and most
> fertile fount of literature—freedom, I mean. So we end up nothing
> but flatterers in the grand style.'
>
> He went on to say that for that reason, though other capacities
> could be acquired by servants, no slave could ever be an orator.
>
> 'For instantly there boils up in his mind his incapacity to speak
> freely and his sense of being a prisoner, always battered into him
> by the blows of habit. "Half his manhood (says Homer) the day of
> slavery takes from a man." As, for instance, (if what I hear is true),

28. The attitude is constant in Lucian (sometimes negatively expressed
in satire) and, for example, Pausanias 8. 52. 1 echoes Plutarch (*Philopoemen*
1. 4) in saying that there was no great Greek after Philopoemen, and in
general he is contemptuous (like Aristides) of modern Greeks.

29. My translation owes much to the translation by D. A. Russell (1965).

30. I translate δικαίας 'just' rather than 'justified' (Russell) because the
point here seems to be (as in 44. 5 below) that Roman rule is just—the point
Plutarch makes in *Marcellus* 20 when he calls the Romans δικαιοτέρους.

the cages in which Pygmies or dwarfs are kept not only stop the prisoners growing but also cripple them because of the fetter surrounding their bodies; so one could term all slavery, even the most just, as a cage for souls, a universal gaol.'

I, however, answered him thus: 'It is easy, my good friend, and characteristic of humankind to find fault with the present. But consider whether it is not the peace of the world that destroys great talents, but much rather this unlimited war that grips our desires, and, heavens, what is more, these passions that besiege our life, ravaging and pillaging it completely. Greed for money, the insatiable disease from which we are all suffering, and also luxury enslave us, or, rather, sink our ship of life with all hands. Avarice is a mean disease, luxury a base one. I cannot see how we can honour or (to put it more accurately) deify unlimited wealth without receiving straight into our souls the evils that naturally belong to it. Wealth, when it is unlimited and uncontrolled, is accompanied by extravagance, sticking to it and (as they say) keeping step with it; and when wealth opens the gates of cities and the doors of houses, extravagance comes too and lives with it. These evils, becoming chronic in men's lives, nest (as philosophers say) and quickly set about breeding—greed, pride, luxury are their children, not bastards but all too legitimate. If these offspring of wealth are allowed to grow up, they soon breed in men's souls inexorable tyrants—hybris, lawlessness, shamelessness. For it is inevitable that this should happen and that men should cease to notice or to care for their reputation with posterity; but in a cycle of such happenings the destruction of their lives is gradually accomplished. Greatness of soul droops, withers, and loses its attraction, while men concentrate on their mortal parts and neglect to develop their immortal. A judge who has been bribed could no longer be a free and sound judge of the right and the good (a bribed man must think his own side right and good); yet nowadays bribes arbitrate the whole life of each and all of us, not to mention the hunting after the deaths of others and the ambushing of their wills. Enslaved by love of money, we buy at the price of our souls the ability to make money out of everything. In such a pestilential destruction of life, can we think that there is left to us any free and uncorrupt judge of things that are great and of permanent value and that he is not being corrupted too by the lust for profit?

And so, perhaps it is better for such as we are to be ruled rather than free? Our lust for gain, if it were completely released and set free from prison against its neighbours, would flood the world with evil.'

I went on to say that the ruin of present day talents was that laziness in which all but a few of us live, making efforts and undertaking anything only for praise or pleasure, and not for beneficial ends that are worthy of honour and imitation . . . .

There are some difficult and peculiar features in this. First, the word λόγοι can mean 'literature', but it can also mean 'words' or it can mean 'speeches', i.e., 'oratory'. Now it is in the nature of the political explanation of decline to account for the decline of oratory but not really for that of literature and art in general. The philosopher talks mainly of oratory but contrives a certain ambiguity by the use of λόγοι and by a somewhat implausible attempt to extend the political explanation by suggesting that slavery imposes a sort of psychological paralysis on great minds (though this can only be made concrete in the proposition that no slave can be an orator).[31] The type of political explanation deployed goes back to Aristotle's demonstration that oratory arose in Sicily when tyranny disappeared. This position is expanded by Cicero in his *Brutus*[32] so that Athens becomes the great centre of oratory as long as she remained a democracy. No orator, so Cicero says, came from states like Sparta. Consequently, when the philosopher talks about 'democracy' he is probably not contrasting the Roman Republic with the Empire, but Athenian democracy with Roman domination of Greece.[33] The correctness of this interpretation is con-

31. This is on the model of the argument from moral decline, which speaks of slavery but means the slavery of the individual to his desires: see the passage of Pliny above or Longinus' own arguments in 44. 6 ff., or Philo *quod omnis probus liber sit* 62–74. But 'slavery' is highly metaphorical and exaggerated used in the political context.

32. *Brutus* 45–52.

33. It seems unlikely in any case that a Greek of the Empire would use the word δημοκρατία of the Roman Republic. When Plutarch advises a Greek who is given some authority by the Romans, he uses the advice which Pericles gave himself when he became a general (*praecepta gerendae rei publicae* 813E): 'Give heed, Pericles, it is free men you are commanding, Greeks, citizens of Athens'—that is, he goes back instinctively to Athenian democracy. In the same work, Plutarch expresses the attitude of Longinus' philosopher but with sound political sense and without exaggeration: 'you who rule are also a subject and the state is subject to proconsuls, agents of

firmed by the philosopher's assertion that 'we end up nothing but flatterers in the grand style', for with this phrase he reiterates the common Greek theme of the danger that Greeks may become oversubservient to their Roman masters (not merely to the Emperor).[34] It would be naive to suppose that Longinus is really quoting some philosopher's actual argument. Rather Longinus has shaped the argument he attributes to the philosopher in the way that will best elicit the case he himself wishes to state. Consequently, at the cost of some violence, he has warped the exposition so that it will cover all literature. This is the reason for the early assertion of 'a worldwide dearth of literature'; here λόγων must have the wider meaning of literature', and yet this assertion comes in oddly after a statement of the problem (highly reminiscent of the opening formulation of Tacitus' *Dialogus*) that ought to confine it to the field of oratory. He has also tried to attribute to loss of political freedom a psychological effect of wide generality.

The reason why Longinus himself favoured the moral explanation was, no doubt, that it not only naturally covered all

---

Caesar . . . you should not have great confidence in your office since you see the governor's boots [on the interpretation see Jones (1971), 133] above your head' (813E). 'The [Greek] statesman should not only show himself and his state blameless towards our rulers [the Romans]. . .' (814C). 'However the [Greek] statesman, while rendering his state completely obedient to our rulers [the Romans], should not humble it further, nor, after the leg has been put in chains, also put the neck under the yoke, as some do who, because they refer all matters, great and small, to our rulers, acquire the slur of slavery' (814E-F). All of this expresses the attitude of a sensible Greek to Roman rule, but Plutarch is grateful for the Roman gift of peace and harmony.

34. The theme of Greek subservience to Roman masters and the consequent need to avoid flattery is constant in Greek writers under the Empire. For instance, Dio Chrysostom in his speech to the Rhodians (*oratio* 31), probably belonging to the early years of Vespasian (see Momigliano [1951], 149–53), warns the Rhodians against losing their dignity in flattering the Romans, hoping to retain their freedom (157 ff.). Here the idea of slavery is used—'it is better in every way for you to be slaves than to cling to an undignified freedom' (112). It is also a theme emphasized by Plutarch: see Palm (1959), 38.

literary effort, but also diagnosed a remediable situation. This wide-ranging exposition needed the correspondingly extended form of the political explanation as its foil. But Longinus takes up the philosopher's argument by an odd reference to the destructive effect of 'the peace of the world'. The philosopher had said nothing about this. Longinus' motive is twofold: the first is rhetorical (his speech is very highly rhetorical and artificial)— to construct a contrast between the 'peace of the world' and the 'unlimited war that grips our desires'; the second is that in the Greek mind there was a close association of ideas between Roman domination and the concept of peace,[35] which allows Longinus to substitute the idea of peace for that of slavery. The slavery which Longinus envisages, however, is the slavery of men to their desires, particularly to greed for money. This formulation leads to an original touch towards the end, where he declares that for men in such a state of moral degeneracy it is better to be ruled than to be free, since at least some control is thereby exercised over their greed. In this way, he takes the philosopher's political explanation and turns it into a moral benefit: it is better for Greeks to be ruled by Romans than to be free.[36] There is a certain optimism in this. But there is more in his final remarks where he exempts himself and his friends from the general laziness that inhibits creative effort;[37] the situation is clearly remediable: what is needed is moral reform, and then great literature will be written again. Optimism was obligatory in a teacher of sublimity in writing.

Longinus sees literature completely from the Greek point of view. His only mention of a Roman is of Cicero (12. 4), who is briefly compared to Demosthenes with the apologetic conclusion: 'but that is a comparison which your countrymen can

35. This is to be seen in writers like Dio Chrysostom, Plutarch, and Aelius Aristides: see Palm (1959), 16–82.

36. That theme too—the idea that the Roman government is good for Greeks—is frequent, for instance, in Dio Chrysostom, Plutarch, and Aelius Aristides: see Palm (1959).

37. See the similar sentiment of Pliny above.

make better than I'. It was conventional that Greek writers should not mention Roman:[38] they had no need to, and discretion may have reinforced that fact. Yet Longinus is addressing a Roman, and without violating the convention, he makes his argument as universal as possible. This he does by small touches: there is the assertion of a 'worldwide' dearth of literature; the formulation of the political explanation is wider than usual and, especially in the point about political rewards (44. 3), has a Roman relevance; the detail of will-hunting is frequent in Roman writers (44. 9) and seems unsuited to Greek economic conditions;[39] and, finally, the very adoption by Longinus himself of the moral explanation shows his own desire for an explanation that will not only exonerate Roman rule but also rise above national boundaries. Greeks were, and would in future be, responsible for great literature, but the decline which paralyzed them affected the whole of the world too. When Longinus makes his philosopher emphatically assert a worldwide dearth of literature, he must therefore have the Roman world, to some extent, in mind too. This makes it implausible that he was writing in the time of Augustus and even in the first century A.D. The reign of Nero particularly was marked by a much-advertised renaissance of literature.[40] The assertion suits the second and third centuries far better, and there is a good case for the traditional identification of Longinus as Cassius Longinus,[41] the distinguished rhetorical writer who lived most of his life in Athens but who joined Zenobia in Palmyra as an adviser and was executed in 273 when the city was captured by Aurelian.

Consequently, as I see it, Longinus gives an analysis of literary decline from the Greek point of view, probably in the third century A.D., using two traditional types of explanation,

38. See, for instance, Grube (1965), 212–13. That the reason was not ignorance is shown, for example, by the debate at dinner between Greeks and Romans on both literatures described by Aulus Gellius 19. 9.

39. See Wilamowitz (1956), 2. 539.

40. For the literary renaissance under Nero see Index s.v. 'Nero'.

41. The case is made persuasively and in detail by G. Luck (1967), who deals convincingly with the stylistic arguments.

both basically Greek. The first, put in the mouth of a philosopher, is the political explanation, very briefly touched on from
one aspect (which Longinus also includes)[42] by the elder Seneca,
that subject nations cannot produce great literature.[43] The second is the moral explanation, favoured by most analysts of decline and expressed by Longinus in a form very close to that of
Pliny the elder. There were two reasons for the popularity of
the moral analysis: in general, causal explanations in ancient
historical thinking ultimately came down to the characters of
the participants (both individuals and nations), but, in particular, the ancient world was deeply committed to the belief
that literature was in a real sense educative and thus closely
related to morality. Longinus has touches of originality in his
formulation of both explanations, but both lie firmly in a
strong Greek tradition,[44] and to this fact we can attribute the
echoes with Philo[45] (writing about the time of Tiberius or Gaius).

42. In chap. 44. 3.
43. The decision to put this explanation into the mouth of a philosopher
in order to refute it seems designed to spare Roman sensitivities. Further,
the exaggerated form of the freedom-slavery antithesis (with both extremes
emphasized), together with the unsuccessful attempt to make the explanation cover all literature, suggests the possibility that Longinus had some
knowledge of the *Dialogus* of Tacitus and that his aim was to shape the
final argument of Maternus into a form that could be refuted by the explanation from morals. (The *Dialogus* would have a depressing effect on
any teacher of rhetoric.) In that case, the Greek form of the argument (as
seen, for instance, in Cicero *Brutus* 45–52), combining freedom and peace,
has been adapted in the light of the end of the *Dialogus*, and, consequently,
all that is left of Maternus' political optimism is Longinus' own puzzling
reference to 'the peace of the world' (44. 6).
44. The tradition is to be seen clearly in Plato *Laws* 8. 831, and Seneca
(*Epistles* 87. 31) refers it to Poseidonius. But it can also be seen—with a
warning to Rome—in Polybius 6. 57, and it was also used by Dionysius of
Halicarnassus and by Diodorus (see Palm (1959), 12–13).
45. On the echoes with Philo see especially Norden (1954) and Goold
(1961) 174–78. The echoes are linguistic and, while the closest is Longinus
44. 3 with Philo *de ebrietate* 198, they are with widely scattered passages of
Philo. The significance of the echoes is reduced by the fact that in each case
Philo is simply moralizing, and there is nothing either of the political or of
the literary dimensions that are a feature of the philosopher's discourse in
Longinus.

7. *The* Dialogus de oratoribus *of Tacitus*

Both the date and authorship of the *Dialogus* have been ques-
tioned. But doubt over authorship can only be sustained by a
misunderstanding of the manuscript tradition,[46] and the argument from style can no longer be used.[47] Positively, the work
bears the stamp of the author of the *Historiae* and *Annales*, not
only in the sharpness of analysis but also in the characteristic
habit of putting contrary views side by side and leaving them
more or less unresolved. This extends even into details—as in
2. 1–2, where one set of opinions about the talents of Aper and
Secundus is introduced by *maligne* and a quite different set by
nam (picking up and explaining *maligne*). The reader wonders
why the former opinions have been mentioned at all.[48] It is a
technique found often in Tacitus.[49] It will be assumed here that
Tacitus wrote the *Dialogus*.

The question of date is less simple. The dramatic date of the
Dialogus is A.D. 75,[50] in which year the author described himself
as *iuvenis admodum*; that excludes the possibility that the work
was written in the six years from A.D. 75 to the accession of Domitian,[51] and the political conditions make it certain that it was
not written under Domitian. A post-Domitianic date is suggested by a series of positive arguments: the work shows acquaintance with the *Institutio Oratoria* of Quintilian,[52] which
was written at the end of Domitian's reign; Tacitus in his *Agricola* (3. 2–3) makes it plain that he wrote nothing in the fifteen
years of Domitian's reign; the work is dedicated to Fabius Iustus

---

46. See especially Mendell (1957), 5 and 241 ff.
47. This argument was demolished by Leo in 1898.
48. See further below.
49. R. Güngerich (1956), 147 n. 2 makes the interesting point that the
formulation of the problem in *dial.* 1 shows a technique of deriving consequences for cultural history from philological observations that is a peculiarity of Tacitus.
50. For the date see Syme (1958), 670.
51. This is decisively demonstrated by Hass-von Reitzenstein (1970),
20–21.
52. See Güngerich (1951).

who held the consulship in A.D. 102, and there is evidence to suggest that dedication to a man in or about the year of his consulship was something of a convention;[53] there is clear evidence
that Pliny knew the *Dialogus* when he was composing the
version of the panegyric intended for publication, which he
delivered to Trajan in A.D. 100[54]—Pliny was certainly working
on it in 101 and perhaps subsequently.[55] It seems the most prob-
able assumption, therefore, that the *Dialogus* was composed in
A.D. 101 or the following year or so; the fact that Pliny and Tacitus together conducted the prosecution of Marius Priscus in a
famous case in A.D. 100 recommends putting the date of composition as late as possible after that date. The date has considerable importance for the interpretation of the work.

The ostensible motive for writing *Dialogus* was Fabius Iustus'
constant questioning why previous ages were distinguished by
glorious orators of genius while the present age is totally bereft
of any, even the name of orator having disappeared (there are
only technically trained professional men like lawyers, solicitors,
barristers, and so forth). The form of the question assumes an
advanced state of decline, and Tacitus is glad to be able to avoid
passing an adverse judgement on his own contemporaries; he
will answer the question by reporting a debate by experts at
which he was present when he was 'pretty young'. (The date
is subsequently fixed more or less precisely in A.D. 75; see 17. 3.)[56]

After more introductory remarks, the scene is set in the house
of Curiatius Maternus. He is revising his tragedy *Cato*, which
he read the previous day 'to the great offence of powerful people, since he had totally immersed himself in Cato and forgotten
his own situation'. Two friends arrive (bringing Tacitus with
them): one is Julius Secundus, who will not take a prominent
part in the debate; the other is Marcus Aper, a self-made man
from Gaul, a powerful and abrasive orator. They warn Ma-

53. See Syme (1958), 112 and 672.
54. See Bruère (1954) and Güngerich (1956).
55. Pliny *Epistles* 3. 13 and 18, with Sherwin-White's commentary.
56. See Syme (1958), 670.

ternus and inquire hopefully if he is toning down his play. He says 'No: quite the opposite; and if anything was left unsaid in my *Cato*, it will be said in my next play, *Thyestes*!' Aper rebukes Maternus for wasting his time writing plays, and Maternus' reply indicates that this has been a frequently debated topic of disagreement between them; he appeals to Secundus to be arbiter. Secundus declares an interest: he is a friend and admirer of the poet Saleius Bassus and so cannot be impartial. Aper answers that that does not matter: he is not attacking poets as such, but only poets who are capable of the higher art of oratory, and in particular Maternus. So Secundus is appointed arbiter.[57]

This little drama is an important guide to the first debate: it is not just a confrontation of the relative merits of oratory and poetry, but a discussion of whether, and in what terms, a man like Maternus is justified in abandoning oratory for poetry. (The real answer does not, in fact, come till 41. 4–5.) Aper speaks first, and his speech is twice as long as Maternus':[58] he speaks of oratory as a useful weapon, of the pleasure a man feels in the sense of power it gives him, and of its fame. Poetry gives none of this, creates danger for its composer, and is in any case only a subsection of oratory. The argument is very revealing of the speaker's brashness and pragmatism and of his vulgar sense of values.[59]

Maternus' speech[60] is in no sense a direct reply. In total contrast he builds up an idyllic picture of the poet's remoteness from the world's anxieties and of the truly lasting fame that the poet achieves through men's valuation of his work. He expresses extreme distaste for oratory that feeds on men's perils.

57. This is made virtually certain by Hass-von Reitzenstein (1970), 65–66, 70, 101, 108–9, arguing from the Ciceronian parallel in *de natura deorum* and the conventional use of the prejudice motif. Dialogues after the first century A.D. follow Tacitus in using an *arbiter*. I should be inclined to emend 5. 1 to '*Securus sis* [MSS *sit*]' *inquit Aper'et Saleius Bassus et quisquis alius. . . . sed ipsum solum apud te* [MSS *cos*] *arguam*. This use of *apud* is a technical term for stating a case 'before' a judge.

58. Chaps. 5 to 10.

59. Especially 6. 2; 9. 1–2, 3, 6.

60. Chaps. 11 to 13.

Apart from the fact that Maternus is clearly someone for whom the word *orator* has disappeared (in the terms of Fabius Iustus' opening question), it is hard to see the relevance of all this to the proposed topic of the dialogue: why has oratory virtually disappeared? Nor is it clear that Maternus has refuted Aper: two totally different views have been dramatically contrasted, and they touch at very few points. But the debate is neatly motivated and arises directly out of the situation in which his friends find Maternus, for Aper is really trying to persuade him to return to being an orator.[61] If he succeeds, the question of Fabius Iustus will turn out to have been falsely formulated.

He does not succeed, and there now follows a dramatic interlude of a type common in dialogues—the arrival of an important character at a strategic point in the debate; the archetype is the late arrival of Alcibiades in Plato's *Symposium*. Here the Senator Vipstanus Messalla arrives and joins in. The late arrival is very nicely timed, for in the exchanges that follow there is just the merest reference to (15. 1) 'the eloquence of your brother' (*fratris tui eloquentiae*). No name is mentioned, but the reader is intended to realize that this is none other than M. Aquillius Regulus, the most notorious of the *delatores* in the second half of the first century; his remark on his own technique was the celebrated 'I instantly see my opponent's throat and spring at it'.[62] He was, in fact, Messalla's half-brother; and Messalla just succeeded, by a well-judged speech, in saving him from condemnation as a *delator* in A.D. 70 at the beginning of Vespasian's reign. Messalla's late arrival ensures that he has not had to suffer Maternus' reference (12. 2) to 'that blood-stained oratory, intent only on financial gain' (*lucrosae huius et sanguinantis eloquentiae*), a description that would above all fit the wealthy and successful Regulus. A further advantage is that Messalla can speak without being constrained by the arguments of the debate so far, and the debate can take a new direction.

61. So Secundus interprets the speech in 14. 2.
62. The anecdote is reported by Pliny in a letter (1. 20) to Tacitus.

Messalla is characterized by Aper in the terms of Fabius Iustus' question: Aper describes him as frequently asserting (15. 1) that no *orator* exists today. Messalla now reveals that he often reflects (15. 2) on the causes of the great gulf between the past and the present, and he suggests that they debate the whole question. Both Secundus and Maternus urge Messalla to express his own views, but before he can get a word in, Aper, very much in character, rudely interposes with a long speech (16–23).

This speech expresses some important ideas. All the explanations of decline examined above were united in ignoring the fact of historical change. Aper makes two points. The first concerns the relativity of the time scale: from a distant historical perspective one's own age will look very different, and even its chronological limits will probably be wider (so that, for instance, Cicero may well be reckoned as belonging to Aper's own age). Second, everything changes and must change: what suits one set of circumstances will need to be altered to suit another. He includes a brief attack on Cicero to show that Cicero had faults, recognizable even in his own time, and also a demonstration that at all times men have displayed a love—even a preference —for literature of the past. The latter is particularly interesting in a work written at a time when the archaizing movement was well under way in Rome,[63] but both points underpin the interlocking relativity of taste and time and style.

The primary reason why Tacitus made use of the dramatic possibilities inherent in Aper's character to insert this speech at this particular point was to maintain a conspicuous feature of the *Dialogus*: the speeches of the debaters do not answer one another, but set forth points of view that are more or less independent and that touch on one another only in limited respects; each speech is in this way more or less self-contained. The points which Aper makes are largely unanswerable, and Messalla immediately (25) concedes Aper's arguments from relativity (though he is allowed the satisfaction of calling the relativity of time a quibble—*nominis controversia*). The point he himself is

63. See chap. VI sect. 8.

allowed to make is twofold: that each age—and especially the Ciceronian age—has, for all its diversity, a recognizable character of its own, and that men are justified in regarding one age as the peak of achievement to which preceding ages lead up and from which subsequent ages lead down. So Cassius Severus, whom Aper saw as the beginning of the modern age, is regarded by Messalla as the end of the great age. At this point Messalla begins to blame Aper for not mentioning the names of modern orators of worth, and Maternus intervenes to cut him off.[64] But it is noticeable that Messalla has not been able to modify Aper's views; what he has done has been to suggest other factors to be taken into consideration with, not substituted for, Aper's views.

Maternus insists that Messalla need not demonstrate that the earlier orators were greater; his task is to explain the causes of the decline. With this, a third section of the *Dialogus* begins (28), consisting, like the others, of two speeches.[65] Messalla, assuming decline, therefore, traces it basically to educational causes, inadequate grounding in morals and philosophy, and the unreality of the declamations used in training orators. His attitude is, however, optimistic since all that is needed is educational reform. There is a lacuna after chapter 35 of about one and a half pages;[66] when the text resumes Maternus is speaking (36–41). His speech has almost no relationship to Messalla's. Instead, he takes Aper's point about historical change and uses

64. For discussion of this motif, see below.

65. The structure of the *Dialogus*—three pairs of speeches by three speakers, with Messalla's speech divided into two parts at 27—seems now to be generally agreed on. See Barwick (1954), 4, Häussler (1969), 66–67, and Hass-von Reitzenstein (1970), 109–10. On the part of Secundus see above, and note 66, below.

66. That the extent of the lacuna after chapter 35 is small has been convincingly shown by Barwick (1954), 33–39 and Häussler (1969), 25–30. That Secundus made no real contribution in this gap is shown by the fact that he is not mentioned at the end and that it is Messalla who comments on Maternus' speech (42), thereby showing that Maternus spoke immediately after him. Also, in general the Ciceronian pattern is of no more than three main speakers. See Hass-von Reitzenstein (1970), 109–11 and 119–28, whose discussion of the problem has convincingly settled it.

it to give a devastating analysis of the prospects for oratory; liberty of the type in which oratory flourishes is characteristic of an unstable society and is simply incompatible with strong central government such as has brought peace and prosperity to Rome in recent times. Oratory, consequently, is finished since the effect of social peace and stability has been to remove all the stimuli to, and occasions for, the practice of oratory in the Ciceronian sense.

The *Dialogus* ends with smiles and friendly farewells and a suggestion for continuing the debate on a later date of a type conventionally used to round off a dialogue on a subject that is incapable of being brought to a decisive conclusion. The reader is left to ponder some difficult problems. This, for instance. The dialogues of Plato and of Cicero deal with timeless problems of philosophy or rhetoric or the ideal constitution of the state. Such problems can be given adequate treatment regardless of the period chosen as the dramatic date. Plato's dialogues are all set in the past, and the author represents himself simply as a reporter. Many of Cicero's dialogues also are set in the past,[67] with the author functioning as reporter; some are set in the recent past, and Cicero himself is a major participant. The *Brutus* is an example of the latter, and the motives for setting it at a recent date and for Cicero's own participation are that the problem posed was one of immediate concern and that Cicero was the leading expert of the time. The *Dialogus* of Tacitus was set in A.D. 75 but was written and published over twenty-five years later. Yet the generation from 75 to about A.D. 102 had seen fundamental changes in society and politics which completely altered the situation of oratory. How could Tacitus, without gross anachronism, set a debate in A.D. 75 that would still be relevant to the situation of A.D. 102?

Consideration of this problem must start from a notable series of contradictions or contrasts that can be seen both in the views

67. The best discussion of the Ciceronian background to the *Dialogus* (with careful assessment of earlier literature on the subject) is that of Hass-von Reitzenstein (1970).

of individual characters and between the views expressed by different characters. These are most noticeable in the case of Maternus in whom there are at least four such contradictions or contrasts:

1. In his final speech he makes the point that *libertas* in the sense of 'freedom of speech' is inconsistent with strong central government: he says, for instance (38. 2) 'a long period of peace, unbroken tranquillity on the part of the people as a whole, continuous quiet in the senate, and the imposition of very strong discipline by the emperor had pacified eloquence like everything else' (*postquam longa temporum quies et continuum populi otium et assidua senatus tranquillitas et maxima principis disciplina ipsam quoque eloquentiam sicut omnia depacaverat*). 'Like everything else' is very strong and outspoken, but it takes not the slightest account of Maternus' own activity. At the beginning of the *Dialogus* the tragedies of Maternus are mentioned—*Cato*, *Thyestes*, *Medea*, and *Domitius*. From these titles it is clear that Maternus was using tragic themes to reflect dramatically on tyranny and opposition to it; furthermore, it is clear from his offending powerful people (2) that he was expressing in his dramatic tyrants an analogue to the imperial system. This literary activity had certainly not been tamed by peace and the principate.

2. In his last speech Maternus expresses himself as strongly in favour of the imperial system. There may be a certain irony in this—and the exact nature of the irony will need to be considered[68]—but, on the face of it, his last speech is in some contradiction to the implicit criticism of the imperial system represented by his tragedies.

3. There is another contradiction in Maternus' own picture of the poet's ideal existence amid groves and streams, remote from the world of politics and ambition, and the all-too-real participation in that world which is figured in the reading of his *Cato* and the offended reaction of the powerful to that activity.

4. This contradiction is linked to an interesting contrast.

68. See below.

Maternus says in his first speech (11. 4): 'So far I have protected my position and security better by my innocence than by my eloquence, and I have no fear that I shall ever have to speak in the senate except on behalf of some threatened friend'. At the end of the speech (13. 6) he prays for a quiet end to his life. But on a number of occasions his friends warn him of the offence to the mighty that he is causing by his tragedies and of the consequent dangers that threaten. This contrast needs to be seen in relation to two facts. First, probably in the year before the dramatic date of the *Dialogus*, Helvidius Priscus, former friend of Vespasian and outspoken critic of the regime, was exiled; it was perhaps in the very year in which the *Dialogus* was set that Helvidius was killed on the orders of the emperor. Both he and his attacker, Eprius Marcellus, are briefly mentioned in the speech of Aper (5. 7); Aper is referring to the beginning of Vespasian's reign when buoyant senators were prosecuting *delatores* who had previously persecuted them; among them was Helvidius Priscus, who indicted Eprius Marcellus. The prosecutions were stopped by Vespasian. A hint was intended to the knowing reader in Tacitus' choice of A.D. 75 as the year for the debate. Second, many dialogues, both Greek and Latin, have their dramatic date set a short time before the death of the host or principal speaker.[69] The date A.D. 75 was certainly chosen by Tacitus because of the proximity of the exile and death of Helvidius Priscus, the first really sinister sign in the new regime. The reader has a nagging sense of dramatic irony in the contrast between Maternus' equanimity, even complacency, and the worries of his friends on his behalf. It seems a likely conjecture that Tacitus was conscious of a fact, certainly shared by his readers: Curiatius Maternus, so attractively portrayed in the *Dialogus*, was condemned and executed soon after the scene of the debate, and that death was foreshadowed with precise dramatic irony in Maternus' own prayer for the opposite (13. 6) and in a more general way in his friends' warnings.

Such are the contradictions and contrasts expressed in the

69. See especially Cameron (1967) and Hass-von Reitzenstein, 37.

central character of Maternus, but before considering the reasons for them, it is worth taking account of a contrast between the views of Aper and Maternus. In his speech rudely interrupting Messalla, at the beginning of the second part of the debate, Aper uses his concept of historical relativity to justify a most optimistic view of the present situation of oratory and of its future prospects. Yet in his final speech Maternus uses the same concept of historical relativity, applied this time, however, to the relation between oratory and politics, to give a devastatingly pessimistic account of the prospects for oratory. The fact that the two speeches are widely separated means that the contrast need not obtrude on the reader—otherwise he would be inclined to believe that Maternus simply did not listen to Aper. But on closer inspection it appears that the contrast was deliberate and that the two speeches were widely separated on purpose—another motivation for Tacitus' using Aper's character as an excuse to insert his speech ahead of that of Messalla.[70] Maternus' final speech reflects the political situation of about A.D. 102, and the terms of his analysis are close to those that Tacitus himself uses when he speaks in other works of the period at which he was writing—that is, the time of Trajan.[71] Aper's speech, in contrast, is directed to setting the oratory of his own particular time in a historical framework extending from Cicero's time to A.D. 75.

This remoteness of Maternus' final speech from A.D. 75 is underlined by a curious fact. In his very first speech Maternus referred to (12. 2) 'that blood-stained oratory, intent only on financial gain', and he characterized it as a recent invention. Such oratory, the oratory of the *delatores*, could not be ignored by Tacitus when he purported to set a dialogue in A.D. 75, but he placed the references to it in the earliest section of the debate, allowing Aper to name a series of distinguished *delatores* (not omitting the high regard that the emperor had for them—8. 3), and giving Maternus the opportunity here for moral condemnation. Apart from this, the very choice of Vipstanus Messalla as a

70. See above.
71. Notably *Agricola* 3 and *Hist*. 1. 1.

participant in the debate is significant; his half-brother was Regulus, the most famous *delator*, who may not even have been dead[72] at the time when Tacitus wrote the *Dialogus*. Though his name is not used, he is very delicately and inexplicitly mentioned—again at an early stage. Regulus in his own person spanned the period from Nero to Trajan; he was a symbol of the great, wealthy, influential past of oratory. But he was also a symbol of something quite different. When Maternus in his final speech asserts conclusively that good government by one man does not need oratory, the oratory it most conspicuously does not need was that on which all emperors from Tiberius to Domitian had most heavily relied for the protection of the regime, the oratory of the great *delatores*. But the most decisive difference between the situation of 75 and 102 lay in the fact that Trajan had once for all (following a brief initiative by Titus, reversed by Domitian) abolished *delatores*.[73] That this was the most important form of oratory emerges from any consideration of the years A.D. 14 to 96; the fact is also reflected in Pliny's boredom and his paradoxical longing for the detested Regulus.[74] Maternus' final speech is designed to be an analysis of the immediate situation of A.D. 102 and so must omit all consideration of that type of oratory. This is neatly done since his argument destroys oratory, regardless of *delatores*; or, to put it differently, Trajan's abolition of *delatores* proved Maternus' argument by showing that they were no longer needed in the imperial administration.

Thus this contrast between the second speech of Aper and the final speech of Maternus reflects the gap between 75 and 102; it looks as if the other contradictions mentioned above have the same explanation. The question, how does Tacitus bridge the gap between 75 and 102? can now be examined by looking at the main characters in turn. Each character as he speaks confronted

72. On this, see Syme (1958), 663.
73. Suetonius *Titus* 8. 5; Pliny *Panegyricus* 34–35.
74. *Letters* 6. 2.

the author with the problem of locating his views in A.D. 75 in such a way as would make them relevant to A.D. 102; but the problem varied with each case.

The obvious way to establish the dramatic date of the *Dialogus* was to sprinkle it with references that belonged to the years about A.D. 75. Tacitus does this, in fact, but all such references are confined to the first section of the work, and there is none after the dramatic arrival of Messalla, in chapter 15. The exemplary poet chosen is Saleius Bassus, who had recently received a donation from Vespasian (9. 5), and he is most highly praised both by Secundus (5. 2) and also by Aper (9. 2). The neatness of this dating mechanism can be seen from Quintilian's assessment of him (10. 1. 90): 'impetuous and poetic was the genius of Saleius Bassus, but it did not become mellow with age' (*vehemens et poeticum ingenium Saleii Bassi fuit, nec ipsum senectute maturuit*): that is, Saleius showed great poetic power in his youth which did not develop in later years; also he was dead by the time Quintilian was writing in the early 90s. It is the view that critics would have had of Saleius in A.D. 75 that Tacitus attributes to his friend and also to Aper (who would naturally have been a hostile critic). A further poetic reference is the comparison of Pomponius Secundus[75] to Domitius Afer, both of whom had died fifteen years or so earlier and would be relevant to the period of A.D. 75—*nostris quidem temporibus* (13. 3). The practice of *delatio* was encouraged by Vespasian,[76] and so the leading *delatores* are mentioned, Eprius Marcellus and Vibius Crispus (5. 7 and 8. 1); also mentioned is a notorious case of the period, that of Helvidius Priscus against Marcellus (5. 7), and when Maternus mentions *delatio* he describes it as *recens* (12. 2). All this is in the early part of the *Dialogus*. There is a reference to Nicostratus (10. 5), who in A.D. 36 at Olympia won the boxing and pancration contests on the same day, a most unusual feat. Quintilian, who saw him (2. 8. 14), makes full use of the extraordinary nature of the feat;

75. On Pomponius Secundus, see Cichorius (1922), 423-32.
76. See especially Winterbottom (1964), 93.

but Tacitus, using him only as a dating mechanism, probably took the reference from Quintilian and ignored all its finer points.[77]

There is an odd little contradiction that has some bearing on the relation between the levels of A.D. 75 and 102. Messalla, in chapters 34 and 35, regrets the loss of the custom whereby a young barrister's training was completed by a sort of long apprenticeship to a leading barrister of the day. This was the practice in Cicero's day, and Messalla contrasts it with the present-day habit of training young men in the declamation schools. He implies that the Ciceronian practice has completely died out; yet among his four hearers is a young man who is present simply because he is apprenticed in just this way to Secundus and Aper (2. 1). What is meant here is not just the guidance in making the young orator's actual début, which Quintilian describes in 12. 6. 2, the type of introduction to the forum that Pliny gave to his young senatorial friend Cremutius Ruso (*Epp.* 6. 23). What is meant is the practice Quintilian describes at 10. 5. 19 and 12. 11. 5; in both passages Quintilian's language suggests a nostalgic longing for a practice long since outmoded (*quod apud maiores fieri solebat, more veterum*). It is entirely possible, then, that at the time Tacitus was writing, the custom had disappeared.[78] Was it still in vogue in A.D. 75? Caution is needed. The motif is used in a number of Ciceronian dialogues, especially in *de re publica* and *de oratore*. Its significance is that it supplies perfect motivation for the presence at a debate of a young man who can report the debate long after the deaths of the participants. Tacitus makes special use of Ciceronian motifs for his own purposes, and who is to say that the practice was not still observed, at any rate by old-fashioned families, in A.D. 75? What

77. Güngerich (1951), 161–2.
78. Cf. the complaint of Pliny (*Letters* 2. 14) that young men come straight from declamation school to the courts and are not even introduced by a senior, 'some person of consular rank', as used to happen; and his description of *tirocinium fori* in *Epp.* 8. 14. 4–8 suggests nostalgia for a past custom.

we should notice is that, like other touches which would convey the sense of an earlier period, it occurs in the first section of the *Dialogus*.

This is immediately accompanied by another Ciceronian motif: the author corrects opinions about the talents of the main speakers that had a wide currency. This is closely parallel to the *magna opinio* which Cicero in *de oratore* 2. 1 reports about Crassus and Antonius, only to refute it. Cicero has a particular aim in mind: he will later be stressing the importance of education and *doctrina*, so he emphatically mentions and denies an opinion that would have refused these two qualities to his main protagonists. Tacitus has no such motive. His aim can only be to substantiate for his reader his own inside knowledge of the two orators, and his refutation depends on intimate acquaintance with both men and their inmost thoughts: 'the style of Secundus was fluent to a satisfactory degree' (a judgement that could only be based on constant critical listening to his actual speeches) and 'Aper was highly educated and spurned literature rather than was not acquainted with it, thinking he would have a greater reputation for hard work if his genius were seen not to depend on the help of alien arts' (where Aper's private thoughts are the evidence). Again a Ciceronian motif is turned to his own special use by Tacitus.

All the evidence above on dating mechanisms reveals that Tacitus was well aware of the gap between the two levels of the *Dialogus*, that of A.D. 75 and that of 102; he has made every effort dramatically to substantiate the historical setting of the debate in A.D. 75, but has confined all such details to the first section of the work. It is now necessary to look at the characters and their ideas from this point of view.

First, then, Maternus. The problem for Tacitus was that Maternus' final speech forms a dramatic and conclusive end to the work, yet the views he expresses most impressively at the end of his speech belong firmly in the context of A.D. 102. The problem was to draw him back into the context of A.D. 75. Tacitus has done this in three main ways:

1. The warnings of danger by his friends and the foreshadowing of his own death locate Maternus as a person in a past belonging to the circumstances of Vespasian's reign, with a pretty clear implication that he did not long survive the occasion of the *Dialogus*.[79]

2. Maternus is firmly dated by the literary genre that he practises. Mythological and historical tragedy, used to convey Republican sentiments and criticism of the monarchy, was already old-fashioned by the time of Vespasian, and it had completely died out long before A.D. 102.

In both of these respects Maternus is very much a figure of his time, that is of A.D. 75, but the more this fact is emphasized, the greater becomes the apparent contradiction with the views and tone of his last speech. Here a particular feature needs to be interpreted.

3. The degree of this contradiction can be (and often is) exaggerated and Maternus' speech therefore interpreted as deeply ironic.[80] The degree of contradiction needs careful definition. It is less than it seems, for Maternus is speaking about oratory (not any other branch of literature), he is speaking to men who consider themselves orators, and he is speaking in the character of a poet who has been urged to return to oratory. From this point of view, society and politics exhibit certain characteristics that Maternus himself may well regret (and attack) but that are not only valued by most people but are most relevant to the condition of oratory: these are peace, security, and obedience on the part of the governed. Thus Maternus says that as doctors are not needed by healthy peoples and medicine makes least

79. See above.
80. This is particularly the thesis of Köhnken (1973), but he goes so far as to regard it as irony on the part of Tacitus. The weakness of his thesis lies in the fact that he compares Maternus' last speech with material taken from Tacitus' views on the period A.D. 14–96; but the relevant comparison is with Tacitus' views on the time of Trajan. Furthermore, Köhnken's examples of Tacitean irony (pp. 34–36), especially *Annals* 11. 3 and 12. 53. 3, demonstrate conclusively that Tacitus lets his irony appear quite clearly in the sarcastic tone which is betrayed by the unexpected vocabulary. The essential straight-facedness of Maternus' speech is not paralleled elsewhere.

progress in such conditions, so 'the greatness of orators is lessened and their glory obscured when people behave well and are ready to obey a ruler'. It is wrong to treat that last phrase (*in obsequium regentis paratos*) as equivalent to *servitium*[81] and refer to Maternus' words in 13. 4, where he characterizes *delatores* like Eprius Marcellus as 'insufficiently servile in the views of their masters but insufficiently free in ours'. Many points of view are possible on freedom: one when you think of sensible political behaviour, another when you think of extremists. Thus in 41. 3 Maternus is speaking of sensible moderates, but in 13. 4 he speaks of *delatores* who exert themselves to crush opposition to their masters; in (40. 2)–'that great and famous eloquence is a nurseling of the licence which fools call freedom' (*licentiae quam stulti libertatem vocant*)–he refers to extreme Republicans, among them the Stoic opposition for whose political sense Tacitus sometimes showed scant respect;[82] finally, in (27. 3)–'make use of that old-fashioned freedom of speech from which we have degenerated further than from eloquence'–he uses *libertas* in the restricted sense of 'freedom of speech', but the sense is restricted further than such a translation suggests, for it is nearer to what we mean when we say 'feel able to speak freely'.[83] There is nevertheless an element of exaggeration or elevation[84] in the way Maternus speaks of the regime, particularly in his description (41. 4) of the emperor and his *clementia*. Yet the sentiments here are very close to those of Tacitus himself in his introductions to his *Agricola* and *Histories* where he speaks of the reign of Trajan. The effect of this exaggeration or elevation on the part of Maternus

81. This is the procedure of Köhnken (1973), 49. But *obsequium* is a technical term for 'obedience required by the laws' and *regere* is used intransitively a number of times by Tacitus, and other writers such as Quintilian, of the rule of the *princeps*. The tone must be assessed from the context, especially *bonos mores*.

82. See Syme (1958), 547–65; Murray (1965), 58–59.

83. And so it could be restricted by social convention as well as by imperial censorship. For the outspokenness of the Ciceronian period see Aper's remarks in *dial.* 21 and Messalla's in 25.

84. Syme's apposite description of a characteristic technique of Tacitus: see Syme (1958), 349.

is more that of slightly rueful good humour than of irony; but, however one defines it, this tonal nuance bridges the separation between the Maternus of A.D. 75 and the views for which he is made the vehicle by Tacitus at the end of the final speech, and which belong firmly to about A.D. 102.

The problem with Aper was almost the opposite. Nowhere is it said (or implied) that he was a *delator*, but both in his style and in his attitude to oratory he is very much a man of the mid-first century A.D. He represents in one person all the orators of the period, including *delatores* like Regulus and Eprius Marcellus.[85] Consequently, everything about him could sound very dated in A.D. 102. The problem, therefore, was to draw him forward, as it were, from A.D. 75 to 102. This is done by one very effective method.

In several Ciceronian dialogues, notably in *de oratore* and *de re publica*, one character is made to play the devil's advocate,[86] to take a point of view that he himself does not hold but that needs to be expressed if the debate is to deal adequately with its subject. Cicero makes it clear that the character does not share the views he expresses not only in comment from others but in the character's own words. Thus in the *Dialogus*, Messalla twice (15. 2 and 28. 1) and Maternus twice (16. 3 and 24. 2) say that Aper is taking a part in the debate which is not his own position. To clinch the reader's impression Tacitus has already said in the introduction (1. 4) that one of the characters took the opposite point of view, and his language seems to imply (though not definitely) the deliberate acceptance of something alien. In Cicero, when this happens, the motive is clearly to ensure that a distinguished Roman is not burdened with a view that is simply refuted later in the dialogue. The Ciceronian background to this feature of the *Dialogus* is made clear by Maternus when he says (24. 2): 'after the ancient custom, often displayed by our

85. See Winterbottom (1964), 94.
86. On the Ciceronian background to this motif, see the excellent account in Hass-von Reitzenstein (1970), 131–43.

philosophers, he [Aper] has accepted the task of taking the opposite point of view'. But there is a major difference between Ciceronian practice and the *Dialogus*. In *de oratore* and *de re publica*, Antonius and Philus themselves proclaim that they are undertaking to defend a point of view they do not hold. In the *Dialogus*, Aper never gives the slightest hint that the views he expresses are not his own. The motive must be different: Aper is clearly not being excused from his views nor are they really refuted.

The effect is twofold: first, a deliberately theoretical exposition of a generalized point of view is motivated, freed from specific reference to a particular period. Second, the effect is rather to undercut Aper's views in one particular aspect—the idea that Aper and his contemporaries are as good as Cicero and his contemporaries; Maternus urges Messalla to take it for granted that everyone admits the inferiority of contemporary oratory (24. 2, 27. 1). It is notable that there is no similar isolating or undercutting of Aper's first speech; quite the opposite, for Secundus describes Aper's aim (14. 2) as having been to 'persuade Maternus to devote all his talent and interests to oratory'. The case that Aper makes, pragmatic and self-interested, could equally be made in A.D. 102; the totally opposed senses of values expressed by Aper and Maternus are timeless. But Aper's second, very long speech needed to be undercut in that one particular aspect because it was in that aspect that it was most liable to be out of date in A.D. 102. The value of his speech lies not in its assertion of the equality of contemporary oratory to Ciceronian but in the exposition of general factors that need to be taken into account in any analysis of decline.[87] The one serious difficulty for Tacitus lay in the fact that if Aper's case was to be made plausible, he should name contemporary orators and compare them to Cicero and his contemporaries; but that would date his speech hopelessly to A.D. 75. So, in a splendidly dramatic touch, Tacitus makes Messalla complain about this omission of names and im-

87. See above.

petuously offer to supply the deficiency himself; but at that very point Maternus interrupts to forbid it and turns him towards another line of argument.

And so to Messalla. When Maternus interrupts his speech (27. 1), he does not characterize the whole of it as a digression but only the latter part, where Messalla asserts that contemporary oratory is degenerate and offers to demonstrate the point by referring to specific names. In the dialogues of Cicero digressions occur, but there is an important difference from the case of Messalla: in all instances in Cicero—with a very minor exception[88]—the speaker himself calls a halt and apologizes, while his hearers express their appreciation of the digression. The fact is that Messalla's speech is no digression but makes important points,[89] and Maternus' interruption has two functions: (1) to give a dramatic reason for the absence of contemporary names by conceding the inferiority of contemporary oratory to be generally admitted, and (2) to motivate an important change of direction in Messalla's argument and mark the beginning of the third and final section of the debate.[90] But this was the only real difficulty that Tacitus had with Messalla. His conservative and basically optimistic views had been expressed some ten years earlier by Quintilian (though Messalla's views are by no means identical with those of Quintilian), and, by and large, they seem to have been held at the time of Tacitus' writing by Tacitus' friend and Quintilian's pupil, the younger Pliny.[91] Essentially they were old-fashioned views that were contrary to the general

88. See Hass-von Reitzenstein (1970), 88. The single exception occurs at *de oratore* 3. 226 at the end of the work. Crassus tells an anecdote about Gracchus, especially addressed to Catulus. Catulus then acknowledges and expresses admiration for Gracchus. But then Crassus starts to deplore Gracchan politics and, after one sentence, is recalled politely to the anecdote. The dialogue has by now become more like general conversation, and the motif is consequently totally different in tone and purpose from that in Tacitus.

89. See above.

90. See n. 65 above.

91. For a survey and bibliography, see Sherwin-White (1966), 86–89; add Quadlbauer (1958).

movement of oratory in the first century A.D. in calling for a revival of Ciceronianism,[92] and, to the extent that they saw such
a revival as perfectly possible, they were highly optimistic. Such
views would have been no less and no more plausible in A.D. 75,
at which time too they would have been old-fashioned. There
is a certain contradiction between Messalla's assumption that the
practice of apprenticing a young man to a great orator had died
out and the presence of Tacitus, who provides an example of the
custom, but the latter may be no more than a convention from
Ciceronian dialogues used by Tacitus for his own purposes.[93]

By means of all of these artistic devices Tacitus has attempted
to bridge the gap between A.D. 75, the dramatic date of the *Dialogus*, and A.D. 102, the time of writing. The question can now be
asked: What views emerge from the *Dialogus*?

There is one fact (not always noticed) to be stated firmly: no
speech is refuted, and almost the only view generally denied is
that contemporary oratory has not declined from Cicero's time;[94]
certain views are countered by other speakers, however, as, for
instance, when Maternus in his first speech condemns on moral
grounds the oratory of the *delatores* which Aper had so highly
valued on social and political and self-interested grounds. In
addition, none of the three main characters simply expresses an
identifiable doctrine: Maternus no more expresses Tacitus' views
than Messalla does Quintilian's or Aper those of Regulus. The
greatness of the *Dialogus* lies in the author's capacity to see the
strength of different points of view and to demonstrate that none
can be simply dismissed. Consequently, it is not easy to say what
finally emerges, but inquiry can start from considering the relevance of the first debate between Aper and Maternus and the
way in which it fits into the *Dialogus*.

Two points can be made immediately. The first is that the
effect of the two statements on behalf of oratory and of poetry is
to assert the primacy in terms of basic human values of imagina-

92. See Winterbottom (1964), 94–95.
93. See above.
94. See above.

tive literature[95] over oratory, which is practical and career-orientated, and so to validate in those terms the retirement of Maternus from oratory (but not, of course, in terms that form the basis of Aper's case).[96] The second point arises from another strange contradiction. Aper makes much of the fame that the orator can win, and several times he satirizes the difficulty poets have even in getting audiences to listen to them. In this he ignores the opening scene, which showed Maternus not only all too capable of attracting an audience but—far more important—actually preparing his *Cato* for publication. That publication guaranteed a much wider audience and a longer life to literature than to oratory[97] is especially evident from Maternus' treatment of Virgil (12. 6–13. 2), who even in his lifetime was venerated by theatre audiences as if he were Augustus.

These two points are not made explicitly; they are left (with Tacitean unobtrusiveness) for a discerning reader to see at an early stage of the dialogue—if they were set later or even at the end they would inevitably suggest a doctrine on Tacitus' part. In fact, of course, a reader can reflect that Aper's first speech carries a message embodied in Tacitus' own early career, while, to some extent, Maternus' first speech represents Tacitus' later career, the theoretical connection between the two being provided by Maternus' final speech. But at the early stage of the *Dialogus* both points serve to assert the primacy of imaginative literature over oratory in humane and moral terms. In his final speech Maternus deploys an argument that destroys the possibility of any real future for oratory, but on political grounds. Clearly, however, a reader in A.D. 102 would be fully aware that Maternus' own type of politically orientated tragedy was also

95. I use this phrase to avoid a too narrow definition of the type of activity which Maternus describes, for at times he himself loses sight of the precise nature of his own activity.

96. Hence Maternus cannot be said to meet and refute Aper's case.

97. An impressive witness to this attitude is provided by the somewhat pathetic letter of Pliny to Titinius Capito (5. 8) in which he longs for lasting fame and knows clearly that it only comes from published works.

doomed to extinction—and Maternus does not mention it in his last speech. What, then, is left?

Two important facts finally emerge. First, Maternus' final argument only destroys oratory; literature in general is something different and will not, as Longinus discovered,[98] be covered by any political argument. Second, Aper made a very important point when he defined *eloquentia* (10) as a concept wide enough to accommodate any and every kind of literature. He was, in fact, doing nothing new, simply expressing the normal view of the ancient world. He used the concept to assert the primacy of oratory and to recall Maternus to a proper sense of values. But the concept will also serve a different purpose: it removes the necessity to assert general literary decline on the basis of demonstrated decline in particular branches of literature—for instance, oratory.[99] It opens the way, in fact, for Maternus to assert an equally proper, but entirely different, sense of values, embodied in a quite different literary activity.

Maternus is given so important a part in the *Dialogus* because, like all the others present (including the young Tacitus), he has been an orator and knows what they are talking about but is now a poet and represents an attitude to literary composition that is pretty well the opposite of the orator's. He emphasizes (and indeed exaggerates) the lonely life of the intellectual outside the ways of men, and yet, by what seems a contradiction, he can assert the political power of his tragedies by recalling a triumph of his own under Nero (11. 2).[100] The contradiction is neither resolved nor made explicit, but it does represent a real feature of imaginative literature and its influence in the world—one which makes censorship dear to authoritarian regimes. Here Aper's concept of relativity, expressed in his second speech, comes in: the idea that literary standards and modes must change with the

98. See p. 21 above.

99. Maternus carefully separates poetry from oratory in *dial.* 12. 2–4.

100. On the text and interpretation of this passage, see especially Barwick (1954), 40–42.

times is impotent to save oratory from the consequences of Maternus' last speech, but it leaves all forms of reflective and imaginative literature not only unharmed but positively encouraged.[101] What is needed is change and modernization, an injection of new life and ideas, a breaking down of rigid categories and genres.[102] At this point another concept of Aper's is relevant: Aper (21. 6) hits out in a cutting aside at poetry as a leisure activity of orators—it must be either oratory or nothing. It is useless, Aper's point is, for an orator who thinks he recognizes the obsolescence of oratory to compensate by taking up poetry. That this was hitting at a real target of A.D. 102 can be seen from Pliny's letters: for instance, the letter of A.D. 105 to Titinius Capito (5. 8): 'oratory and poetry meet with little favour unless style is perfect; history pleases however it is written; for men are by nature inquisitive and avid for information however baldly presented—seeing they are captivated by small talk and anecdotes'. This dilettante attitude would have excited Aper's anger, and Tacitus' too, no doubt. Aper is the thorough professional, engaged on a hopeless pursuit, it is true, but with the right attitude to literary effort.

This highly professional attitude, even a certain perfectionism, was shared by Tacitus, and it need be no accident that historiography comes safely under the umbrella of Maternus' arguments; several times Tacitus views historiography as functioning socially in something like the way that Maternus saw his tragedies functioning.[103] Tacitus saw historiography in terms in which some have seen the modern documentary novel—as a work of nonfiction in which imagination obeys the impulse of fact.[104]

101. The encouragement lies in the quiet confidence and optimism of Maternus' first speech.

102. All of these literary ideals, expressed in Aper's second speech (18–23) can be detached from the sphere of oratory to which he applies them.

103. Notably *Annals* 3. 65.

104. See George Steiner's essay 'Humane Literacy' in *Language and Silence* (London, 1969), especially p. 25.

8. Conclusion

Tacitus clearly asserted the decline, even the death, of oratory. But in doing so, he paid scant attention to the theories and explanations that were offered by other writers examined above. He did not so much as give a mention to the theory of a universal law of rise and decline.[105] Nor does the argument from morals appear in a recognizable form. Instead he put into Messalla's mouth a view of declined educational aims and standards (and too little discipline in homes and schools) together with a condemnation of the practice of declamation. To a limited extent these views coincide with those of Quintilian in the *Institutio oratoria* (and perhaps also in the lost *de causis corruptae eloquentiae*),[106] but, whereas Quintilian's moral attitude would go far towards condemning the use of oratory in *delatio*, Messalla's would not.[107] There is nothing here, however, of the hackneyed and loose thinking that characterizes the way in which other writers express the argument from morals.

Tacitus brought a completely new, deeply historical, insight to bear on the explanation of decline—the insight of a senator and magistrate and orator and historian. That insight is to be seen no less in the second speech of Aper (with its deep sense of historical relativity) than in the brilliant final analysis of Maternus, which gives a new dimension to literary history. What finally emerges (apart from technical questions of style and composition) when oratory is disposed of is the dilemma of the artist torn between the tensions of Republican free speech *(Dial. 2)*

105. However, in *Annals* 3. 55. 4, in the context of sumptuary legislation, he allows himself to speculate on the possibility of cycles of taste and morals, changing with the times, as an explanation for moral changes under Vespasian.

106. For a collection and examination of the evidence on Quintilian's *de causis corruptae eloquentiae,* see Reuter (1887). Reuter's idea of the work is, however, too narrow and technical, and needs to be supplemented by the examination in Barwick (1954), 10–14 (note, in turn, the reservations of Güngerich [1955], 440).

107. See Winterbottom (1964), 94–96.

and the autocracy, benevolent as it may be, of the monarchy (*Dial.* 40–41). This is presented mainly in the person of Maternus and in two ways: first, through the dangers that threaten him and, second, through the portrait of the remote, satisfying life of the intellectual. Tacitus in other works expresses gratitude for the peace and freedom he enjoys under Trajan, but in the *Dialogus* the problem of the writer under a monarchy remains, as it must— and did—unresolved.

Yet there are considerations to give one pause. Near the beginning (3. 1) of the *Agricola* Tacitus speaks of the benefits that have come with the reigns of Nerva and Trajan—the happy combination of principate and liberty, the increased felicity of the times, the strong sense of public security; but 'by nature the remedies for human infirmity act more slowly than the diseases, and just as our bodies grow slowly but perish quickly, so it is easier to snuff out talent and intellectual activity than to revive it. One even finds oneself feeling the charm of laziness, and inertia, hateful at first, comes to be loved'. Peace, prosperity, and security produced a certain boredom; even Pliny could find the senate boring—'everything is under the control of one man who, for the common good, has alone taken on himself the worries and troubles of all men' (*Letters* 3. 20. 12).

In spite of his optimism for imaginative literature, Tacitus may have sensed that literature can die as easily amid peace and plenty and a well-ordered society as amid persecution and suppression. The literary activity in which he was the star was to be very short-lived, and even Pliny is to be found (*Letters* 9. 2) comparing his situation unfavourably with Cicero's: there was lots for Cicero to write about that was interesting and important, but Pliny himself has run out of subject matter. Tacitus could not foresee how quickly literature was going to die out in the second century. There was the brief renaissance after Domitian's death, the reasons for which will have to be considered, but first it will be worthwhile to go back to the beginning of the period and consider Tacitus' portrait of Curiatius Maternus in the light of the career of Ovid; and here the similarities will turn out to be more important than the differences. For one unspoken, but nevertheless very strongly held, doctrine emerges from the *Dialogus*: it is that there is an essential connexion between literature and the life of its time. It was because that connexion was broken that oratory died. Maternus may talk about groves and streams and the remote paths of the poet, but his work is deliberately aimed at contemporary political features of his own society. It is that fact which puts him in danger, while at the same time allowing him to claim a status even greater than that of the orator: he can do everything that the orator does (and more), but his work finds its target without causing bloodshed or compelling him to compromise his principles. It was that essential involvement in his own contemporary society and its politics that Ovid tried desperately to avoid or at least to keep under control, without success; for his very stature drew him into the engagement, with most important consequences for writers who came after him.

II

Ovid:
the Poet
and Politics

THE originality of Ovid's poetry invites a new misinterpretation by each succeeding generation. But there is no mistaking the weight of his influence (whether for good or bad) on the literature of the first century A.D. He stands next to Virgil in frequency of quotation by writers like the elder Seneca and his son; and it is impossible to read poets like Lucan and Juvenal without sensing that in all ways Ovid meant at least as much to them as Virgil himself[1]—and even a confirmed Virgilian like Silius Italicus can be shown to owe an incredible debt to Ovid.[2] He was writing at a major point of change in Roman literature, and was himself no small part of that change. Some of his work (his earliest poetry) can be read as putting the finishing touches to earlier types of poetry; but the major part of it looks unmistakably to the future. His importance was increased by the fact that he found it impossible to avoid becoming involved in politics, and he was the first poet to fall a victim to the clash between republican ideals and the imperial system. And herein lies a

1. See particularly Thomas (1959).
2. See, for instance, Bruère (1958) and Bruère (1959).

paradox: his poetry seems, to a degree most unusual in Roman poetry, to have been created basically for its own sake, with no ulterior purpose, no message—art for art's sake; yet his personal life became so deeply involved in the public life of his times that a major problem concerns the interpretation to be placed on the many passages in his poems that touch on politics. What sort of example did he provide for later writers on the delicate question of treating political themes, and particularly on the question of the relationship between the writer and the emperor?

1. *Ovid's isolation*

Ovid's poetic autobiography (*Tristia* 4. 10), written in exile, gives more information about him than we have for most Roman poets. He was born in 43 B.C., after the assassination of Julius Caesar and not long before the triumph of Antony and Octavian at Philippi. He was, consequently, at least a generation—and, in terms of historical change, a whole era—younger than the other great Augustan poets: Virgil was born in 70 B.C., Horace in 65 B.C., Tibullus and Propertius probably about 60 B.C. or slightly later. The historian Livy had probably been born about 64 B.C.[3] Ovid's social rank was that of *eques*, and he was of independent means. His father, however, who had the careful attitude to money characteristic of his class and provincial origin, said, when Ovid wanted to be a poet: 'Why take up a useless career? Homer had no money to leave in his will'. Ovid obeyed and embarked on a political career; but, on the point of entering the senate, he gave it up: 'The burden of office was beyond my strength; my physique could not stand it, and my mind was unsuited to the work and recoiled from the anxieties of ambition' (36–38). Poetry was what he wanted, and it came spontaneously to his lips. There was a long tradition in Rome that senators did not write poetry—not seriously at any rate.[4]

Ovid describes his early days as a poet (*Tristia* 4. 10. 41–56):

3. R. Syme (1959), 40–42.
4. Williams (1968), 449–50.

> temporis illius colui fovique poetas,
>   quotque aderant vates rebar adesse deos.
> saepe suas volucres legit mihi grandior aevo,
>   quaeque nocet serpens, quae iuvat herba, Macer.
> saepe suos solitus recitare Propertius ignes,   45
>   iure sodalicii, quo mihi iunctus erat.
> Ponticus heroo, Bassus quoque clarus iambis
>   dulcia convictus membra fuere mei.
> et tenuit nostras numerosus Horatius aures,
>   dum ferit Ausonia carmina culta lyra.   50
> Vergilium vidi tantum: nec avara Tibullo
>   tempus amicitiae fata dedere meae.
> successor fuit hic tibi, Galle, Propertius illi;
>   quartus ab his serie temporis ipse fui.
> utque ego maiores, sic me coluere minores,   55
>   notaque non tarde facta Thalia mea est.

I sat at the feet of poets of that time [5]—any poet I revered as a god on earth. Macer, considerably my senior, often read me his lines on birds or dangerous snakes or beneficial herbs; often Propertius used to read me his love poetry (45)—as you would expect from the closeness of our friendship. Ponticus the epic poet and Bassus with his iambics were agreeable members of my circle. The musical Horace held my attention as he struck out his polished odes on an Italian lyre (50). Virgil I merely set eyes on; and the greedy Fates did not allow time for me to become friends with Tibullus. Tibullus was Gallus' successor, Propertius was Tibullus', and I was fourth in line of these. Just as I revered my elders, so the younger generation revered me (55), and my poetry quickly became famous.

These lines, looking back over more than thirty years to the high point of Augustan poetry, have a pathos that is separate from the pathos of the poet's view of happy young days seen from the misery of exile. It comes from the way in which the last three poets are mentioned: the schematic ordering of the succession of elegiac poets is rough literary history, but it makes the point that very soon Ovid was alone. By the time he was twenty-four, in 19 B.C., Tibullus and Virgil were both dead, and Propertius was dead within the next six years, probably sooner. By the time Ovid

5. This must have been about 20 B.C.

was thirty-five, in 8 B.C., Horace was dead. Ovid was then isolated: there was no poet remotely near him—even Varius had died in 14 B.C. This isolation is underlined by the fact that except in his earliest work, there is little sense in his writing of belonging to an established tradition. No doubt he was surrounded by minor poets writing conventionally in outworn modes (like Macer and Ponticus). But by 8 B.C. he was acknowledged as the greatest living poet. He stresses that fame came to him early and that it was— most unusually—unaccompanied by Envy; and, though he himself puts the great poets of his age ahead of himself, the world has not agreed but considers him their equal, so that his fame extends over the whole earth (121–132). The words convey a tranquil recollection of acknowledged poetic supremacy. The historical facts, no less than one's own literary judgement, confirm this as a realistic assessment of Ovid's situation in the years after 8 B.C. He was, consequently, severely exposed to a certain type of pressure.

His first poetic work was the most traditional, for which he claimed to be the successor of Gallus, Tibullus, and Propertius. The *Amores* was completed in five books, perhaps about 10 B.C. In a second edition of the work, Ovid reduced it to three books;[6] this was published perhaps about 2 B.C.[7] Between these two editions came a work for which, in spite of certain precedents, Ovid justifiably claimed originality; this was the *Heroides*, a collection of letters from abandoned mythological ladies to their lovers or husbands. Such letters form the first fourteen poems (it is not certain that the fifteenth is Ovidian). The idea for the later pairs of letters, including replies from husbands or lovers, was suggested to Ovid by his friend Sabinus (*Amores* 2. 18. 27–34). The work is a tour de force of brilliant originality. Of an even greater degree of originality was the *Ars Amatoria*, two books intended for the instruction of men, with a third added by popular request from

6. Specially stated in the poet's own prefatory epigram.
7. On Ovid's literary career the most useful work is S. Mariotti (1957). For careful examination of the date of *Heroides*, see Jacobson (1974), 300–318.

female admirers—no need to take that witticism literally. This was followed soon by the *Remedia Amoris*. All of this was completed by A.D. 2.[8]

Ovid then turned to the simultaneous composition of two major works, both also highly original, the *Fasti* and the *Metamorphoses*: that their composition (in two different metres) was more or less simultaneous is shown by the fact that both were unfinished in A.D. 8. For suddenly in A.D. 8 Ovid was exiled to Tomis. The offence which the *Ars Amatoria* gave to Augustus was the main reason, but one must ask why Augustus delayed at least six, and perhaps eight, years after the work was published.[9] Ovid lived on for about nine more years, but he never undertook another major work of originality; the *Tristia* and *Epistulae ex Ponto* have great merits and a certain originality, but they are mostly a pale reflection of the genius that he had been. He completed the *Metamorphoses* for publication (it was clearly much further advanced by A.D. 8); but he published only half of the projected *Fasti*, and that was at a date later than A.D. 14. Removed from the stimulus of the literary milieu at Rome, he lost not his facility but his inspiration, the poetic vision that reshaped material into original conceptions. But why had Augustus waited for six or more years?

2. *Literature and politics*

Augustus, while still Octavian, had put into practice a concept which had some precedents at Rome but none remotely on the new scale:[10] he collected the major writers of his age under his patronage (and, to some degree, control) through the skilled management of Maecenas. The poets included Virgil, Horace, Varius, and Propertius. The patronage was generous and the control—if that is the right word—tactful; the poetry written under these conditions included the greatest that Rome ever produced.

8. A. S. Hollis (1973), 101 and n. 34.
9. Ovid himself complains of the delay: *Tristia* 2. 539 ff.
10. Williams (1968), 41–44.

Augustus clearly took an interest and gave active encouragement and a ready hearing to new poetry, but he stood at a distance and was generally not addressed directly in poems before 19 B.C. About that time, however, there must have been an important change, the evidence for which is largely indirect.[11] Maecenas only makes a single third-person appearance in a few words of *Odes* 4. 11 after the publication of Horace's *Epistles* 1, about 19 B.C., whereas every earlier work of Horace had been dedicated to him and many individual poems were addressed to him. In 17 B.C. Horace was officially appointed to compose the *carmen saeculare* for the very important *Ludi Saeculares* of that year; this can only have been at the direct instigation of Augustus. Suetonius, who had easy access to good evidence as imperial secretary under Hadrian, reports in his *vita Horati*: 'Augustus so approved his writings and considered them likely to live for all time that he not only requested him to compose the *carmen saeculare*, but also odes on the victory over the Vindelici won by Tiberius and Drusus, and he then got him to add, after a long interval, a fourth to his three books of *Odes*'. Of the composition of *Epistle* 2. 1, Suetonius relates: 'After reading certain *Epistles* of his, (Augustus) complained that no mention was made of himself, thus: "Please understand that I am angry with you because amid very many compositions of this sort you do not address yourself to me particularly. Are you afraid that the appearance of being on familiar terms with me will bring you infamy with posterity?" And so he extorted the special composition whose beginning is *cum tot sustineas* [*Epist.* 2. 1]'. The *Epistle* 2. 1 dates from soon after 17 B.C.[12] In it, and in many odes of book 4, Horace addresses Augustus directly. These facts suggest that after the settlement of Spain and Parthia, Augustus (about 19 B.C.) dispensed with Maecenas' help and took over control of literature directly in his own person. Further evidence of this may be seen in the changed nature of Propertius' poetry in book 4. He had been a member of the circle of Maecenas and had expressed sup-

11. Williams (1968), 86–88.   12. Williams (1972), 38–40.

port for Augustus in his earlier poetry but by means of a sophisticated literary formula which left him, the love poet, at one extreme and the realities of political life far removed at the other.[13] In book 4, however, he directly treats current issues—outstandingly in the epitaph on Cornelia but also in the sixth elegy celebrating the victory at Actium.

Evidence is meagre, but the evils of the situation may have remained merely potential till as late as A.D. 6, when the books of Titus Labienus, containing historical comment reflecting adversely on Augustus, were condemned and burnt.[14] It may have been about A.D. 12 that Cassius Severus, whom anecdote links with Labienus (Cassius said that he too should be burnt since he knew Labienus' works by heart), had his speeches and pamphlets condemned; he himself was exiled first to Crete and then to the island rock of Seriphos.[15] The situation was one in which Ovid could not but feel subjected to pressure, for after 8 B.C. all Augustus' hopes for poetry worthy of the subject matter, which he himself provided, must have been concentrated on Ovid. But here another factor needs to be taken into account.

That is Augustus' obsession with the idea of moral reform—particularly legislation regulating sexual behaviour—as essential for the reconstruction of Roman society.[16] His first attempt, in 28 B.C., was rejected, presumably by the senate. His ideals were, however, taken up and given powerful expression by poets, especially by Virgil and Horace, and also by the historian Livy. By 19 B.C. the time had come for another attempt. Of that year, on his return from abroad, Augustus reports: 'the senate and people of Rome agreed that I should be appointed supervisor of laws and morals without a colleague and with superior power (*summa potestate*), but I would not accept any office inconsistent with the customs of our ancestors'.[17] From Dio (54. 10. 5) it appears that

13. For an analysis see Williams (1968), 51 ff. and 557 ff.
14. Seneca *contr.* 10 *pr.* 4 ff.; Suetonius *Caligula* 16. 1.
15. Tacitus *Annals* 1. 72. 3; 4. 21. 3; Suetonius *Cal.* 16. 1.
16. Williams (1962) and Brunt and Moore (1967), 45–47.
17. *res gestae* 6. 1.

Augustus accepted the office of 'supervisor of morals for five years with censorial powers'. Augustus says that he carried out the measures that the senate ordered by means of his tribunicial power.[18] The reference is to the *Leges Juliae de maritandis ordinibus* and *de adulteriis* of 18 B.C. In that year Augustus was in a strong enough position to pass this legislation (by no means 'ordered by the senate') through the plebeian assembly. It was the first stage of his moral legislation, but more was needed. It can be no mere coincidence that the evidence points to his also taking over control of literature at this very time. He may well have been disenchanted with Maecenas on moral and, perhaps, also on political grounds,[19] but his main motive must have been to encourage support for his moral attitudes. He seems always to have felt a close link between literature and morality.[20]

The second stage of the moral legislation had to wait a further twenty-seven years. The *lex Papia Poppaea of* A.D. 9 no longer required the personal *auctoritas* of Augustus; his control had by then become so firm that the legislation was simply put through by the consuls of the year.[21] Augustus expressed his view of this legislation in the *res gestae* (8. 5): 'By new laws passed on my proposal, I brought back into use many exemplary practices of our ancestors which were dying out in our time, and I myself handed on exemplary practices to posterity for the guidance of their conduct'. Not only was his obsession with sexual reform unique in Roman history, but the idea that such private matters should be made the subject of criminal legislation was unprecedented. There could be no mistaking Augustus' seriousness: he persisted with the idea for thirty-six years and made use of his legislation—for instance, putting to death Polus, one of his most favoured freedmen, for adultery (*adulterare matronas*).[22] And there were more painful scandals. In 2 B.C. Julia, his daughter

18. See Brunt and Moore (1967), 27–28.
19. On this see Syme (1939), 341–42 and 409–12.
20. Suetonius *Augustus* 89.
21. See Last (1934), 452–56.
22. Suetonius *Aug.* 67. 2.

and now wife of Tiberius, was exiled by her father to an island
for adultery; five *nobiles* were also involved, of whom Iullus
Antonius (the son of Antony, a distinguished member of Augustus' own household, and the consul of 10 B.C.) was executed
and the other four exiled.[23] Attempts have been made to see a
treasonable conspiracy in this, since the penalties go beyond
those of the *leges Iuliae*;[24] but this is not convincing and, given
both Augustus' obsession and the facts that the scandal was in his
own house and must have been going on for some time (Tiberius
had retired to Rhodes in 6 B.C.), not necessary. Then in A.D. 8,
Julia, the granddaughter of Augustus, was also involved in a
scandal and banished to an island; her noble lover, D. Junius
Silanus, was exiled.[25] Ovid was somehow implicated in this
affair—that implication will have been his *error*—and exiled to
Tomis.[26]

The date of this can no more be a coincidence than the date of
Augustus' taking over control of literature: Augustus was certainly cleaning up Rome in preparation for the final instalment
of the moral legislation in the next year; a continuing scandal
in his own house would have been a source of weakness and—
worse—ridicule. He succeeded also in entangling Ovid in the
purge, though, no doubt, in a very marginal way since Ovid's
real offence must have been his failure to live up to Augustus'
expectations as a poet. The reason for the delay of at least six
years after the publication of the highly offensive *Ars Amatoria*

23. Syme (1939), 425–27.
24. Syme (1939), 426–27. Reliance is sometimes placed on a gossipy
passage of the elder Pliny, who in *NH* 7. 149 talks of *consilia parricidae
palam facta*; the context here contains quite absurd innuendoes about
Augustus' suspicions of Marcellus' ambitions and Agrippa's *pudenda able-
gatio*, and even suspicions that Augustus himself caused the deaths of Gaius
and Lucius. The rhetorical motive of the passage is to show what an unhappy life the great *princeps* really led, and Pliny (or his source) caught at
every piece of gossip (of which there was much) to substantiate it. The
reality was seen by Tacitus (*Annals* 3. 24. 2): Augustus treated adultery that
affected his own family as treason. See chap. 4, sect. 1.
25. Rice Holmes (1931), 123–25.
26. *Tristia* 4. 10. 89–90.

must have been that the opportunity only came in A.D. 8, together with the desirability of a salutory example (and, no doubt, a certain amount of personal acrimony).

3. Ovid's earlier poetry and Augustus

Ovid mentions Augustus and Augustan themes a number of times in his early poetry, and these have often been taken to show an anti-Augustan attitude. But caution is needed. The greatest characteristic of all Ovid's work is wit—wit of a special kind, unknown in Rome before him and only occasionally (and remotely) paralleled in Greek epigrams. His wit, unlike, for instance, the humour of Horace, does not proceed from a particular *persona* adopted by the author (except in so far as he dramatically presents himself as a lover), but from the intrinsic nature of the theme, of which it serves to reveal one aspect; it is a highly conceptual and verbal wit, and it can coexist with seriousness in another aspect of the theme: in the elegy on the death of Tibullus,[27] Cupid is pictured in detail as present at the funeral; the poet then finds himself reminded of Cupid's similar appearance at the funeral of his brother Aeneas.[28] The wit of this unexpected conjunction—the wit of a mind that constantly makes surprising associations—should not affect a reader's judgement of the basic seriousness of the poet's feelings on Tibullus' death.

It is in this light that references to Augustus in *Amores* need to be judged. In *Amores* 2. 14, the poet is arguing Corinna out of undergoing an abortion, and he collects, as is his way, a series of warning examples, among which is (17–18): 'if Venus, pregnant with Aeneas, had done violence to her womb, the world would have been robbed of the Caesars'. In *Amores* 1. 2, in the course of an address to Cupid, we suddenly read (51–52): 'see the successful weaponry of Caesar, your relative: where he has conquered, his hand protects the conquered'. In both passages, the legend of the Julii is treated with a wit that achieves surprise, while a compliment is paid at the same time to Augustus. This

27. *Amores* 3. 9.   28. 7–14.

way of judging the literary effect of the passages is separable
from the question of whether Augustus might justifiably have
felt that his majesty was diminished by appearing in such contexts. Ovid was certainly not attacking Augustus; he was doing
what he saw the other Augustan poets doing, and giving him
honour and respect, but in his own literary terms and accommodated not only to his own style but also to very particular
contexts.

The most shocking lines in *Amores* are 1, 8, 39–42:

> forsitan immundae Tatio regnante Sabinae
> noluerint habiles pluribus esse viris:
> nunc Mars externis animos exercet in armis,
> at Venus Aeneae regnat in urbe sui.

Perhaps it may be true that those scruffy Sabine women in olden
times really were unwilling to give themselves to more than one
man: but now our martial soldiery have their attention occupied
in foreign wars, and Venus reigns in the city of her son Aeneas.

It is bad enough to suggest that women of ancient Rome did not
really cherish the honorific title of *univirae*;[29] it is a shocking
surprise to find it asserted that since the army is abroad on pa-
triotic ventures, men in Rome can now have fun with soldiers'
wives. But the sentiments are spoken by the wicked old *lena*
Dipsas and we wittily view Rome through her opportunistic
eyes.[30] Ovid loves this sort of surprise—that of seeing a familiar
situation in a way that stands convention on its head: like Phae-
dra in *Heroides* (4. 129–32) reassuring Hippolytus that it is boor-
ish to be shocked at the idea of wives going to bed with stepsons.
That is Ovidian wit at its most characteristic: the familiar is
suddenly transfixed by a line of thought from an unexpected
direction.

29. Williams (1958), 23 ff.
30. Misjudgements are often made by ignoring the context of a speech
and the element of characterization; the views expressed are then referred
directly to Ovid: a conspicuous instance is the speech of Pythagoras in *Metamorphoses* 15. See below.

There is no calculated attack on Augustus, for any material can be, and is, given such treatment. What is clear is that the whole attitude to life and love expressed in Ovid's early poetry was quite alien to the obsessive views of Augustus. Further, the sophisticated wit is predicated on a way of life and a system of values that do not appear in any of the other Augustan poets. The reality of this is occasionally expressed in direct, if humorous, terms: for instance, in *Ars Amatoria* 3. 121–28:

> prisca iuvent alios, ego me nunc denique natum
>   gratulor: haec aetas moribus apta meis,
> non quia nunc terrae lentum subducitur aurum
>   lectaque diverso litore concha venit,
> nec quia decrescunt effosso marmore montes,   125
>   nec quia caeruleae mole fugantur aquae,
> sed quia cultus adest nec nostros mansit in annos
>   rusticitas priscis illa superstes avis.

Let others take pleasure in the ancient way of life. I congratulate myself on being alive at this moment in time. This is the age that suits my way of life—not because pliant gold is now being dug out of the earth, nor because the murex is being brought from distant shores, nor because mountains are being lowered by the quarrying of marble (125), nor because the blue waters of the sea are being driven back by harbour moles, but because nowadays there is style, and the countrified inelegance that characterized our distant ancestors has not lasted to my time!

Such joy in the here and now, in the sophisticated life of the city, is not to be found in the other Augustan poets who, as love poets, are absorbed in their passion, or, like Horace, predicate enjoyment of the present on the ground that the morrow may be taken from you. In fact Ovid's wit and sophistication reflect an element in Augustan society that does not otherwise appear in the literature. Instead it appears in a series of splendidly witty anecdotes, some of them about the Julias and their circles, but also about Augustus—even hitting clearly at the moral legislation.[31] The milieu of all this is unmistakably aristocratic, and the social reality that underlay it is expressed in a fixed phrase that echoes

31. See especially the collection in Macrobius *Saturnalia* 2.

through Roman literature—*in circulis et in conviviis.*[32] So, for instance, L. Aemilius Paullus, about to set out for Macedonia in 168 B.C., complained in a speech that the war was being fought for him in comfort (Livy 44. 22. 8): *in omnibus circulis atque etiam, si dis placet, in conviviis sunt qui exercitus in Macedoniam ducant* ('at all social gatherings, and also—dammit!—at parties you find people leading armies against Macedonia'). In 59 B.C. Cicero complained to Atticus about loss of freedom and fear of violence, yet (*ad Att.* 2. 18. 2) *hac tamen in oppressione sermo in circulis dumtaxat et in conviviis est liberior quam fuit* ('yet amid all this oppression, conversation is less inhibited than it used to be, at social gatherings, at least, and at parties'). Cicero put into the mouth of Cato in *de senectute* (43–47) an extensive reflection on the pleasures of these aristocratic activities. Later, Tacitus, purporting to quote a letter from Tiberius to the senate in A.D. 22, has him say (*Ann.* 3. 54. 1): *nec ignoro in conviviis et circulis incusari ista et modum posci; sed si quis legem sanciat, poenas indicat, idem illi civitatem verti, splendidissimo cuique exitium parari, neminem criminis expertem clamitabunt* ('I am quite well aware that such behaviour is condemned at social gatherings and parties, and moderation is demanded; but just let someone pass a law, fix a penalty, and those same people will be shouting that the state is being subverted, the most brilliant members of society threatened with death, and that no one will be exempt from indictment'). Tiberius was talking about sumptuary legislation and the power of aristocratic resistance; he had good reason to know. But this context also serves to recall an important coincidence in the circles in which Ovid moved. The aristocratic coteries in which he delighted and whose approval he sought would have contained the very people who were most opposed to the moral legislation of Augustus, and whose power to block it clearly diminished only gradually from 28 B.C. to A.D. 9.[33] They

32. See, for instance, Boissier (1875), 58 ff.; Sutherland (1951), 25.
33. Cassius Dio 56. 1 ff. and Suetonius *Aug.* 34. 2 concentrate on the opposition of the *equites*, but only because senatorial opposition could be taken for granted and was not expressed in the dramatic public form de-

were the aristocratic avant-garde of Rome, to whom the Julias were naturally attracted, and their lovers and, no doubt, Ovid. Who were they?

4. Ovid's patron

Ovid's patron was Marcus Valerius Messalla Corvinus, a member of one of the oldest and most distinguished patrician families in Rome. Its greatest period of fame lay in the far past, but that fact was only likely to recommend its living members to Augustus the more. To show his respect and regard, Augustus put up a statue of Messalla's ancestor, Valerius Corvus, in the Forum. Messalla's own career was symptomatic of the man.[34] He was probably born in 64 B.C. and thus was a year older than Augustus. In 42 B.C. he was with Brutus and Cassius at Philippi, and he held command under Brutus on the successful right wing. After the final defeat, he joined Antony and went east. The stature and importance of the man and his family is fairly indicated by the fact that he was put on the supplementary list of the proscribed in 42 B.C., but his name was soon removed from it.

Some time soon after 40 B.C. he became disillusioned with Antony and transferred his allegiance to Octavian. He was Octavian's right-hand man in the struggles of the 30s, both military and propagandistic. His reward came in 31 B.C. when he held the consulship with Octavian and shared the command at the battle of Actium. Plutarch tells in his *Life of Brutus* (53. 2)—perhaps depending, as he often does in that life, on Messalla's own memoirs—how Augustus once praised Messalla for being his greatest enemy at Philippi, out of loyalty to Brutus, and yet most zealous on his behalf at Actium; and Messalla said 'I have

scribed by Dio. Furthermore, the opposition of the *equites* is described by Dio only in the context of the legislation of A.D. 9, by which time Augustus was more confident of his control of the senate, which, in any case, could (perhaps like himself) benefit from the difference between preaching and acting (as the marital status of the consuls of A.D. 9 showed).

34. On the life and career of Messalla see Hammer (1925) and Hanslik in P-W s.v. (nr. 261).

always belonged, Caesar, to the better and the juster side'. An aristocratic—if diplomatic—reply. Messalla clearly possessed every quality to recommend him to Augustus, yet a series of facts demonstrate an unusual and surprising degree of independence.

First, sources constantly link him with Asinius Pollio, and they were not only friends but were often partners in trials. Messalla was unique in being so close to the difficult and intransigent Pollio, and Pollio was, at least from 40 B.C., an implacable enemy of Augustus.[35]

Second, when Augustus went off to Spain in 26 B.C., Messalla was left as *praefectus urbi*. He gave up the post after a few days, and there are two accounts of his reason. Tacitus (*Ann.* 6. 11. 3) says: *primusque Messalla Corvinus eam potestatem et paucos intra dies finem accepit, quasi nescius exercendi* ('Messalla Corvinus was the first to receive that office and in a few days its end, on the ground that he did not know how to execute it'). Jerome, under the year 26 B.C., reports: *Messalla Corvinus primus praefectus urbi factus sexto die magistratu se abdicavit incivilem potestatem esse contestans* ('Messalla Corvinus, the first *praefectus urbi*, abdicated the office, arguing that it was no office for a citizen'). Some take it that Tacitus gave the true account and that Jerome reported a source hostile to Augustus (perhaps Cremutius Cordus). The office was one of police control over Rome and its surrounds. It had existed in the early Republic (a good reason for Augustus to revive it and give it to Messalla);[36] most recently, in 45 B.C., Caesar had used it, but in the form of a board of six *praefecti urbi*. There is no real contradiction between Tacitus and Jerome—the latter was using a careful and detailed source. The zeugma *accepit* in Tacitus' account is, as often with him, both a sarcasm and a syntactical enactment of the astonishing brevity of Messalla's tenure. The ironical use of *quasi* in reporting the ostensible reason shows that Tacitus was epigrammatically referring to a well-known story. How well known it was becomes clear from Seneca's *Apocolocyntosis* (10). There Augustus speaks,

35. Syme (1939), 320, 482, and 512; and Syme (1958), 569 ff.
36. Mommsen (1887), vol. 2, 1059–60.

but words fail his indignation at Claudius: *confugiendum est itaque ad Messallae Corvini, disertissimi viri, illam sententiam 'pudet imperii'* ('so I must just take refuge in the famous saying of that most eloquent man, Messalla Corvinus, "I am ashamed of my office" '). Messalla gave up the office because his sense of Republican and constitutional propriety was offended by his having to exercise unofficial power over his fellow citizens.

Third, in the fashion of aristocrats of an earlier period, who, using Alexander as their model, developed the habit of gathering poets round them to immortalize their exploits (the archetype was M. Fulvius Nobilior in 189 B.C.), Messalla too gathered poets round him.[37] Tibullus was the greatest of these poets in the earlier period; more than a third of his poems mention Messalla, while four of them explicitly celebrate the fame and family of Messalla. The panegyric style is also represented in two inept compositions, the *panegyricus Messallae* and the *elogia in Messallam*, if these works are not later forgeries. But this was only one aspect of the poets in the circle of Messalla. There were also genuine poets of great talent who wrote in the genre of erotic elegy. By the time that Ovid became a member of the circle, Messalla's days of military exploits were over, and Ovid in those days showed no tendency to panegyric. The greater part of Tibullus' production belongs also to this category, and also that of Sulpicia and that of 'Lygdamus'—though there is reason to think the last, at any rate, is a much later forgery.[38] The way in which these two aspects of the poetry reflect a close bond between poet and patron (so that, for instance, Tibullus does not mention Augustus) is only paralleled in the relationship between Horace, Virgil, and Propertius with Maecenas and Augustus.

Fourth, Messalla was himself a literary man: a most distinguished orator, a philosopher, a writer on grammar and language, and a composer of memoirs. He was also a poet of a significant type. If the *elogia in Messallam* is to be trusted, he wrote bucolic poetry in Greek, and the younger Pliny is witness

37. On the poetic circle of Messalla see Hanslik (1953) and Davies (1973).
38. See, most recently, Hooper (1975), with bibliographical survey.

to erotic poetry by him.[39] So Messalla's own poetry belonged to
the personal, erotic genre, most clearly represented by the poets
whom he gathered round him.

All of these features in Messalla suggest a man of proud independence and of a particularly Republican disposition in his
tastes and outlook. A guess at the identity of those who successfully opposed Augustus' moral reforms in 28 B.C. would certainly
put Messalla very high among the near certainties (though he was
most probably not in Rome at the time). In spite of this—and
Messalla was clearly no Pollio—Augustus valued such people,
who were both willing to work with him and who were of the
ancient nobility: Messalla was both. There can be no question
of Messalla's loyalty to the regime—nor of his rewards: he was
appointed *augur* in 36 B.C., ὕπερ τὸν ἀριθμόν ; he celebrated a Gal-
lic triumph in 27 B.C.; along with Agrippa, he occupied Antony's
house on the Palatine; and in 11 B.C. he succeeded Agrippa
in the very important administrative office of *curator aquarum*,
a post he held till his death. Perhaps his greatest act of loyalty
was in 2 B.C. to proclaim Augustus, in the name of the senate
and Roman people, *pater patriae*.[40] Suetonius quotes the exact
words:[41] ' "And may this", he said, "prove a good and fortunate
omen for you and for your house, Caesar Augustus. For thus we
think we can pray for the perpetual felicity of our state and the
happiness of this city. The senate in agreement with the Roman
people salutes you Father of your Country". To him, in tears,
Augustus replied—I give the exact words, as in the case of Messalla—"Having been granted all my wishes, senators, what else
can I beseech the immortal gods than that I may be allowed to
enjoy this harmony of yours to the last moment of my life" '.
Emotional words, but the time and the title were important, and
in A.D. 13 Augustus saved the record of this title for the final

39. *Letters* 5. 3. 5.
40. The title had previously been used informally of Augustus (Nisbet
and Hubbard [1970], pp. 38–39) so it may be inferred that the date of its
official conferring was deliberately chosen.
41. *Augustus* 58.

paragraph of his *res gestae* (35): 'In my thirteenth consulship the senate, the equestrian order, and the whole Roman people hailed me as Father of my Country, and voted that this should be inscribed on the porch of my house'.

In 2 B.C. Augustus assumed the consulship to introduce his younger adopted son into public life. In August of the same year he dedicated the temple of Mars Ultor, with enormous and lavish entertainments for the Roman people; the temple housed the deities of Mars, Venus Genetrix, and Divus Julius—a symbol of the family and of the providence that had brought him to power. Again in the same year a terrific sexual scandal was revealed which involved Julia and various aristocratic luminaries. One of these was executed, the rest were banished, and Julia, the mother of Augustus' two adopted sons and designated successors, was exiled to an island. Augustus communicated the details to the senate in a letter (Seneca *de beneficiis* 6. 32. 1): 'Adulterers were admitted to her house in flocks; the whole state was overrun in nocturnal debaucheries; the very Forum and the Rostra from which her father had promulgated his law on adultery were chosen by his daughter for her sexual vices; there was a daily rush to the statue of Marsyas since, turning from an adultress into a prostitute, she sought out every possibility of licentiousness in partnership with adulterers unknown to her'. The obsession of Augustus can be seen in this public exposure and the enthusiastic details of the rhetoric. Some have wanted to see a political conspiracy against Augustus in the affair, but the picture of the aging tyrant, less and less tolerant of opposition, and no doubt stung by the laughter and persistent gaiety of Rome's aristocracy, is convincing enough by itself.[42]

The scandals cannot have been sudden: Tiberius, Julia's husband, retired from Rome in 6 B.C.; in 5 B.C. Augustus held the consulship to introduce Gaius to public life. So he may well have learnt of Julia's disgrace in the following three years and deliberately planned for his consulship the cleanup, the title of *pater patriae*, and the dedication of the temple of Mars Ultor. If

42. See n. 24 above.

so, how far were Messalla and his house and friends implicated
in the scandals of Julia? Was Messalla, in proposing the title,
being compelled to make a public declaration of loyalty and soli-
darity? The moment chosen, the nature of the title (invoking the
paternalistic attitudes of Augustus to the country), the official
wording, with the emphasis on home and family, all suggest the
characteristic device of an authoritarian regime surviving a crisis
—this time a personal crisis in his own family with ramifica-
tions beyond. Augustus needed and demanded support, and the
twenty-fifth year of his reign was the perfect occasion. Where did
Ovid stand in all this?

5. *The* Ars Amatoria *and Augustus*

The *Ars Amatoria* was probably actually being written during
the crisis of 2 B.C., since Ovid refers to the mock sea battle (part
of the celebrations to mark the dedication of the temple of Mars
Ultor in August) as having taken place 'recently' (1. 171 *modo*).
The poem seems to bear the mark of times of stress in two major
features.

The first is this. In the *Amores*, as in the love elegy of predecessors, there is no reason to doubt that basically the women who
figure in them were conceived as respectable women of good
family, generally provided with the interesting complication of a
husband.[43] But the *Ars Amatoria* is explicitly directed to *hetaerae*
and away from married women. Ovid makes the point in his
introduction (1. 31–34):

> este procul, vittae tenues, insigne pudoris,
>   quaeque tegis medios instita longa pedes:
> nos Venerem tutam concessaque furta canemus
>   inque meo nullum carmine crimen erit.

Stay far away, all slender head-dresses, the mark of chastity, and
the long dress that stretches to the ankles: I shall be singing of a
Love that is safe and of affairs that are permitted by law; in my
poem there shall be no material for accusation.

43. See Williams (1968), 525–42.

The prohibition against married women is slipped in now and again in the course of the poem, for instance at 3. 57–58 where, after the introduction (in which he said that only [27] *lascivi amores* would be his subject), he addresses girls: 'while genius favours, get your lessons from me, girls—those of you who are permitted by chastity, the laws, and your own status'. At 2. 597–600, after he has told with disapproval of the way in which Vulcan snared Mars with Venus, he says:

> ista viri captent, si iam captanda putabunt,
>   quos facient iustos ignis et unda viros.
> en iterum testor: nihil hic nisi lege remissum
>   luditur; in nostris instita nulla iocis.

Let those men use such tricks (if they judge they ought to be used) whom fire and water shall mark as legal husbands. Again I assert: there is no play in my poem except what is permitted by law; in my frivolities no ankle-length dress appears.

In such a passage there is no escaping the ironic implication that husbands may of course behave boorishly and inhumanely. Irony is to be detected also in passages like 3. 611–16:

> qua vafer eludi possit ratione maritus
>   quaque vigil custos, praeteriturus eram.
> nupta virum timeat, rata sit custodia nuptae:
>   hoc decet, hoc leges iusque pudorque iubent.
> te quoque servari, modo quam vindicta redemit,
>   quis ferat? ut fallas, ad mea sacra veni.

My intention was to pass over ways in which a shrewd husband or a watchful guard may be eluded. A married woman ought to fear her husband, a married woman should be kept in custody: that is proper, that is what the Laws and Justice[44] and Chastity enjoin. But who could bear that a freedwoman should also be guarded? Let her approach my poetry and learn to deceive.

---

44. The alternative *duxque* offered by some MSS for *iusque* makes a quite implausible sequence, whereas *ius* and *lex* are often connected: cf. *AA* 3. 58, and, for example, Cicero *de domo* 33; *de legibus* 1. 56; *Phil.* 9. 11.

Here the ironical implication that of course marriage is a
prison for women is clear. Ovid, however, sometimes goes even
further. At 3. 483–84 he says:

> sed quoniam, quamvis vittae careatis honore,
>   est vobis vestros fallere cura viros

> But since, although you lack the headband of marriage, you have
> an interest in deceiving your men . . . .

The implication here that married women naturally want to
deceive their husbands is as clearly expressed as when Ovid tells
the story of Venus and Mars, and remarks that Venus did not
behave like a churlish boor when he asked her to go to bed *(nec
Venus oranti . . . rustica Gradivo difficilisque fuit)*, or when (2.
359–72) he tells the story of Helen and Paris, and attacks Menelaus for his lack of understanding—of course, when Menelaus
was away, it was perfectly right and natural for Helen to have
Paris warm her bed.

But these are all examples of normal Ovidian wit: he takes the
commonly held point of view and treats its opposite as obviously
true. It becomes irony when in stating the common point of view
he lets it appear by clear verbal signals (such as *timere* and *custo-
dia* in 3. 611–16) that he really holds the opposite view. What
Ovid does is to undercut his iterated claim that *Ars Amatoria* is
addressed to *hetaerae*. That this claim was no mere literary theme
is shown by the space and emphasis given to its defence in a
passage of nearly forty lines set prominently in the centre of
Remedia Amoris (361–98). There he asserts that his poetry has
been attacked as *Musa proterva*, and he defends himself on two
grounds: first, the attack is the result of sheer envy; second, every
subject matter has its appropriate treatment. He ends (383–98):

> quis ferat Andromaches peragentem Thaida partes?
>   peccet in Andromache Thaida quisquis agat.
> Thais in Arte mea est: lascivia libera nostra est;   385
>   nil mihi cum vitta; Thais in Arte mea est.
> si mea materiae respondet Musa iocosae,
>   vicimus et falsi criminis acta rea est.

rumpere, Livor edax: magnum iam nomen habemus;
    maius erit, tantum quo pede coepit eat.   390
sed nimium properas: vivam modo, plura dolebis,
    et capiunt anni carmina multa mei.
nam iuvat et studium famae mihi crevit honore;
    principio clivi noster anhelat equus.
tantum se nobis elegi debere fatentur,   395
    quantum Vergilio nobile debet epos.
hactenus invidiae respondimus: attrahe lora
    fortius et gyro curre, poeta, tuo.

Who could stand Thais playing the part of Andromache? Whoever acted Thais when playing Andromache would be badly wrong. It is Thais who appears in my *Ars*: it is uninhibited lasciviousness (385): I have nothing whatever to do with married women: it is Thais who appears in my *Ars*. Since, then, my poetry suits my subject matter, my case is won and my poetry is falsely accused. You have burst yourself, biting Envy: I have a great reputation, and it will be greater provided I continue as I began (390). But you are going too fast: provided I live, there will be more to cause you anguish, and my years give promise of much poetry. For that is my pleasure, and my desire for fame has fed on praise: my horse is only panting on the beginning of the climb. Elegiac poetry admits a debt to me (395) as great as that of Epic to Virgil. That is sufficient reply to Envy: draw tight your reins, poet, and continue your circuit.

There is no mistaking the basic seriousness of this whole passage. The reassertion of the claim made in *Ars Amatoria* that married women had no part in his poetry is linked to a twofold defence: first, each genre has its appropriate style and subject matter; second, the attack is really a sign of Envy at Ovid's great reputation (he is the Virgil of elegy), which will grow even greater. Here the emphasis on the fact that he has plans for further poems is clear, and, indeed, he may well have already started on *Fasti* and *Metamorphoses* when these words were being written; at least we may safely assume that he had both poems planned in his mind. It seems clear that Ovid was worried, that the elaborate defence built into *Ars Amatoria* had not worked, and that explicit defence was needed—a defence under-

pinned by the seductive suggestion of yet greater poetry to come
which would not be erotic elegy (394–95). Augustus was intended
to take note.

The second feature that marks *Ars Amatoria* is the explicit
treatment of political themes. A minor example is 3. 387–92:

> at licet et prodest Pompeias ire per umbras,
>   Virginis aetheriis cum caput ardet equis;
> visite laurigero sacrata Palatia Phoebo
>   (ille Paraetonias mersit in alta rates)
> quaeque soror coniunxque ducis monimenta pararunt
>   navalique gener cinctus honore caput.

> But it is permitted and a good idea to walk in the portico of
> Pompey when the Virgin's head is hot with the sun's horses;[45] visit
> the Palatine consecrated to laurel-wreathed Phoebus (he it was who
> sunk the ships of Egypt in the deep) and the monuments erected
> by the sister and the wife of our Leader and his son-in-law crowned
> with the wreath of naval victory.

Girls are being advised where they should walk if they want to
pick up men. The passage corresponds closely to similar advice
given to men (1. 67 ff.), and the places naturally correspond to
a large extent—the porticoes of Pompey, Octavia, and Livia and
the temple of Apollo on the Palatine. In this later passage Ovid
has added a reference to the battle of Actium, the main reason
for Augustus' dedication of the temple to Apollo. But both passages pick out for special mention the magnificent new buildings
in Rome—particularly those associated with the imperial family—
of which Augustus was so proud. A compliment is paid to Augustus without disrupting the tone of the context; the technique
is the same as that in the passages of *Amores* examined above. But
did Ovid—as is sometimes asserted—intend mockery of Augustus
by mentioning the buildings as fruitful places of assignation?
Another important passage needs consideration before an answer
can be attempted.

In *Ars Amatoria* 1. 67–262, Ovid lists the various places in
which girls may be picked up—the porticoes, public celebrations,

45. That is, in August.

the temple of Isis, the Fora, the theatre, the Circus, gladiatorial games, the *naumachia* of Augustus, the triumph, banquets, Baiae, and, finally, the grove of Diana at Aricia. The gladiatorial games are seen taking place in the Forum (164–70); Cupid is also present and deals out as many wounds as the gladiators. Then (171–76):

> quid, modo cum belli navalis imagine Caesar
>   Persidas induxit Cecropiasque rates?
> nempe ab utroque mari iuvenes, ab utroque puellae
>   venere, atque ingens orbis in Urbe fuit.
> quis non invenit turba quod amaret in illa?   175
> eheu, quam multos advena torsit amor!

Or remember when Caesar recently put on show Persian and Athenian ships in the representation of a naval battle? From all over Italy flocked young men and girls; the city became one huge world. Did anyone fail to find a lover in that crowd? (175) Ah! how many felt the pangs of a love that came from far off!

This refers to the great pageant which Augustus put on in August 2 B.C. to celebrate the dedication of the temple to Mars Ultor. Then the poet goes on without pause, by a sort of artistic association of ideas, as if the recent celebration reminded him of something yet to come (177–86):

> ecce, parat Caesar, domito quod defuit orbi,
>   addere: nunc, Oriens ultime, noster eris.
> Parthe, dabis poenas; Crassi gaudete sepulti
>   signaque barbaricas non bene passa manus.   180
> ultor adest primisque ducem profitetur in annis
>   bellaque non puero tractat agenda puer.
> parcite natales timidi numerare deorum:
>   Caesaribus virtus contigit ante diem.
> ingenium caeleste suis velocius annis   185
>   surgit et ignavae fert male damna morae.

What is more, Caesar is making ready to add what was missing to our world empire: now, Far East, you shall belong to us! Parthians, you shall be punished: Crassi, in your graves, rejoice, and legionary standards that did not easily brook barbarian hands! (180) The avenger has come, and in his earliest years a boy shows

himself as Leader and wages war, no task for a boy. But in the case
of gods one should not anxiously count birthdays: to Caesars man-
liness has always come long before its time. Divine genius rises
more swiftly than its years (185) and cannot bear the idle loss of
time.

The association of ideas that introduced this theme was fa-
cilitated by the fact that the temple of Mars Ultor, although
originally intended to commemorate the avenging of Julius
Caesar's murder, came to be associated with the idea of vengeance
exacted on the Parthians.[46] After some examples of boyhood
genius taken from Greek mythology, the young Hercules and
Bacchus, the poet continues (191–204):

> auspiciis animisque patris, puer, arma movebis
>   et vinces animis auspiciisque patris.
> tale rudimentum tanto sub nomine debes,
>   nunc iuvenum princeps, deinde future senum;
> cum tibi sint fratres, fratres ulciscere laesos,   195
>   cumque pater tibi sit, iura tuere patris.
> induit arma tibi genitor patriaeque tuusque;
>   hostis ab invito regna parente rapit.
> tu pia tela feres, sceleratas ille sagittas;
>   stabit pro signis iusque piumque tuis.   200
> vincuntur causa Parthi, vincantur et armis:
>   Eoas Latio dux meus addat opes.
> Marsque pater Caesarque pater, date numen eunti:
>   nam deus e vobis alter es, alter eris.

With the auspices and spirit of your father you will go to war,
boy, and you shall conquer with the spirit and auspices of your
father. With such a name as yours you owe us a first initiation in
war like that, leader of our youth just now, destined to be leader
later of our older men. You have brothers, avenge the insult done to
them (195); you have a father, uphold his rights. He who is Father
both of the country and of you has clad you in your armour: the
enemy is stealing your father's kingdom without his assent. The
weapons you shall bear will be loyal and devoted: the enemy's will
be stained with crime; before your standards Justice and Loyalty
will take up position (200). The Parthians are inferior in their
cause; let them be shown also inferior in war: may my Leader add

46. Weinstock (1971), 128–32.

the wealth of the East to Latium. O Father Mars and Father Caesar, give him your blessing as he sets out: for one of you is a god and the other will be.

Throughout this and the previous passage Ovid plays on the concept of Augustus' divine descent, treating him at times as a god, at others as about to be. At the beginning of the second passage Ovid recalls the technique of Horace's panegyrics of Drusus and Tiberius (*Odes* 4. 4 and 14): the son is praised by being given the qualities of the father; and the fact that he will succeed Augustus is stressed (194). Augustus is praised as *pater patriae*, the title given to him earlier in the year. The tone of panegyric throughout is unmistakable. The occasion was the setting out of Gaius for the East in 1 B.C. There had been further trouble with the Parthians,[47] and the poet treats the expedition as marking total Roman domination of the Eastern world. He continues (205–22):

> auguror en, vinces, votivaque carmina reddam   205
>   et magno nobis ore sonandus eris:
> consistes aciemque meis hortabere verbis
>   (o desint animis ne mea verba tuis!);
> tergaque Parthorum Romanaque pectora dicam
>   telaque ab averso quae iacit hostis equo.   210
> qui fugis ut vincas, quid victo, Parthe, relinques?
>   Parthe, malum iam nunc Mars tuus omen habet.
> ergo erit illa dies qua tu, pulcherrime rerum,
>   quattuor in niveis aureus ibis equis;
> ibunt ante duces onerati colla catenis,   215
>   ne possint tuti, qua prius, esse fuga.
> spectabunt laeti iuvenes mixtaeque puellae,
>   diffundetque animos omnibus ista dies;
> atque aliqua ex illis cum regum nomina quaeret,
>   quae loca, qui montes quaeve ferantur aquae,   220
> omnia responde, nec tantum si qua rogabit;
>   et quae nescieris ut bene nota refer.

See, I foretell the future: you shall conquer and I shall offer votive hymns (205) and I shall have to proclaim you in epic tones: you shall stand there and urge on the troops using my words (oh!

47. Rice Holmes (1931), 101.

let not my words be forgotten!): of Parthian backs and Roman breasts shall I speak and of the shafts the enemy fires as his horse runs away (210). Since you run away in order to conquer, what, Parthian, will you leave for the conquered to do? Parthian, now your War God is already ill-omened. So that day shall dawn on which you, most fortunate in all the world, shall proceed in gold on four white horses; before you will walk kings with their necks bowed under chains (215), no longer capable of being saved by running away. Crowds of happy young men and girls among them will watch, and that day will put new heart into everyone. And when a girl shall ask the names of the kings, and of the regions, mountains, and rivers painted on the pictures carried in procession (220), answer every question—and do not wait to be asked—and, even if you do not know, answer as if you did!

Here Ovid foresees victory as a subject for panegyrical poetry (a well-known Augustan form of *recusatio* in which, however, the subject is not so much refused as satisfied by being anticipated); he makes tentative moves towards treating the war poetically (207–12), and then turns to picture the triumph procession through Rome and up the slope to the Capitol.[48] The route will be crowded. The poet is now back to his theme: this will provide an excellent opportunity to pick up a girl. The return is neatly managed through the questions that she will be eagerly asking.

This whole passage is an extended panegyric of Augustus and the plans which he formulated in 2 B.C.—the title of *pater patriae*, the dedication of the temple of Mars Ultor, the designation of his adopted son Gaius as his own successor and the marking of this by an expedition against those ever-ready old enemies, the Parthians (for this purpose Gaius had been designated to the consulship of A.D. 1, at an unprecedentedly early age). Gaius set out in 1 B.C., but the plan must have been known much earlier; in fact, the situation already existed (as far as Armenia was concerned) in 5 B.C., when Gaius was designated to the consulship, and in that year Augustus had tried to send Tiberius on the mission (instead, Tiberius retired to Rhodes, seeing clearly that Gaius

48. For the divine associations of the particular detail of white horses in a triumphal procession, see Weinstock (1971), 68–71. Ovid here increases the panegyrical element by using this feature.

was being designated Augustus' successor). No doubt this was a
long-heralded expedition, and Augustus' plans for Gaius were
long clear; they were stated in so many words in a letter written
by Augustus on his sixty-fourth birthday, 23 September A.D. 1,
and sent to Gaius in the East.[49] Consequently, Ovid's panegyric
was most timely in all its details and corresponds closely to other
contemporary panegyrics (though it far outdoes them in length
and precision of detail).[50] This was also the period of the exiling
of Julia, and Augustus' need for support was great.

The whole passage is, however, sometimes explained as being
deliberately anti-Augustan and ironical, on the ground that both
occasions (the celebration of the temple dedication and the expected triumph) are treated as opportunities for picking up girls.
But that is what Ovid's poem is about, and it can be said at once
that there is no irony here: not only are no criteria of irony
satisfied,[51] but Augustus would have to be reckoned both as a
discerning reader and also as the prime (indeed, the only) victim
of it. It is, however, no less absurd to assert Ovid's intention as
anti-Augustan; this simply looks at the context from the wrong
end. The problem that Ovid has solved was not how to make fun
of Augustus, but how to accommodate panegyric artistically to
the context of his poem without painful disruption. Ovid, in
fact, reused the same technique to accommodate the same theme
in *Remedia Amoris* 153–58. There he is pointing out the dangers
of *otium* if you want to fall out of love; the remedy is to find
something to do—how about the law and defending one's friends?
Or, Ovid suggests (153–58):

> vel tu sanguinei iuvenalia munera Martis
>   suscipe: deliciae iam tibi terga dabunt.
> ecce fugax Parthus, magni nova causa triumphi,
>   iam videt in campis Caesaris arma suis.
> vince Cupidineas pariter Parthasque sagittas
>   et refer ad patrios bina tropaea deos.

49. Aulus Gellius 15. 7. 3.
50. See chap. III, sect. 3.
51. On criteria for judging this type of irony see Wayne C. Booth (1974),
esp. 33 ff.

Or take up a young man's part in bloody warfare: amorousness will flee at the sight of you. For instance, the runaway Parthian, the recent cause of our great triumph, already sees the weapons of Caesar in the midst of his own country. Overcome the arrows of Cupid and of the Parthians at the same time, and bring back twin trophies to the gods of our country.

The central couplet is panegyrical, but beautifully accommodated to its context. Of course, one can judge that the panegyric has been ruined in both cases by the frivolity of the contexts. Probably Augustus thought that too. But that Ovid did not is shown by the way he fitted his certainly serious defence of *Ars Amatoria* into its very undignified context in *Remedia Amoris*.[52] In all his poetry Ovid composed in small units and exercised his ingenuity in creating clever transitions.[53] In *Ars Amatoria* 1. 171 ff., he borrowed the technique from Propertius, who, in 3. 4, combined the theme of panegyric through description of a triumph with the theme of the totally devoted lover by including a tiny vignette of himself in his girl's arms as part of the crowd watching the procession.[54] There, too, critics have been ready to talk of irony. The difficulty of accommodating panegyric to various poetic genres runs right through Augustan literature, and many ingenious solutions were invented (not least these two of Propertius and Ovid). There is no sign of anti-Augustanism in the *Ars Amatoria* or *Remedia Amoris*—apart from the very fact that such works were conceived in Augustan Rome.

One can imagine that Messalla's circle encouraged Ovid with admiring delight in both works. But Ovid became worried, and tried to retrieve the situation, both by substituting *hetaerae* for married women and by explicit panegyric of Augustus. The banishing of Julia and the execution and exile of men who no doubt belonged to that very circle must have chilled enthusiasm. And one may speculate on Messalla's attitude. However great his aristocratic independence, he was renowned (as was his son) for

52. 361 ff.
53. See further below.
54. See Williams (1968), 431–33.

his *pietas* to Augustus.[55] The proposal of the title *pater patriae* was his act of duty in the fateful year 2 B.C., and he would have been in the position to give Ovid some sober advice. If so, Ovid took it and executed it as best he could. That he hoped to have done the trick is shown by the words he addressed to Augustus in the long plea *Tristia* 2. 53–76.[56] There Ovid refers specifically to the *Ars Amatoria*, and he is thinking not only of major passages like 1. 171–228, but also of many passages in which he deferred respectfully to Augustus (some have been mentioned above), or described him as 'my Leader' or 'our Leader'. There is no reason to take the passage as anything but clear evidence of Ovid's motives in so astonishingly extending the element of deferential panegyric in the *Ars Amatoria*. Augustus was not mollified because it was the work itself that offended. That this was so, that the erotic works were considered by Augustus to be ideologically offensive, is shown by the fact that they were specifically banned from public libraries in Rome after Ovid's exile.[57] Suetonius (*Aug.* 89. 3) records: 'He encouraged the literary talents of his age in every way. He listened with patience and sympathy to recitations, not only of poems and histories, but also of speeches and philosophical works. He was offended, however, if anything was written about himself except in a serious way and by the most distinguished writers'. The words might express Augustus' precise reaction to the *Ars Amatoria*. His anger had two sources: the frivolous amorality of the poetry, and the fact that Ovid was indeed the greatest living writer. However, he waited. The affair of Julia must have caused the postponement of further moral legislation; then the successive deaths of Lucius in A.D. 2 and of Gaius in A.D. 4 must have occupied him fully. He did not need to move till A.D. 8, but then he avenged to the full his long-standing resentment of Ovid, as well as of other members of the circle, like the younger Julia and her friends. Rome was to be clean for the last stage of the moral legislation.

55. Weinstock (1971), 258.
56. Quoted on p. 87 below.
57. *Tristia* 3. 1. 59–82; 3. 14. 5–18.

That Ovid was well aware of the situation is shown by a passage of *Tristia* 2 in which he assures Augustus that he had tried to write on the battle of the Giants (a frequent means in Augustan poetry of figuring the struggle of Augustus against enemies).[58] He asserts (317 ff.) that epic subjects like Troy, or Thebes, or Rome, or Augustus were always beyond his powers, and then says (331–48):

> forsan (et hoc dubitem) numeris levioribus aptus
>   sim satis, in parvos sufficiamque modos:
> at si me iubeas domitos Iovis igne Gigantas
>   dicere, conantem debilitabit onus.
> divitis ingenii est immania Caesaris acta   335
>   condere, materia ne superetur opus.
> et tamen ausus eram. sed detractare videbar,
>   quodque nefas, damno viribus esse tuis.
> ad leve rursus opus, iuvenalia carmina, veni,
>   et falso movi pectus amore meum.   340
> non equidem vellem: sed me mea fata trahebant,
>   inque meas poenas ingeniosus eram.
> ei mihi, quod didici! cur me docuere parentes,
>   litteraque est oculos ulla morata meos?
> haec tibi me invisum lascivia fecit, ob Artes,   345
>   quis ratus es vetitos sollicitare toros.
> sed neque me nuptae didicerunt furta magistro,
>   quodque parum novit, nemo docere potest.

Perhaps (yet I should doubt even this) I am suited to more frivolous verse and good enough for minor poetry; but if you should command me to speak of the Giants tamed by Juppiter's fire, the weight will be too great for my efforts. It needs a rich genius to write poetry on the tremendous deeds of Caesar (335) and avoid seeing the work overborne by its subject. And yet I have tried; but it seemed that I detracted from and—what is criminal—even belittled your powers. So I turned back to the work of my youth, frivolous poetry, and stirred my spirit with a fictional love (340). Would that I had not! But my destiny dragged me on, and I was talented to my own destruction. Alas for my learning! Why did my parents teach me? and why has writing ever held my attention? This wantonness of mine made you hate me because of the *Art* (345), in which you

58. See, for example, Buchheit (1966), 100–101.

thought I was disturbing lawful marriage. But no wives learnt amorous intrigues from my teaching—and no one can teach what he does not know.

Here Ovid refers to a frivolous passage of *Amores* (2. 1. 11–20) where he claimed to have tried to write about the Giants only to have his girl stop him. That passage is an amusing *recusatio* in which the poet pretends to explain his rejection of epic themes in order to expound his own view of love poetry. In *Tristia* 2 Ovid claims that the attempt was genuine, not because he hoped to convince Augustus of that implausible assertion, but in order to make a genuine *recusatio* here: if he attempted to write the sort of serious poetry on political themes that Augustus wanted, he would only harm Augustus (a clear reference to Augustus' views, as reported by Suetonius). This then leads him to regret his love poetry, recognize that the *Ars Amatoria* only gave offence to Augustus, and defend it once again. It was realization of that fact (together, no doubt, with a more positive sense of real danger after 2 B.C.) that had led him to introduce serious and extended panegyric into the *Ars Amatoria;* but that was not what Augustus wanted. Open hatred of Ovid was expressed in A.D. 8 in the calculated cruelty of the place chosen for the exile.

6. Fasti *and* Metamorphoses

Ovid, however, had not been idle or insensible of his situation in the intervening years. By about A.D. 2 he was engaged in more or less simultaneous composition of *Fasti* and *Metamorphoses*.[59] He claims in the letter to Augustus (*Tristia* 2. 549–52):

> sex ego Fastorum scripsi totidemque libellos,
> cumque suo finem mense volumen habet,
> idque tuo nuper scriptum sub nomine, Caesar,
> et tibi sacratum sors mea rupit opus.

I have written twelve books of *Fasti*, with each volume containing one month: that work, written under your name and dedicated, Caesar, to you, my calamity interrupted.

59. See sect. 1 abve.

A couplet is then given to his *Medea* before he speaks of *Metamorphoses* (555–62):

> dictaque sunt nobis, quamvis manus ultima coeptis
>   defuit, in facies corpora versa novas.
> atque utinam revoces animum paulisper ab ira
>   et vacuo iubeas hinc tibi pauca legi,
> pauca, quibus prima surgens ab origine mundi
>   in tua deduxi tempora, Caesar, opus:
> aspicies quantum dederis mihi pectoris ipse,
>   quoque favore animi teque tuosque canam.

And though the attempt lacks its final touch, I have sung of bodies transformed into new shapes. Would that you could just call back your heart a short time from anger, and, when you have time, bid a few passages from it be read to you, just a few in which, beginning from the first creation of the world, I have brought the work down, Caesar, to your epoch. You will see how much inspiration you yourself provided me with, and with what heartfelt devotion I celebrate you and your family.

The implication here is that the *Fasti* was finished at least to the same degree as the *Metamorphoses*. But only six books of *Fasti* have been preserved, and it is impossible to escape the conclusion that Ovid was deliberately dangling before Augustus the completion of the *Fasti*, a work which would be more congenial to him. He had, however, completed less than six books of the *Fasti* by A.D. 8, though the work had certainly been dedicated to Augustus. He went on writing it in Tomis, since the sixth book contains what can only be a reference to his exile. It occurs towards the end of *Fasti* 6 (the end of that book is a perfunctory composition, with only one certain reference to Augustus, through Atia, at 809–10 and a general address to Caesar at 763). Ovid is telling of the retirement of flute players to Tibur: *exilium quodam tempore Tibur erat!* (666: 'there was once a time when Tibur could mean exile!')—a wry comment on his own distant place of exile. This oblique reference contrasts strongly with the one passage outside book 1 that was certainly revised after A.D. 14. In *Fasti* 4. 19–62, Ovid goes through the pedigree of Augustus' family, with ring composition on the name of Venus (27 and

61); the second mention of Venus prompts the remark that April (the month of book 4) was named from the Greek word for 'foam'. Then, to explain Greek influence in Italy, Ovid goes through a list of Greek heroes who came to Italy, including, of course, Aeneas 'who had a comrade named Solymus from Phrygian Ida: from him the town of Sulmo takes its name—cool Sulmo, my native region, Germanicus. Pitiable am I, so far is it from the land of Scythia. Therefore so far away I—but cease your laments, Muse: sacred themes should not be sung on a mournful lyre' (79–84). This violent intrusion of the poet as a private individual was clearly added to an already completed passage after the death of Augustus in A.D. 14, and it is the only certain instance of such revision outside book 1 (which was heavily revised in preparation for a dedication of the whole work to Germanicus).

The *Fasti* is filled with deference to, and flattery of, Augustus that goes far beyond that of the *Ars Amatoria*.[60] There is no reason to suppose that this flattery was inserted after the exile. In fact, there is no reason to suppose that Ovid did much work on the *Fasti* at Tomis, apart from completing book 6 (including the oblique reference to his exile), which is far less ingenious in its flattery than the earlier books. Further, the *Fasti* does not show evidence of the more advanced types of imperial flattery employed by Ovid in *Tristia* and *ex Ponto* (for instance, the only time in *Fasti* that Augustus is called Juppiter is in an address to Germanicus at 1. 650–obviously a late composition). The reasonable hypothesis, then, is that the *Fasti* reflects the Ovid of A.D. 2 to 8, the years between the *Ars Amatoria* and the exile. Augustus now appears as a god on earth in the prophecy of Carmentis (1. 530). In the course of an extended *laudatio* of Augustus (1. 590–616), he is treated as being alone the equal of Juppiter, by virtue of the title Augustus. He is twice given the epithet *aeternus*[61] and is associated with Vesta,[62] or toasted with the

---

60. See Allen (1922) and Scott (1930).
61. 3. 421 and 4. 954.
62. 3. 425 ff.

Lares.[63] Ovid in the *Fasti* gives firm expression to the concept of the *gens Iulia* and of Augustus as descended directly from Troy and Mars and Venus—a concept only doubtfully suggested by Livy and only vaguely adumbrated by Virgil.[64] Perhaps most significant is the extensive praise that Ovid gives to Augustus as *pater patriae* and the way in which he connects this title with the moral legislation; he even goes on to assert that the rule of law, which characterizes the age of Augustus, makes him superior to Romulus (*Fasti* 2. 127–44). This reveals Ovid fully exploiting the opportunity for panegyric offered by 5 February. It hardly needs saying that throughout the *Fasti* there is a constant note of patriotism and pride in the *urbs aeterna* (3. 72).

All of this panegyric Ovid succeeded in accommodating to a treatment of myth and religion that moves between the extremes of Hellenistic prettiness, sheer burlesque, and antiquarian seriousness. The exposition is dominated by the *persona* of the poet as an eager inquirer into religious antiquities[65] (for which reason the intimate glimpse of the real individual, P. Ovidius Naso, at *Fasti* 4. 79–84, the composer of *Tristia* and *ex Ponto*, is disruptive and embarrassing). Only by violent misinterpretation can the large element of imperial panegyric in *Fasti* be treated as ironic or parodic. For instance, anyone who wishes to interpret *Fasti* 2. 119–26 (the introduction to the praise of the *pater patriae* and his moral legislation) as parody of the formula whereby a poet calls for epic tones to treat such a subject, should reflect that Roman readers would have agreed that epic verse was appropriate to the topic; they would have interpreted Ovid's call for epic sonority as an extra ingredient of the panegyric itself. The Ovid of the *Fasti* is an Ovid committed to the poetic praise of Augustus and his regime; this probably reflects a tighter grasp exerted by Augustus in the years following 2 B.C. and Ovid's increasing recognition of his danger.

63. 2. 631 ff.
64. Allen (1922), 253–55.
65. On this see especially the excellent analysis by Fränkel (1945), 145–46 (and notes), and L. P. Wilkinson (1955) 247 f.

Nor is it otherwise with *Metamorphoses*. Ovid's own assessment has already been quoted in one passage from *Tristia* 2; there is another at 53–80. He begins with a general statement of his loyalty and devotion to Augustus (53–60):

> per mare, per terras, per tertia numina iuro,
>   per te praesentem conspicuumque deum,
> hunc animum favisse tibi, vir maxime, meque   55
>   qua sola potui mente fuisse tuum.
> optavi peteres caelestia sidera tarde,
>   parsque fui turbae parva precantis idem,
> et pia tura dedi pro te, cumque omnibus unus
>   ipse quoque adiuvi publica vota meis.   60

By the sea, by the land, by the gods of the third sphere, by you yourself, a god present and visible amongst us, I swear that this heart of mine was devoted to you, greatest of men, and that I (55) was yours in the only way I could be—with my intellect. I prayed that your ascent to heaven would be long delayed, and I formed a tiny part of the throng whose prayer was the same. I offered up reverential incense on your behalf, and, a single individual amid the whole mass of the people, I helped with my own the nation's prayers (60).

Here Ovid asserts a personal devotion expressed in two ways: by private and public association with national expressions of loyalty, and by his intellectual labours (in 56 he contrasts *mente*—intellectual effort—with physical effort such as service in the army or the senate). He then turns explicitly to his writings, and especially to *Metamorphoses* (61–76):

> quid referam libros, illos quoque, crimina nostra,
>   mille locis plenos nominis esse tui?
> inspice maius opus, quod adhuc sine fine tenetur,
>   in non credendos corpora versa modos:
> invenies vestri praeconia nominis illic,   65
>   invenies animi pignora multa mei.
> non tua carminibus maior fit gloria, nec quo
>   ut maior fiat crescere possit habet.
> fama Iovi superest: tamen hunc sua facta referri
>   et se materiam carminis esse iuvat,   70
> cumque Gigantei memorantur proelia belli,

credibile est laetum laudibus esse suis.
te celebrant alii quanto decet ore, tuasque
ingenio laudes uberiore canunt:
sed tamen, ut fuso taurorum sanguine centum,   75
sic capitur minimo turis honore deus.

Need I mention that my books—even those that are used to
accuse me[66]—are filled with your name in a thousand places. Examine my major work (which is held up and still unfinished) on
bodies changed in miraculous ways: there you will find encomia of
your name (65), you will find many pledges of my devotion. I
know your glory is not increased by poetry nor can it possibly grow
greater than it is. But Juppiter's glory is pre-eminent, yet he is glad
that his deeds are told and that he is the subject of poetry (70); and
it is plausible to suppose that when the battle of the Giants is told,
he is delighted to be praised. Others celebrate you in fitting style
and sing your praises with richer genius, yet a god is captivated no
less by a tiny offering of incense than by the spilt blood of one
hundred bulls.

Ovid depreciates his talent in comparison with that of other
poets, but asserts that *Metamorphoses* contains much panegyric
of Augustus. So too, he claims, did his earlier work, and this leads
back to the claim that he is being unjustly condemned (77–80):

a, ferus et nobis crudelior omnibus hostis,
delicias legit qui tibi cumque meas,
carmina ne nostris quae te venerantia libris
iudicio possint candidiore legi.

But cruel and more brutal to me than all was that enemy who
read you my erotic passages in order to make you biassed in your
judgement of passages in my books that venerate you.

Ovid's claim is that his work should be read with careful attention to changes of tone in different passages. Understood in this
way, his *Ars Amatoria* will reveal a proper balance. In the same
way, his *Metamorphoses* shows the same panegyrical aim as the
Fasti, but, as also in the *Fasti*, cleverly accommodated to the work
as a whole and to particular contexts. Augustus is not obtrusively
praised; it is rather that modest opportunities are seized upon—

66. That is, the *Ars Amatoria*.

often with the wit (characteristic of all his work) that sees an unexpected connexion, as in *Met.* 1. 175–76. There, after an epic *ecphrasis* of Juppiter's dwelling, he says:

> hic locus est quem, si verbis audacia detur,
> haud timeam magni dixisse Palatia caeli.

This is the place which, if words are permitted the audacity, I should not hesitate to call the Palatia of great heaven.

The wit lies only partly in the mock-hesitant tone and far more in the fact that the equation between Augustus on earth and Juppiter in heaven is left unspoken. Again, later in the book, Apollo pursues Daphne till she is turned into a laurel. Ovid pictures the god kissing the tree and the tree shrinking from his kisses (555–56). Then Apollo speaks (557–67):

> cui deus 'at quoniam coniunx mea non potes esse,
> arbor eris certe' dixit 'mea. semper habebunt
> te coma, te citharae, te nostrae, laure, pharetrae.
> tu ducibus Latiis aderis, cum laeta Triumphum   560
> vox canet et visent longas Capitolia pompas.
> postibus Augustis eadem fidissima custos
> ante fores stabis mediamque tuebere quercum,
> utque meum intonsis caput est iuvenale capillis,
> tu quoque perpetuos semper gere frondis honores!'   565
> finierat Paean: factis modo laurea ramis
> adnuit utque caput visa est agitasse cacumen.

And the god said to her, 'Since you cannot be my wife, you will certainly by my tree. My hair, my lyre, my quiver shall always display the laurel. You shall accompany the generals of Latium when joyful voices raise the Triumph song (560) and the Capitol sees the long processions of victory. The most faithful guardian of his doorposts, you shall also stand before the gates of Augustus, keeping watch on either side, with the oak leaves in the centre. And as my head is youthful with unshorn hair, do you too wear the glory of everlasting foliage' (565). The Healer had finished: the laurel nodded with her newly created branches and seemed to shake her top as if it were a head.

Predictably, scholars have tried to distort Ovid's intention. For instance: 'Can Ovid really have intended to honour Augus-

tus—as distinct from seeming to honour him!—by thus introduc-
ing him into the context of a fanciful tale of metamorphosis and
a god's frustrated amours, especially when that god is none other
than the chosen imperial patron?'[67] The only possible answer is
yes—but the distinction between 'honouring' and 'seeming to
honour' is false. What matters here is Ovid's witty and unexpected connection between Apollo (the patron god of Augustus),
the laurel, and Augustus—with the laurel now agreeing to the
god's less demanding propositions. Ovid has accommodated a
touch of panegyric to what seems an unlikely context. But no
more here than in his earlier works is the panegyric injured by
its context. It is done far more skilfully by Ovid, but Greek poets
of the same period can also be seen moulding a frivolous and
trivial subject to carry a seriously meant compliment. For instance, this epigram of Crinagoras (*Anth. Pal.* 9. 562):[68]

> ψιττακὸς ὁ βροτόγηρυς ἀφεὶς λυγοτευχέα κύρτον
> ἤλυθεν ἐς δρυμοὺς ἀνθοφυεῖ πτέρυγι,
> αἰεὶ δ' ἐκμελετῶν ἀσπάσμασι Καίσαρα κλεινόν
> οὐδ' ἂν' ὄρη λήθην ἤγαγεν οὐνόματος·
> ἔδαμε δ' ὠκυδίδακτος ἅπας οἰωνὸς ἐρίζων
> τίς φθῆναι δύναται δαίμονι 'χαῖρ'' ἐνέπειν.
> Ὀρφεὺς θῆρας ἔπεισεν ἐν οὔρεσιν, ἐς σὲ δέ, Καῖσαρ,
> νῦν ἀκέλευστος ἅπας ὄρνις ἀνακρέκεται.

A parrot, imitator of man, leaving its wicker-work cage, went on
flowery wing to the woods, and, always practising for its greetings
the glorious name of Caesar, did not forget it even in the hills.
Hence all the birds, quickly taught, came running, rivalling one
another as to who should be first to say 'Greetings' to the god.
Orpheus made wild animals obedient to him in the hills: to you,
Caesar, every bird now tunes up without being ordered.

Crinagoras found great favour with Augustus.[69] Ovid hoped
for similar favour. To make Apollo ordain the laurel as Augustus'
own tree (to be seen by every passer-by in front of Augustus'
doors) was a compliment whose serious intention is clear from

67. Coleman (1971), 466 n. 1.
68. Gow and Page (1968), Crinagoras XXIV.
69. See especially Bowersock (1965), 36 and 133.

Apollo's simultaneously ordaining its use in Roman triumphs. Greek myth was made to subserve Roman history here; and the same technique is used in a more obviously serious passage, *Met.* 1. 200–205, where the dismay of the gods at the cannibalism of Lycaon and his attack on Juppiter is thus conveyed:

> sic, cum manus impia saevit
> sanguine Caesareo Romanum extinguere nomen,
> attonitum tanto subitae terrore ruinae
> humanum genus est totusque perhorruit orbis,
> nec tibi grata minus pietas, Auguste, tuorum est
> quam fuit illa Iovi.

So when a wicked band of fanatics tried to extinguish the Roman state with Caesar's blood, the human race was struck with just as great a fear of instant destruction, and the whole world shuddered. No less pleasing to you, Augustus, is the loyal devotion of your subjects than was that of the gods to Juppiter.

This deliberate condemnation of the murder of Julius Caesar goes far beyond anything Horace or Virgil was capable of; the emphasis on the *impietas* of the assassins and on the *pietas* of Augustus' subjects together with the parallelism between Augustus and Juppiter make this a passage of serious (but cleverly accommodated) panegyric. But it has an additional element. The immediate meaning is condemnation of the assassination of Julius Caesar. However, not only is this worded in a very general way (especially *manus impia saevit*), but Ovid seems to have invented the detail that Lycaon actually threatened the life of Juppiter. This fact, together with both the generalized wording and the equation of Augustus with Juppiter, makes reference to various conspiracies against Augustus equally a part of the meaning. In that way the murder of Julius Caesar is being regarded by Ovid as just the first of a series of attacks on Augustus himself. Lists of such conspiracies are given by Seneca and Suetonius.[70]

Metamorphoses is a ring composition in the sense that book 1 has several passages referring to Augustus, who then returns in book 15, so that the work culminates in the deification of Julius

70. Seneca *de clementia* 1. 9. 6; Suetonius *Aug.* 19.

Caesar and (prospectively) of Augustus. Here again a witty and unexpected connexion enabled Ovid to introduce this theme, for he views deification as a form of metamorphosis, and, in harmony with that connexion, concentrates in an unparallelled way on the physical changes in Julius Caesar as he is translated to the heavens (15. 843–51). The whole passage (745–870) is a wonderful example of Ovid's mythopoeic technique, blending fact and fantasy into a unity dominated by the poet's genius for phrasing and the quicksilver of his verbal wit. But it has become fashionable to treat the passage as a sort of attack on Augustus: typical is this judgement: 'Deification too is a metamorphosis, and the deified Aeneas, Romulus, and Caesar, by being included in the same poem with Lycaon, Daphne, and the rest are reduced to the same level. The whole grandiose Augustan mystique is turned into a fanciful divertissement'.[71] Or, again: 'For Ovid thus sets his long poem of fanciful caprice up against both the heroic mythology of the Ennian epic tradition and the Augustan orthodoxy represented, at least on occasion, by Horace. . . . Ovid was "playing the Augustan game" all right, but he was playing it in his own way'.[72]

71. Coleman *CR* 17 (1967), 50 (in a review of Brooks Otis, *Ovid as an Epic Poet*, Cambridge, 1966).

72. Coleman (1971), 476–77. Both quotations happen to be from the same scholar, but many similar quotations may be found in modern writers on Ovid. As exemplary of the method may be taken the article by G. Karl Galinsky 'The Cipus Episode in Ovid's *Metamorphoses* (15. 565–621)', *TAPA* 98 (1967), 181–91. Valerius Maximus 5. 6. 3 gives a brief summary of the legend of Cipus under his examples of *pietas*. Briefly, the method of this article is to emphasize the differences from Valerius' account and assert that Ovid is mocking Augustus (for instance, Cipus, in Ovid's account, used a laurel wreath to conceal his horns: such a wreath, says Galinsky, was 'habitually worn by Augustus'—an assertion whose validity depends on treating coins and portraits as if they were everyday photographs). But basically the theory depends on a misreading of the text: e.g., (184) 'Ovid's Cipus has no desire to exile himself, he is not concerned about his *pietas*; he returns—and it is never made quite clear whether he actually enters the city—calls an assembly of the senate and the people, and finally settles outside of the city. Ovid leaves it entirely open whether Cipus himself or the *proceres* (15. 616) insisted on the withdrawal'. Not one of these assertions

Not only does this point of view ignore the close thematic connexion between *Metamorphoses* and *Fasti,* but it is open to other more serious objections. First, it is irrelevant and unhistorical to pose the problem in terms such as, was Ovid writing 'a serious Augustan poem'? or indeed to talk about 'Augustanism' and 'anti-Augustanism'. When a critic speaks of 'the explicitly anti-Augustan themes of passion and violence', he confuses life and letters—as if the tales of Greek mythology in themselves had the slightest relevance to Augustan politics. In fact, there was nothing in the time of Augustus corresponding to concepts like 'Augustanism', except in so far as such concepts meant 'what Augustus wanted'—and the evidence for that is plain to read in the *res gestae.* There was no 'Augustan orthodoxy' in the sense required nor any organized 'Augustan mystique'. The apotheosis of Julius Caesar was a poetic concept, but that was literature; in

---

survives a reading of the text: Cipus will exile himself (588–89); he does not enter the city (592–93); Cipus passes sentence on himself (600–602). The distortion continues: 'Above all his *pietas* is not even mentioned, let alone made the moralistic point of the story' (184). Of course not: such stuff was left to writers like Valerius. Then, again: 'The phrase *meritis clarum caput,* which in no way is prepared for. . . suggests that Ovid was not thinking only of Cipus' (i.e., but really of Augustus). The phrase is in fact clearly prepared for in 569–Cipus is returning from a great victory. Again, the mention of an *augur* is, of course, taken to allude to Augustus and the twin sculptures of horns on the city gate to the two laurels at Augustus' doorway. This is mere assertion. 'Finally, a paraphrase from Vergil is used to make the identification of Cipus and Augustus even more explicit. The appearance of the twin horns on Cipus' forehead is described as a *monstrum* (571). The same term is used by Vergil (*Aeneid* 2. 680) in the description of the lambent flame on Ascanius' head, which is recalled by the appearance of the twin flames springing from Augustus' temples in *Aeneid* 8' (cf. *Aen.* 8. 680 and *Met.* 15. 611). With the failure of the rest of the theory to survive a reading of the text, this sort of arbitrary assertion is left to fend for itself. The fact is that Ovid loved bizarre stories, of which there were many in Greek mythology and very few in Roman; here all his variations from Valerius Maximus are successfully designed to create drama (with Cipus concealing his horns with his merited laurels and bidding the people find the man with horns). This utterly implausible article has, however, been assumed by later writers on Ovid to be self-evidently true, and is normally used as undisputed evidence of Ovid's mockery of Augustus.

real life, deification meant a temple and a ritual, not a belief or a
legend. Augustus himself seems to have favoured the idea of personal descent from Apollo rather than the poetically favoured
connexion with Venus.[73] So little, in fact, was there a set orthodoxy that a strong case can be made for regarding the 'orthodoxy'
and 'mystique' conceived by modern scholars as largely the
creation of Ovid himself, in that it was he who shaped the
mythology.[74]

Second, in choosing *Fasti* and *Metamorphoses* as his forms for
poetic composition after A.D. 2, Ovid had certain considerations
clearly in mind. One must have been the opportunity to rival
Greek poets, especially Callimachus, in types of poetry that they
had invented, where the challenge lay in linking discrete episodes; he indicated the intended rivalry in his humorous use of
the phrase (*Met.* 1. 4) *perpetuum . . . carmen.* Another consideration must have been the desire to avoid problems of large-scale
construction. Both works are essentially episodic, and each episode has its own tone and *color*.[75] Large-scale symmetry and sub-
tly significant arrangements are missing from all Ovid's work.
The reason is that in all his work the unit of composition was
small and such that his imagination could comprehend it as a
whole and devise the most appropriate *color*. Thus within each
unit there are all the devices of sophisticated artistry, but widely
spaced episodes are independent of one another. The choice of
subject matter in *Fasti* and *Metamorphoses* reflects this technique
of composition; the challenge was to link the episodes, and here
Quintilian recognized the genius of Ovid, somewhat grudgingly
(4. 1. 77): 'There is a childish and pedantic affectation in vogue
in the schools of marking transitions by an epigram and hoping to
win applause for this cleverness. Ovid is given to this affectation
in *Metamorphoses*, but he has some excuse since he is compelled

73. The connexion with Venus was important to Julius Caesar: Nisbet
and Hubbard (1970), p. 31 and Weinstock (1971), 15 ff. For Augustus'
descent from Apollo, see Suetonius *Aug.* 70. 1 and 94.

74. On Ovid's mythopoeic faculty, see further below.

75. On the significance of episodic composition see chap. V, sect. 4.

to weld the most diverse subject matter into the appearance of a
unified whole'.

Those two considerations were literary. A third must have been
the desire to find a safe subject matter that was capable of accommodating elements of panegyric. Both works provided this; they
also provided material perfect for the exercise of that wit which
was inseparable from Ovid's process of poetic composition; and
they also provided material which could be moulded, re-formed,
and altered at will. Ovid is no more seriously interested in the
facts of Roman religion in the *Fasti* than he is in those of Greek
myth in *Metamorphoses*. What Ovid did at the end of *Metamorphoses* was to accept the deification of Julius Caesar as poetic
material of the same status as Greek myth so that it could accommodate his usual flashes of wit and lightness of touch as well as
seriousness, as, for instance, when Juppiter is made to say (15.
832–37):

> pace data terris animum ad civilia vertet
> iura suum legesque feret iustissimus auctor
> exemploque suo mores reget inque futuri
> temporis aetatem venturorumque nepotum
> prospiciens prolem sancta de coniuge natam
> ferre simul nomenque suum curasque iubebit.

After he (Augustus) has given peace to the world, he will turn
his attention to civil legislation and will with absolute justice propose and pass laws, and by his own example will control morality,
and, looking to the future and the line of his descendants, will
require the son born of his sacred wife to adopt his name and with
it his responsibilities.

Here the moral legislation (the real cause of all Ovid's troubles) is unmistakably praised and in the terms that Augustus
himself used of it in *res gestae* 8. 5. Then the hereditary principle
of the succession to Augustus is asserted, just as it was asserted in
Ars Amatoria. A few lines later (860) the title of *pater patriae* is
referred to, and the same relationship between Augustus and
Juppiter is asserted as was used in book 1. Seneca nicely recognized the nature of the panegyric in *Metamorphoses* when he

made Juppiter say, early in *Apocolocyntosis* (9): 'I propose that from this day forth Blessed Claudius be a god, to enjoy that honour with all its appurtenances in as full a degree as any other before him, and that a note to that effect be added to Ovid's *Metamorphoses*'. It is in harmony with Ovid's own assertions in *Tristia* 2 about his intention in *Metamorphoses*, and these, with some allowance for the exaggeration essential to rhetorical *insinuatio*, should be used as a valuable guide in interpreting the work. Ovid was no more an old-fashioned Republican, survivor of Philippi, bitterly chipping away at the regime, than he was a solemn supporter of Augustus, like Horace or Virgil or Agrippa. Ovid gradually learnt to live easily with the necessity for panegyric.[76]

7. The letters from exile

Ovid lived on in exile at Tomis for more than eight years (he probably died in A.D. 17), and in that period, apart from the *Ibis* (an attack on the one man in Rome who betrayed him), he composed ninety-six verse epistles—something like one a month. There was no real model for this literary form; the nearest was the *Epistulae* of Horace, but they were not intended as real letters (they made use of the autobiographical form for discussion of philosophical and literary topics in an informal way).[77] Ovid's *Tristia* and *Epistulae ex Ponto* were, in a real sense, intended as letters—particularly the latter, which were addressed to individuals. Ovid asserts that it took a year from the time that he sent a letter to the time that he received a reply.[78] Unlike Horace's, every one of them really concerns Ovid's own situation —his miseries, his surroundings, his reactions to news from Rome, and his hopes and prayers for pardon. Yet, in spite of this,

76. A clear literary analogue to Ovid's description of Julius Caesar's apotheosis in *Met*. 15 is Lucan's description of the apotheosis of Pompey (9. 1–18): humor is, of course, lacking in the later work, but both show the same capacity to suspend questions of truth and reality in mythopoeic invention. (Lucan clearly had Ovid's description in mind.)

77. See McGann (1969) and Williams (1972), 36–38.

78. *ex Ponto* 3. 4. 59–60; 4. 11. 15–16.

they are poems, and Ovid shows concern for a wider audience in frequent addresses like *vos* and *o lector*; or, again, in the publication of *ex Ponto* 1–3 as a unit, with prologue and epilogue addressed to Brutus; or in his sad sense that his poems from exile are monotonous (3. 7. 1 ff.); or in the care lavished on their construction;[79] or in the sheer *doctrina* of the writing—the volume of referential material from (often obscure) Greek mythology is in the very best tradition of Alexandrian composition. Finally, Ovid several times expresses the hope and the confidence that his poems from exile will find as appreciative an audience as his other works.[80]

This is highly original poetry, but a considerable element of its originality derives from the originality of the poet's situation and his readiness to exploit it poetically. No doubt Ovid could have written poetry anywhere, but a prime motive was his desire to obtain the grace of pardon or at least an amelioration of exile. His method (like that of Seneca later)[81] was flattery of the emperor. It is a pity to take a high moral tone over this; he was in a dilemma—dignity with exile or pardon with abasement. What is fascinating and important for the literature of the early Empire is to see that in respect to the large element of panegyric *Tristia* and *ex Ponto* stand as the culmination of a tendency that steadily grew throughout Ovid's poetry. Here is the finished creation of an Augustan poetic mystique of ruler worship:[82] Augustus (identified with the state) is of divine ancestry and a god on earth (addressed as Juppiter) and worshipped as a god in the poet's own private shrine. After Augustus' death the poet described his apotheosis (in Getic, but summarized in *ex Ponto* 4. 13. 19–30).[83] This creation of a mystique is to be attributed to Ovid; only scattered hints exist in other Augustan writers. The special mark of Ovid's activity lies in his mythopoeic invention; from the

79. See, for example, Kenney (1965), 37–49.
80. *ex Ponto* 2. 5. 19–24; 2. 6. 33–34; and perhaps 3. 2. 29–36.
81. See below.
82. See especially Scott (1930).
83. Also mentioned in *ex Ponto* 4. 6. 17–18; 4. 8. 63–64; 4. 9. 127–34.

amusing idea of Cupid as the brother of Aeneas and, consequently, a relative of Augustus in *Amores* 1. 2. 51 to the more serious
use of the motif in *ex Ponto* 3. 3. 62, there is a steady accumula-
tion of mythic details around the concept of the ruler as a god
and of this particular ruler's kinship with a series of gods. What
Ovid does with this element in his poetry is parallel to the free
inventive treatment which he gave to many particular Greek
myths. This mythopoeic faculty goes right through all Ovid's
work and is itself parallel to that faculty in his erotic poetry by
which he used for his own purposes, adapting them as required,
the themes, inventions and situations found in earlier love poets
like Tibullus and Propertius (and, no doubt, Gallus). That
particular strain continued on into nonerotic works like *Metamorphoses*, where Ovid made equally creative use, for instance,
of themes from the *Aeneid*. But the mythopoeic faculty was reinforced by another capacity in Ovid—and it was something new
in Roman poetry—that of taking poetic material and giving it a
new and appropriate treatment on its own terms, regardless of
questions about truth or relationship to reality or indeed to anything but the artistic question, How can this concept be given
new poetic life? Put differently, this can be seen to represent one
of the most significant features of imperial literature: the desire
to find originality, not in subject matter or ideas, but in the
novelty and ingenuity of a treatment which could give life to
material already used by others (and the more often it had been
used the greater was the challenge).[84]

When this technique is seen to have been applied to panegyric,
judgement is made difficult. The trouble is that when flattery is
carried to an extreme, a modern reader wants to read irony or
satire into it, partly through embarrassment, but mainly because
he does not believe it himself to start with and projects his own
incredulity onto the writer. There is an added difficulty in understanding the literary pleasure of thematic exploitation when the
material is basically repugnant; but that pleasure is a major
source of poetic inspiration in the writers of the early Empire.

84. See chap. V below.

In so far as Ovid can be seen to have given increasing poetic attention to shaping what may be called the myth of Augustus, to that extent he may be regarded as being—or, at any rate, as feeling himself—under increasing pressure to include the emperor among the topics of his poetry. The pressure probably came from Messalla and people like him in the first instance, but increasingly Ovid must have felt the pressure of events closing in on him— especially after 2 B.C.—and it can be no accident that his first extensive essay in panegyric came in *Ars Amatoria*. In A.D. 8 the pressure came directly from Augustus; and one would like to know what was said in the interview that preceded the exile. That Augustus felt confident that he had Ovid completely under control after the interview and exile is shown by the conjunction of two facts: first, though he banned Ovid's books from public libraries, he made no attempt to silence—or even censor—his communications from Tomis; second, the letters of *Tristia* did not mention names of specific addressees (except for his wife) lest they should be put in danger by such mention, but for the epistles *ex Ponto* all but one of his addressees gave permission for their names to be used. This can only mean that Augustus let it be known that Ovid was no longer considered an enemy. In fact, Augustus may very well have approved of the poetry from exile and felt that, at last, the most distinguished poet of his time was achieving something of what had been expected of him. Not only is there a much more extensively reverential treatment of the emperor, but Ovid, in his efforts to exculpate himself, came to share and express Augustus' view of a close relationship between literature and life—particularly morality (*Tristia* 2 is good propaganda for the point of view). That must have been extremely satisfactory to Augustus, and the fact that Ovid, in his vigorous defence of himself, could seem at times as if he were actually attacking Augustus and sounding a note of defiance, did no more than lend life and verisimilitude to the debate.[85]

85. This point is misinterpreted by those who take seriously the possibility that Ovid was in actual fact attacking Augustus—characteristic is Marache (1958).

8. *Ovid and the future*

Ovid was a poet deeply out of tune with what hindsight can identify as the main stream, the whole political trend, of his time; and he was the first such in Rome. He was a genius who struggled to keep poetry to itself and out of politics. When he failed he was lost, and he became the most influential guide to later writers of the Empire who were equally lost in an intolerable tension (portrayed by Tacitus in the *Dialogus*) that was really a reflection of the large-scale tension between the Republic, still alive (usually by means of artificial respiration) in many of the forms and attitudes of public life, and the imperial system. Ovid showed such writers three ways of escape or retreat: first, into antiquarianism and safe re-creation of Rome's past—especially of her far past (as in *Fasti*); second, into Greek mythology (as in all of his writing, but most of all in *Metamorphoses*); and, last, into a flattery of the monarch, in which imagination and fantasy could feel free to invent ever greater ingenuities.

In assessing Ovid, the younger Seneca easily comes to mind. He certainly differed from Ovid in being actively interested in a political career.[86] But, just as Ovid transformed poetic style, Seneca revolutionized the style of Latin prose. Like Ovid, he was exiled on charges of sexual misconduct; and he also tried to buy his way back with flattery. He too, in the end, was forced to face the reality of the tension between despotic power and the ideals of the Republican past kept alive in Stoic philosophy. Both men, in their different ways, were geniuses deeply at variance with the realities of their own time, and for neither did the innocent path of compromise work.

Both of them differed from Curiatius Maternus as he appears in Tacitus' portrait, for Maternus deliberately set out to offer public criticism of the imperial system, well knowing that he was causing offence. Neither Ovid nor Seneca did that, and the reason for Tacitus' choosing to emphasize that trait in Maternus was certainly to provide him with a literary activity that corre-

86. Seneca *contr.* 2 *pr.* 4.

sponded as closely as possible to oratory in having an active social function. In the important respect, however, of giving offence to the emperor, Ovid and Maternus were alike, and so was Seneca; and all three illustrate the dilemma of the writer under the imperial system.

Of the three ways of escape devised by Ovid, two were of prime importance and need wide examination. The escape into antiquarianism was not to become significant in the history of Roman literature until it was transformed in the middle of the second century A.D. into the archaizing movement. But the retreat into Greek mythology raises the whole question of the relationship between Greek and Roman culture; and the device of flattering the emperor was only one aspect of a retreat into irrationality that had many facets. It will be examined after the problem of Greek culture has been considered.

III

The Dominance
of Greek Culture

IT IS the thesis of this lecture that in the first centuries of the Roman Empire there was a reciprocal movement between the two civilizations of Greece and Rome, a movement whose beginnings can be seen already in the last century of the Republic but which accelerated greatly under the conditions of monarchical rule. The reciprocity operated in such a way that Greeks came to value, and participate in, the secular goods offered by the Roman Empire—firm rule, peace, good administration, Roman citizenship, and Roman careers; Rome dominated the material world. On the other hand, Romans were admitted to status in Greek culture and came to interpret artistic excellence in Greek terms and ultimately to regard things Greek—even their language—as superior to Roman equivalents. Romans thus came to feel inferior when they contemplated the cultural achievements of Greeks and responded increasingly by sheer imitation. This was a powerful factor in the decline of Roman literature.

The interaction of these two cultures is a vast subject and can only be treated here impressionistically and selectively, beginning with a sketch of their relationship in the early period.

1. The period before 100 B.C.

The evidence of Greek cultural influence on Rome goes back to the earliest period. In the religious sphere it can be seen in

forms of prayers, ritual regulations, and, particularly, in the
carmen Arvale.[1] In law it can be seen in the formulations of the
Twelve Tables.[2] It can be seen very extensively in Greek bor-
rowings in the Latin language that became regarded as native
words, and in very early transformations of Greek myths into
Roman terms. It can be seen in art in the earliest signatures of
artists, as found on the *Lapis Niger* or the fibula from the tomb
at Praeneste. It can even be found in the early organization of
characteristically Roman festivals like the *ludi maximi*.[3] But
this last example points up a peculiarity that was universal. It
might have been expected that such a national festival would
continue to grow into an equivalent to the great Greek festivals;
but it degenerated into a festival for the masses, patronized from
a distance by the aristocracy. Besides this we should note two
further facts: first, before the time of Lucilius, no member of the
aristocracy, that is, of the senatorial class, took any interest (other
than external) in rivalling what we should regard as the greatest
achievement of Greek culture, its literature; second, when Greek
literary genres were introduced after 240 B.C., their composition
was left exclusively to men of inferior social status, freedmen
and noncitizens. All of this suggests that, perhaps due to the
social divisions marked by the so-called struggle of the orders,
the upper class in Rome developed an attitude that regarded the
fine arts as frivolous, foreign, and unsuited to the practice of a
serious public figure. The fine arts, practised by foreigners and
inferiors, could serve for adornment, occasional entertainment,
or public ritual.

What the aristocracy could accept and use was the impact of
Greek sophistication on practical activities like law or religious
performances or personal comfort.[4] They were even ready to

1. Norden (1939).
2. Norden (1939), 254 ff.; Ciulei (1944); Schulz (1953), 5; Kunkel (1966),
5-6, 23-24.
3. Still the most stimulating account of early Roman culture, despite
evidence that has accumulated since he wrote, is that of Mommsen in the
first two books of his *History of Rome*.
4. See, for example, Fraenkel (1960), 415-16.

adopt Greek formulae of politeness and civilize their daily in-
tercourse with the inherited courtesies of Hellenistic society.
This had certainly happened before the time of Plautus, since
he delights in the comic effect of elaborate politenesses between
likely and unlikely characters. These politenesses have parallels
in Aristophanes and in Plato, but they are extremely infrequent
in Greek New Comedy. They are later found in Terence (who
was much closer than Plautus to the idiom of everyday life) and
in the letters of Cicero. They cover a wide range of situations:
greetings and farewells, apologies, invitations, acceptances and
refusals, the requesting and granting of favours, expressions of
gratitude and congratulation. There can be no question that
Plautus mechanically incorporated formulae in his 'translations', for not only are they rare in New Comedy, but the comic
impact would be totally lost unless his audience could recognize
the genuine ring of polite upper-class manners. The conclusion
must be that the upper stratum of Roman society had learnt and
appreciated the idiom of polite manners, common throughout
Hellenistic society and readily available in the Greek cities of
South Italy.[5] A similar influence of Greek social ideals can be
seen in one phrase in the epigram[6] (itself a purely Greek innovation) on the tomb of L. Cornelius Scipio Barbatus, consul in
298 B.C.: *quoius forma virtutei parisuma fuit* ('his physical perfection was the perfect match of his moral qualities') is a translation into Latin of the Athenian ideal of καλοκἀγαθία.

All of this had happened at least by the end of the third century B.C. By then Greek literary genres had been introduced into
Rome; at first only plays (beginning in 240 B.C.), and those written by the Greek freedman from Tarentum, Livius Andronicus.
But soon he recast the *Odyssey* into Latin, and, by 207 B.C., had
acquired sufficient distinction to be asked, when the *quinde-
cemviri* had consulted the Sibylline books at the order of the
senate, to compose the *carmen* which they prescribed should be

5. See Fraenkel (1957), 350 n. 4, and (1962), 69–71; Crosthwaite (1956).
6. *CIL* I.2. 6–7.

sung through the city by a choir of boys and girls[7]—the whole procedure entirely Greek in spirit and in ritual. Later authors, while still composing plays for the aediles, found in poetry on contemporary history and in panegyric verse a way of interesting the Roman aristocracy in patronage, at least, of poets.[8] Thus Ennius accompanied his patron M. Fulvius Nobilior on his Aetolian campaign, writing a poem on it and later adding several books on the subject to his *Annales*.

The great acceleration in the influx of Greek intellectual culture particularly and the way in which it was resisted by the more conservative among the aristocracy[9] can be seen in the events of just twenty years: in 173 B.C. two Epicurean philosophers were expelled from Rome; in 169 B.C. Crates of Pergamum began his influential stay in the city; in 161 B.C. philosophers and rhetors were expelled; and in 155 B.C. Carneades, Critolaus, and Diogenes, the three most distinguished philosophers of the contemporary Hellenistic world, came to Rome on an embassy and stayed to lecture. Less significant—but only because a mixture of motives enters into religious changes—was the acceptance of the cult of *Magna Mater Idaea* (more oriental really than Greek, except that Alexander had unified that region of the world) into Rome in 204 B.C., and the prerogative claimed by the aristocracy to celebrate it in a yearly festival (with performances of plays added to the festival in 194 B.C.).

7. Livy 27. 37. 7.
8. Williams (1968), 37–39.
9. The attitude of contempt and doom is well caught by Cato's words to his son (quoted by Pliny *NH* 29. 14): 'About those Greeks, Marcus my son, I shall speak in the proper place, of the result of my inquiries in Athens, and the fact that it is right to inspect their literature but not to study it closely. I shall convince you that they are an utterly worthless and undisciplined race. And consider this the word of a prophet: when that race shall give us their literature, they will corrupt everything—even more so if they send their doctors here. They have made a conspiracy to murder all foreigners by their medicine, but even this they ask a fee for doing so that they may win credit and destroy us easily. And they keep calling us barbarians, and they foul us more disgustingly than they do other peoples by calling us Opici. I forbid you to have anything to do with doctors'. See also Plutarch *Cato* 22–23.

The same impulse to a closer acquaintance with Greek culture can be seen in Terence's more faithful adherence to the
plays of Menander and Apollodorus and to the implications of
their being set in a Greek city. At the same time he established
and expressed in his *Prologues* a conception of originality that
viewed it as not being in the least inconsistent with the use of
a Greek model, a conception that was to be most important for
later writers. It is clear from the *Prologues* that Terence was
appealing to the upper stratum in Roman society, and his views
will certainly have appealed to his patrons. It is at this point
that the rift, based on class, becomes obvious in Roman culture;
and it widened throughout the second century B.C. till drama
as such virtually ceased to be written for the Roman stage. The
rift was between the cultural interests of the upper classes, which
were more and more concerned with Greek culture, and those
of the lower classes, the voting masses, who needed to be enter-
tained and were alienated by writers like Terence. Yet, by a
powerful and persistent convention, the writing of poetry was
regarded as beneath the dignity of senators; they wrote indeed,
but they produced instructive works on farming and the law and,
since they themselves made it, history. They could condescend
to enrich the world with the fruits of their experience, but artistic frivolities—perfectly acceptable when dedicated to them[10]
—were for Greeks and social inferiors. This whole situation was
changed when Lucilius (not himself a senator but of senatorial
family) invented a completely new type of poetry that com-
ported with the dignity of a senator.[11] From then on, poetry became possible for senators as an occupation of their (naturally
few) idle hours. But this also meant that the most educated
classes in Rome became vitally interested in understanding and
giving Roman form to the greatest and most up-to-date achieve-

10. Whether by Romans or Greeks: cf. Alcaeus of Messene *Anth. Pal.*
7. 247, making use of an epigram on the Macedonian dead at Cynoscephalae
to attack Philip, and in *Anth. Plan.* 5, celebrating Flamininus as the liberator of Greece (the occasion of the proclamation at the Isthmian games of
196 B.C.).

11. Fraenkel (1957), 80, 150–53; Williams (1968), 443–59.

ments of Greek writers. For Lucilius' poetry showed itself fully aware of contemporary Hellenistic ideals and ideas. Like all great literature in Rome, it was an amalgam of Greek and Roman elements.

The versatility of these men and their deep knowledge of Greek culture[12] is clear in many examples: for instance, in P. Rutilius Rufus, consul in 105 B.C., who wrote his autobiography in Latin but a history of his own times in Greek:[13] that is, the defence of his own career was directed to fellow senators, but with his history he wanted to reach the cosmopolitan audience of the Hellenistic world (including Romans, of course).[14] Nor was the traffic only one way: the conservative Cato insisted on using an interpreter when he addressed Greeks—that is understandable; and Greek embassies were only heard by the senate when they spoke in Latin. But Greeks also took a close interest in Roman culture, and there were Greeks of this period who even took a Roman point of view[15]—the outstanding example was Polybius. It was in this period too that documents and decrees that were translated into Greek began to use Latinisms where no exact Greek equivalent was immediately to hand; this was natural for dates and technical terms, but Latin idioms were also translated, like *operam dare ut* . . . (διδόναι ἐργασίαν ἵνα . . .).[16] Such locutions can also be found fairly frequently in Polybius. Finally, the Latin language became an object of study

12. For Greek education of children, cf. on Aemilius Paullus, Plutarch's life of him 6; on Tiberius Gracchus, Cicero *Brutus* 104, and on the mother of the Gracchi, Plutarch *Life of C. Gracchus* 19. 2.

13. That he was in exile in the East does not affect the issue, as the later histories in Greek by Lucullus and by Cicero himself show. Lucullus actually claimed that solecisms in his history were deliberate and intended to show that he was no Greek; Cicero refused to do that (*ad Att.* 1. 19. 10). There is no good reason to suppose that the history of Rutilius was a mere translation of his autobiography.

14. Cf. Cicero *pro Archia* 23 *Graeca leguntur in omnibus fere gentibus, Latina suis finibus, exiguis sane, continentur.*

15. See, for example, Hahn (1906), 40 ff. Hahn's collection of material is extensively used in what follows.

16. Hahn (1906), 38.

and comment in Alexandria;[17] but not till the middle of the first century B.C. did Latin come to be treated linguistically as a dialect of Greek.

2. *From 100 B.C. to the time of Augustus*

The real contrast between this period and the previous one lay in the speed and self-confidence of the Roman take-over of Greek culture. Within half a century Greek culture was assimilated, dominated, and used to create a specifically Roman culture. The single great intellectual force in this conquest was Cicero, and the self-confidence is clear, for instance, in the words he gives to Scipio in *de re publica* (1. 36): 'On the one hand, I am not satisfied with the works on this subject which the greatest and wisest men of Greece have left us; on the other hand, I am not so bold as to set my own opinions above theirs. So I request that you hear me neither as one who is quite ignorant of Greek ideas nor as one who prefers theirs, especially on this subject, to our own, but as a Roman widely educated by a father's care and fired from boyhood with a desire to learn, yet also schooled by experience and advice at home much more than by books'. Here the voice of Cicero himself speaks: Greek philosophy was useful for giving shape to hard Roman experience and native wisdom. The attitude is clear from a different direction in *de legibus* 1. 53. There, when Cicero has come to the point of discussing what he considers both relevant to the consideration of law and also the most difficult philosophical problem—the question of what is the highest good—he throws in the amusing story of L. Gellius Poplicola (consul in 72 B.C.) when he first arrived in Athens as proconsul of Greece. He called together the heads of the philosophical schools and earnestly beseeched them to settle their differences; he promised his own good offices as arbiter. The joke is attributed to Atticus, but Cicero uses it seriously to introduce his own philosophical synthesis.

This note of extreme confidence, the sense of being able to

17. Hahn (1906), 52.

use Greek culture where it had anything valuable to offer but of
starting from a firm base that was essentially Roman, permeates
all Cicero's writing. In his work on the history of oratory (*Brutus*
254), Brutus is made to report a compliment from Caesar: 'I
regard you—which was praise enough—as the virtual founder
and inventor of this fluency in speaking, but, more than that,
as having performed a notable service to the fame and prestige
of the Roman people: for, in this one respect in which we used
to be outdone by the conquered Greeks, that victory has been
snatched from them by you—or at least shared'. With such attitudes, Romans had clearly come to feel that they did not need
to be overawed by Greek culture: on the contrary, it was there
for them at their disposal to use appropriately.

The attitude is clear too in rhetoric. This was a purely Greek
science[18]—even Roman rhetorical treatises omit any reference
to funeral orations, which, though very important in Roman
society, were not a Greek custom at all. The basic training con-
sisted of declamation in Greek, and it was practised by the great
Crassus and by Cicero himself. There had earlier (in 161 B.C.)
been hostility to Greek rhetors; the last flicker of conservative
resistance can be seen in 92 B.C. in the expulsion of Latin rhetors
(they had too immediate an influence on Roman education).[19]
But already the *ad Herennium* shows antipathy to Greek rhetors
and uses Roman examples. Cicero, with the same confidence
with which he dealt with Greek philosophy, took over what
was an arid academic discipline in Greek and turned it into a
humane, wide-ranging critique of the literary form of oratory,
which he regarded as a product of the creative imagination. In
consequence, Cicero was able to feel justified in regarding poetry
and the fine arts as both inferior to oratory (*Brutus* 3). Cicero's
achievement here was so impressive that even in the next generation a Greek rhetor like Caecilius of Caleacte can be found

18. See, above all, Kennedy (1972), 72–300.
19. Cicero (*de oratore* 3. 93–95) puts a less plausible view in the mouth
of Crassus, whose censorial edict it had been, that the Latin rhetors were
incompetent and immoral.

declaring him the equal of Demosthenes. In this, however, Caecilius had long been preceded by Apollonius Molon, who con-
fessed to the young Cicero in Rhodes that the only good things
that had been left to Greeks, literary culture and eloquence, had
now passed over to the Romans.[20] And the strength of Roman
rhetorical influence in the late Republic can be gauged by the
fact that young Cicero wrote to Tiro in 44 B.C. from Athens to
tell him that he had been practising in Latin *apud Bruttium
philologum*. Greek rhetoric was simply taken over and transformed. And it was really in Rome that the controversy over
Asianism and Atticism was decided in favour of Atticism—a victory that cost Greek literature dear.[21]

In law, this period saw the same sort of advance.[22] Roman
legal science came to terms with Greek philosophy in such a way
as to use the generalizing capacity provided by it to formulate
basic structural concepts. This was a very considerable intellectual achievement, slowly and carefully carried out, the guiding
attitude being, as Sallust made Caesar say (*Catiline* 51. 37), that
'our ancestors never lacked either good sense or courage, and
no false pride ever prevented their adopting the institutions of
others if they approved them'. In the process, Roman legal science developed into an organized professional science on the
Hellenistic pattern, and it was no mere mixture or juxtaposition
of Greek and Roman; as in Cicero's philosophy, the two elements
were blended into an organic unity.

The changes in Roman poetry in the period fit into the same
pattern. Not only did it become an activity acceptable to the
leisure hours of senators like Q. Lutatius Catulus and Cicero
himself, but the genius of Catullus, building on the invention
of Lucilius, created a type of personal poetry that had been unknown in Greece since the sixth century B.C. He also invented
the totally new genre of love elegy, and this (like most of his
poetry) was created out of a fusion of Greek and Roman ele-

20. Plutarch *Cicero* 4.
21. See sect. 3 below.
22. See especially Schulz (1953), 60–86.

ments. One mark of the period was continuous invention and exploitation of the inventions of predecessors. So Horace used the model of Lucilius for his own highly original *Satires* and *Epistles*—the latter a most ingenious invention of his own;[23] and, building to some extent on the work of Catullus, he created a new type of lyric poetry in his *Odes*. Propertius and Tibullus likewise extended the work of Catullus into new fields, and by new methods transformed love elegy into a major poetic genre. Virgil successively challenged comparison with Theocritus, Hesiod, and Homer, similarly using his predecessors in the process, and he put a new stamp on the genres of pastoral, didactic, and epic. Another mark of the period is most clear in his work, though it is certainly clear also in the works of all the other poets mentioned above: that is the extraordinary self-confidence with which these poets faced and made use of the greatest Greek poets.[24] All of them consciously exploited the great Classical Greek poets, but they also used and challenged the great Hellenistic poets who had established new canons of accuracy and perfection in poetic composition. In the process they achieved an astonishing originality and displayed another type of self-confidence: their poetry was extremely subtle; it meant far more than it appeared to say, and confidently demanded the imaginative cooperation of the reader.[25] (For reasons to be described in later lectures, that confidence proved, in the long run, to be misplaced.) The fusion of Greek and Roman elements was, however, the basis of all their poetry, and the greatest originality was shown here. For instance, Greek mythology had been the staple material of Greek poetry at all times. Roman poets in this period invented ways of using Greek mythology that had had no parallel among Greek poets since the fifth century B.C. (and then only to a very limited extent).[26]

23. See Williams (1968), 518–23.
24. Williams (1968), chap. 5.
25. Williams (1968), chap. 4.
26. I hope to explore this point of view in a monograph soon to be published.

Greek myths, as these Roman poets used them, were made to work for their place in poems: they were seldom merely exemplary or ornamental or used for their own sake. In fact, one of the greatest contrasts between Ovid on the one hand and the poets of the late Republic and of the earlier Augustan age on the other is that he reverted to using the material of Greek mythology in ways that were basically Greek.

Every aspect of Roman intellectual culture in this period can be seen undergoing confident reshaping in the light of a growing acquaintance with Greek culture. But the meeting of the two cultures took other forms too. Increasingly, in the last century of the Republic, close ties were formed between important Romans and leading members of Greek city-states, to the mutual advantage of both: Romans gained inside knowledge and help in governing Greeks, and Greeks gained benefits for their states and for themselves.[27] But this also meant that Romans were more and more initiated, in a natural day-to-day way, into the Greek way of life, and many of them liked what they saw and adapted their own way of life accordingly—even to the extent of wearing Greek dress.[28] Some Romans even chose to go and live in the Greek East and were initiated into mystery cults.[29] Reciprocally, many Greeks were given Roman citizenship, successively and increasingly, by Marius, Sulla, Pompey, and Caesar. In fact, Caesar went so far as to confer citizenship on all medical doctors and teachers of the liberal arts in Rome in order to induce others to come and settle there too.[30]

The influx of Greeks into Italy and especially into Rome in this period was great. Already in 166 B.C. Polybius could speak of a great flood pouring from Greece;[31] and the drawing power of Rome hugely increased in the last century of the Republic.[32]

27. This aspect of the life of the period is extensively examined by Bowersock (1965), and I am much indebted to his work in what follows.
28. See Bowersock (1965), chap. 6.
29. Hahn (1906), 70.
30. Suetonius *Caesar* 42. 1.
31. 30. 32. 10.
32. The basic survey of Greeks in Rome during this period who were

Those who came found various levels of admission. At the highest level, distinguished Greeks came at the invitation of important Romans: so Panaetius was invited by Scipio, Poseidonius came as a friend of Pompey, Antiochus of Ascalon came as a friend of Lucullus, and L. Calpurnius Piso brought back Philodemus with him. Far more came, in the first instance, as slaves and freedmen, and worked their way into the confidence and esteem of their sometime masters. These men of course brought with them valuable expertise in Greek literature, philosophy, and rhetoric; but of even more interest are a whole series who brought their expertise to bear on Roman studies. Such, for instance, was Epicadius,[33] freedman of Sulla, who completed his master's unfinished autobiography. More surprising, however, are men like M. Pompilius Andronicus,[34] who wrote what seems to have been a polemical work against commentators on Ennius —very much in the style of the later Alexandrian scholars. Or, again, Nicias of Cos (first mentioned by Cicero in a letter of 50 B.C.)[35] wrote a number of books on Lucilius which were approved by the grammarian Santra.[36] Similarly, L. Crassitius,[37] a freedman from Tarentum, wrote a commentary on the *Zmyrna* of Catullus' friend, C. Helvius Cinna. Linguistic studies were not missing: Philoxenus,[38] a grammarian from Alexandria who taught in Rome, wrote a work περὶ τῆς Ῥωμαϊκῆς διαλέκτου, and the Younger Tyrannio,[39] taken captive after Actium, wrote περὶ τῆς Ῥωμαϊκῆς δαλέκτου ὅτι ἔστιν ἐκ τῆς Ἑλληνικῆς; both titles represent the view, common later, that Latin was a dialect of

---

grammarians, rhetors, poets, and writers (excluding philosophers), is still that of Alfred Hillscher (1892), and constant use has been made of his work in what follows.

33. Hillscher (1892), 363–64.

34. Suetonius *de gramm.* 8; Hillscher (1892), 366–67; Vahlen (1903), p. xxix.

35. *ad Att.* 7. 3. 10.; Hillscher (1892), 373–74.

36. For his unpopularity as tyrant of Cos and the despoiling of his tomb, see Crinagoras *Anth. Pal.* 9. 81; Bowersock (1965), 45–46.

37. Hillscher (1892), 382–83.

38. Hillscher (1892), 371; Pfeiffer (1968), 273–74.

39. Hillscher (1892), 375–76.

Greek, and it will have been in this period that the theory became popular that Romans were, in fact, originally Hellenes. A freedman of Pompey, Lenaeus,[40] translated Greek medical texts into Latin—this was the same man who wrote a satire against Sallust for insults against his patron in the *Histories*. Two Greek rhetors, Empylus of Rhodes and Straton of Epirus,[41] were on the Republican side: the former wrote a *Brutus* (Brutus had been his patron) on the death of Caesar; the other wrote a self-commendatory account of his own practical assistance at the suicide of Brutus during the battle of Philippi—thus he recommended himself to Caesar.

What emerges from these facts is that during the last century of the Republic, Alexandria, as it were, was transferred to Rome: not only libraries came in abundance, but all the scholarly activity associated with the great library of the Ptolemies. Nor were poets missing. From the early second century B.C., Greek poets had been ready to compose panegyrical poetry, especially in the form of epigrams, that was acceptable to their conquerors. Alcaeus of Messene wrote so for Flamininus and against Philip (thus altering an earlier standpoint). But it is highly doubtful whether he ever came to Rome.[42] However, increasing numbers of Greek poets came to Rome after 100 B.C. Publilius Syrus[43] was one of the most remarkable since his compositions in Latin won him enduring fame, and his wit influenced not only similar composers but even, according to the elder Seneca,[44] Cicero himself. The wit of M. Otacilius Pitholaus[45] was thought worthy of quotation by Macrobius,[46] and Caesar bore, with gentlemanly restraint, his *epigrammata maledicentissima* that attacked his reputation; the epigrams were probably in Greek and perhaps belonged to the freedom as-

40. Pliny *NH* 25. 5; Hillscher (1892), 377.
41. Hillscher (1892), 391–93.
42. Hillscher (1892), 400–401.
43. Hillscher (1892), 401.
44. *contr.* 7. 3. 9.
45. Hillscher (1892), 401.
46. *Sat.* 2. 2. 13.

sociated with a triumph, but the witticism was certainly in
Latin since it depends on a Latin pun. Then there was the distinguished A. Licinius Archias from Antioch, the client of
Cicero; he seems to have promised his patron the much-desired
epic on his consulship, and he certainly wrote an epic-type poem
on Lucullus' part in the Mithridatic war. He had come to Rome
originally in 102 B.C., and Cicero's words imply that he celebrated the achievements of the consuls, Marius and Catulus.[47]
That was done, perhaps, in epigrams, thirty-seven of which have
survived under the name Archias, though none has political
content.[48] Thyillus[49] was perhaps a freedman of Cicero (he was,
at any rate, living with him in 67 B.C.).[50] Three pleasantly medi-
ocre epigrams by him on general themes have survived.[51] Tullius
Laurea[52] was certainly a freedman of Cicero; he not only wrote
in Greek (three quite nice epigrams are extant), but Pliny[53]
quotes a very competent epigram that Laurea wrote, after Cicero's death, on the spring that suddenly appeared in the Puteolan
estate, with miraculous powers to cure eye troubles. Philodemus,[54] more attractive as a poet than a writer of prose, the
friend of L. Calpurnius Piso, scarcely needs mention.[55] But
Parthenius of Nicaea came to Rome as a slave in the Mithridatic
war.[56] He was considerably influential with Roman poets and
may have been one of Virgil's teachers;[57] he was closely associated with C. Cornelius Gallus and perhaps with the development of Latin love elegy.

47. *pro Archia* 5.
48. See Gow and Page (1968), pp. 432–35.
49. Hillscher (1892), 403.
50. *ad Att.* 1. 9. 2.
51. *Anth. Pal.* 6. 170; 7. 223; 10. 5.
52. Hillscher (1892), 403.
53. *NH* 31. 7.
54. Hillscher (1892), 403–4.
55. In one epigram (*Anth. Pal.* 11. 35) he can, interestingly, be seen
gathering his Greek friends for a dinner party. See the commentary of
Cicorius (1922), 297–98.
56. Hillscher (1892), 404–5.
57. Macrobius *Sat.* 5. 17. 18.

What seems to have happened during this period was that
Rome came to be recognized as the intellectual centre of the
Mediterranean world. The reasons for this were not primarily
intellectual, but, rather, political, economic, and social. The
lengthy disturbed period in the Hellenistic world, when small
states fought in rivalry, brought about a steady decline in the
intellectual life of the Greek East, and as Rome gradually
brought order and stability, she came to be a place that important Greeks wished at least to visit, quite apart from the pressure brought to bear on them by Roman magistrates in the East.
But Rome did more than that; and it is possible to discern in
this period a really positive force exercised by Romans in their
eagerness to assimilate all they could of a declining Greek culture;[58] this inspired Greek scholars and poets of all sorts to see
a new purpose in their activities. The influence, in this form,
did not last for long; but in the late Republic and in the Age
of Augustus it is a fascinating sight to see Romans keeping Greek
culture alive so that it might minister to their own self-confident
aspirations.

The point of view is well expressed by Cicero (*Tusc.* 2. 5): 'So
I exhort all who can do it to snatch the glory of this field of study
too [philosophy] from the failing hand of Greece and transplant
it to this city, just as our ancestors, by their spirit of enquiry and
their tireless efforts, transplanted all the rest that were worth
searching out. And in oratory certainly our fame has grown
from humble beginnings to the greatest possible height, in such
a way, however, that, as nature ordains with almost everything,
it is now declining and seems likely in a short time to come to
nothing; while, on the other hand, philosophy is coming to
birth in Latin literature as a result of the times we live in, and
we are giving it assistance. . . .'.

The *Tusculans* was written in the evil year 45 B.C., and Cicero's
pessimism appears in his view that oratory is in decline. His
reasons for thinking that oratory will 'soon come to nothing'
are explained at the end of the *Brutus*; they are there based on

58. See Pfeiffer (1968), 274.

the political situation—the breakdown of Republican government and the tyranny of Julius Caesar. Here he avoids making
that diagnosis because his interest is concentrated on philosophy.
So he allows the argument that there is a natural law of growth
and decline just to appear and attaches it to the metaphor in
senescere. Then, after expressing his pessimism briefly in a most
extreme form, he hurries on, with a difficult syntactical connexion, to the assertion that the evil times (which, it is implied,
will kill off oratory) are propitious to the birth of philosophy
as a Roman literary art. This was no more than the truth. It
was late in 46 B.C. that Cassius was converted to Epicureanism,
and he and Cicero were corresponding about it in 45 B.C.[59] In
March of the following year, he and Brutus took the lead in
assassinating Julius Caesar. It was in 46 B.C. that Cato had committed his famous suicide at Utica rather than endure the clem-
ency of Caesar: he was a Stoic. Brutus, like Cicero to some extent,
was an Academician. The letter of Cassius—taken, of course,
with Cicero's late philosophical works—gives the best clue to
what was happening. Cassius there presents a point of view
quite different from that of conventional Epicureanism, with
heavy emphasis on justice and activism. These Romans were all
making use of conceptual frameworks provided by Greek philosophy to come to practical decisions about Roman politics.
Different philosophical systems could lead to the same conclusion. Greek culture was being set to work for practical Roman
ends.

It is important, too, that in this period the two cultures began
to converge, and not only through the activities of Romans who
fused Greek with Roman; Romans were also found composing
in Greek and—more significant—Greeks were writing in Latin.
The convergence was assisted by theories that Romans were
really Hellenes and that Latin was a dialect of Greek. Relevant
here is the work of the younger Aristodemus of Nysa,[60] teacher
of Pompey's children, who lived in Rome in the middle of the

59. *ad Fam*. 15. 16 and 19. See Momigliano (1941), 151–57.
60. See Hillscher (1892), 435–39 and Robert *Hellenica* (1940), 148.

first century B.C. He wrote a work demonstrating that Homer
was really a Roman, on the basis of the Roman customs to be
found in him. His comments, mostly idiotic, commended themselves to Eustathius, and are preserved to some extent in the
Homeric scholia.

But basic Roman attitudes still remained. Greeks were welcome as artists, writers, and scholars, but, ultimately, they were
inferiors—at least socially. Even so distinguished a Greek as
Philodemus is found composing an invitation-epigram to Piso
in which he explicitly adopts the status of a *cliens*.[61] Pliny,[62]
writing about silversmith's chalk, and reflecting on the use of
the inferior type to whiten slaves' feet at auction, draws a contrast between Greek slaves in the late Republic, who were able
to gain fame as writers or wealth by opportunism in the civil
wars, and those of his own time, who were actually being elevated to Roman magistracies. It is one aspect of Roman regard
for Greek culture in the late Republic that they valued it for
what it could contribute to Roman culture, but its practitioners, however pleasant and stimulating their company, were never rivals, never in any way a threat to Romans. Greeks knew
their place. The monarchy was to change that situation somewhat; and the intrinsic vitality of Greek culture was to do the
rest.

3. Greek culture in the age of Augustus

Greeks of the relevant class universally welcomed monarchy
at Rome. It replaced with one clearly supreme patron the dangerous ambiguity of varying patrons thrown up by the civil
wars and even by the ordinary process of Republican government.[63] Cicero's friends wrote with pained astonishment in 43
B.C. of the madness displayed by Greeks who felt no interest in
supporting the better cause.[64] Philo neatly summed up Greek

61. *Anth. Pal.* 11. 44; Williams (1968), 125–28.
62. *NH* 35. 199–201.
63. Bowersock (1965), 2.
64. *ad fam.* 12. 13 and 14.

feeling when he spoke of Augustus as 'the first and greatest and universal benefactor who entrusted the universal ship to a single helmsman instead of many'($ἀντὶ\ πολυαρχίας$).[65] So, under Augustus (though the process had started with Julius Caesar), it is no surprise to find the greatest Greek writers all living at least a part of their lives at Rome.[66] A high proportion of them played double roles as ambassador and writer, as some of their predecessors had also done, but the pattern became permanent with Augustus; and such men played a significant role in the government of the Empire. No statistics are available, but it is clear that the influx of Greeks into Rome greatly increased in this period and that it was Augustus' policy to encourage it.

A fundamental change in Greek artistic tastes and attitudes becomes clear in this period. Dionysius of Halicarnassus gives a particularly interesting analysis of it in his essay *On the Ancient Orators*. He expresses gratitude that he lives in the present age because of the progress in the arts and especially in oratory. He dates the beginning of the collapse of oratory to the death of Alexander; by his own time it had almost vanished. Its place had been taken by the shameless and decadent style known as Asianism. But the present generation has restored the ancient rhetoric, and taste is noticeably improving. The real cause of this he attributes to Rome and especially to her rulers 'who govern their country on the highest moral principles and are men of education and fine taste'.[67] So, he says, histories and fine speeches and even philosophy are being written both by Greeks and by Romans; and he looks forward to the complete disappearance of bad taste (i.e., Asianism) in the present generation.

With due allowance for a natural flattery, this makes two very important points: first, that Romans in this period were exercising a decisive influence on Greek culture; second, that the influence came from Roman admiration of Classical Greek models which lay four centuries or more in the past. This marks

65. *leg. ad Gaium* 149.
66. In general, see Bowersock (1965), chap. 10.
67. *On the Ancient Orators* 3.

the origin of the archaizing movement in Greek literature, and it was ultimately destructive of it; but certain earlier general trends can be detected. The idea that in Greece perfection was reached in the far past coexisted with Cicero's idea, for instance, that oratory was only just reaching its perfection in his own time; and this was clearly likely to create a buoyant confidence in Romans at the same time that it infected Greeks with nostalgia and regret. But then Cicero reached perfection, and in the Augustan age he was followed by Virgil and Horace and Propertius. Here the gloomy theory of inevitable rise and fall (found in the elder Seneca and in Velleius Paterculus)[68] expressed an attitude that Romans were pretty well compelled to adopt by the force of their own logic. At that point there was a strong upsurgence of Greek literary vitality. But that is to anticipate.

Augustus was clearly a vital figure in Dionysius' analysis— justifiably, for Augustus had a great admiration for the Greek past. That Roman interest in Greece, of course, goes back much further: it is very clear in Cicero's admiration for Plato and Demosthenes; and, during the last century of the Republic, Greeks no less than Romans came to feel justified in looking back over the Hellenistic age to the great Classical age of Greece. But Augustus was vital, for he had pre-eminent authority, and he infected Greeks no less than Romans with his own historicist view of the great past as the model of excellence in all fields. Just as he tried to reconstitute Rome on the ancient pattern by reviving old moral ideals and the ancient religion, so he did also for Greeks: there are inscriptions from Athens, Aphrodisias, and Kyme, dating from early in his reign (the inscriptions from about 27 B.C., but the decisions from 29 B.C.), which set up machinery for restoring to state control temple property and both sacred and public lands that had fallen into private hands.[69] From acts like these, which were no doubt widespread in the Greek world, there began that renascence of Greek cities and

68. See chap. I above.
69. Oliver (1972).

Greek life which made itself strongly felt from the latter half of the first century A.D. onwards. Parallel with this was the propagation of Roman ideas through the medium of classicizing art: the outstanding (but not unique) example of this was the temple of Roma and Augustus in Athens,[70] with its fine neo-Attic inscription.[71] Here too Augustus was building on earlier preparations; for Roman patronage had long before influenced a strong revival of the old Attic style in painting and sculpture. Many Greek artists came to work in this style in Rome—outstanding among them for his theoretical as well as for his practical activity was Pasiteles, who came to Rome in the time of Pompey.[72] The new impulse given by Augustus was to encourage such artistic activity in Greek cities as well, and Roman architects seem to have helped with their own technical skills.[73]

Simultaneously, Romans (of the relevant class) had come to feel a strong attraction for the Greek way of life, an attraction that actually extended to dressing in Greek style and speaking Greek. For instance, when Antony was in Athens in the winter of 39–38 B.C., he dressed as a Greek and behaved in every way as a Greek, only returning to Roman habits when he had to return to the army.[74] Cicero reflected this in his speech for C. Rabirius (26–27): 'I have often seen not only distinguished Roman citizens but also young noblemen and even senators of highest birth dressed for their pleasure and delight in Greek style—and not in their gardens or villas, but amongst all the crowds in Naples'. In fact, Naples was one of the most conservatively Greek of Greek cities, preserving its way of life and customs and institutions under a thin Roman veneer till late into the Empire.[75] Thus it provided a ready retreat in which wealthy Romans could indulge their longing for the Greek way of life.

70. For descriptions see Judeich (1931), 256 ff.; Travlos (1971), 494 ff. and plate 626.

71. *IG* II. III. 2. 3173. Plate in Kirchner (1948), nr. 118.

72. See especially Pollitt (1974), 78 ff.

73. Bowersock (1965), 74–75, 95.

74. Appian *BC* 5. 76. Hahn (1906), 71; Bowersock (1965), 10.

75. Hahn (1906), 62.

It became especially attractive after Julius Caesar passed a law that no citizen, aged between twenty and forty, could be out of Italy (except with the army) for more than three years; and senators' sons were forbidden to leave Italy except to accompany a magistrate.[76] Clearly, many Romans chose, like Propertius' friend Tullus (nephew of the consul of 33 B.C.), to live permanently in the Greek East.[77] Augustus himself enjoyed and admired Greek life. In 31 B.C. he became an initiate of the Eleusinian mysteries,[78] and he visited the mysteries when he was in Athens again in 20 B.C.[79] Not only were the games at his own city of Nicopolis Greek (the city had been founded to celebrate Actium), but so were the quinquennial games instituted in A.D. 2 at Naples; and Augustus encouraged the continued indulgence of Greek customs on his own island of Capri.[80] That island was the site of a remarkable scene in his last year: Augustus caused Romans and Greeks to exchange clothing and speak each other's language. That can only have been a symbolic demonstration of the community of the two cultures; but it makes sense of an important aspect of Augustus' activity as *princeps* to view it as directed to creating a unified Greco-Roman civilization out of the Empire.

Culturally, however, the most important of Augustus' activities was his patronage of writers. Among Greeks, these included a galaxy of talent: Dionysius of Halicarnassus (who spent twenty-two years in Rome), Strabo, Nicolaus of Damascus, Caecilius of Caleacte, Parthenius, Crinagoras, Diodorus of Sardis, Antipater of Thessalonice, and many others. The activity of these men in Rome stimulated a corresponding activity—that of Romans who wrote in Greek. The examples known to us must represent only a small fraction of such practitioners. One of the most interesting was Q. Sextius Niger, who had been offered

76. Suetonius *Caesar* 42. 1.
77. Hahn (1906), 70–71.
78. Cassius Dio 51. 4. 1.
79. Cassius Dio 54. 9. 10.
80. Suetonius *Augustus* 98. 3.

the *latus clavus* by Julius Caesar but refused it for a career devoted to philosophy.[81] He wrote in Greek and became a professor of philosophy in Athens, lecturing in Greek and counting among his pupils distinguished men like the Alexandrian Sotion.[82] He was there during the principate of Augustus. A different literary style, and very Greek, was adopted by two senators. Cn. Lentulus Gaetulicus,[83] consul in A.D. 26, wrote erotic Greek epigrams well enough to be claimed as a model by Martial. Tuticanus Gallus, a senator and son of a senator, a friend to whom Ovid addressed two poems from exile,[84] also wrote erotic epigrams in Greek. Both men wrote in a thoroughly Greek style and technique. In these ways the two literary cultures became interchangeable, with Greeks reasserting their dominance through re-creation of their ancient glories, equally the envy and the model of Roman writers.

The Greeks whom Augustus patronized repaid his interest. There was only one sour note: Timagenes, a prolific writer, quarrelled with Augustus, and, retiring to the house of Asinius Pollio, burnt his panegyric on the deeds of the emperor.[85] But there was adequate compensation: the great historian, Nicolaus of Damascus, wrote a biography of Augustus based largely on Augustus' own autobiography. What Cicero had pleaded for in vain, Augustus had no difficulty in obtaining. Strabo wrote two complementary works: his *Historical Sketches* ($\dot{\nu}\pi o\mu\nu\dot{\eta}\mu\alpha\tau\alpha$) in forty-seven books and his *Geography* in seventeen books; both were political works, designed to be useful to a governing class, specifically the Roman aristocracy. The latter work was dedicated to Aelius Gallus, prefect of Egypt, who took Strabo with him on his unsuccessful Arabian expedition.[86] Dionysius

81. Seneca *Epp.* 98. 13. On Sextius see especially Oltramare (1926), 155 ff.; he is probably wrong, however, in distinguishing a Sextius Niger, the medical and botanical writer, as a son—the two were identical.

82. Seneca *Epp.* 59. 7; 108. 17–22; *Nat. Quaest.* 7. 32. 2.

83. Cichorius (1922), 323–25.

84. *ex Ponto* 4. 12 and 14.

85. Seneca *contr.* 10. 5. 22; Seneca *de ira* 3. 23.

86. Bowersock (1965), 128–30.

of Halicarnassus[87] addressed the same people,[88] with some note taken of possible Greek readers.[89] Dionysius gave a firm basis to the thesis that Rome was a Hellenic state and that the best of Roman culture was Greek—to such an extent that Romans even outdid Greeks in Hellenism.[90] Such doctrine was as pleasing to Greeks (who did not need to see themselves as conquered by inferiors) as it was to Romans (who were relieved of any cultural inferiority complex).[91] He, in common with earlier Greek writers like Polybius and Diodorus, diagnosed a moral decline in the present as compared with the past of Rome.[92] His formulation, with the optimistic assertion that there were some by whom Rome's greatness was still being upheld, was well designed to give strong support to the moral reforms of Augustus.

Greek poets, however, played an even more interesting role with similar themes. A Greek epigram, preserved on papyrus, celebrates the battle of Actium in an address to a statue of Apollo, erected to commemorate the battle:[93]

"Ακτιον ἀμ[φιέπων, ἄνα ν]αύμαχε, Κ(αί)σαρος ἔργων
    μνῆμα κ(αὶ) ε[ὐτυ]χέων μαρτυρίη καμάτων,
Αἰῶνος σ[τό]μασιν βεβοημένε· σοὶ γὰρ "Αρηος
    π[νεύμα]τα καὶ σακέων ἐστόρεσεν πάταγον,
Εἰρήνης μόχθους εὐώπιδος ἔνθα κλαδεύσας
    γῆν ἐπὶ Νειλῶτιν νίσε(τ)ο γηθαλέος,
εὐνο[μίης] φόρτοισι καὶ εὐθενίης βαθυπλούτου
    βρι[θό]μενος βύζην Ζεὺς ἅτ' ἐλευθέριος,
δωροφόροις δὲ χέρεσσιν ἐδέξατο Νεῖλος ἄνακτα
    κ(αὶ) δάμαρ ἡ χρυσέοις πήχεσι λουομένη
ἀπτόλεμον καὶ ἄδηριν ἐλευθερίου Διὸς ὄμβρον,
    ἀτρεκὲς ἐσβέσθη δ' οὔνομα κ(αὶ) πολέμου·
χαῖρε, μάκαρ Λευκᾶτα, Διὸς [Κρον]ίδαο Σεβαστοῦ
    νικ(αί)ων ἔργων ἐν πρυτάνευμα καλόν.

87. For the analysis of the attitude to Rome of Dionysius of Halicarnassus, Dio Chrysostom, Plutarch, Lucian, Aelius Aristides, Pausanias, Galen, Appian, Philostratus, and Cassius Dio, the most useful overall view is given by Palm (1959), and I am much indebted to this work.
88. *Roman History* 1. 6. 4.
89. *Roman History* 16. 4. 1. (cf. 1. 5. 3–4).
90. *Roman History* 7. 70 and 72.
91. Palm (1959), 13–16.
92. Palm (1959), 13.
93. Text and commentary in Page (1942), 468–71.

Lord of Actium, sea-fighting prince, memorial to the deeds of Caesar and witness to his successful labours, your name is shouted aloud on the lips of Time, for in your honour Caesar calmed the blasts of war and the clash of shields, and, there bringing to an end the sufferings of beautiful Peace, he came rejoicing to the land of Nile, heavy laden down with a cargo of Law and Order and Prosperity's abundant riches, like Zeus, God of Freedom. And Nile welcomed his lord with arms full of gifts, and his wife (Egypt), whom with golden arms he bathes, received the shower, free from war or strife, that came from Zeus, God of Freedom, and assuredly the very name of War was abolished. Hail, blessed Lord of Leucas, one and only handsome president over the victorious deeds of Augustus, our Zeus, Son of Kronos.

What is remarkable here—apart from the wretched poetry— is the thematic coincidence with Roman poets. The political references suggest a date later than 17 B.C., and the themes recall the *carmen saeculare* of Horace in particular, with emphasis on moral reform, prosperity, and peace; but the account of Actium recalls Propertius' poem on the battle (4. 6), while the welcoming Nile suggests a tactful adaptation of Virgil *Aeneid* 8. 711– 13 (where Nile receives the conquered Cleopatra).[94] All of this Roman poetry would have been quite new about 17 B.C. The poem is composed from the point of view of Egypt, but the poet is careful—and extremely clumsy—in mediating his identification of Augustus and Zeus: Augustus is first like Zeus Eleutherios, then it is only implied that he actually is Zeus Eleutherios, and finally he is Zeus in the eyes of Egyptians. The poet was closely enough in touch with feeling at Rome to know Augustus' expressed aversion to deification—in fact, the poem may well have been written in Rome about 17 B.C., when the poet already knew the poems of Horace, Propertius, and Virgil.

It is not rash, then, to suggest direct influence not merely of Greeks on Roman poets[95] but of Roman poets on Greeks. The

94. It is noteworthy too that, as is also true of Virgil and Horace, the war that the Greek poet envisages as abolished in favour of Peace is civil war. That, from the Roman point of view, was the only type of war that needed to be abolished.

95. For instance Horace (*Sat.* 1. 2. 92–93) paraphrases an epigram of Philodemus (*Anth. Pal.* 5. 132) and mentions him by name (120 ff.) while

best explanation of the lines of Erucius of Cyzicus (*Anth. Pal.* 6. 96. 1–2), Γλαύκων καὶ Κορύδων οἱ ἐν οὔρεσι βουκολέοντες, Ἀρκάδες ἀμφό-τεροι, is that they imitated Virgil *Eclogue* 7. 2–4, since it was Virgil who first set pastoral in Arcadia (that fact rules out both the possibility of the opposite, and of a common source). Erucius was a Roman citizen who lived in Rome in the early years of Augustus.[96] But use by Greek poets of Roman poets can be demonstrated elsewhere.

Apollonides, probably the rhetorician from Nicaea, whose activity in Rome is most closely connected with Tiberius, though he was writing there before A.D. 14,[97] wrote this epigram (*Anth. Pal.* 9. 244):[98]

> δειματόεις ἐλάφων κεραὸς λόχος, εὖτε κρυώδεις
> πλῆσαν ὀρῶν κορυφὰς χιόνεαι νιφάδες,
> δείλαιαι ποταμοῖσιν ἐφώρμισαν ἐλπίδι φροῦδοι
> χλιῆναι νοτεροῖς ἄσθμασιν ὠκὺ γόνυ,
> τὰς δὲ περιφράξας ἐχθρὸς ῥόος ἀθρόον ἄφνω
> χειμερίηι στυγεροῦ δῆσε πάγοιο πέδηι,
> πληθὺς δ' ἀγροτέρων ἀλίνου θοινήσατο θήρης,
> ἢ φύγεν ἁρπεδόνην πολλάκι καὶ στάλικα.

An antlered troop of deer, taking fright when snowy clouds had filled the icy tops of the mountains, wretched creatures, found haven in a river, going there in hope to warm their swift limbs in its moist exhalations. The hostile stream suddenly imprisoned them, all caught together, and bound them in wintry fetters of hateful ice. And a crowd of country folk feasted on an unnetted catch that had often escaped their cords and nets.

This is the sort of nonsensical fantasy to which an itch for originality drove Greek epigrammatists—or so it seems till one

---

paraphrasing another epigram that is not extant. Or, at *Fasti* 1. 355–58, Ovid imitated an epigram of Leonidas of Tarentum (*Anth. Pal.* 9. 99), the six lines of which Evenus, probably contemporaneously with Ovid, reduced to a single couplet (*Anth. Pal.* 9. 75).

96. See Cichorius (1922), 304–6.

97. For, despite Cichorius (1922), 335, *Anth. Pal.* 9. 287. 6 Ζῆνα τὸν ἐσσόμενον must refer to Tiberius. The phrase does not mean, as Gow and Page ([1968], II, p. 160) say, 'the man who will be *Divus* some day', but 'the man who will be *princeps*'; it therefore belongs to the period between A.D. 4 and 14.

98. Gow and Page (1968), n. XVI.

looks at Virgil *Georgics* 3. 367–75. There Virgil is describing winter in Scythia, and says (360–61) 'sudden ice-crusts form on the flowing river, and the tide soon bears iron-bound wheels on its surface'; and he follows this with other details, such as splitting wine with an axe. He then turns to another feature (367–75):

> interea toto non setius aere ningit:
> intereunt pecudes, stant circumfusa pruinis
> corpora magna boum, confertoque agmine cervi
> torpent mole nova et summis vix cornibus exstant.
> hos non inmissis canibus, non cassibus ullis
> puniceaeve agitant pavidos formidine pennae,
> sed frustra oppositum trudentis pectore montem
> comminus obtruncant ferro graviterque rudentis
> caedunt et magno laeti clamore reportant.

No less meanwhile does snow fill the whole sky: cattle perish, the great frames of oxen stand sheathed in frost, deer in a crowded herd are numb beneath the strange mass, and the tips of their horns scarcely appear above it. Men hunt them, not with dogs unleashed or nets nor terrified by the purple-feathered scare, but, as their breasts vainly strain against the mountainous mass that confronts them, men come right up to them, butcher them with swords as they bellow piteously, and bear them home with loud shouts of joy.

This is no case of a common source. Virgil was the source, and the Greek poet was trapped by the word 'sudden', used to describe the ice forming on the river, into connecting the killing of the deer with the phenomenon of the river freezing over and not with the paralyzing effect of deep snow on swift runners. Apollonides can only have got his connexion of these two disparate elements from Virgil's description of Scythia.

A very important Greek poet in Rome under Augustus was Antipater of Thessalonica, who composed this epigram (*Anth. Pal.* 9. 297):[99]

99. Gow and Page (1968), n. XLVII.

στέλλευ ἐπ' Εὐφρήτην, Ζηνὸς τέκος, εἰς σὲ γὰρ ἤδη
ἠῷιοι Πάρθων αὐτομολοῦσι πόδες.
στέλλευ, ἄναξ, δήεις δὲ φόβωι κεχαλασμένα τόξα,
Καῖσαρ, πατρώιων δ' ἄρξαι ἀπ' ἐντολέων,
'Ρώμην δ' 'Ωκεανῶι περιτέρμονα πάντοθεν αὐτός
πρῶτος ἀνερχομένωι σφράγισαι ἡελίωι.

Speed on your journey to the Euphrates, son of Zeus: already the
feet of the Parthians in the East are deserting to your side. Speed
on your way, O prince; you shall find their bows unstrung in terror
of you, Caesar. Rule in accordance with the precepts of your father,
and be the first to confirm to the rising sun that the Roman Empire
has the Ocean as its boundary on every side.

There is considerable similarity between this and Ovid's
much lengthier passage in *Ars Amatoria* (1. 177–228),[100] which
extends to details like the reference to the father's instructions
(191–92), and, just as Ovid praises Gaius without ever losing
sight of Augustus, so does Antipater. He too, like Ovid (177–78),
treats the expedition as intended to add the last piece of the
world to the Roman Empire.

Antipater and Ovid show other connexions. When the Greek
addressed Cotys (*Anth. Plan.* 75), he said to him: ἐποιήθης δ' ἔργον
ἀοιδοπόλων, 'you have been made the subject of poetry'; and it is
easy to understand this as a reference to the poem that Ovid addressed to Cotys from exile (*ex Ponto* 2. 9). A quite clear imitation
seems to be *Anth. Pal.* 5. 3, where the theme, used by other epigrammatists (including Meleager), of the lover's hatred of the
crowing cock[101] has the decisive addition of Tithonus' senility,
worked out so amusingly by Ovid in *Amores* 1. 13. Here the only
real possibility is that Ovid was the source. In *Anth. Pal.* 5.
30, Antipater certainly seems to have got the theme from Tibullus 2. 4. 27–34, since the details are so close; and in this
case not only the unique treatment of the theme but also the
relative dates of the two poets make the priority of the Ro-

100. See chap. II, sect. 5 above.
101. Meleager *Anth. Pal.* 12. 137 was imitated by Argentarius *Anth. Pal.*
9. 286. Meleager invented the variant of curses on the Morning Star, *Anth.
Pal.* 5. 172 and 173.

man certain. If so, there seems to be a strong probability that Ovid and Antipater were friends, and that the similarity of their treatments of Gaius' eastern expedition came from discussion at least as much as from imperial dictation. This is additional confirmation of the view expressed above that irony was far from Ovid's thoughts when he composed the panegyric.

The most important Greek poet in Rome under Augustus was Crinagoras of Mytilene,[102] who emerges as a distinct personality from his poems and who also had the good fortune to be mentioned on a series of inscriptions that have survived.[103] He had the further distinction of being the subject of a poem by the great Parthenius. He was also important politically and a member of three embassies from Mytilene to Rome.[104] He was poetically active in Rome in 25 B.C. (his poem on Marcellus must belong to that period).[105] His themes were more than usually factual and autobiographical, and many of his epigrams have a political interest. Among the latter is the following (*Anth. Pal.* 9. 283):[106]

> οὔρεα Πυρηναῖα καὶ αἱ βαθυαγχέες Ἄλπεις,
> αἳ Ῥήνου προχοὰς ἐγγὺς ἀποβλέπετε,
> μάρτυρες ἀκτίνων, Γερμανικὸς ἃς ἀνέτειλεν
> ἀστράπτων Κελτοῖς πουλὺν Ἐννάλιον.
> οἱ δ' ἄρα δουπήθησαν ἀολλέες, εἶπε δ' Ἐννώ
> Ἄρεϊ 'τοιαύταις χερσὶν ὀφειλόμεθα'.

Mountains of the Pyrenees and deep-valleyed Alps that look away to the nearby streams of the Rhine, [you were] witnesses of the lightning flashes which Germanicus raised up as he hurled the bolts of war in profusion on the Celts. They were flung every one of them crashing to the ground, and Enyo said to Ares 'To hands like these should we be entrusted'.

There has been much dispute about the reference of the poem. It most obviously refers to Drusus, brother of Tiberius, who

102. See especially the treatment by Cichorius (1922), 306–23.
103. The original discovery and treatment was by Cichorius (1888).
104. Bowersock (1965), 36, 123–24.
105. *Anth. Pal.* 6. 161.
106. Gow and Page (1968), n. XXVI.

was killed in 9 B.C. But it is always assumed that the poem could only have been written during his life, yet the award of the title Germanicus was posthumous; also the geography indicates the campaign of 15 to 13 B.C., not that of 12 to 9 B.C. Consequently, odd suggestions have been made: for instance, 'a quite minor incident will suffice' in which Germanicus (son of Drusus and adopted son of Tiberius) was engaged in A.D. 13.[107] But the poem does not sound like that, and it would be of much later composition than any other poem of Crinagoras can be shown to be. It is hard to see why the poem should not be an epitaph in the traditionally crisp style of Greek epitaphic epigrams. A number of epigrams look as though they were intended to have an explanatory or dedicatory heading;[108] and poems like Propertius 3. 18, the epitaph on Marcellus which nowhere mentions his name, or *Eclogue* 8, dedicated to Pollio[109] without mentioning his name, or Tibullus 1. 7 in honour of Messalla, seem likely to have had headings at one time. Our manuscripts have, in the course of time, lost these headings, as can be shown, for instance, from the *Silvae* of Statius, where the headings have been preserved and are guaranteed by the introductory letters to each book.[110] In Crinagoras' poem, its epitaphic nature would have

107. Gow and Page (1968), vol. II, 235-36.

108. For example, poems of Antipater in honour of Piso which do not mention his name—*Anth. Pal.* 9. 92 and 428 (Gow and Page, nos. II and I); or *Anth. Pal.* 6. 238 (Gow and Page, n. II), where Apollonides does not mention the name of the deity; similarly *Anth. Pal.* 6.239 (Gow and Page, n. III); or *Anth. Pal.* 9. 555 (Gow and Page, n. XXXI), where Crinagoras omits the name of the island; or *Anth. Pal.* 9. 230 (Gow and Page, n. V), where Honestus has omitted the name of the addressee. Similarly, a number of epigrams of Martial are clearly addressed to a specific individual but do not name him in the form in which they appear in the MSS: e.g., 2. 85; 9. 54; 12. 67.

109. *Pace* Bowersock (1971). The genuine information in the Philargyrius commentary and under *alii* in Servius will go back to the original heading, while Servius' misdirected guess, *o Auguste*, will be no more than that. *Ecl.* 6. 11-12 suggests that the dedicatee's name could appear as a title to a poem.

110. Even in the fifth book, where the prefatory letter only mentions the first poem, the habit was sufficiently established to preserve the titles—even if not in the exact form in which they had been written by the author; see

been made clear by the heading. The poem's ending, with emphasis on τοιαύταις, is a neat epitaphic ending, expressing hope of others like him as well as regret. The real clue to the interpretation lies in the extraordinary tautologous sequence ἀκτίνων . . . ἀνέτειλεν . . . ἄστραπτων. . . . Here the poet was using a Roman image which was basically a Virgilian invention (*Georg*. 4. 560–61, *Caesar dum magnus ad altum fulminat Euphraten bello*; cf. *Aen*. 12. 654). But there is another oddity in the passive use of δουπήθησαν. Crinagoras had two Horatian poems in mind, which commemorated the campaign of 15 to 13 B.C., the one (*Odes* 4. 4) celebrating Drusus, the other (*Odes* 4.14) first honouring Drusus briefly, then Tiberius. Drusus is pictured flashing down on the Vindelici like an eagle (*ministrum fulminis alitem*) on his prey, and this suggested the lightning images. Drusus and Tiberius are honoured for the destruction that they inflicted on the enemy (9–13 and 29–32):

> milite nam tuo
> Drusus Genaunos, implacidum genus,
> Breunosque velocis et arces
> Alpibus impositas tremendis

> deiecit acer plus vice simplici. . . .

> ut barbarorum Claudius agmina
> ferrata vasto diruit impetu
> primosque et extremos metendo
> stravit humum sine clade victor.

In Crinagoras, the lightning image in its tautology catches the extent of the destruction, but the adaptation of Homeric language in δουπήθησαν captures the feeling of *et arces Alpibus*

Vollmer (1898), 207. The reason why the headings were preserved was only partly due to the introductory letters; the real reason must lie in the unique nature of the collection: every poem, with the exception of *Somnus,* is dedicated to an individual and an occasion. I suspect that where poems with headings were scattered in collections of poems that were mainly without headings, the headings tended to be omitted and the information went into commentaries (where appropriate).

impositas tremendis deiecit acer and *stravit humum* particularly. Crinagoras, therefore, thinking of an epitaph for Drusus, used the Horatian poems as a starting point. He was then able to work in the later campaign, not only in the very title Γερμανικός, but also in making the two great north-facing mountain ranges the witnesses (for Drusus started off in Gaul on both campaigns).[111] He was also able to refer to the enemy as Κελτοί (extended to 'Germans' only by later Greek authors) because, again, the title Γερμανικός was sufficient reference in itself to Germany. The essence of an epigram is brevity combined with suggestiveness.[112] It is easy to imagine a lengthier, but hardly a better, epitaph for Nero Claudius Drusus Germanicus in the year 9 B.C.

One is constantly aware, reading the Greek epigrammatists who are represented in the *Garland of Philip*, that they were acquainted with the work of their great Roman contemporaries and that they used them as a source for material. In fact, one feature that most marks off the *Garland of Philip* from the *Garland of Meleager*—the topicality of many of the poems, the authentic sense of real events—may be viewed as one way (and a very important one) in which Roman culture gave a new lease on life to Greek poetry. This came through the influence of Roman poets like Catullus, Horace, Virgil, and Propertius, and, to a lesser extent, that of Tibullus and of Ovid.

There was another way in which Greek and Roman poets came closer together. For some time (in fact the practice went back at least to Ennius) Roman poets had been accustomed to create a poetic language in Latin (which was otherwise missing) in various ways, including the transference of Greek syntactical usages to Latin poetic style. It was in this age that Greeks for the first time began to use Latin structures in Greek. Some of these correspond to the way in which Greeks had long since been accustomed to translate Latin idioms straight into Greek, par-

111. Rice Holmes (1931), 63–81.
112. Crinagoras is distinguished for such brevity: see below on *Anth. Pal.* 9. 291 and 419 (Gow and Page, n. XXVII and n. XXIX).

ticularly those that belonged to administrative or legal or constitutional contexts. This became customary in documents,[113]
but it penetrated into artistic writers too. So, for instance, Dionysius of Halicarnassus[114] can be found writing πυρὶ καὶ σιδήρῳ
λωβᾶσθαι = igni ferroque vastare, or ὑπὸ δόρυ πωλεῖν = sub hasta
vendere, or ἐγγύην ὁμολογεῖν = vadimonium promittere, and
many others. It was the same interest that prompted Bassus
to write (Anth. Pal. 9. 236. 1) ἄρρηκτοι . . . ὅρκοι on the analogy
of Latin fidem or foedus frangere. When Crinagoras wrote
(Anth. Pal. 6. 229. 6) ὁ πᾶς ἐπὶ σοί, Λεύκιε, Κριναγόρης, he was thinking of the Latin idiom of devotion (as in Horace Sat. 1. 9. 2 totus
in illis). And Geminus, writing (Anth. Plan. 205) μὴ θεὸς ἀντὶ
τέχνης σύμμαχα τόξα λάβῃ ('in case the god take up his bow to defend
art'), was using ἀντί on the analogy of pro. When Macedonius
wrote (Anth. Pal. 11. 39. 1) περὶ ἧς λόγος ἔρρει he must have been
thinking of it fabula. Philip was perhaps thinking directly of
Horace Epist. 1. 5. 12 quo mihi fortunam . . . (a line which also
came into Ovid's mind—Amores 2. 19. 7) when he wrote (Anth.
Pal. 11. 347. 3) ποῖ γὰρ ἐμοὶ ζητεῖν . . .; for no other Greek used the
idiom. Most striking, however, is an imitation of the Latin ablative by Parmenion (Anth. Pal. 9. 304):[115]

> τὸν γαίης καὶ πόντου ἀμειφθείσαισι κελεύθοις
> ναύτην ἠπείρου, πεζοπόρον πελάγους,
> ἐν τρισσαῖς δοράτων ἑκατοντάσιν ἔστεγεν ἄρης
> Σπάρτης· αἰσχύνεσθ', οὔρεα καὶ πελάγη.

The man who, when the paths of earth and sea were inter-
changed,[116] was a sailor on dry land, an infantryman by sea, this
man the fighting quality of Sparta held off with three hundred
spears. Feel shame, mountains and seas.

Here the dative ἀμειφθείσαισι κελεύθοις, with the defining genitives, consorts so ill with the genitives ἠπείρου and πελάγους and

113. Material in Hahn (1906), 114–20.
114. See Hahn (1906), 120–29.
115. Gow and Page (1968), n. X.
116. For the commonplace see Mayor on Juvenal 10. 173–84 (commentary, vol. 2, p. 127).

creates a tautology so clumsy as to compel belief that the poet was imitating in Greek the Latin construction of the ablative absolute. What would have made this easier was the long-standing stereotype on documents of translating the Latin dating system by consuls directly into Greek,[117] substituting a dative for the ablative absolute.[118] This was the equivalent, of course, not of a Greek genitive absolute but of ἐπὶ ὑπάτων . . ., but the system is found as early as 39 B.C. and will have become so normal that it was ready to supply Parmenion with a syntactical opportunity which existed outside any reference to the Greek structure of the genitive absolute.

What all of these features present is, as it were, a practical demonstration of the theoretical relationship of the two cultures, as expounded, for instance, by Dionysius of Halicarnassus. They show the interchangeability of Greek and Latin language and literature, and it was in this period that Romans seriously began to write in Greek on the same level and in the same genres as Greeks. The other aspect of this was that little by little Romans were robbed of their own specific literary identity and heritage; they began to stand in direct competition with Greeks and to adopt their habit of looking back over the Hellenistic age to the great Classical age of Greece.

Another way in which Greek and Roman poets came together in this period was within the system of patronage. Even Greek poets who, at first sight, do not appear to be connected with Augustus turn out to be so on closer inspection. Antipater of Thessalonica addressed ten epigrams, which found a place in the *Garland of Philip*, to L. Calpurnius Piso Frugi, consul in 15 B.C. This man was clearly Antipater's patron, yet one epigram, written between 10 and 8 B.C., is this (*Anth. Pal.* 10. 25):[119]

117. On documentary Latinisms, see, for example, Debrunner and Scherer (1969), 82–87 (with bibliography), and Sherk (1969), 13–19, 208–9. For nondocumentary Latinisms the best general source is still Hahn (1906) *passim*.

118. Josephus actually used this formula in artistic writing: Hahn (1906), 237.

119. Gow and Page (1968), n. XL.

Φοῖβε Κεφαλλήνων λιμενοσκόπε θῖνα Πανόρμου
ναίων τρηχείης ἀντιπέρην Ἰθάκης,
δός με δι' εὐπλώτοιο πρὸς Ἀσίδα κύματος ἐλθεῖν
Πείσωνος δολιχῆι νηὶ συνεσπόμενον,
καὶ τὸν ἐμὸν βασιλῆα τὸν ἄλκιμον εὖ μὲν ἐκείνωι
ἵλαον εὖ δ' ὕμνοις ἄρτισον ἡμετέροις.

Phoebus, harbour watchman of the Cephallenians, dweller on
the beach of Panormus opposite rough Ithaca, grant that I travel
towards Asia through seas fair for sailing, following the long
ship[120] of Piso. And make my powerful monarch well disposed to
him, well disposed also to my poetry.

The last couplet forms a surprise ending and is clearly intended to catch the eye of Augustus.[121] It shows the Greek poet's
sensitive understanding of Augustan patronage: though he is a
client of Piso, when it comes to Augustus, both he and Piso
stand on the same level—or, rather, not he so much as his poetry.
Piso can contribute directly in his own person to Augustus,
Antipater only as a poet. Consonant with this plea for regal
patronage, there are two epigrams addressed to Gaius,[122] the
adopted son and designated successor of Augustus. Antipater's
relationship to Piso can be seen as analogous to that of Tibullus
or Ovid to Messalla Corvinus: the lesser relationship did not in
the least rule out the rewards—and obligations—of the greater.

The relationship of Crinagoras to Augustus was also that of
client and patron, but, no doubt because of Crinagoras' high
social standing in Mytilene, he seems to have been on more direct terms with the family of the *princeps*, though not with Augustus himself. So he addressed two epigrams to Marcellus (on
the dedication of his first beard and with the gift of a copy of the
Hecale of Callimachus);[123] both reflect the dynastic plans that
Augustus had for Marcellus. Apart from addresses to Antonia,[124]

120. A Latinism: *navis longa.*
121. Hillscher (1892), 411–12 unconvincingly refers the last couplet to
Piso.
122. *Anth. Pal.* 9. 59 and 297 (Gow and Page, XLVI and XLVII).
123. *Anth. Pal.* 6. 161 and 9. 545 (Gow and Page, X and XI).
124. *Anth. Pal.* 9. 239 and 545 (Gow and Page, VII and XI).

daughter of Antony and Octavia, he wrote epigrams about Drusus and Tiberius and Augustus, without addressing them directly. One epigram is particularly interesting (*Anth. Pal.* 9. 291):[125]

> οὐδ' ἢν Ὠκεανὸς πᾶσαν πλήμυραν ἐγείρηι,
> οὐδ' ἢν Γερμανίη Ῥῆνον ἄπαντα πίηι,
> Ῥώμης δ' οὐδ' ὅσσον βλάψει σθένος, ἄχρι κε μίμνηι
> δεξιὰ σημαίνειν Καίσαρι θαρσαλέη.
> οὕτως καὶ ἱεραὶ Ζηνὸς δρύες ἔμπεδα ῥίζαις
> ἑστᾶσιν, φύλλων δ' αὖα χέουσ' ἄνεμοι.

Not even if Ocean should rouse up its whole flood, not even if Germany should drink up the whole Rhine, not in the slightest will that injure the power of Rome, so long as she stays confident in Caesar that his dictates are right.[126] In the same way, the sacred oaks of Zeus stand firm in their roots, while winds scatter the withered leaves.

The many attempts to tie this down to a particular disaster seem misplaced and founded on an over-rigid preconception of Crinagoras as a poet of 'real' events. But this preconception, while basically justified, is not always true, and Crinagoras can also use the devices of rhetorical exaggeration like any of his contemporaries. This is clear from *Anth. Pal.* 9. 419:[127]

> κἢν μυχὸν Ὀρκυναῖον ἢ ἐς πύματον Σολόεντα
> ἔλθηι καὶ Λιβυκῶν κράσπεδον Ἑσπερίδων
> Καῖσαρ ὁ πουλυσέβαστος, ἅμα κλέος εἴσιν ἐκείνωι
> πάντηι· Πυρήνης ὕδατα μαρτύρια.
> οἶσι γὰρ οὐδὲ πέριξ δρυτόμοι ἀπεφαιδρύναντο,
> λουτρὰ καὶ ἠπείρων ἔσσεται ἀμφοτέρων.

Even if most august Caesar should travel to the depths of Hercynia or to farthest Soloeis and the fringe of Libyan Hesperides, everywhere his glory shall go with him. Witness the waters of the Pyrenees: not even nearby woodcutters washed in them, yet they shall be the baths of both continents.

125. Gow and Page (1968), n. XXVII.
126. Hillscher (1892), 425 n. 2 rightly compares Aratus *Phaen.* 5 (of Zeus) ὁ δ' ἤπιος ἀνθρώποισι / δεξια σημαίνει.
127. Gow and Page (1968), n. XXIX.

Augustus seems to have taken the waters at Dax in southwest France, near the Pyrenees, and the poet claims that he conferred such fame on them that the whole world will now come to them. To illustrate Augustus' fame, he envisages his travelling to the *silva Hercynia* on the upper Rhine or to the most western extreme of the Mediterranean. The 'Even if . . .' formula marks rhetorical amplitude. So, in the political epigram, the poet envisaged an enormous national disaster and, coupled with that, a military threat to the borders of the Empire (the Germans growing so numerous that the Rhine simply dries up and ceases to be a barrier). To envisage a threat to the Empire in terms of Germany would be relevant any time between 16 and 6 B.C. The interest lies in the fact that Crinagoras echoes a constant theme of Horace. For instance (*Odes* 3. 14. 14–16) *ego nec tumultum | nec mori per vim metuam tenente | Caesare terras,* or (*Odes* 4. 5. 25–7) *quis Parthum paveat, quis gelidum Scythen, | quis Germania quos horrida parturit | fetus, incolumi Caesare?*[128] In fact, the last quoted passage, from an ode dating from 13 B.C., may well have suggested the idea to Crinagoras. It does not need saying that the formula ἄχρι κε μίμνῃ . . . does not imply any doubt. Here Crinagoras speaks in the tone of Augustus' favoured laureate, creating a context in which the rule of Augustus could be equated (by literary echo) with that of Zeus (another Horatian device).[129]

The possibility seems likely that when Horace died and Ovid failed him, Augustus turned more and more to Greek poets for the sort of literary support to which he had become accustomed. They also represented a type of poetry that Augustus himself indulged in. For, apart from his ill-fated *Ajax*—a notably Greek genre and subject—and the Hellenistic-sounding poem *Sicilia*, he composed a book of epigrams. At least some of these were in Greek: the elder Pliny reports[130] that Augustus composed a Greek epigram for the painting of Aphrodite Anadyomene by

128. Cf., for example, 4. 14. 41–52; 15. 17–24.
129. See Williams (1968), 160 ff.
130. *NH* 35. 91.

Apelles, which he received from Cos as an offset against taxes[131] and which he dedicated to Julius Caesar. Pliny says: 'the work was eclipsed but made famous by the Greek verses in its praise'. Macrobius has an amusing story[132] of a *Graeculus* trying for days to present an epigram to Augustus, who instead presented the Greek with an extempore epigram and was given a few denarii in payment—the Greek got a handsome payment in return. The story was, no doubt, an invention, but its framework rings true. These were poets with whom Augustus could feel at home and on easy terms. His interest lent authority to their writings, and they responded with enduring expressions of Augustan ideals.

Thus Augustus himself integrated Greek poetry more and more into Roman culture, reinforcing the existing tendencies to a unification of both cultures.

4. *Cultural fusion in the early Empire*

The most fascinating picture of the fusion of Greek and Roman culture is found in the writings of the elder Seneca, where Greeks and Romans alike use Greek or Latin indifferently, call on the resources of Greek or Latin literature, and behave in such a uniform way that they can often only be distinguished as Greeks rather than Romans or vice versa with the help of Seneca or extraneous research.

The emperors provide a clear picture of the growing dominance of Greek culture,[133] but in doing so they are only an indication of the upper class as a whole in Rome. Theories that Petronius was satirizing Nero in the figure of Trimalchio quite miss the mark. In the detail of his dedicating his first beard, he is shown observing a Greek custom that caught on in Rome in the first century;[134] the fact of the golden box is just an added

131. Strabo 657.

132. *Sat.* 2. 4. 31.

133. The evidence for the literary activity and interests of the emperors is collected and examined by H. Bardon (1940). This has been used in what follows.

134. Cf., for example, Crinagoras *Anth. Pal.* 6. 161 (Gow and Page n. X) to Marcellus.

detail of ostentatious luxury. Trimalchio is also portrayed as having two libraries, one Greek and one Roman (48). In all this Petronius is satirizing the pretensions to Greek culture of someone who aspires to the way of life of a class far above him in society.

Tiberius had a Greek education with the Stoic Nestor of Tarsus[135] and the rhetorician Theodorus of Gadara. His love of obscurity was proverbial and that, no doubt, dictated his pleasure in Hellenistic poets like Euphorion and Parthenius and Rhianos,[136] and especially in the *Silloi* of Timon, on which Apollonides of Nicaea wrote a commentary dedicated to Tiberius.[137] But Tiberius himself composed in Greek, imitating his favourite authors.[138] Apart from that, he wrote a lyric, *conquestio de morte L. Caesaris*, in Latin and wrote epigrams, probably in both languages. He clearly loved the Greek way of life, and when he retired to Rhodes in 6 B.C. he wore Greek dress, attended Greek lectures, went to the gymnasium, and sent chariots to compete at the games at Olympia and Thespiae. In Rome he showed strong philhellenism in his circle of friends. Tiberius is especially significant, for he was an old-fashioned aristocrat, a strict traditionalist who felt himself a senator; he was an archaist in literary tastes and a purist.[139] He is a measure of the extent to which the two cultures had become one.

Germanicus, father of the emperor Gaius, had been skilled in Greek and Latin, and had written comedies in Greek as well as an adaptation of Aratus into Latin. Josephus reports Gaius as an excellent orator both in Greek and Latin.[140] Gaius put on Greek games at Syracuse in imitation of Augustus and presented Attic plays at Lyons. Claudius went much further, making Greek an official language and even using it in the senate;[141] this was a

135. Ps.-Lucian *macrob.* 21.
136. Suetonius *Tib.* 70.
137. Diogenes Laertius 9. 12. 109; Hillscher (1892), 387–88.
138. Suetonius *Tib.* 70.
139. Cassius Dio 57. 17. 1–2.
140. *Antiqu. Iud.* 19. 208.
141. Suetonius *Claud.* 42.

significant step towards giving Greek a preference over Latin. On the other hand, Claudius demanded a knowledge of Latin in citizens, and deprived of his citizenship a Lycian who could not speak Latin in the senate. He himself wrote in Greek a history of the Etruscans in twenty books, and a history of Carthage in eight. He then founded a second Museum in Alexandria and ordained that on fixed days each year his histories should be read aloud, one in each Museum. Nero, notoriously, went further again, speaking Greek, adopting Greek customs, instituting Greek festivals in Rome.[142] After his eighteen-month tour of Greece in A.D. 66 to 68, he imitated the return of Greek victors and entered Naples, Antium, Alba, and finally Rome in a chariot drawn by white horses through a breach made in the walls. His most famous act was at the Isthmian games of A.D. 67 to declare Achaea free from direct rule and tribute. For that Plutarch described him as 'one to whom the gods owed some benefit because he freed the best and most dear to them of all his subjects'.[143]

This was a high point for the moment, and of Galba only silliness is recorded: being no Julio-Claudian, he compensated by tracing his father's ancestry back to Juppiter and his mother's to Pasiphae; and when he found a statue of Fortuna / Τύχη after dreaming of her, he performed monthly sacrifice to her and a yearly vigil, like a Greek. Vespasian, on the other hand, was proud of his obscure origin and mocked flatterers who tried to improve it. He was skilled in Greek, and he subvented the arts and education—particularly Latin and Greek rhetoric—but he was really only interested in the practical results, and the one poem certainly addressed to him,[144] an epigram by Leonidas of

142. His deliberately Greek attitude can be gauged from the fact that he actually invited the Vestal Virgins to view the wrestling because at Olympia the priestesses of Demeter were allowed that privilege (Suetonius *Nero* 12. 4). That may be contrasted with Augustus' total exclusion of the female sex from wrestling bouts (Suetonius *Aug.* 44. 3).

143. *de sera numinis vindicta* 567E.

144. Apart, of course, from the dedication of the *Argonautica* of Valerius Flaccus: see chap. VI, sect. 6 below.

Alexandria on the favoured Aquae Cotiliae,[145] is without significance, except that it calls attention to a strange poet. Titus, however, less concerned to dissociate himself from Nero, while he conducted cases in Latin, composed poetry and tragedies in Greek.[146] More significantly, he was a good musician. This means that the influence of the Greek way of life had by then made this acceptable, and that when Juvenal or Tacitus satirizes or condemns such performance, they were relying on old-fashioned prejudice. The elder Pliny used and praised[147] a poem by Titus, probably in Latin, on a comet. There is no indication that Titus indulged these activities as emperor, but he was already emperor when Pliny dedicated his *Natural History* to him and, in the preface (5), praised the emperor's skill as a poet.

After A.D. 69, Domitian gave up active life for poetry. Both Tacitus and Suetonius characterize this as simulation, designed to cloak his real intentions.[148] He wrote what appears from the single fragment to have been an ironical work, *libellus de cura capillorum*, on the treatment of hair: he himself was already going bald.[149] But epic was his real interest, and he composed and himself recited poems on the wars of A.D. 69, the wars in Judaea, and perhaps on his own wars against the Chatti in A.D. 83 and 88. His poetry was dynastic in intent: it concerned the deeds of the Flavians. It is not known whether it was in Greek or Latin—probably the latter. Domitian set up two poetic festivals on a purely Greek pattern, with prizes for poems in Greek and in Latin: the Capitoline were five yearly, those of Minerva, yearly. He wore Greek dress, and his real interest in Greek culture came out when he accepted the archonship at Athens.[150] He

145. *Anth. Pal.* 9. 349. For Vespasian's attitude towards the arts see Woodside (1942).
146. Eutropius 7. 21.
147. *NH* 2. 89.
148. Suetonius *Dom.* 2. 2; Tacitus *Hist.* 4. 86. On this innuendo see Thiele (1916), 240 ff.
149. Suetonius *Dom.* 18.
150. *IG* II². 1996.

not only proclaimed support for the art and literature of Greece, but also rebuilt the temple of Apollo at Delphi.[151] It was in his reign that the consulship was held for the first time by a man from the Greek East (the first senator had come under Nero, when in A.D. 55 Balbillus, a highly favoured astrologer, was appointed prefect of Egypt).[152]

Trajan, though he was very free with the admission of men from the Greek East to honours and office at Rome,[153] reverted to Vespasian: he was uninterested in their culture; it was their political capacities that he exploited. He wrote, as emperor and after A.D. 107, an account of the Dacian wars, but in the style of Caesar's *commentarii*; the work differed oddly, however, from Caesar's in being written, apparently, in the first person plural. Naturally, he knew Greek, and fragments of letters in Greek by him have survived, but he did not collect literary men around him; he preferred jurists and men of political experience like Licinius Sura. His feeling against Greek customs may be seen in his readiness to permit the abolition of the gymnastic *agon*, which had been established at Vienne;[154] his basic prejudice here was founded on a common Roman idea that such contests encouraged homosexuality.

Hadrian was an extraordinary contrast both with Trajan and even with himself: he was a gifted artist and a serious, hard-working emperor. Cassius Dio (69. 3) summed him up well: 'By nature he was φιλόλογος in both languages, and has left prose writings and poetry of all kinds. His ambition was insatiable, and he practised all arts, even the least important: he sculpted and painted. . . '. He was also a musician and an expert astrologer. His Latin style shows frequent Hellenisms and his Greek was fashionably neo-Attic.[155] He founded the Athenaeum in Rome and favoured Greeks in his entourage. Under Hadrian,

151. *ILS* 8905. Syme (1958), 510.
152. See Walton (1929).
153. But he required that they hold at least a third of their property in Italian land: Hahn (1906), 157.
154. Pliny *Epp.* 4. 22, and Sherwin-White (1966), p. 301.
155. See especially P. J. Alexander (1938).

in fact, Greek culture became dominant and Latin became largely administrative. Greek was the language of artistic composition.

This picture, derived from the emperors, of Greek culture steadily advancing at the expense of Roman can confidently be predicated of the upper classes in general in Rome. There were, no doubt, frequent displays of chauvinism. Juvenal, writing most of his work under Hadrian, had a real target for his satire in Greeks; though, as is his way, he attacks them indirectly through Greeks of the lower class at Rome (they could not retaliate). The fact is that the higher strata of Roman society were not only riddled with real Greeks, they were also deeply Greek themselves in culture and attitudes. Even Trajan could allow himself a moment of irritation, writing to Pliny: *gymnasiis indulgent Graeculi* 'wretched Greeks are mad on the gymnasium',[156] but he still admitted them to the senate. Less attractive is the doctrinal chauvinism of a Paetus Thrasea complaining about the change in times:[157] 'Once not only praetors and consuls, but even private individuals were sent to visit provinces and make recommendations on the obedience of each; and foreigners went in fear of the opinions of such individuals. But now we cultivate foreigners and kowtow to them...'. He was talking about a Greek from Crete, and the senate applauded him.

Seneca, too, from time to time sneers at Greek frivolity and triviality: Rome, he says, has been infected with their pedantry.[158] But in his writings there is little to tell a reader that he was a Roman, except that he wrote in Latin. His tragedies belonged to a cultural sphere that was no more Roman than Greek, but stem from an unconscious fusion of both. In his so-called philosophical works there is nothing of the sense of Cicero intellectually stimulated by Greek ideas and eager to use them in constructing

156. Pliny, *Epp.* 10. 40. 2.
157. Tacitus *Annals* 15. 21. 1. The same man was ready to offend Nero by being inconspicuous at the Juvenalia; yet he actually sang himself *habitu tragico* at a festival in his home town (true, the festival only took place every thirty years—Cassius Dio 62. 26. 4): *Annals* 16. 21. 1.
158. *de brevitate vitae* 13. 1–3.

a system that is Roman. Seneca was a Hellene for whom ideas
were Greek in origin. And this carried over into his own life. At
the end he gave dramatic evidence of a deep, spontaneous Hellenism in himself. He was compelled to commit suicide by Nero in
A.D. 65. Tacitus describes the last scene: [159] 'He requested that
Statius Annaeus (long of proven worth to him in true friendship
and in the art of medicine) bring out the poison already prepared, the same poison used by Athenians to execute those condemned in public trial. Seneca drank it with some difficulty, for
his limbs were chilled and his body closed against the power of
the poison. Finally he got into a bath of warm water, and, sprink-
ling the nearest of his slaves, spoke these words: "I give this
liquid as a libation to Juppiter, God of Freedom" '. There are
two elements in this scene: one is the deliberate imitation of the
death of Socrates; [160] the other is the libation not to a Roman god,
but to the Greek conception of Zeus as the Liberator or Saviour [161]
—a very ancient concept, going back at least to the early fifth
century B.C.

When Thrasea Paetus had to commit suicide a year later, he
added the melodramatic touch of cutting the veins in his arms

159. *Annals* 15. 64. 3–4.

160. Cf. the double herm of Socrates and Seneca, probably to be dated
to the late first century A.D. See Murray (1965), 50, n. 50. It is illustrated in
MacMullen (1966), plate I (opposite p. 50).

161. This has been denied by Degrassi (1963), 520 (October 13–18: cf.
April 13 and September 1), who refers this passage and also coins of Nero
inscribed IUPPITER LIBERATOR to the early Roman *Iuppiter Liber* or
Libertas. This is totally unconvincing. The calendar of Philocalus (*CIL*
I². p. 274) belongs to the fourth century, and it shows the assimilation with
Ζεὺς Ἐλευθέριος. Also Nero figured himself early in his reign as Iuppiter
Liberator, especially in the decree of Greek freedom at Corinth, where he
used the term Ζεὺς Ἐλευθέριος, and the coins—one of which was minted in
Greece (Mattingly [1923], 214)—derive their inscription from this (two of
them are associated with *Roma restituta* on the obverse; see Mattingly
[1923], 295). On the freedom decree see Holleaux (1888). In general, see
Latte in P-W XIII. 1 col. 93, s.v. *Liberator*, who makes clear the Greek
connexion. On early Roman *Iuppiter liber* see Roscher *Lexicon* s.v. *Iuppiter*
cols. 661–65. On Ζεὺς Ἐλευθέριος, see Farnell (1896), I, pp. 61 ff. and Cook
Zeus, Index s.v.; also Fraenkel (1950), 653, n. 1; and, on the religious significance, Nilsson (1955), 417–18, (1961), 184–85.

and using the blood as his libation—again to Zeus the Liberator. There was clearly conscious imitation in Thrasea's death, but the significance lies in the fact that both men, wishing in their last moments to make a gesture of deep import to Romans, used a Greek god as their vehicle. Romans of that class, at what they felt to be a crisis in their lives that had profound exemplary value for posterity, spoke and thought as Greeks.

Another philosopher provides illustration from another direction. Gaius Musonius Rufus, often called in ancient times the Roman Socrates, was born some time before A.D. 30 in Volsinii, of Etruscan family. He was a Roman *eques* and became a Stoic philosopher of great influence. Successive emperors from Nero onwards exiled him, and he spent large parts of his life abroad, either on a rocky island or in Athens. But even in Rome he conducted all his teaching and lectures in Greek. His most famous pupil was the Greek Epictetus. Philosophy had so far retreated into being a Greek discipline that Musonius Rufus (among many others) found it more convenient to use that language to expound it.

5. *The poetic fascination of Greek*

Arrius Antoninus was a senior consular who had supported Nerva; he had held the consulship twice, in A.D. 69 and, probably, in 97; he had been proconsul of Asia about A.D. 78. He wrote erotic epigrams and iambic mimes. Pliny wrote about them (4. 3. 3–5):

> Nam et loquenti tibi illa Homerici senis mella profluere et, quae scribis, complere apes floribus et innectere videntur. ita certe sum adfectus ipse, cum Graeca epigrammata tua, cum mimiambos proxime legerem. quantum ibi humanitatis venustatis, quam dulcia illa quam amantia quam arguta quam recta! Callimachum me vel Heroden, vel si quid his melius, tenere credebam; quorum tamen neuter utrumque aut absolvit aut attigit. hominemne Romanum tam Graece loqui? non medius fidius ipsas Athenas tam Atticas dixerim. quid multa? invideo Graecis quod illorum lingua scribere maluisti. neque enim coniectura eget, quid sermone patrio

exprimere possis, cum hoc insiticio et inducto tam praeclara opera
perfeceris.

As you speak, the honey of Homer's Nestor seems to flow, and
bees seem to fill and fasten together with flowers the written words.
That was certainly how I felt when recently I read your Greek epigrams and mimes. What sensitivity, what grace! How charming
they are, how full of love, how witty, how correct! I felt as if I
were holding Callimachus or Herodes or someone better; and yet
neither of them touched, still less perfected, both genres. Could a
Roman write in Greek so well? Believe me, I should not say that
Athens herself was so Attic. So I envy the Greeks because you have
preferred to write in their language, and no guess is needed as to
how you could express yourself in your native tongue when you
produce such masterpieces in a foreign and acquired one.

Arrius is being compared to Callimachus and Herodes, but he
writes in the most correct Attic style. In later letters we find Pliny
translating Arrius' epigrams into Latin; he has difficulty because
of the poverty of the Latin language (4. 18. 1), and his 'imitation'
(in Latin) falls far short of the original (5. 15).

The atmosphere of all this can be gathered from another letter
in which Pliny quotes a poem of Q. Gellius Sentius Augurinus,
later to be proconsul of Macedonia. He heard Sentius giving a
recitation and he wants to recall particularly one poem in which
Sentius took Pliny as his subject. He hopes that he can remember
the second line (4. 27. 4):

> canto carmina versibus minutis,
> his olim quibus et meus Catullus
> et Calvus veteresque. sed quid ad me?
> unus Plinius est mihi priores:
> mavolt versiculos foro relicto
> et quaerit quod amet, putatque amari.
> ille o Plinius, ille quot Catones!
> i nunc, quisquis amas, amare noli.

I write poetry in delicate metres, like those in which my revered
Catullus and Calvus and the ancients long ago wrote. But what
are they to me? Pliny alone is worth all predecessors to me: putting
aside the law courts, his preference is for lyrics, as he seeks a love
and finds that it is returned. Oh that one Pliny is worth all your
Catos! And, lovers, you may as well confess yourselves defeated!

Pliny invites his addressee to admire the skill and polish of the composition, and he promises that this is a true specimen of the book as a whole. He also lets fall that the young man spends a lot of time with Arrius Antoninus and with Spurinna. Clearly the poems of Arrius and of Sentius and of Pliny himself were all in the same manner, only differing in language. The Spurinna mentioned was T. Vestricius Spurinna, one of the most distinguished of the senior consulars; he held the consulship three times—once in an unknown year, then in A.D. 98 and 100. This man spent his leisure hours writing *lyrica doctissima* in Greek and Latin, and Pliny praises them (3. 1. 7) for the same qualities that he found in those of Sentius. In the same circle, Calpurnius Piso, probably the consul of A.D. 111, wrote καταστερισμοί in elegiac couplets, pretty certainly in Greek, and he gave recitations of the work, which Pliny praises particularly for the skilful modulations of tone (5. 17. 2–3).

Among the most surprising examples of poetic activity in Pliny's circle is that of Caninius Rufus. Pliny addressed seven letters to him, in four of which he urges him to write seriously. Caninius finally proposes an epic on the Dacian wars in Greek. By that time, Trajan's own account of the war had probably appeared. Pliny was highly enthusiastic; his only worry was how to get all those barbarous names into Greek hexameters, but he reflects that Homer was permitted all sorts of metrical licences.[162] An epic in Greek on a Roman historical subject marks the point at which a Roman feels the two literary cultures to be interchangeable. Such things had happened earlier: for instance, Messalla Corvinus seems to have written bucolic poetry in Greek; but the steady increase in this activity over the century indicates the despair of men who felt that they could no longer achieve anything adequate in their own language. Another friend of Pliny's actually composed Aristophanic comedy. This was Vergilius Romanus, who also wrote iambic mimes, and imitations of Menander, which Pliny rates as the equal of Plautus and

162. A conventional reflection: cf. Martial 9. 11. 13–17, and the point goes back to Lucilius.

Terence.[163] These plays, like those of Seneca and Pomponius Secundus, were composed for recitation.

The cases of Caninius and Vergilius and of Pliny himself show the difficulty of finding suitable and inspiring subject matter. And this difficulty also was crucial. From the time of Ovid, more and more poets took refuge in one or another of the escape routes he had established, but particularly in Greek mythology. Persius was hitting at real targets in his first satire when he ridiculed, on the one hand, poetic composition in Greek and, on the other, the use of hackneyed Greek myths as subject matter. Juvenal similarly satirizes poets endlessly composing huge poems on such Greek subjects. Martial (who refrains from satirical comment on such poetic compositions) provides abundant evidence, however, of the truth of the accusation. But the sad fact is that Persius and Juvenal themselves use material from the Greek myths. Horace, in the first book of his *Epistles*, for instance, uses no exemplary material from that source; the material is thoroughly Roman, and this fact represents a genre distinction from his *Odes*. Such a distinction had broken down by the time of Persius, and the Greek myths had become again what they had always been for Greek poets—the prime source of material for all types of poetry. From Ovid's *Medea* to the Greek *Medea* of his friend Pompeius Macer to the tragedies of Pomponius Secundus and of Seneca is as clear a movement as from Ovid's *Metamorphoses* to the epics of Valerius Flaccus and of Statius.

Many of these poets had great technical gifts—Statius is an outstanding example—but they treated poetry as though it were an activity whose scope and subject matter had been definitively laid down centuries before by the great poets of Classical Greece; all that was left for them was to exercise their technique within those guide lines. They did not direct their minds as poets to the sort of issues that stimulated the intellect and the emotions at the same time. Romans sometimes sought material in the great past of Rome, as did contemporary Greeks in their great past before the death of Alexander. But the result was either a poetic

163. Pliny *Epp.* 6. 21.

activity directed to issues as dead as those of the Greek myths or, if the issues still contained the original fire, the poem became impossible to publish—as was the case with Lucan. But within little more than a quarter of a century even the issues raised by Lucan's poem were dead by sweet agreement, and Roman history was totally available to the poet. The trouble lay in finding the means to bring such material alive. It needed a Greek to look at the Roman tradition with fresh eyes and inspired confidence in order to reinterpret it; that did not happen till Claudian came to Rome from Alexandria.

The poets who appear in Pliny's letters were not great, but they are the more useful on that account as symptoms of the despair that Roman writers felt. There were two writers certainly at the time who belied expressions of despair in the power of their writing; Tacitus and Juvenal were exceptional, and the reason for that must be considered later. Meanwhile, it is possible to see some reasons underlying Roman literary despair. First, a strong opinion had grown in the first century A.D., which was expressed a number of times even by Quintilian,[164] that Latin was far inferior to Greek in respect particularly of the qualities that were needed for poetic composition. The tone of these complaints is quite different from that of Cicero who, when he complained of the relative poverty of Latin, felt it as an inspiring challenge (as Lucretius did also). Second, the richness of the Greek heritage was always before the eyes of Romans, and they were constantly consorting with Greeks who now felt not the least need to take note of Roman literature (except for technical information). Furthermore, there had been a striking renascence of Greek culture, and though its greatest achievements were in prose and rhetoric, Greek poets were still producing a stream of poetry. It was indeed mechanically reproduced on ancient formulae, but, with the fusion of the two cultures and the increasing preference of Romans for the Greek, such poetry produced an instant sense of inferiority in poets trying to imitate Greek genres in Latin. This inferiority was increased by another

164. 10. 1. 100; 12. 10. 27; 12. 10. 33–34.

factor: it is clear that Roman poets of the period felt that Augustan writers had attained the ultimate perfection and had set a standard of achievement that left little possibility of imitation, let alone emulation. Yet the Augustans were also too close; they lacked the inspiring distance of Homer and the writers of Classical Greece, whose remoteness in time and language and material held out the inspiring possibility of a renascence. Statius was acutely conscious of the pre-eminence of Virgil, but he could do little more than follow the epic pattern that had so recently been laid down. Admiration for Martial should begin from the fact that he challenged the Greeks in a genre that was peculiarly theirs, and outdid them.

Greek poetry, with certain exceptions such as the epigrammatists, had fallen into this depressed condition as far back as the third century B.C. The first scholars of the Hellenistic world were poets, and there was an exciting conjunction of the impulse to knowledge of the great past with the idea that such knowledge could provide a basis for a new type of poetic inspiration. But already in the third century B.C., scholarship and learning were fast advancing, while poetry was retreating into dead stereotypes, and the union of the two was broken. The ideal of φιλόλογος was taken up by Roman poets in a period when poetry, no less than learning, was advancing again—by poets of the quality of Lucilius and Catullus and others in the late Republic. But the greatest example of the combination of learning and creative power in the late Republic was Cicero (whose poetry only earned him ridicule). No contrast with the end of the first century A.D. could be more startling than the sight of the confident genius of Cicero covering every branch of learning and philosophy (except the mathematical sciences) and using the achievements of Greeks to create a great series of highly original Roman works. In his range and confidence he can well be compared with great Alexandrian polymaths like Eratosthenes—and that in the intervals of an active political career. Nor was he alone.

Greeks found a solution for their literary dilemma: it was to allow the Hellenistic age to fall largely into oblivion and to look back over it to the Classical age. It was a way of looking at Greek culture that obtained added impetus from Roman political domination. By the end of the first century A.D., Romans found themselves culturally doing the same things as Greeks and swamped by the richness of Greek culture, which no longer provided the stimulus required for adaptation and assimilation. They wrote indifferently in Latin or Greek, and they were oppressed by the achievements of their own too-recent Classical age. It was only late in the first century A.D. that Romans began to adopt the Greek expedient of looking back to their earlier literature; [165] but for them this meant looking back over their great Classical age to the rude beginnings of literature. (Such an expedient was impossible for poets of the stature of Statius, for it would have meant denying the very basis on which the poetic genres were founded.) It was a counsel of the despair examined above, and it led to the virtual extinction of Roman poetry for a number of generations. Instead of attempting poetry, Romans again took a hint from contemporary Greeks and used the earliest Roman literature to transform Latin prose and escape from the oppressive genius of Cicero. Even then they had to fight a losing battle against Greek superiority. Aulus Gellius tells [166] of a dinner party in the late second century, when some Greeks who were both cultured and very knowledgeable in Latin literature began to attack the rhetor Antonius Julianus, not just because he was from Spain but because 'he taught exercises in a tongue without charm and without any sweetness of Venus and the Muses'; they asked him what in Latin could compare to Anacreon except a few poems of Catullus and perhaps a few of Calvus. His

165. The way in which writers are mentioned by Manilius in the prooemium to book 2 is significant: he is highly dismissive of Hellenistic poets. For Statius it was not Antimachus who was important, but Sophocles and the cyclic epic poets: see Vessey (1970). In the opposite direction, Calpurnius Siculus and the *Einsiedeln Eclogues* depend on Virgil, not on Theocritus. It is further notable that the Alexandrians, with the exception of a few passages quoted to illustrate Virgil's *Eclogues*, hardly appear at all in Aulus Gellius.

166. *Attic Nights* 19. 9. 7–14.

answer was to recite verses of Valerius Aedituus, Porcius Licinus, and Quintus Catulus. Gellius comments that nothing neater or more graceful or more polished or more elegant could be found in either Greek or Latin. But, equally, it was Gellius and his friends who read the *Plocium* of Caecilius and then the original play of Menander, and were astonished at the utter inferiority in every respect of Caecilius.[167]

Such confusion was born from despairing Roman attempts to resist the paralysis induced by the dominance of Greek culture,[168] and this dominance was increased by what was recognized by Greeks to be an outstanding benefit conferred on the world by Romans. In the words of Aelius Aristides *in Romam* (13): 'The word Roman you have caused to be the label not of membership in a city but of a common nationality, and that not just one among so many but one balancing all the rest'. He was talking of Greeks as Roman citizens, linked in a cultural and political unity against the rest of the world. But culturally the unity was Greek in character.

The way of escape into Greek mythology, devised by Ovid, was only too consonant with what has turned out to be a general movement towards Greek culture in the period as a whole that was to absorb and dominate Roman originality and inspiration, and ultimately to silence it. The other escape route, into flattery of the emperor, was also deeply consonant with yet another deep-rooted tendency in the age as a whole; this will be examined in the following lecture.

167. 2. 23.
168. Aulus Gellius often readily admits the superiority of Greek—see Marache (1952), 183–85—but he can report even a patriot like Fronto as admitting it too: *Attic Nights* 2. 26. 7 *tum Fronto ad Favorinum 'Non in-fitias' inquit 'imus quin lingua Graeca, quam tu videre elegisse, prolixior fusiorque sit quam nostra'.* Favorinus, the Gaul, Greek philosopher and orator, is also a most interesting phenomenon from this point of view: see Bowersock (1969), 35 ff.

IV

Authoritarianism
and Irrationality

PLINY the elder complained bitterly in his excursus on sources of knowledge of trees about the intellectual degeneracy of his own time:[1] not only were men so interested in making money and indulging in all sorts of luxury that they had no time for scientific research, but they even failed to preserve the knowledge that had been accumulated through long years of patient research in the far past. The complaint has elements of self-justification, but also of truth. There is a sense in which a number of features in the cultural life of the early Empire can be viewed as a flight from reason; there are fields in which previous ages had made advances by hard systematic thinking that were turned, in the first century A.D., into playgrounds for the emotions. New ways of formulating experience grew up that seem deeply irrational. It is the thesis of this lecture that a loss of intellectual confidence and a retreat into exploitation of irrationality in many of its aspects characterize the cultural life of the early Empire, and that the growth of this phenomenon was connected with the growth of authoritarianism in the monarchy. The emphasis throughout is on the ways in which literature of the period was affected by this trend.

1. See chap. I, sect. 5 above.

1. *Imperial authoritarianism*

The younger Pliny, in a letter of A.D. 107,[2] expresses his delight: the emperor, Trajan, summoned him to act as assessor with him at Centum Cellae. 'Nothing' says Pliny 'could give me more pleasure than to have firsthand experience of our ruler's justice and wisdom'. There were three cases. The first concerned a provincial worthy from Ephesus, loyal to Rome, who had been accused by an informer. The case was dismissed. The third case concerned a will and was complex; the emperor carefully consulted his assessors. There is no indication of any consultation in the first case; Roman government depended on the support of such men. Nor in the second case. The wife of a military tribune 'had brought disgrace on her own and her husband's position by having an affair with a centurion'. The centurion was cashiered and exiled. The tribune, however, loved his wife and had taken her back, and they were living together again. He was, most reluctantly, compelled to divorce, and give evidence against, his wife. He was severely reprimanded for his reluctance; his wife was deprived of half her dowry and banished to an island. The emperor handled the case himself because he wanted his decision to be exemplary and to create the precedent for all such cases.

The emperor's attitude here and the readiness with which he translated his own sense of discipline and his own moral concepts into law go immediately back to Augustus' moral legislation and the unparallelled interference in the private lives of Roman citizens (particularly of the upper class) which it represented. Successive emperors kept Augustus' legislation in force. Trajan was a 'good' emperor, but the office had grown into a Hellenistic, autocratic monarchy.

Augustus was already of this cast of mind. Tacitus remarks that in the case of sexual offences among distinguished people, Augustus not only far exceeded the *clementia maiorum* but even his own laws, since he treated adultery that affected his own family

2. 6. 31.

as treason.[3] His interference was often petty and expressive of his own attitudes: for instance, he forbade women to be present at wrestling bouts,[4] and he rebuked by letter the young nobleman L. Vinicius for calling on Julia at Baiae.[5] Tiberius also took on himself the regulation of public morals,[6] enacting sumptuary legislation,[7] issuing an edict forbidding people to kiss when they met,[8] and, of course, taking a special interest in legislation on sexual misconduct.[9] Both emperors alike exercised a tight literary censorship.[10] Caligula reacted against Tiberius and started well, but in fact went further than any Julio-Claudian in turning the principate into a Hellenistic monarchy. His rule quickly deteriorated into a whimsical tyranny, typified by his warning *memento omnia mihi et in omnes licere* 'remember that I am permitted to do anything to anyone'.[11] Claudius too began well, but soon again restrictions began and executions—his most promising sign of liberalism was a projected edict to permit farting at dinner.[12] Nero likewise began well and degenerated into arbitrary despotism (there were even executions to raise money).[13] Vitellius seems to have been a sadist who used his position to gratify his tastes.

The Flavians began most promisingly,[14] but with a very high moral tone—intended to create the most notable contrast with Nero—which soon needed exile and execution to uphold it; this reached a high (or low) point with Domitian who was also, on the evidence, a sadist. Nerva's rule was a short and uncertain period, but everyone seemed happy with Trajan. Pliny said in his *Panegyric*, addressed to Trajan on his accession (65): 'On the tribunal you, with the same oath, subjected yourself to the laws— laws, Caesar, that no one intended for an emperor. But you want

3. *Annals* 3. 24. 2.
4. Suetonius *Aug.* 44. 3.
5. Suetonius *Aug.* 64. 2.
6. Suetonius *Tib.* 33.
7. Ibid. 34. 1.
8. Ibid. 34. 2.
9. Ibid. 35.
10. Ibid. 61.
11. Suetonius *Calig.* 29. 1.
12. Suetonius *Claud.* 32.
13. Suetonius *Nero* 32.
14. Cf. Tacitus *Hist.* 4. 42. 6.

no more power for yourself than for us (that is, the senate); the result is that we want more for you. This is something I now hear for
the first time, for the first time I am told it: the emperor is not
above the laws, but the laws are above the emperor, and what is
forbidden to the rest of us is also forbidden to the emperor'. However, after expressing suitable astonishment at this news, he goes
on to say 'You command us to be free: we shall be. . .'.

The fact was that, as every previous emperor had shown, Trajan's subjection to the laws was purely voluntary. At the end of
the second century A.D., the lawyer Ulpian interpreted the position thus:[15] 'What the emperor has decided has the force of law;
for with the law conferring the succession on him, the people also
confers this power on him'. And Gaius says much the same
thing:[16] 'It has never been doubted that the decision of the emperor has the force of law'; and he defines 'decision' as 'what the
emperor has laid down either by decree or by edict or by letter'.
The basis for this concept was Greek: it was the explanation
Greek philosophers had worked out for a relationship between a
monarch and the law—the Hellenistic monarch was the incarna-
tion of the law ($νόμος$ $ἔμψυχος$, 'law incarnate').

This concept had far-reaching consequences for one area of
intellectual activity in which Romans were pre-eminent: the law.
Pomponius, a jurist of the second century A.D., gave a brief history of the *ius respondendi*:[17] 'Before the time of Augustus, the
right to give legal opinions was not conferred by great men of
the state, but those who felt confidence in their legal researches
gave opinions to anyone who consulted them. . . . Augustus
first, with the intention of increasing the authority of the law,
laid down that opinions could only be given on his authority;
and from that time the right began to be petitioned as a favour'.
Since, however, as is clear from Trajan as well as Augustus, the
authority of the emperor outweighed any other, *de facto* the right

15. *Digest* 1. 4. 1.
16. *Institutiones* 1. 5: see de Zulueta (1953) ad loc, and for more general
discussion, Wirszubski (1950), 132 ff.
17. *Digest* 1. 2. 2. 49.

of interpreting the law was reserved for the emperor. Gaius tried to reserve the right exclusively for the emperor by law,[18] but he was not successful, and the *de facto* position of the emperor was not made *de iure* till Hadrian.

This brought a change to the study of law.[19] The time of great innovating geniuses went with the Republic; the intellectual excitement of a Cicero seeing for the first time the implications of Greek philosophical concepts for the very Roman fields of law and jurisprudence was a thing of the past. The period of the early Empire was a period of consolidation and elaboration to the last detail of the ideas of the great Republican jurists. The period beginning with Augustus was also one of increasing bureaucracy, and, like everything else, this was centralized in the hands of the emperor. With Vespasian a new type of jurist made his appearance: professional, bureaucratic, salaried—in short, a civil servant. Study of the law was concentrated on private law, and it typically descended into close scrutiny of minute, often insignificant, problems; in the same way, and closely reminiscent of contemporary rhetoric, jurists delighted in the invention of ingenious difficulties, like eccentric testamentary clauses. Classical jurists were typically uninterested in generalizations or legal philosophy or even in the history of jurisprudence.[20] The culmination of their efforts is to be found in the codification of the praetor's edict under Hadrian. At this point the organization of legal administration and practice became the sole concern of the *consilium principis*. In all this there was nothing irrational, except perhaps in the love of fantastic problems; but authoritarianism was the natural attitude of jurists—illustrated by the proverb 'to answer like a jurist'[21]—and their instinct was to work within the framework laid down by the emperor. The age lacked the stimulus to creative thinking about law that the challenge of

18. Suetonius *Calig.* 34. 2.
19. See especially Schulz (1953), 124–40; Watson (1970), 27 ff., 90.
20. For a typical example see Aulus Gellius *Attic Nights* 16. 10. 1–8; Schulz (1936), 100 ff.
21. Seneca *de benef.* 5. 19. 8; *Epp.* 94. 27. Schulz (1953), 125.

the Empire, with its enormous scope for every conceivable legal problem and the need for expanding definitions, should have provided.

The situation can be viewed from another angle. The concept of *clementia* had meant that instinct to humanity which exercises mercy when guilt, of whatever sort, has been established. With Julius Caesar it meant the arbitrary concession of pardon to those whom he regarded as enemies. Augustus claimed it as one of his four cardinal virtues.[22] In A.D. 28 an *ara Clementiae* was voted to Tiberius.[23] In A.D. 39 Caligula treated the senate as a body of traitors, and it praised his *clementia*.[24] The word appears on coins of Vitellius, and its equivalent, *Indulgentia Augusti*, on coins of Hadrian. In this series two literary works are of especial importance. On Nero's accession Seneca addressed to him a treatise *de clementia*.[25] The basic idea was a version of the Hellenistic concept of the king as νόμος ἔμψυχος: Nero is *de facto* above the law; the distinction that matters is between a tyrant and a king who obeys the laws of right reason. In this way, Seneca admits absolutism but hopes to mitigate it. A further concept is inevitably attached to this. Seneca asks Nero to speak with himself thus: 'Was I from all mortals elected and chosen to take the place of gods on earth? To be arbiter of life and death for the world? Has the power been given me to decide the lot and status of every individual? Does Fate speak with my lips her decrees for each mortal? Only upon my verdict do peoples and cities find reasons for joy? Does no part of the world flourish unless it is at my will and pleasure?'[26] The last words are *nisi volente propitioque me*, an archaic formula of prayer to a god. Again Seneca says: 'A subject looks upon his ruler with the feeling that it is the immortal gods who permit him to be seen. Why not? For he

22. *res gestae* 34. 2: on this and on what follows, see especially Charlesworth (1937).
23. Tacitus *Annals* 4. 74. 2—dated incorrectly in Charlesworth (1937), 112 to A.D. 22.
24. Cassius Dio 59. 16. 10.
25. See especially Büchner (1970).
26. *de clem.* I. 1. 2.

holds next place to them who conducts himself in accordance with the nature of the gods as beneficent, generous, and powerful for good. This is what should be aimed at, this is the pattern: to be considered all-highest in such a way that you are also considered best'.[27] The adjectives here are *maximus* and *optimus* and refer to the national god of the Roman state, Iuppiter Optimus Maximus.

This is the ultimate irrationality: the emperor prefigured as a god on earth, the equivalent of Juppiter, and his basic relationship with his subjects expressed in the arbitrary ideal of *clementia*, totally bypassing the great Roman intellectual structure of the law and the ideal of equality before the law.[28] Nor was this the particular problem of Seneca faced with a Nero whose propensities he perhaps recognized. Pliny in his *Panegyric* spoke in a similar way to Trajan of *clementia* (80): 'These are duties worthy of an emperor and even of a god: to reconcile rival states, to restrain arrogant peoples by reason no less than by authority, to step in when magistrates are unfair, to undo what has been done wrongly, and, finally, like the swiftest of stars, to watch over everything, to hear everything, and wherever invoked as a god to be ever present to help. Such I should believe to be the affairs that the Lord of the Universe controls at a nod whenever he casts his eyes to earth and deigns to count the fates of mortals among his divine concerns; of all that duty he has now been relieved and has been set free to concentrate on heaven, since he has given us you to discharge his duties towards the whole human race'. Seneca's *de clementia* signified the end not only of political philosophy but also of any broad-based legal science; Pliny's *Panegyric*, to some extent based upon it, drove the point home.

2. *Emperor worship as a literary theme*

In real life deification was honorific. The emperor was not a god, except as an object of veneration and gratitude; no one

27. ibid. I. 19. 8–9.
28. Cf. Cicero *pro Cluentio* 146 *legum idcirco omnes servi sumus ut liberi esse possimus.*

would pray to a dead emperor for help. Deification was a metaphor for expressing the relationship between the emperor and his
subjects. Pliny expressed the concept with a nice sense of what
terms like *providentia* and *aeternitas* meant for the continuity
of the monarchy.[29] He addressed Trajan in his *Panegyric* (11):
'You installed your father (Nerva) in the stars, not to strike fear
into your citizens, not to insult the gods, not to honour yourself,
but because you really regard him as a god. But, though you
reverence him with all sorts of ceremonies, yet you do not make
him a god and prove him to be such for any other reason than
that you are of the same sort'. The continuity of the Empire and
the divinity of the ruler were mutually supportive concepts.

For centuries Greeks had developed the concept of the Hellenistic king as a god, and contemporary Greek poets treated
Augustus, Tiberius, Gaius, or Nero as gods, equivalent to Zeus.
These were highly respected poets like Crinagoras or Apollonides
or Philip or Leonidas of Alexandria. Used in this way in poetry,
the concept of the emperor as god had a status that formed one extreme; the other was formed by the state cult of emperors, and the
midpoint was occupied by a formulation like that of Pliny, quoted
above. In poetry the concept was strictly a myth, a way of pro-
cessing the institution of monarchy for treatment in poetry. Both
Virgil and Horace, in their earliest exuberance as they experi-
mented with the concept, produced formulations from which
everything that they subsequently wrote was a retreat; Horace
Odes 1. 2 was dependent on Virgil *Georgics* 1. 24–42, and both
passages treat Augustus as in some degree actually a god on earth,
before the point when Augustus returns to heaven to become an
actual god. But it may well have been under the influence of
such Greek poets as Crinagoras that Ovid progressively moved
in the direction of treating Augustus as a god on earth. At a late
point, Ovid actually united the two extremes of myth and real
life: in *ex Ponto* 2. 8 and 4. 9. 101 ff., he tells how Cotta Maximus
sent him silver reliefs of the 'Royal Family' which he has en-
shrined in his house; he also honours the birthday of Augustus

29. See Charlesworth (1936).

with as lavish a festival as he can. But at the end of the latter poem, he breaks out of real life back into myth to offer a prayer to Augustus for help. The idea of worshipping Augustus in a real-life way by putting him among the Lares and celebrating his birthday was for Ovid a poetic way of exhibiting his loyalty, for Augustus was no longer alive and Tiberius was emperor; nor was the prayer to Augustus for the ears of Augustus.

The poetic figuring of the emperor as already a god on earth went further and further in later writers. Lucan's invocation of Nero is particularly important both as a close reworking of the passage of Virgil's *Georgics* and because its sentiments catch a reader by surprise. Lucan opens his epic reflecting on the crime of civil war. Then (24–32), by means of a perfectly handled crescendo on the theme of Italy ruined, depopulated, and turned into wasteland, he reaches the climax that this was the result of no enemy's action but only her own. This climax then carries over into (33–45):

> quod si non aliam venturo fata Neroni
> invenere viam magnoque aeterna parantur
> regna deis caelumque suo servire Tonanti   35
> non nisi saevorum potuit post bella gigantum,
> iam nihil, o superi, querimur; scelera ipsa nefasque
> hac mercede placent. diros Pharsalia campos
> impleat et Poeni saturentur sanguine manes,
> ultima funesta concurrant proelia Munda,   40
> his, Caesar, Perusina fames Mutinaeque labores
> accedant fatis et quas premit aspera classes
> Leucas et ardenti servilia bella sub Aetna,
> multum Roma tamen debet civilibus armis
> quod tibi res acta est.   45

But if Fate found no other way for Nero to come, and if their eternal kingdoms are bought dearly for the gods, and heaven could be ruled by its own Thunderer (35) only after battling with the fierce Giants, then, O gods, we have no complaint: all that crime and guilt are agreeable at this price. Yes, let Pharsalia fill her terrible plains and let Carthaginian ghosts be glutted with blood; let the final battle be joined at deadly Munda (40); to these disasters, Caesar, let there be added the famine at Perusia and the horrors of

Mutina and the fleets that stormy Leucas keeps under her waves and the slave wars near burning Aetna. In spite of all that, Rome owes a great debt to civil war because it was fought for you.

This is a carefully shaped passage which ends on the theme of its opening. Its arrangement—A (33–37), B (37–38), B¹ (38–43), A¹ (44–45)—allows B and A¹, A and B¹ to balance each other. Also the historical vision has widened to extend the civil wars down to Actium and so to the foundation of the principate. The historical concept is that Nero is a direct result of the civil wars. This could be interpreted in two ways: the civil wars were bad enough, but Nero is worse; or (as Lucan has chosen here) the civil wars were bad, but good has come out of them.

Lucan then turns to Nero himself (45–66):

> te, cum statione peracta
> astra petes serus, praelati regia caeli
> excipiet gaudente polo: seu sceptra tenere
> seu te flammigeros Phoebi conscendere currus
> telluremque nihil mutato sole timentem
> igne vago lustrare iuvet, tibi numine ab omni   50
> cedetur, iurisque tui natura relinquet
> quis deus esse velis, ubi regnum ponere mundi.
> sed neque in Arctoo sedem tibi legeris orbe
> nec polus aversi calidus qua vergitur Austri,
> unde tuam videas obliquo sidere Romam.   55
> aetheris inmensi partem si presseris unam,
> sentiet axis onus. librati pondera caeli
> orbe tene medio; pars aetheris illa sereni
> tota vacet nullaeque obstent a Caesare nubes.
> tum genus humanum positis sibi consulat armis   60
> inque vicem gens omnis amet; pax missa per orbem
> ferrea belligeri conspescat limina Iani.
> sed mihi iam numen; nec, si te pectore vates
> accipio, Cirrhaea velim secreta moventem
> sollicitare deum Bacchumque avertere Nysa: 65
> tu satis ad vires Romana in carmina dandas.

When, your watch on earth finished, long in the future, you shall rise to the stars, the celestial palace you choose will receive you and the heavens shall rejoice. You may choose to be the supreme ruler, or to mount the fiery chariot of Phoebus and circle with your am-

bient flame an earth that feels no fear at the change of the sun—
every deity (50) will give way to you and Nature will put it in your
control to choose what god you wish to be, and where to establish
your kingdom of the universe. But do not choose your abode in
the northern sky nor where the hot circle of the opposing south
sinks down: for there you would look upon Rome with slanting
light (55). If you put your weight on one section of the infinite
heavens, the axis will feel the burden. In the centre of the whole,
keep the weight of the universe in balance. May that region of the
heavens be clear and bright, and may no clouds obstruct the view
in Caesar's direction. Then may the human race put aside weapons
and plan its own welfare (60); may the nations all be bound in mutual love; may Peace, sent forth through the world, close the iron-
bound gates of warring Janus. But to me you are already a god:
and if I receive you in my poetic heart, I need not trouble the god
who reveals his secrets at Cirrha, or turn Bacchus aside from
Nysa (65): you give me sufficient strength for Roman poetry.

This too is a very careful composition. The awkward idea of
looking ahead to Nero's death is expressed in the soldier's metaphor of guard duty, and it occupies only the second half of a
line with a syntactical structure that subordinates it to the climax
which follows—*astra petes*. Then two passages (46–52 and 53–
59), of seven lines each, amplify two ideas: what god will Nero
be, and where will he reside in heaven? A surprising climax follows in the last four lines. All that preceded looked to the future
in which Nero will be a god: that reaches its own climax in a
prayer for universal peace and love at that time (60–62). But in
63 the poet asserts that as far as he is concerned, Nero is already
a god and an inspiration for Roman poetry; he therefore needs
no conventional appeal to Greek deities like Apollo or Bacchus
for inspiration.

All three sections are highly original reworkings of the three
themes in Virgil *Georgics* 1. 24–42. The one entirely new element is the appeal for peace and love, which is strongly motivated
by the theme of Lucan's epic as he had already expounded it in
his prooemium. There is an emotional climax at this point. From
the time of the earliest scholia, the whole passage has been taken
as ironic, and the scholiasts quite absurdly and wrongly explain

that Nero was obese and squint-eyed and so forth.[30] But an ironic reading of the passage imports mere vulgarity into the deeply impressive opening to the epic, and ignores not only the deliberate use of Virgilian themes and the emotional climax on peace, but also the careful artistry of the composition at all points. Since Nero would be both the sole victim of the irony and the sole unprivileged reader, the choice is not between an ironic and a serious reading, but between a direct attack on Nero and a seriously intended, but highly stereotyped, tribute. What disturbs the reader is the fact that the sentiments expressed here deeply contradict the Republican ideals in the rest of the epic. There is one general explanation: this is another example of the way in which poets in this period could take material and give it appropriate rhetorical treatment without involving themselves in the truth or falsity of the subject matter, using skilful devices to incorporate it appropriately into the movement of the poem. Thus Lucan leads in by using the climax as a bridge (31–34) and leads out of it on the idea of inspiration (67): *fert animus causas tantarum expromere rerum*. Other particular explanations are relevant to this specific passage. The early years of Nero saw a great renascence of literature in Rome, inspired by the emperor himself, and several other poets at this time burst out with enthusiastic flattery. Lucan published the first three books of the *Bellum Civile* separately, and it is easy to suspect that his affection and admiration for Nero were still unimpaired and that he could still hold the basic Stoic view that monarchy was not necessarily bad, and that judgement on it depended on the character of the monarch. That this was Lucan's meaning is confirmed by the relationship he sets up between the battle of the Giants and the reign of Juppiter as analogous to the civil wars and the reign of Nero—except that the analogy of the battle of the Giants and the civil wars collapses if pressed. It also seems clear that Lucan (and perhaps others at the time) optimistically interpreted the early

30. Modern scholars continue to repeat the scholiast's view in spite of the conclusive demonstration by Grimal (1960).

years of Nero as the beginning of an era of world peace,[31] no less than of domestic peace. But, beyond all this, it also seems likely that Lucan was still unaware of the ways in which the very composition of the epic would crystallize his own ideas about the monarchy, while growing antagonism to Nero focussed his attention on them and compelled expression of them.[32]

An extreme point was reached in Roman poetry with Statius and Martial. This is partly explained by the extreme demands made by Domitian, demands which compelled even Quintilian to use the concept of the emperor's divinity in prose after Domitian had entrusted the education of his grandnephews to him (4. praef. 4–6): 'No one feels surprise that the greatest poets have often invoked the Muses at the beginning of a work; but also later, when they came to an especially important section, they repeated their vows and offered, as it were, new prayers. So I may be forgiven if I do now what I did not do at the beginning when I was entering on this task, and invoke the assistance of all gods, and especially of Himself, than whom there is no deity more present to help nor more well disposed to these studies, beseeching him to inspire in me genius in proportion to the hope he has shown in me, and to be present to aid me, kindly and propitious, and make me such as he has believed me to be. Now this, though the greatest, is not the only reason for my devout prayers, but my work as it proceeds faces me with ever greater and more difficult problems'.

How far Quintilian has gone can be measured by comparing

31. The concept of peace expressed by Lucan is quite new in that he takes the point of view of the world as a whole, and that peace is to be accompanied by universal love. When Virgil and Horace reflected on peace, it was generally freedom from civil war; but in any case it was a peace not only imposed by Romans, but viewed from the Roman standpoint.

32. See, for instance, Marti (1945). The view of Brisset (1964) that there is no real change of attitude in the Bellum Civile is unconvincing, and not only requires that the panegyric of Nero was ironical, but also that Lucan be separated from other Neronian writers who hailed the accession as marking the coming of a Golden Age.

that with Valerius Maximus' invocation of Tiberius (Book 1 *praef.*): 'So I invoke your help in this undertaking: in your hands the consent of gods and men has been pleased to place the rule over sea and land: by your heavenly wisdom [*providentia*] those virtues of which I am about to speak are most generously fostered, the vices most severely punished. For if orators of old properly began with Iuppiter Optimus Maximus, if the most distinguished poets took their beginnings from some deity, my own insignificance will more rightly take refuge in your beneficence, since the divinity of others is inferred from general opinion, but yours is seen on firsthand evidence to be the equal of your father's and your grandfather's stars from whose shining light much distinction and brightness has been added to our religious acts: for the rest of the gods are given to us, the Caesars we create'.

Valerius Maximus, though his treatment of the topic may have influenced Quintilian, stopped well short of viewing Tiberius as a god—as distinct from praising him as godlike—and he made the proper distinction between the traditional gods and the Caesars (the deification of the latter is honorific for qualities shown and services done). Quintilian, however, was writing sixty years later, and he used the practice of poets (which Valerius had used to contrast with his own form of invocation) as a direct analogy to his own invocation of Domitian.

Flattery of the emperor had become a necessary poetic theme, and poets, accepting the topic on the same terms as any other topic, exerted themselves to devise new ingenuities by which to surprise and delight their hearers. So Domitian was treated by Statius and Martial as Saviour (a Greek concept),[33] as bringer of the Golden Age, as darling of the gods, as God on Earth, as Juppiter, as Hercules or Dionysus, as *aeternus, maximus, sanctus*, and so forth. Both also address him as *Dominus*, and Martial alone addresses him by the title which he particularly liked, *Dominus et Deus*. The emperors up to Nero avoided the title *Dominus* because it suggested autocracy. As a polite form of address it could be used between inferiors and social superiors (or if one

33. Material collected by Sauter (1934).

had forgotten an equal's name), and thus it was the normal form of address used by Pliny in his letters to Trajan. But when Domitian wished to be called *Dominus et Deus*, he was not only regarding himself as a god in his lifetime but was using *Dominus* as an imperial title, a use not otherwise found before the age of the Severi.

Some of Martial's writing on this topic has merit, where he learnt from Ovid and used the technique of framing the flattery in a witty setting. For instance, 7. 99:

> sic placidum videas semper, Crispine, Tonantem
>   nec te Roma minus quam tua Memphis amet:
> carmina Parrhasia si nostra legentur in aula
>   (namque solent sacra Caesaris aure frui)
> dicere de nobis ut lector candidus aude:
>   'temporibus praestat non nihil iste tuis,
> nec Marso nimium minor est doctoque Catullo'.
>   hoc satis est: ipsi cetera mando deo.

> If you want to see the Thunderer always placid, Crispinus, and Rome to love you no less than your native Memphis does, then, when my poems shall be read out in the hall of the Palatine (for they are wont to enjoy the favour of Caesar's holy ear), be brave, speak out as a frank reader and say this of me: 'He brings some distinction to your times and is not far inferior to Marsus and the erudite Catullus'. That is sufficient: I leave the rest to the God himself.

There is a fine wit in the setting of this flattery and appeal for patronage, and in the treatment of the very important upstart foreigner Crispinus. But it is seldom that Martial hits flattery off with such lightness of touch, and Statius never does. The understandable change and relief that came with Trajan was nicely expressed by Martial in a poem in which he addressed the personified troop of Flatteries (10. 72):

> frustra, Blanditiae, venitis ad me
> adtritis miserabiles labellis:
> dicturus dominum deumque non sum.
> iam non est locus hac in urbe vobis;
> ad Parthos procul ite pilleatos

> et turpes humilesque supplicesque
> pictorum sola basiate regum.
> non est hic dominus sed imperator,
> sed iustissimus omnium senator,
> per quem de Stygia domo reducta est
> siccis rustica Veritas capillis.
> hoc sub principe, si sapis, caveto
> verbis, Roma, prioribus loquaris.

In vain, Flatteries, you come to me, wretched creatures with whore's lips: I am not about to address any man as Master and God.[34] There is no place in this city for you: off with you to the turbaned Parthians, and, you base crawling creatures, kiss the soles of painted kings. No Master is here—only an army commander, a senator most just of all, who has led simple Truth, with unperfumed hair, up from the Stygian abode. Under this emperor, Rome, see, if you are wise, that you do not speak those former words.

This, of course, is flattery too, and Martial was embarrassed; but it is a neat and witty conception to take the initiative and give good advice to his fellow citizens—at the same time implying his own regret and hatred of his conduct under Domitian. The imperial cult went on, but Roman poetry died for a long time (except for one of the greatest, who, because he wrote under Trajan and Hadrian, did not have to flatter). The theme of the emperor-god was left to Greek poets in the second century A.D. and later. It was quite irrational material, forced on Roman poets by the imperial autocracy; and not only was it derived from the Greek East, but it got much of its earliest impetus in the time of Ovid from the practice of contemporary Greek poets writing in Rome.

Three characteristics of the treatment of this theme by Roman poets are of particular interest: first, it was a theme that had to be explored without any regard for its truth or falsity; second, normal poetic treatment of the theme led easily, indeed inevitably, to conceit and fantasy; third, at least in this area, the poet was compelled to ask what his audience wanted to hear and so had to regard his poetry as a commodity designed to meet certain

34. Cf. Pliny *panegyricus* 2. 3; 7. 6; 45. 3.

wishes in his customers. Later we must ask whether, and to what extent, these characteristics were determined by a particular type of material, or whether they can be seen as general in the poetry of the early Empire. The weakness of the invocation in Lucan's *Bellum Civile*, for instance, can perhaps be defined in terms of a distinction between ideas and ideology. In the opening section of the epic, the reader is aware of the poet's mind actively confronting and dominating ideas that arouse strong emotions; but when he turns aside to address Nero, what he says is false (if only by hindsight) and clever: a predetermined ideology is being imposed upon the facts, and no emotion is involved except in the climactic prayer for peace. It will need to be asked whether there are other digressions in Lucan that show similar characteristics.

3. *Some consequences of the terror*

The terror of life under the emperors (from Tiberius to Domitian—and, perhaps, at least the later period of Augustus) needs little illustration. It was a terror that weighed on exactly those men who were likely to exercise literary talents and pursue intellectual enquiry. Suetonius says[35] of the later reign of Tiberius: 'no day passed without executions of men'; and Seneca tells[36] of the *eques* Pastor under Gaius: the emperor had imprisoned Pastor's son, disliking his hair style and clothes. The father begged that the son's life be spared, but Gaius instantly executed him and invited Pastor to dinner. He had the father watched all the time for the least sign of grief, but the father showed only enjoyment— he had a second son.[37] When Seneca describes men, who feared they might be indiscreet in their wine cups, asking friends to

---

35. *Tib.* 61. 2. *nullus a poena hominum cessavit dies.*
36. *de ira* 2. 33. 3–5.
37. Cf. the similar story of Julius Canus: *de tranq. an.* 14. 4–9. It is clear that such stories were collected not just for their anecdotal value but because they helped to stiffen the resistance and bolster the courage of those who had cause to fear similar threats to themselves, quite apart from the delicious sense of terror they conveyed (see chap. V, sect. 5).

watch and remove them before that happened,[38] he suggests not just a careful regard for politeness but something that is made explicit by a passage of Epictetus:[39] 'A soldier sits beside you in plain clothes and begins to abuse Caesar; then you, thinking you have a pledge of his trustworthiness in that he began the abuse first, say what you think yourself, and then you are dragged off to jail'. Here Epictetus was talking of the time of Domitian. Seneca speaks similarly of the time of Tiberius:[40] 'Under Tiberius Caesar the frenzy to make charges (of treason) was widespread, indeed almost universal, and it took a heavier toll of our citizens' lives than the whole of the civil war: the words of drunk men were overheard, also the frank speech of men telling jokes. Nothing was safe: every opportunity to do injury was taken, and no one wanted to find out the fate of those accused—there was only one outcome'.

Such accounts underline Tacitus' praise[41] of the time of Trajan—'when you can hold what opinions you want and express your opinions openly'. The pages of Tacitus and Suetonius are filled with continuous executions in the upper classes, among *equites* and senators. It is a major moral preoccupation of Tacitus that crimes of the emperors had to be met with *adulatio*. He is most outspoken in his own person after the horrible murder of Octavia:[42] 'Anyone who, reading me or other authors, learns the disasters of those times, should take it for granted that on each occasion that an emperor commanded exile or death, invariably thank-offerings were made to the gods, so that what had previously been the sign of prosperity then became the sign of disaster to the state. In spite of that I shall record each decree of the senate that displayed originality in adulation or a new low point in servility'.

This condition of life, which persisted to the death of Domitian

38. *de ira* 3. 13. 5.
39. 4. 13. 5. It is clear that Epictetus is talking of Domitian: see Starr (1949). Cf. Tacitus *Agricola* 2. 3, and *Annals* 4. 69. 3 (Tiberius).
40. *de beneficiis* 3. 26. 1.
41. *Hist.* 1. 1. 2.
42. *Annals* 14. 64. 3; cf. 3. 65. 2.

almost continuously but was transformed (on the evidence of
Tacitus and Pliny) under Trajan, can be seen to have affected
the intellectual life of the period in a number of ways. Most
obviously, it limited subject matter—though at times even Greek
mythology was dangerous. In a more personal and psychological
way, it brought about, or at least helped to bring about, three
remarkable changes in the intellectual climate, all of them irrational in the sense of encouraging a withdrawal from reason
into emotion. One of these has been described as a passionate
surrender to the charms of Fate. Another was the new sense of
the individual isolated and driven in on himself. The third was
a deliberate cultivation of the irrational in various forms of
superstition.

Fate and ecstasy.—The passionate surrender to Fate is not
properly so termed. What was involved is illustrated by words
Seneca quotes of Demetrius of Sunium, a Cynic philosopher, who
taught in Rome under Gaius and Nero.[43] In *de providentia* (3.
3), Seneca quotes with great admiration words of his that he has
just heard: 'No man, in my opinion, is more unhappy than one
who has never met with ill-fortune.' Then, later, Seneca explains
how things like wealth are of no interest to good men (5. 4–6):
'Good men toil, spend, are spent—and gladly so; they are not
dragged along by Fortune: they follow and keep pace with her.
If they had known how, they would have preceded her. This is
another inspiring speech which I remember Demetrius, that most
stalwart man, made: "There is just one complaint I can make
against you, immortal gods: you did not previously make known
your will to me. For I should have, of my own accord, reached
that state that I am now in after being summoned there. Do you
want to take my children? It was for you I brought them up.
You want some part of my body? Take it: it is no great thing that
I offer you; soon I shall leave it completely. Do you want my life?
Why not? I shall make no bones about your taking back what you
gave me. You will be taking from a willing giver anything you

43. See the excellent study of his views by Oltramare (1926), 232 ff.

want. What then is my point? I should have preferred to offer than to hand over. What need was there to take? You were in a position to receive as a gift. But not even now will you be taking things from me, since nothing can be taken unless a man resists". I am under no compulsion, I suffer nothing against my will, and I am not a slave to God, but his supporter—the more so because I know that everything proceeds in accordance with a law that is fixed and laid down for all time. Fate guides us . . . '.

This is a typical passage. Its characteristic is the emotional ecstasy of the martyr who feels completely his own man because he delights in going to meet all the trials that can be presented to him. It has a large element of the masochistic in that the fortune he goes to meet is envisaged as, in ordinary terms, evil and painful. Seneca increased the emotional tension by expressing himself often as a determinist, which earlier Stoics like Chrysippus certainly were not.[44] No evil can be done to a good man (much less can he do any evil) because he is absolutely in control of his emotions—in Seneca's way of putting it, he has no emotions. Evil, then, is not only always the creation of evil men, but it is always subjective in that it cannot affect the good man. What is remarkable in so unemotional a philosophy is the extraordinarily emotional presentation of it. Seneca works himself into a solipsistic religious fervour. It is an ecstasy to be tested by misfortune, and the words Seneca uses of this are metaphors from physical torture: the good man hands himself over or is given over (*praebere*) to Fate as to his torturer.[45] The essential isolation of the good man as conceived by Seneca appears in the fact that, in the typical moral situation as he envisages it, the good man only acts negatively in relation to himself by standards known only to him, and he reacts to the acts of others by withdrawing into himself: Fate is, typically, what others do.

44. For the position of Chrysippus see Rist (1969), 118 ff.
45. Cf., for example, *de providentia* 4. 11–12; 5. 8. In *Epp.* 64. 3–4 he has been reading Sextius, and feels inspired to issue a challenge to Fortune: '*libet omnes casus provocare, libet exclamare: 'Quid cessas, Fortuna? Congredere! Paratum vides!'*

Lucan was clearly under the influence of his uncle, and these ideas form the intellectual framework of his epic. The various words for Fate are used by Lucan (as by Seneca) in several ways that form no coherent doctrine.[46] But most often in Lucan Fate is best regarded as a sort of literary device for foreshadowing future events: Fate is what is going to happen before it happens, and the poet exercises his superior knowledge over the reader. When Lucan omitted the divine machinery, he may have had several reasons for doing so; but one certain motive, both doctrinal and dramatic, was to put human beings in direct contact, without any mediation, with the events, thus allowing each event to take its moral colouring from the human participation alone. Situations were invented to exploit this. Cato has the opportunity to consult the oracle of Juppiter Ammon,[47] and Labienus urges him to 'find out the future of wicked Caesar and examine the future condition of our country—will Romans be allowed to enjoy their laws and liberty, or has the civil war been wasted?' Cato converts these questions into moral questions about the conduct of the good man, and asserts (rightly) that the answers need no oracle.[48]

Lucan quickly skates over any killing done by Cato (the taking of Cyrene is described thus:[49] 'The next task was against the walls and fortifications of Cyrene: excluded from it, Cato took no angry revenge, and the only penalty he exacted from the conquered was to have conquered them'). Instead, Lucan concentrates on something else. Seneca (de prov. 2. 9) asserted that a spectacle worthy of God's eyes is a good man pitted against ill-fortune—and especially if he has himself provoked it. This is the situation in which Lucan placed Cato on his forced march across the worst parts of Africa—and he lengthened the march

46. Attempts—for example, Brisset (1964), 51–78—to view *fatum* in Lucan as determining the fall of the Republic in the manner of a just and benevolent deity ignore the poet's manipulation of the concept to suit each particular context. See also Schotes (1969), 110 ff., 169 f.

47. *Bellum Civile* 9. 558–61.

48. Based on Seneca *Epp.* 88. 14–17.

49. *Bellum Civile* 9. 297–9.

from seven days to two months. Cato's ecstasy at the thought of the perils to be faced on this pointless march is his motive for undertaking it, as he explains in a speech (9. 379–406), and he revels in accepting more hardship than his men. A similar ecstasy on an equally pointless undertaking is shown by Caesar when he sets out in a terrible storm in a tiny fishing boat to Italy;[50] but whereas Cato's wrestling with Fate was approved by the poet, Caesar's was not: Caesar merely does it to test his own very high rating of his private Fortuna—he is boastful, self-centred, and a victim of all the worst emotions. Pompey, who improves morally[51] right through the epic from the point where Lucan asserts that no one can say which of the two took up arms more justifiably (1. 126–27), reaches his moral climax when he leaves everything and gets into the Egyptian boat, suspecting that he is going to be murdered but totally submitting to it, and dying with fully self-conscious regard for the opinions of spectators and posterity.[52] Lucan's own judgement is (8. 621) *seque probat moriens.*

That Lucan's use of Fate and Fortuna was directly connected to his omission of the divine machinery, can be seen from the contrary situation in Statius. There Fortuna plays a very reduced role, while Statius overuses the divine machinery. For instance, he builds up distinct and convincing characters for Tydeus and Capaneus, but he carefully makes Tisiphone instigate their final acts, which are otherwise very much in character.[53] Or, again, the single combat of the two brothers in book 11 is very elaborately arranged by Tisiphone andMegaera. A more disappointing instance of this form of overkill occurs in book 1. There Statius purports to analyse power at Thebes—the inevitable progress from dyarchy to tyranny—using Lucan's ideas and his analysis

---

50. The undertaking is described at length (*Bellum Civile* 5. 504–677). For expressions of ecstasy see, for example, 654–71.

51. See, for example, Marti (1945).

52. *Bellum Civile* 8. 560–636.

53. *Thebaid* 8. 751–66 and 10. 827 ff. (in the latter case it is one of a series of possible motivations).

of Caesar and Pompey in *Bellum Civile* 1; but he still brings in Tisiphone to arrange the split between Polynices and Eteocles. Again, Statius creates a more sympathetic character for Polynices throughout the *Thebaid*, but when the unnamed critic (1. 173–96) mentions this fact specifically (189–91), he explains it by saying *non solus erat*—a circumstance which applied equally to Eteocles. The basic fact was that the conflict between destiny and self-determination became acute in the terms of Statius' treatment: since nothing could happen without divine intervention, character had little or no room for manoeuvre in the epic. The foreboding, irrational Fate of Lucan gave far more weight to the individual and his specific qualities.

Of course, none of the other epic poets had anything like the moral fervour of Lucan or his intense commitment to his subject matter or, indeed, his intellectual strength. In the case of Seneca's tragedies, the emotional intensity came from a reshaping of the Greek material, designed to make evil subjective and the product of emotion; while the very few good characters are such in virtue of their submission to torture and death: outstanding examples of these are Astyanax and Polyxena in the *Troades*.[54] Evil men tower over the plays, giants of emotional intensity and violence; in the *Oedipus* the whole course of the play is simplified because Oedipus himself becomes an evil man, a slave to his emotions.[55]

It is easy to see how ideas of this sort were related to the physical conditions of life under the terror. But philosophy in the period had its own peculiarities. The great creative period was far behind; Cicero's confident grasp of systems (with all his errors) and his imaginative creation of a Roman philosophy from Greek had collapsed. Even the desire had gone. Seneca had no interest in systematic philosophy (and said so),[56] and philosophy quite changed its nature with him and with later so-called philosophers. It degenerated into a series of set topics in the same way

54. 1091–1103 and 1137–64.
55. Well analyzed by Pratt (1948).
56. For instance, *de vita beata* 3. 2; 13. 1; *de brev. vitae* 14. 1–5; *Epp.* 21. 9.

as did contemporary rhetoric and, to some extent, even poetry; the rhetoricians actually listed *loci philosophoumenoi* and *problemata philosophoumena*[57] which they used on appropriate occasions (the topics must have had titles very like those of Seneca's *dialogues*). But, more than that, philosophy had become totally preoccupied with the moral and religious problems of the individual, conceived as a lonely soul in an alien world. Epictetus says that 'the philosopher's lecture room is a hospital'.[58] Seneca recommends a daily self-examination, stressing the importance of the individual conscience and the sense of sin;[59] hence his tragedy is not between man and Fate, but consists in conflict in the individual soul. What is perhaps most surprising, however, is the novel emotional tone which is clear not only in Seneca, but also, for instance, in Epictetus and Musonius Rufus. Philosophy had really become a religion, and initiation language was often used to describe the grasping of philosophical truth: '[philosophy] leads one thither, thither she opens the path. What are evils she reveals; she strips all vanity from our souls. . .'.[60] Musonius Rufus and Epictetus were really preachers, and neither was interested in publication. Seneca's *dialogues* are more like sermons than essays[61] because of the emotional intensity of the language in which they are expressed and the peculiarity of the style.[62] When Seneca writes letters to Lucilius he sounds more like a spiritual

57. Seneca *contr.* 1. 7. 17; 1. 3. 8.

58. 3. 23. 30; cf. Seneca *Epp.* 27. 1.

59. *de ira* 3. 36; cf. Horace *Sat.* 1. 4. 133 ff. It is a theme of the Cynic diatribes: see Oltramare (1926), 55, 278. Seneca *de ira* 3. 36. 1 says of Sextius: *faciebat hoc Sextius ut, consummato die, cum se ad nocturnam quietem recepisset, interrogaret animum suum: 'Quod hodie malum tuum sanasti? cui vitio obstitisti? qua parte melior es?'* Musonius Rufus insisted on the philosopher's duty to produce a sense of sin and shame and repentance in his audience's minds: Aulus Gellius 5. 1. 2–4.

60. Seneca *Epp.* 90. 27–28. Cf. *Epp.* 6. 1 *intellego, Lucili, non emendari me tantum sed transfigurari.*

61. Seneca requires the philosopher and even the historian to display the moral fire of an evangelical preacher: cf., for example, *Epp.* 40. 5; 100. 10. The contrast with Cicero's view could hardly be more dramatic: cf. *orator* 64.

62. The style should be regarded as devised for the purpose of making this type of impact: see chap. V, sect. 3 below.

adviser.[63] And indeed 'philosophers' are often found throughout this period in important private houses, like chaplains; and, like chaplains, they attended on the dying and those condemned to die.[64]

The sense of isolation.—The novel concept of the individual as isolated in a more or less hostile world can be seen, for instance, in the insistence on a personal god who has a close relationship with the individual. Seneca says to Lucilius: [65] 'You do not need to lift up your hands to heaven, or beg a temple custodian to let you go up to the ear of a statue (as if you could be better heard in that way): God is beside you, he is with you, he is within you. So I tell you, Lucilius, a sacred spirit dwells within us, the watcher over, and guard of, our evil and our good deeds. As we treat him, so he treats us. No man can be good without God'. But, most strikingly, this highly emotional sense of isolation is clear in Seneca's morbid concentration on his own death.[66] The theme of death dominates Seneca's writing; it is, for example, the main theme of at least half of the one hundred and twenty-four letters to Lucilius that have survived.[67] He developed the paradox that life is a preparation for death,[68] but not on the ground that would have been comprehensible, for instance, to a Christian, that there is an afterlife; *meditari mortem* was a favourite instruction of Seneca, and life for him was a *meditatio mortis* (almost 'a practising for death' or 'a rehearsal of death').

Suicide had been condemned generally by Greeks as a coward's retreat, and Romans had taken the same view. That was changed

63. A typical expression is (*Epp.* 8. 3) *rectum iter, quod sero cognovi et lassus errando, aliis monstro.* On this aspect of Seneca see especially Guillemin (1952) and (1953).

64. Cf., for example, Tacitus *Annals* 16. 34. 1. For the attitude of mind which Seneca desired to achieve, see the story of Julius Canus, *de tranq. an.* 14. 4–10.

65. *Epp.* 41. 1–2. See Guillemin (1952), 209.

66. There is a similar strain of thought in certain aspects of the Renaissance: see, for instance, Howard (1974), 56–58.

67. See particularly Leeman (1971).

68. *Epp.* 61. 4.

by the political symbolism of Cato's suicide at Utica.[69] But in no
one does the fascination with suicide become so neurotic as in
Seneca. He stresses the power that a man has over his own death,
and, like no previous Stoic, elevates the concept of suicide to a
central position in his morality.[70] The basis for it is the idea that
life and death are 'indifferents': what matters is whether a life is
'good' and, even more, whether a death is 'good'—a 'good death',
he says, 'is to escape the danger of a bad life'.[71] He works out his
own concept of freedom:[72] 'Freedom is man's aim: this is the
reward for all our efforts. But what is freedom, you ask? To be a
slave to no thing, to no compulsions, to no chance happenings;
to treat Fortune as on one's own level. The day I shall know that
I am stronger than Fortune, she will have no power. Shall I put
up with her when I have death in my hands?' Freedom is no
longer political freedom, but a new personal and private freedom. Seneca was fascinated with this concept of death as freedom
(the more so, no doubt, as real freedom receded), and he often
expresses it with excited emotion: for instance (de ira 3. 15. 4),
he offers this advice: 'To anyone to whom chance has given a
monarch who aims arrows at the breasts of his friends, or to
anyone who has a master that gluts fathers on the flesh of their
children, I would say: "Madman, why do you weep? Why wait
for an enemy to avenge you by the destruction of your nation, or
for a powerful king to fly from afar? Everywhere you look there
is an end to your troubles. See that precipice? That is a path to
freedom. See that ocean, that river, that well? Freedom sits at
the bottom of it. See that tree, stunted, burned, and barren?
From it hangs freedom. See that throat of yours, that neck, that
heart? They are escape routes from servitude. Do I point to escape

69. On this whole development see, above all, MacMullen (1966) chap.
I, esp. 4–5 and n. 3; also Rist (1969), 249. However, note needs to be taken
of what seem to have been views expressed by Varro (frgs. 406–8 Büch.),
based on Cynic ideas (Teles 15. 9–17. 7 Hense) that suicide was not criminal.
See Oltramare (1926), 52–53, 105.

70. See, for instance, Epp. 70.

71. Epp. 70. 6.

72. Epp. 51. 9.

routes that are too difficult, requiring too much courage and strength? Do you ask where is the road to freedom? Any vein in your body!" '. In such a passage the process of reshaping Greek myths to carry the new philosophical message can be seen happening as Seneca writes.[73]

Seneca admits that there are cases where suicide is unjustifiable —when a man is disappointed in love, for instance, or because a master keeps complaining, or to avoid arrest,[74] or (as Epicurus also agreed) out of boredom.[75] A man must not love life too much, but he must not hate it too much either.[76] Seneca's writings are marked by an interest in suicide that is not to be found, for instance, in Epictetus. But it is special to Seneca's character and time. His good man seems to be eagerly looking for the right opportunity to commit suicide. It is no accident that Lucan expresses the same idea, particularly in the character of Vulteius;[77] in Vulteius the irrational ecstasy at having been offered an excellent opportunity for suicide is matched by the emotional heat with which he anticipates it. It was a state of mind that had a morbid—if understandable—fascination for men of the time, and Lucan gives Vulteius words that recall the language appropriate to violent initiation ceremonies of Oriental cults.[78] Petronius was again hitting at a real target in the macabre scene where Trimalchio reads his will and makes all dispositions for his death; slaves and relatives weep all around and even Trimalchio himself breaks down.[79] It is a beautiful additional touch to the scene when Trimalchio is made to compose his own epitaph— and it ends with words of self-praise: 'he never listened to a philosopher'.

73. In the same way he 'mythologizes' the real stories of Stoic heroes, as, for instance, that of Julius Canus (de tranq. an. 14. 4–10), through a process of generalization by mythological reference—so that, for example, he replaces the name Gaius by that of Phalaris.
74. Epp. 4. 4.
75. Epp. 24. 22; de tranq. an. 2. 14–15.
76. Epp. 24. 24.
77. Bellum Civile 4. 462–581.
78. Compare 514–20 with the language of Catullus 63.
79. Satyricon 71.

The actual working out of the suicide theme by Seneca often shows his rhetorical interests, but its intensity and frequency of occurrence come from the isolation of a man who (like many others) knew that sooner or later he would be faced with an intolerable choice. The obsessive concentration on the theme was comforting, and the often-repeated stories of the 'good deaths' of others strengthened resolve. But it was not a rational philosophy. The mark of the early Augustan age was the sense of men sharing a whole series of basic concepts in fields ranging from politics to poetry. The first century A.D. is marked by the isolation of the individual adrift in a world that is far off course, and yet there are no agreed solutions. In men like Seneca, a religious emotion took the place of logic and philosophical inquiry.

Interest in magic, witchcraft, and astrology.—Petronius is, as he is so often, a good guide to the fads and fancies of his own age when he depicts Trimalchio's anxious interest in astrology and in stories of werewolves and witches;[80] he is satirizing a striking feature of the first century A.D.: the growing interest in, and even practice of, magic. Terrible stories were told of the persecution of Nero by the ghost of his murdered mother and of his attempts to exorcise her,[81] and even Statius (though in his poem celebrating Lucan's birthday) has a vivid scene of Nero in Hades, terrified of his mother's torch.[82] An oddity in the scene is the imagined pleasure of Lucan as he witnesses the punishment of Nero; this recalls the fact that Plutarch gives odd details about the torture of Nero's soul.[83] Nero himself was so impressed with the appearances of his dead mother's ghost that, though he sorely wished to, he did not present himself for initiation at Eleusis.[84] It has always been a satisfying practice to redress the wrongs of this world by imagining the vengeance of the next, but what is interesting here is the level of sophistication at which such beliefs were expressed in literature.

80. Astrology: *Sat.* 39; werewolves and witches: *Sat.* 62–63.
81. Suetonius *Nero* 34. 4.   82. *Silvae* 2. 7. 111–19.
83. *de sera numinis vindicta* 32.   84. Suetonius loc. cit.

Interest in magic and the occult is deeply embedded in Statius'
Thebaid. But far more impressive is the extent to which Lucan
made use of it. There is not a book that does not give evidence
of it: outstanding examples are the description of extispicy in
book 1 and the immensely long excursus in book 5 when Appius
consults the Delphic oracle. Most striking, however, is the horrific episode in book 6 when Sextus Pompeius consults the Thessalian witch Erichtho. Lucan seems to have planned this scene
from an early point as a counterpart to Aeneas' descent into the
Underworld in *Aeneid* 6 (though the consultation of Delphi was
intended to challenge another aspect of that scene). Lucan must
have been uncertain when he wrote it about its exact location in
the epic. The scene takes place in Thessaly, and the witch has a
satisfyingly wide choice among the bodies of men slain in war
(625–26); and in 633–35 Lucan says that 'if she had tried to raise
up the whole army on the plain and make them fight again, the
laws of Erebus would have given way to her. . .'. But Pharsalia
has not yet been fought, and there should be no relevant dead
bodies yet. It can be taken, then, that Lucan from the beginning
planned this scene as a central panel in his epic (but he died
before he could accommodate the passage properly to the context). Perhaps as odd is a letter of Pliny in which he consults L.
Licinius Sura, Trajan's closest friend and adviser, consul three
times, diplomat, skilled politician, and man of learning: the
subject is ghosts, and Pliny wonders whether to believe the stories
that he hears.[85]

Hitting as clearly at a real target is Petronius' well-known scene
showing Trimalchio's belief in astrology.[86] And there is a splendid moment in Seneca's *Apocolocyntosis* when Claudius is on
the point of death, and Mercury addresses one of the Fates:[87]
'Cruel woman, why let this poor wretch continue to be tortured?
After all his agonies will he never rest? It is now the sixty-fourth
year since he began the struggle with his breath. Why bear a
grudge against him—and the Empire? Let the astrologers tell

85. *Epp.* 7. 25.   86. *Sat.* 39.
87. *Apocolocyntosis* 3.

the truth for once—since he became emperor they have never let a year pass, never a month, without putting him in his grave'. The fact is that from the late period of Augustus to that of Hadrian (information is, however, lacking on Trajan), every emperor not only believed in astrology, but usually had a particularly trusted astrologer living with him.[88] But this only reflects a general belief among the upper classes in Rome (the lower too, for sure, but they are not relevant) in astrology. This is fairly demonstrated by the fact that in our lacunose sources ten times between 33 B.C. and A.D. 93 (under Domitian) astrologers were expelled from Rome. The more an emperor believed in astrology, the less could he afford to let others have access to its truths, for consultations might encourage undue hopes in senators; and on dozens of occasions senators were involved in *maiestas* trials for consulting astrologers. A paradigm case was that of Servilia, daughter of Barea Soranus (and wife of Annius Pollio). She was nineteen years old. Her father was consul suffectus in A.D. 52, but in the fateful year A.D. 66 he was accused of plotting against the emperor in Asia (he had been proconsul there); he was condemned on the false evidence of his Stoic teacher Egnatius Celer. While this was happening, Servilia consulted astrologers on the fate of her family and particularly on the question of whether Nero would relent against her father. She used her wedding presents and her jewelry to pay. Both father and daughter were condemned, and both committed suicide.[89]

Seneca, in spite of his joke against Claudius, was a firm believer.[90] The belief was the counterpart to his conception of Fate: everything had been foreordained, and astrology was simply one means by which men could glimpse the destiny before them; but his opinion was that the study of astrology could contribute nothing to morality.[91] It was this point of view that Lucan made

88. See, in general, Cramer (1954) and MacMullen (1966), chap. 4.
89. Tacitus *Annals* 16. 30–33.
90. Cf., for example, *Quaest. Nat.* 2. 32. 7–8; *de consol. ad Marciam* 18.8.
91. Seneca *Epp.* 88. 14–16.

Cato express when he had the opportunity to consult the oracle of Juppiter Ammon.[92]

These beliefs fascinated, impressed, and even captivated the writers of the early Empire, and no serious composition, poetry or prose, was complete without some major exploitation of the theme. Even a writer like Tacitus exploits the delicious verbal thrill to be got from contemplation of the mysterious or the magical—in fact, the irrational in general and the apparently inexplicable—but he does it, as is his wont, without necessarily committing himself to belief in it.[93] How far, however, the belief gripped men at the time comes out powerfully when we learn that a hard-bitten, very wealthy and successful *delator* like M. Aquillius Regulus, who made his fortune from men's deaths, timidly consulted astrologers about the outcome of each of his cases.[94] The importance of the failure of rationalism—for it was that as much as it was an indulgence in the sweets of irrationalism —in all this lies in the social level at which it occurred and the degree to which it penetrated intellectual activity of every kind. The investigation can be taken much further into all sorts of religious experiment and aberration (like, for instance, the curious habit which grew up in the late first century A.D. of honouring the beloved dead in the form of various deities);[95] it can be taken into all aspects of the search for individual salvation; the picture remains the same, and it is of an intellectual climate dominated by fear and uncertainty and by the search for ways to escape from both.[96] It is notable in this respect how much of the litera-

92. See p. 173 above.

93. Cf., for example, *Hist*. 2. 2f. (Titus' visit to the temple of Venus on Cyprus) or 4. 83 (Serapis). But it should also be noted that he devotes a lengthy chapter (*Hist*. 4. 81) to Vespasian's 'laying of hands' on a cripple and a blind man; Tacitus himself vouches for the evidence of the cure (eye witnesses are still living, and there is no motive for lying).

94. Pliny *Epp*. 6. 2. 2. Cf. the slaughter of pets by Regulus at his son's funeral, *Epp*. 4. 2.

95. Cf., for example, Statius *Silvae* 2. 7. 124–25 and 5. 1. 231–35: see Vollmer (1898) ad loc.

96. See, in general, Festugière (1950) and Dodds (1956), chap. 8.

ture of the period was sheerly escapist. This can be seen in many ways: for instance, from Ovid's *Metamorphoses* to Pliny's *Letters*, nature and the country become routes of escape, with luxury villas and even the landscape adapted by man; there is no trace of the moral and spiritual value that poets like Horace and Virgil found in the country life. Nature became a carefully processed luxury retreat that reproduced the court life out of reach of the court. The extent to which subject matter in general was escapist, on the pattern set by Ovid, needs no demonstration.

4. *Cruelty and the exploitation of weakness*

A characteristic of the period of the early Empire was the extraordinary growth of publicly exhibited cruelty. This hardly needs illustration, and it appears constantly in literature. A paradigm case was the discovery of Sejanus' treason and the horrific scenes that followed in the city of Rome. Clearly the blood lust was deliberately communicated to crowds in the streets.[97] Juvenal neatly processed the scenes, as it were, for poetry by transferring the violence of the crowds to the breaking up and dragging away of a statue of Sejanus;[98] and then, at the end of the

97. Suetonius *Tib.* 61.
98. But Juvenal also had reality as a model. Crowds could anticipate the blood lust and prejudice decisions by venting their hatred on statues, even dragging them to the *scalae Gemoniae*, as in the case of Cn. Calpurnius Piso (Tacitus *Annals* 3. 14. 4), also under Tiberius and only a few years before the fall of Sejanus. In A.D. 69 Vitellius was further shamed by having his statues dragged with him to the prison and thence to the *scalae Gemoniae* (Cassius Dio 64. 21. 2). Pliny revels linguistically in the destruction of Domitian's statues (*panegyric.* 52. 4–5), recalling 'what a joy it was to smash his arrogant face on the ground, attack with swords, run riot with axes, as if blood and agony were the consequence of each single blow. There was no one to be found so restrained in pleasure and late-won joy that he did not view as pure vengeance the lacerated flesh, torn limbs, and finally the hated and horrific portraits flung into the flames and melted down, so that, from being a terror and threat to mankind, the fires turned them into things of use and delight'. This passage may well have been the direct source of Juvenal's inspiration. But its most striking effect is to show the blood lust nakedly expressed by a man who saw himself as a humane and civilized gentleman.

passage, he shows a nervous senator planning to exhibit his loyal support for the regime by hurrying off to kick the dead body where it lies exposed by the river.[99] Nero's treatment of the Christians made a fireworks show out of mass executions and concentrated hatred on the chosen target.[100] A particularly horrible form of public sadism was exhibited in using condemned criminals to act out the parts of victims in tragedies who were slaughtered or mutilated in the course of a play; and thus what had been left to the decent obscurity of a messenger speech no longer made such demands on the imagination of the audience.[101] And, of course, there was the routine sadism of the amphitheatre. Of this Seneca often speaks, as in a letter to Lucilius (95. 33): 'Man, a sacred object in the sight of man, is now slaughtered for jest and sport; and he whom it were wrong to have trained to inflict and receive wounds is now led out defenceless and unarmed, and it is a satisfactory spectacle to see a man made into a corpse'. In de tranquillitate animi (2. 13) he pictured bored men leaving Rome for one place after another, each different; but finally, he states, 'their ears have for too long missed the shouts and din; and now it is their pleasure to enjoy some human blood: "Let's now get back to the city" '. In another letter to Lucilius,[102] he describes an interval in a gladiatorial show: 'Let's have men's throats slit so that there won't be a blank moment'. Once again this fad is beautifully targeted by Petronius in a splendid speech put into the mouth of a ragpicker (45).

It seems likely that most of this was the deliberate policy of the emperors. Seneca was indulging the private and personal feelings of the good man. The younger Pliny, on the other hand, who heartily agreed with Trajan's abolition of the Greek gym-

99. Sat. 10. 56–113.

100. Nero, although he persuaded senators and equites to act as gladiators, began with extraordinary humanity by ordering that no gladiator should be killed—not even the condemned criminals who were used in the bouts. Suetonius contrasts this with his later cruelty: Nero 12. 1.

101. See, for example, Suetonius Calig. 57. 4; Martial liber spectaculorum 5; 7; 8; 21; Juvenal 8. 187.

102. Epp. 7. 5.

nicus agon at Vienne, on the grounds that it had corrupted the morals of the people of that town,[103] had this to say to Trajan soon after his accession, in his *Panegyric* (33):

> visum est spectaculum inde non enerve nec fluxum, nec quod animos virorum molliret et frangeret, sed quod ad pulchra vulnera contemptumque mortis accenderet, cum in servorum etiam noxiorumque corporibus amor laudis et cupido victoriae cerneretur. quam deinde in edendo liberalitatem, quam iustitiam exhibuit omni adfectione aut intactus aut maior! impetratum est quod postulabatur, oblatum quod non postulabatur. institit ultro et ut concupisceremus admonuit, ac sic quoque plura inopinata plura subita. iam quam libera spectantium studia, quam securus favor! nemini impietas ut solebat obiecta, quod odisset gladiatorem; nemo e spectatore spectaculum factus miseras voluptates unco et ignibus expiavit. demens ille verique honoris ignarus, qui crimina maiestatis in harena colligebat, ac se despici et contemni, nisi etiam gladiatores eius veneraremur, sibi male dici in illis, suam divinitatem suum numen violari interpretabatur, cumque se idem quod deos, idem gladiatores quod se putabat.

Then we saw a show neither nerveless nor feeble nor such as would make men's spirits effeminate and soft,[104] but such as would fire them to the beauty of wounds and contempt for death in that they could see desire for fame and the lust for victory exhibited even in the bodies of slaves and criminals. And then what generosity, what impartiality he [Trajan] exhibited, either untouched by any emotion or rising above it![105] What was asked for was given: there was given more than what was asked for. He [Trajan], without being asked, went further and required us to feel needs—that way too we were given many unexpected gifts on the spur of the moment. But how uninhibited did spectators feel in supporting their favourites, how unafraid was their partisanship! Nobody was accused of disloyalty for disliking a particular gladiator, nobody was made a spectacle instead of spectator to expiate his pitiful pleasures on the [executioner's] hook and flames. The other man was mad and quite ignorant of real honours in gathering charges of treason at the arena and in inferring that he was being despised and belittled

103. *Epp.* 4. 22. Pliny was bored by horse races: *Epp.* 9. 6.
104. The allusion is to the Greek type of games put on by Domitian (see previous note).
105. Like the ideal good man of Stoic philosophy.

when we did not worship his gladiators too, that he was being reviled in their persons, that his own divinity, his godhead was being abused, and in thinking consequently the gladiators his equal, however much he thought himself the equal of the gods.

Domitian is here criticized for his own obsessive aberrations, but the basic policy of the two emperors was the same. Most regimes need to find instruments for mobilizing the allegiance of the people as a whole. At times, institutions like carnivals have been used,[106] or mass rallies, or competitive games. It seems clear that Roman emperors used the amphitheatre for this purpose as a regular event in the life of the people. It was Julius Caesar who first seems to have realized the full potential of this focus for hatred and sadism; he was followed by Augustus, who made special mention of the lavishness of his displays, in the *res gestae* (22). Tiberius had an aristocratic dislike for such public occasions and was criticized for failing to attend; but he provided the shows, and his son Drusus made up for his father's lack of interest by showing a keen sadistic interest of his own.[107] The other emperors all continued a political and social function that had established so important a place for itself in the public life. Then, on occasions of crisis, when a plot had been discovered or alleged, a popular blood lust was easy to arouse. The public arousing of blood lust and its efficient stage management seems to have been put on a properly organized basis by Tiberius, to whom were owed fine touches of detail like the use of the *scalae Gemoniae*.[108]

It is significant that care was taken to see that the institution of gladiatorial games spread over the Empire, and particularly in the cities of the Greek East.[109] Herod I was one of the first to

106. On the social and political function of the carnival in Renaissance Venice, see J. H. Elliott, *New York Review of Books* for 16 May 1974, p. 21, with references.

107. Tacitus *Annals* 1. 76. 3–4.

108. Not, of course, invented by Tiberius (cf. Valerius Maximus 6. 3. 3; 6. 9. 13), but perhaps an ancient custom given new life by his encouragement.

109. See, in general, L. Robert *Gladiateurs* (1940).

introduce the amphitheatre, and he put the sport on in Beirut, as Josephus says,[110] 'so that, on the one hand, criminals might be punished and, on the other, the business of war might become the pleasure of peacetime'. It was a duty of local officials to put on such shows,[111] and inscriptions from all over the Greek East attest the presence of φαμιλίαι μονομάχων. Roman officials themselves naturally put on shows on appropriate occasions—to such an extent that Nero, on the ground that such shows served to inhibit the people from prosecuting extortionate governors, felt obliged to promulgate a (short-lived) decree forbidding the practice.[112] There is much evidence, apart from this, for their popularity with Greeks,[113] and both Dio Chrysostom[114] and Philostratus[115] angrily criticized the Athenians for so much enjoying such shows in no less a place than the theatre of Dionysus.

The exploitation of cruelty and physical suffering as a sort of fantasy theme runs through the literature of the early Empire as one of its most characteristic features. It seems really to have started with the *Metamorphoses* of Ovid. Virgil, closely following a Homeric precedent, signifies his horror of war by describing from time to time the physical consequences of wounds. When Turnus kills Pandarus (he has already killed his brother), Virgil describes the scene (9. 749–55):

> sic ait, et sublatum alte consurgit in ensem
> et mediam ferro gemina inter tempora frontem
> dividit impubisque immani vulnere malas.
> fit sonus, ingenti concussa est pondere tellus;
> conlapsos artus atque arma cruenta cerebro
> sternit humi moriens, atque illi partibus aequis
> huc caput atque illuc umero ex utroque pependit.

So he spoke and lifted his sword, rising high for the blow, and with the steel cleft his head in half between the temples and the

---

110. *Antiqu. Iud.* 19. 335–37; 20. 211.
111. P-W. II col. 1576.
112. Tacitus *Annals* 13. 31. 3.
113. E.g., Epictetus 3. 16. 4.
114. orat. 31. 121ff.
115. *Apoll. Tyan.* 4. 22; cf. Lucian *Demonax* 57.

beardless cheeks, an enormous wound. There was a crash, and the earth was shaken with the tremendous weight. Dying, he strewed on the ground his crumpled limbs and his weapons, covered with blood and brain; and his head hung down equally over both shoulders.

Virgil then goes on to describe the terror which this frightful death caused among the Trojans. The physical details are objective, unemotional, and restricted to a minimum. The poet is the recorder of terrible facts that must be told. When emotion is an ingredient of such scenes in Virgil, it is projected on the victim in pity and remembrance (as, for instance, in the death of Euryalus).[116]

In Ovid there is a quite different literary intention. In *Metamorphoses* 6. 387–91 he describes the flaying of Marsyas:

> clamanti cutis est summos direpta per artus,
> nec quicquam nisi vulnus erat; cruor undique manat,
> detectique patent nervi, trepidaeque sine ulla
> pelle micant venae; salientia viscera possis
> et perlucentes numerare in pectore fibras.

As he screamed his skin was torn from the whole surface of his limbs, and he was one continuous wound; blood oozed everywhere; his sinews were exposed to full view, and the flickering veins pulsed with no covering of skin; you could count the throbbing organs and the transparent lungs in his breast.

The poet here is intent on sharing with the reader (to whose presence he draws self-conscious attention) the horror he himself feels; and to this end, he piles up details and adjectives to make the greatest possible impact, even inviting the reader to count the organs of the body with him. The poet is excited by the concrete details, and he reaches a climax with the final line. The emotion here is the poet's re-enactment, by means of objective details, of his own delicious revulsion. The concentration on realistic precision is morbid and even sadistic. Ovid is also extremely good at conveying larger scenes of horror: for instance, the killing of Orpheus, which occupies the first sixty lines of book 11. The

116. *Aeneid* 9. 420–29.

poet concentrates on the contrast between the murderous women and the beautiful normal world that they invade. Their first victims are the birds that have been overcome by the sweetness of Orpheus' singing; after them, the snakes and wild animals that are in the audience. Then the women themselves become like birds attacking an owl in daylight, as they swoop on Orpheus. Ovid has caught the nightmarish quality of the scene perfectly.

All subsequent poets learnt from Ovid, and constantly exploited the emotion aroused by the sight of the physical results of violence. Seneca's tragedies have as a major poetic theme the ways in which human flesh is modified by the application of gross violence, as well as the whole range of physical effects that can be achieved by changes in psychological states. His nephew, Lucan, shared his interests and devoted his imagination to arranging galleries of horrific wounds, set out with the greatest artistry and ingenuity of variation, wherever the opportunity offered: outstanding are the wounds suffered in the sea battle at Massilia (3. 583–751), where twelve scenes of violence, each one different, are arranged in a climactic series. Another incredible series of artistic and horrific deaths is arranged when Cato's army marches through snake country (9. 734–838): there six fantastic deaths are concluded with a seventh incident in which Murrus spears a basilisk; but the poison runs up his spear so quickly that he can only save himself by chopping off his arm at the shoulder.

Physical horrors form a large element in Statius' *Thebaid* too. And even Tacitus is not free from interest in the literary effects to be won from the communication of horror aroused by the sight of mutilated human flesh.[117] In every instance, the writer is clearly trying to share with an audience sensations that he has found emotionally stimulating and that he relives in words.

A more trivial form of irrational stimulation in this period was something to which the great scholars of Alexandria had succumbed several centuries earlier. This was the interest in παράδοξα or 'wonders' of the world; not, that is, great human

117. See, for instance, his description of the scene after the battle of Bedriacum, *Hist.* 2. 70.

achievements, but rivers running red, peculiar customs of remote tribes, or wild beasts behaving like human beings. The origin of this interest lay far back in the genuinely scientific writing of Aristotle, especially, the *Historia Animalium*, for example. The mark of degeneracy lay in the collecting of such peculiar details for their own sake. Even Callimachus gave way to this in his *Collection of Marvels* (παραδόξων συναγωγή). Philip, who probably enjoyed patronage at the court of Gaius, and who was the collector of the *Garland of Philip*, has two epigrams deriding such interests.[118] The theme is echoed by Seneca in *de brevitate vitae* (13): 'That used to be a Greek disease to investigate how many oarsmen Ulysses had, whether the *Iliad* was written before the *Odyssey* and whether they were by the same author, and other things of this type. If you keep such things to yourself, your quiet soul has no benefit, and if you publish them you seem less scholarly than boring. But now this vain passion for learning useless facts has infected Romans too'. Tiberius was an outstanding example of this peculiar interest.[119] It was an aspect of the flight from reason in that it valued the savouring of discrete facts above the intellectual labour of constructing arguments and works of art. It is illustrated by a tendency in the early Empire for the study of literature to descend into a pedantic concentration on minutiae of grammar and syntax and orthography. In its literary operations it produced works like Valerius Maximus' collection of improving tales.

This interest had, so to speak, a concrete aspect too in a Roman mania in this period for monsters and grotesques and dwarfs, which was strongly criticized by Plutarch.[120] Slave markets were scoured for such oddities. Augustus was afflicted with this mania:[121] Nicolaus of Damascus reported having seen in Antioch a 'living herm', a boy born without arms, whom an embassy

118. *Anth. Pal.* 11. 321 and 347.
119. Suetonius *Tib.* 70. 3. Cf., on Nero as *incredibilium cupitor*, Tacitus *Annals* 15. 42. 2.
120. *de curiositate* 520C.
121. Suetonius *Aug.* 43. 3–4.

from Porus in India was conveying, together with other oddities, to Augustus.[122]

Everywhere one turns in studying the early Empire there is a sense that life and literature alike were dominated by a willingness, even a desire, to avoid or devalue the process of rational thought, and to substitute a concentration on anything that would supply an instant emotional stimulus or create an illusion of spiritual calm through dependence on something outside the individual. The effects of rhetorical practice would be an example of the former; the new type of philosophy would exemplify the latter. One of the most impressive pieces of evidence of a deep irrational streak in the intellectual life of the period comes from scenes where the two professions might well unite. A number of writers describe the wildly emotional excitement, more appropriate to the theatre, which greeted the entrance of a famous rhetor, as people even stretched out their hands for the privilege of touching his cloak.[123] This failure of confidence among the Roman upper classes was related, in some degree at least, to the increasingly authoritarian monarchy and the consequent uncertainty of life. But the emperor himself was also the victim of a similar loss of nerve, and in all his habits and attitudes he was one of the same class. In these circumstances, literature tended, with some notable exceptions, to follow the tenor of the age and find its function in an emotional escapism. In this, as in the final plunge into archaizing, Romans turn out to be suffering what Greeks had already suffered more than a century earlier.

It is now time to trace the more specifically literary and stylistic changes in the period. Some of these can be interpreted as reactions to the factors of change already examined, while others are related rather to the political and social changes that will be examined in the last lecture.

122. Strabo 719; Cassius Dio 54. 9. 8.
123. See, for example, Seneca *Epp.* 52. 12–14.

V

Thought
and Expression

IT QUICKLY becomes obvious to a reader of poetry, or
even of prose, written in the first century A.D. that the basic assumptions about what literature was and what the writer was
supposed to be doing have changed since the time of the late
Republic and even of the Augustan age. It is the purpose of this
lecture to examine some of the most important and striking results of this change. For the most part, they had the effect of
closing the gap between Greek and Latin and of creating the
impression of a literary culture that was largely homogeneous,
whichever language it happens to be written in. The phenomena
here analyzed in Roman literature had, for a large part, become
familiar in Greek literature at a considerably earlier period.

1. imitatio *and* aemulatio

A notional literary scale could be constructed such that unconscious reminiscence was placed at the left-hand extreme and
deliberate challenge and confrontation at the right. On such a
scale, the writers of the late Republic and early Augustan age
would find the echoes of earlier writers in their works charted
mainly on the left half; writers of the early Empire, however,
would certainly occupy the right-hand side—and, to a great extent, the extreme right hand—of the scale. Insistent use of the

same material again and again is clear already in the Greek epigrammatists of the time of Augustus. Death at sea was a frequent theme and also escape from death at sea: in the latter case, a dolphin was the favourite agent of salvation—after the story of Arion. Philip shows how far interest in varying a recognized theme could go in the following epigram (*Anth. Pal.* 9. 85):[1]

> νῆα μὲν ὤλεσε πόντος, ἐμοὶ δ' ἔπορεν πάλι δαίμων
> πλαζομένωι φύσεως νῆα ποθεινοτέρην·
> πατρὸς ἰδὼν γὰρ ἐγὼ δέμας εἰς ἐμὲ καίριον ἐλθόν
> μουνερέτης ἐπέβην φόρτος ὀφειλόμενος.
> ἤλαλεν εἰς λιμένας δὲ καὶ ἔσπειρεν δὶς ὁ πρέσβυς,
> νήπιον ἐν γαίηι, δεύτερον ἐν πελάγει.

The sea destroyed the ship, but Fortune presented to me, as I drifted, Nature's more desirable vessel: for I saw my father's body opportunely coming my way. I climbed onto it, single oarsman, its due and proper freight. The old man carried me to harbour, and so begot me twice—as an infant on land, and a second time at sea.

In origin the themes were not such fantasy themes as this would suggest. They started out sanely, like Myron's cow (going back to Meleager),[2] or the fisherman whose boat was his home and livelihood while he lived but his funeral pyre when he died,[3] or the ship built from the profits of a brothel,[4] or the very much loved theme of the bride dying on her wedding day (either before or after the ceremony).[5] But fantasy was always only a step away. On the last-mentioned theme Antiphanes produced this variation (*Anth. Pal.* 9. 245):[6]

> δυσμοίρων θαλάμων ἐπὶ παστάσιν οὐχ 'Υμέναιος
> ἀλλ' 'Αίδης ἔστη πικρογάμου Πετάλης·
> δείματι γὰρ μούνην πρωτόζυγα Κύπριν ἀν' ὄρφνην

1. Gow and Page (1968), n. XXXIX.
2. See, for instance, Gow and Page (1965), vol. II, 63–64.
3. See, for instance, Gow and Page (1968), vol. II, 13.
4. See, for instance, Gow and Page (1968), vol. II, 140.
5. The theme goes back to Meleager (*Anth. Pal.* 7. 182): see Gow and Page (1965), vol. II, 674.
6. Gow and Page (1968), n. III.

φεύγουσαν, ξυνὸν παρθενικαῖσι φόβον,
φρουροδόμοι νηλεῖς κύνες ἔκτανον· ἦν δὲ γυναῖκα
ἐλπὶς ἰδεῖν ἄφνως ἔοχομεν οὐδὲ νέκυν.

At the doors of the ill-fated bridal chamber of Petale, unhappy bride, there stood not Hymenaeus but Hades. For, as she fled in terror alone through the darkness from the first joining of Love (a common dread to all maidens), savage house-guarding dogs killed her. Whom it was our hope to see a wife, suddenly we could not even see her corpse.

The delight in treating the same theme again and again goes back even to the *Garland of Meleager*, and Cicero specifically praises this ability in Archias (*pro Archia* 18): 'How often, judges, have I seen my friend Archias, without writing down a single letter, extemporize verbally excellent poetry on current topics; and then, encored, repeat the same material with complete change of words and pointed phrases!' In *de oratore* (3. 194), Cicero links Antipater of Sidon with Archias in his skill in extemporary poetry. To illustrate the point in a concrete literary way, four epigrams of Archias have been preserved,[7] all treating the theme of dedications to Pan by three hunting brothers; this theme was also used by Antipater of Sidon in an extant epigram.[8]

From Cicero's words it is clear that Romans still regarded such performances merely as entertaining tricks, and that they found their proper place among rhetorical practices. But in the later Augustan period, as poetry became more assimilated to the practices of the rhetorical schools, Romans became enthusiasts of this essentially Greek literary game. Ovid was an outstanding practitioner: in the *Amores* he used material from Tibullus and Propertius, and in *Metamorphoses* material from Virgil, usually in such a way as to challenge the earlier author by the comparison. But he also went further in the Greek direction, and used material from his own earlier works again and again. The practice especially interested him as between *Amores* and *Ars Amatoria*, and as between *Fasti* (and *Heroides*) and *Metamor-*

7. *Anth. Pal.* 6. 16, 179, 180, and 181. Extemporary poetry is first found clearly in Latin in Martial and Statius. See p. 267 below.
8. *Anth. Pal.* 6. 14.

phoses, because, in both cases, the different styles, metres, and approaches demanded by the various genres stimulated him to varied treatment of the same themes.[9]

What was new here was the challenge to the original source. Such close thematic repetition, with that motive, was virtually unknown in earlier Roman writers. Horace came closest to it when he imitated Lucilius in his *Satires*. But in that case there were two differentiating factors. First, Lucilius was the inventor and legislator (with the qualifications expressed in *Satires* 1. 4 and 10) of the genre; it was, therefore, both complimentary and virtually obligatory to make some use of patterns evolved by him. Second, the genre was still very much in process of development, and Horace was far from challenging Lucilius: he was carrying on where Lucilius had left off, and he had the advantage of having very clear views of his own on the factors that should influence the development.[10] But with writers of the early Empire, there was a distinct sense that poets like Virgil had carried the genre to its perfection, and there were two complementary aspects involved in this point of view. First, to use the same material and literary forms eliminated the burdensome and depressing necessity for invention. Second, there was a positive advantage, in that the poet was compelled to challenge Virgil (however humbly), with the hope of gaining a toehold in literary fame by displaying an acceptable variation on what Virgil had done. With minor authors the process was more ruthless: their work had to be obliterated, or at least dislodged, by a more impressive and distinguished handling of the material.

The element of challenge, then, was what was new in all the close repetition. And the origin of the motivation for such repetition is clear: it came from the rhetorical schools. The elder Seneca relates[11] how Ovid transferred many of Porcius Latro's epigrams (*sententiae*) into his own poetry, and, from the examples quoted, it is clear that Ovid tried to improve on them.

9. The basic demonstration is still that of Heinze (1960), 308–403.
10. Contrast the situation described on p. 271 below.
11. *contr.* 2. 2. 8.

Equally, Seneca says of Ovid: 'he not only filled our age with amatory arts, but also with epigrams', and he goes on to point out how later rhetors used many of Ovid's *sententiae*.

This motive provides one explanation for the great popularity of epic poetry in the quarter-century or so after A.D. 60. It worked in two ways: first, the basic material was ready to hand both in Greek mythology and in Roman poets and historians; second, the Greek and Roman writers who had handled it both in prose and in poetry were well known, distinguished, and challenging. To writers from Ovid onwards, the fact that a particular theme provided ready-made material added greatly to its attraction, and it was made irresistible by the existence of challenging predecessors. But those considerations would apply to any genre. What made epic specially attractive was that it demanded a whole series of formal set pieces—catalogues, descriptions of shields, ἀριστεῖα of heroes, funeral games, sacrifices, descents to the underworld, fellings of trees, and so forth. Poetic genius was challenged to give new treatment to each of these within the epic framework.

For instance, Silius Italicus[12] merely sent Scipio (after the deaths of his father and uncle in Spain) down to visit the underworld—he happened to be resting near Avernus—in a very Virgilian scene, varied, however, most notably with elements from Homer (whom Scipio actually meets there, surrounded by his epic heroes). But Lucan drastically converted the descent into the underworld into the summoning from the underworld and the consultation of the witch Erichtho by Sextus Pompeius. It was no mere coincidence that he put this scene in book 6. On the other hand, Lucan directly challenged Virgil's account of the Sibyl's prophetic ecstasy with his account of Appius Claudius' consultation of the Delphic oracle in the previous book.[13] Statius likewise met the challenge of *Aeneid* 6 by dividing the problem

---

12. *Punica* 13. 400–895. Much less successful is his challenge to Ovid's account of the flight of Daedalus (*Met.* 8. 183–259), which Silius works up with full epic bombast from the homely realism of Ovid: see Hollis (1970), 58.
13. 5. 71–236.

into two. In *Thebaid* 7. 771–823 he describes the descent of
Amphiaraus under the earth; then he invented the opening scene
of book 8 (1–126), which is set in the underworld. Later, in
Thebaid 10. 156–218, he describes the grotesque prophetic frenzy
of Thiodamas. It seems clear that in this divided meeting of the
challenge of *Aeneid* 6, Statius was inspired by Lucan and challenging him in turn.

Statius challenged Valerius Flaccus in a different way. Valerius
had quite legitimately incorporated in his epic the story of the
women of Lemnos, treated on a very modest scale:[14] it was in-
tegral to the legend of the Argonauts. Statius, with little excuse
or relevance, but with skill in inventing both, devotes nearly
three books to a different treatment of the same story, which he
cleverly shaped so as to lead into an enormous funeral games.[15]
It was not easy to accommodate the digression, and Statius had to
use force. It was part of the Theban legend that drought afflicted
the Argive army on its march to Thebes. Statius, after an appeal
to Apollo for inspiration,[16] invented a scene with Bacchus rolling
home drunk from the conquest of Haemus; annoyed by the sight
of the Argives, he blocks up all the rivers, except one. Only
Hypsipyle (whose presence here needed more extraordinary invention) knows the secret of this; and so there is created the opportunity for her to tell her story. No challenge could be more
blatant. Statius' version of the story is not only far longer than
Valerius Flaccus'; it is more overwrought, more emotional, more
horrible,[17] and there is far greater reliance on irrational forces.

Many other opportunities were taken. Virgil was inspired by
a passage of Homer[18] to explore the concept of a god flying over
the earth and to imagine what it would be like to look down.[19]
The idea was taken up in greater detail by Ovid in *Metamor-*

14. *Argonautica* 2. 82–427.
15. For a sympathetic account of this, see Vessey (1973), 165 ff.
16. *Thebaid* 4. 649–51.
17. See, in addition to Vessey loc. cit., Burck (1971), 75 ff.
18. *Odyssey* 5. 44–54.
19. *Aeneid* 4. 238–61.

phoses.[20] Statius then exploited the idea twice in passages not widely separated: the first is of Tisiphone making her way to Thebes in answer to Oedipus' prayer.[21] The second is far more impressive:[22] it is the vision of the ghost of Laius, summoned by Mercury, flying by night to Thebes; and the sense of looking down on a dark world from a great height is well caught.[23]

The theme of one man in single combat against a whole army was favoured by these poets, and here they started from Virgil who, in turn, had used Homer and Ennius.[24] Turnus fights single-handedly against the Trojans (9. 806–14):

> ergo nec clipeo iuvenis subsistere tantum
> nec dextra valet, iniectis sic undique telis
> obruitur. strepit adsiduo cava tempora circum
> tinnitu galea et saxis solida aera fatiscunt
> discussaeque iubae capiti, nec sufficit umbo   810
> ictibus; ingeminant hastis et Troes et ipse
> fulmineus Mnestheus. tum toto corpore sudor
> liquitur et piceum (nec respirare potestas)
> flumen agit, fessos quatit aeger anhelitus artus.

Therefore the warrior cannot sufficiently withstand them either with his shield or with his right hand, so overwhelmed is he by spears hurled from all around him. His helmet resounds with continuous ringing around his hollow temples, and the solid bronze is torn by stones and the crest is broken upon his head, nor can his shield stand up (810) to the blows. Both the Trojans and lightning-swift Mnestheus redouble [the shower of] spears. Then sweat pours over his whole body and makes a dark viscous stream; it is impossible for him to breathe, and his gasping shakes his tired limbs.

20. 2. 708–30.
21. 1. 92–124.
22. 2. 55–92.
23. Lucan transferred the concept to the flight of Pompey's soul (9. 1–18): the soul gazes first on the higher regions and the planets, then it smiles at what has been done to the body it has just left; only then does it fly over Pharsalia and the standards of blood-stained Caesar.
24. *Iliad* 16. 102–11 and *Annales* 401–8V. On the relationship between these and on their interpretation, see Williams (1968), 687–89.

In general Virgil followed Homer, but his vocabulary was heavily influenced by Ennius. As often, one detail is completely new: the 'pitchy river of sweat' (*sudor. . .piceum. . .flumen agit*). Conington and Nettleship say in their commentary: '*piceum* is a strange and scarcely pleasing epithet, expressing, doubtless, the sweat as mingled with dust and gore.' The precise visual detail and the distaste are characteristic of Virgil, and the motif looks forward to Turnus' next move, which is to escape by jumping into the river; he is thereby washed and happily restored to his comrades (815–18).

Lucan used Virgil in his description of Scaeva's lone stand against Pompey's army (6. 192–206, 214–19, 224–25):

> fortis crebris sonat ictibus umbo,
> et galeae fragmenta cavae conpressa perurunt
> tempora, nec quicquam nudis vitalibus obstat
> iam praeter stantis in summis ossibus hastas.   195
> quid nunc, vaesani, iaculis levibusque sagittis
> perditis haesuros numquam vitalibus ictus?
> hunc aut tortilibus vibrata falarica nervis
> obruat aut vasti muralia pondera saxi,
> hunc aries ferro ballistaque limine portae   200
> promoveat. stat non fragilis pro Caesare murus
> Pompeiumque tenet. iam pectora non tegit armis,
> ac veritus credi clipeo laevaque vacasse
> aut culpa vixisse sua tot vulnera belli
> solus obit densamque ferens in pectore silvam   205
> iam gradibus fessis, in quem cadat, eligit hostem. . . .   206
> Dictaea procul, ecce, manu Gortynis harundo   214
> tenditur in Scaevam, quae voto certior omni   215
> in caput atque oculi laevum descendit in orbem.
> ille moras ferri nervorum et vincula rumpit
> adfixam vellens oculo pendente sagittam
> intrepidus, telumque suo cum lumine calcat. . . .   219
> perdiderat voltum rabies, stetit imbre cruento   224
> informis facies.   225

His stout shield rings with endless blows, and the fragments of his hollow helmet crush and chafe his temples; his vitals are bare, and nothing covers them except the spears stuck in the bones above them (195). Mad fools! Why do you keep wasting shots with jave-

lins and light arrows that will never reach his vitals? Only an ar-
tillery missile discharged with flexed bands could overwhelm this
man, or the wall-like weight of a huge rock; an iron battering ram
or a catapult would thrust him from the entrance way (200). He
stands as a strong wall to protect Caesar and hold Pompey back.
Now he ceases to cover his chest with his armour, and, fearing to
have it thought that his shield and left arm were idle or that he
was to blame for surviving, alone he receives all the wounds of
war and, carrying a dense forest on his chest,[25] his steps growing
weary, he looks for an enemy on whom to fling his body (206). . . .
But, see! A Cretan arrow is sped from a distance by a Cretan hand:
truer than any hope (215), it falls upon his head and the ball of his
left eye. He tore the stubborn steel with the ligament of muscle,
and, unterrified, having plucked the arrow out with his eyeball
attached to it, he tramples weapon and his own eye into the
ground (219). . . . Rage had ruined his face, his features were dis-
figured with a bloody rain.

Lucan's treatment challenged Virgil's by its intensification of
heroism, horror, and pathos. The physical ailments that proceed from the body's weakness (sweat, weariness, and breathlessness) are deliberately omitted to make way for a hyperbole of
wounds inflicted by the enemy. Weariness is only very briefly
mentioned (206) to motivate two novel ideas: the first, the hyperbole of finally killing an enemy by falling on him like a stone
(206)—which he does not do; the second, to assert that his weariness vanishes (250–51) as long as there is fighting to be done: he
collapses only when the enemy retreats. The constant entry of
the author into his narrative, both to apostrophize the enemy
as a means of increasing pathos and drama and to explain psychological motivation that would escape a reader since it is so incredible, is characteristic of Lucan's style.[26] He (rightly) cannot
trust his reader to see possibilities that are not personally thrust
on him and specifically guaranteed by the author.

Statius twice used this topic, both times concerning Tydeus.
The first comes in the dramatic night ambush, when Tydeus is
caught alone as he is returning to Argos (2. 668–74):

25. The detail from *Aeneid* 10. 887 (see note 29 below).
26. See further sect. 3 below.

> haec intonat; ast tamen illi
> membra negant, lassusque ferit praecordia sanguis.
> iam sublata manus cassos defertur in ictus   670
> tardatique gradus, clipeum nec sustinet umbo
> mutatum spoliis; gelidus cadit imber anhelo
> pectore, tum crines ardentiaque ora cruentis
> roribus et taetra morientum aspargine manant.

So he thunders; but nevertheless his legs are letting him down, and the blood strikes wearily at his heart. Now his uplifted hand is spent on vain blows (670) and his steps are slowed; and the boss cannot hold together the shield with its ruined hides; a chill rain streams down his panting breast; finally his hair and burning face are flooded with a bloody dew and the filthy spatterings of the dying.

The second time is in the scene leading to the death of Tydeus and his act of cannibalism (8. 700–712):

> et iam corporibus sese spoliisque cadentum
> clauserat; unum acies circum consumitur, unum
> omnia tela vovent: summis haec ossibus haerent,
> pars frustrata cadunt, partem Tritonia vellit,
> multa rigent clipeo. densis iam consitus hastis
> ferratum quatit umbo nemus, tergoque fatiscit   705
> atque umeris gentilis aper; nusquam ardua coni
> gloria, quique apicem torvae Gradivus habebat
> cassidis, haud laetum domino ruit omen. inusta
> temporibus nuda aera sedent, circumque sonori
> vertice percusso volvuntur in arma molares.   710
> iam cruor in galea, iam saucia proluit ater
> pectora permixtus sudore et sanguine torrens.

And now he had enclosed himself with corpses of the dead and their weapons. The enemy army is spent on him alone, for him alone all weapons pray. Some stick in the surface of his bones, some miss and fall on the ground, some Athene plucks out, many bristle on his shield. The boss, sown with dense spears, shakes an iron-bound grove, and on his back (705) and shoulder his native boar-hide gapes in rents; gone is the tall glory of his crest, and the Mars that occupied the peak of his fierce helmet falls, no joyful omen for its owner. The bare bronze is branded onto his temples, stones strike his helmet and fall ringing about his armour (710). Now there is blood in his helmet, now a black torrent of mixed sweat and blood drenches his wounded chest.

Statius has succeeded in giving two totally different treatments to the topic. In the former, the theme of breathlessness is omitted (Tydeus has just made a ringing speech—*intonat*). All the details go to show the hero in a mess rather than physically affected—except by tiredness,[27] which is here the result of continuous killing and which motivates his sparing the life of Maeon to carry the news to Thebes. His shield is ruined, and Statius finds a surprising phrase for the idea: 'the boss cannot hold up the shield, changed [for the worse] in its hides'—that is, the laminated leather has been so torn that it is not stiff enough for the bronze centre to support it.[28] Statius loves to enliven a little scene by a surprising locution. The second passage, however, is an elaborate challenge to Virgil certainly, but also at least as much to Lucan. From Virgil came (705) *fatiscit*, the loss of the crest, the sounding of the stones; and, finally, Statius ends with his own version of Virgil's *piceum. . .flumen*. More comes directly from Lucan. In 702 *omnia tela vovent* recalls (215) *voto certior omni*; but *summis haec ossibus haerent* recalls (195) *stantis in summis ossibus hastas* in such a way that doubt is cast on Statius' understanding of it. In Lucan *summis* meant that the bones protected the vitals, but Statius surely did not mean to contrast bones on the surface with those that lie deeper, no more than he meant to contrast the surface of the bones with a deeper penetration. He seems simply to have used Lucan's phrase. However, where Lucan said (205) *densamque ferens in pectore silvam*, Statius has not only transferred this to the shield[29] but, by manipulating the adjec-

27. The similarity to Lucan's conception of Scaeva is underlined by Statius' borrowing of *imber* (used by Ennius of the shower of weapons) to express the idea of sweat (Lucan did not allow Scaeva even this weakness, and *imber* in line 224 refers to his own blood).
28. That this must be the meaning is convincingly argued by Mulder (1954), 338–39.
29. Thereby returning to the passage of Virgil which Lucan had in mind for the detail—*Aen.* 10. 887 *immanem aerato circumfert tegmine silvam*; Statius used this more directly at *Thebaid* 5. 533.

tives *densis* and *ferratum* and using *consitus*, achieves a double
and much more self-conscious metaphor. Finally, he has toned
down Lucan's hyperbole (193–94) *galeae fragmenta. . .perurunt
/ tempora*, since he, poet of heroic times, was able to imagine a
far grander type of helmet: stripped of its adornments, it is
'branded on his temples'.

Finally, Silius Italicus used the topic for Hannibal in single
combat against the men of Saguntum (1. 522–32):

> hinc saxis galea, hinc clipeus sonat aereus hastis;
> incessunt sudibus librataque pondera plumbi
> certatim iaciunt. decisae vertice cristae
> direptumque decus nutantum in caede iubarum.   525
> iamque agitur largus per membra fluentia sudor,
> et stant loricae squamis horrentia tela.
> nec requies, tegimenve datur mutare sub ictu;
> genua labant, fessique humeri gestamina laxant.
> tum creber penitusque trahens suspiria sicco   530
> fumat ab ore vapor, nisuque elisus anhelo
> auditur gemitus fractumque in casside murmur.

From this side his helmet rings with stones, from that, his bronze
shield with spears. They attack with stakes, and compete among
themselves in whirling and casting lumps of lead. The plume was
shorn from his head, and the glory of the horsehair that nodded
over his killings was torn off (525). And now abundant sweat pours
over his streaming limbs, and bristling weapons stand from the
scales of his breastplate. And he is not permitted rest or change
of armour under the blows; his knees buckle and tired arms let fall
their burdens. Then puffs of steam, drawing gasps from deep within (530), smoke from his dry mouth, and groaning, forced out with
strained panting, is heard and a broken sobbing within the helmet.

Here Silius based himself closely on Virgil, but in his expression of the details it is clear that he used the second passage of
Statius also as a model; and since he ends with an animal simile
(421–25)[30] it seems likely that he had the first passage of Statius

30. Against the transposition of this simile (usually placed after 1. 532),
see Albrecht (1964), 111–13. His defence is not convincing, but neither is
the case for transposition, and circularity would result if the passage of
Statius were adduced as an argument. My argument must, consequently, be
discounted, to that extent.

in mind as well, for there Statius slips into a lion simile. The steam was Silius' own contribution, but it is based closely on the strange phrase of Statius (8. 400), *pariter suspiria fumant*; Silius separated the synaesthetic elements. In this context the sobbing heard within the helmet was also his contribution; but there was a strange interest in all of these writers in the effect of weeping or groaning heard inside a helmet—a macabre interest in a realism remote from their own lives—and Silius, here as elsewhere, had an eye for a fashionable theme.[31]

Valerius Flaccus was more independent, and he had the ability to originate ideas from time to time. During the boxing match between Amycus and Castor, he imagines the shades of those slain by Amycus being let out of Hades to enjoy the sight of their savage killer's defeat (4. 258–60):

> et pater orantes caesorum Tartarus umbras
> nube cava tandem ad meritae spectacula poenae
> emittit: summi nigrescunt culmina montis.

And father Tartarus, at their request, sends forth in a hollow cloud the shades of the slain to see at last well-deserved retribution; and the topmost peaks of the mountain grow dark (with them).

31. Cf., for example, Valerius Flaccus 6. 738; Statius *Theb.* 2. 635; 7. 528–29; 9. 41–42; 10. 275–76; 11. 385–86; Silius Italicus 5. 303–4; 12. 553–54. (Cf. Aeneas kissing through his helmet, *Aen.* 12. 434 *summaque per galeam delibans oscula*.) More generally, the obsessiveness of these writers in the treatment of certain themes would repay study. For instance, their obsession with tyranny and arbitrary violence: this is certainly not a sign of covert attacks on the emperors (the superficial conclusion usually drawn). The emperors were unconcerned with such literary explorations in the absence of any *animus nocendi* (it was the admitted presence of this that placed Curiatius Maternus in danger, as his friends saw). But from Seneca to Statius the violent and arbitrary tyrant was a figure that fascinated writers—probably a subconscious admission of the fears that could easily become a reality no less than a love of the melodramatic and exaggerated. (It was evidence of *animus nocendi* that impelled Sejanus to obtain penalties against Phaedrus: that is, either Phaedrus himself or a senator hostile to Sejanus must have publicly pointed out the relevance of some of Phaedrus' moral fables to the actions of Sejanus; see p. 275 below.)

In the *Thebaid*, when the single combat of the brothers is about to take place, something similar happens (ll. 420–23):

> ipse quoque Ogygios monstra ad gentilia manes
> Tartareus rector porta iubet ire reclusa.
> montibus insidunt patriis tristique corona
> infecere diem et vinci sua crimina gaudent.

Even the king of Tartarus himself bids the gate be opened, and the Theban ghosts proceed to view the monstrous deeds of their kin. They settle on their native mountains and pollute the daylight with their grim circle, and are glad to see their own crimes outdone.

Here Statius has changed into conventional form the bold phrase of Valerius, *pater Tartarus*. But the idea, perfect in its former context where it suggests the long murderous career of Amycus, is less good in the *Thebaid* where the ghosts should be confined to the family of Laius and his ancestors; and their delight in seeing worse crimes than their own gives a poor motive to the king of Hades (whereas in Valerius he is on the side of justice, and kindly lets the souls out to see it done). It is hard to say whether Valerius was inspired by the passage in which Lucan pictures the guilty dream-ridden night of the victors after Pharsalia (7. 768–70):

> ingemuisse putem campos, terramque nocentem
> inspirasse animas, infectumque aera totum
> manibus et superam Stygia formidine noctem.

I could believe that the plains gave a groan and that the guilty land breathed out spirits over them, and that all the air was polluted by the spirits of the dead and the night of the world above by the terrors of Hell.

Lucan's concept is highly impressionistic, and he commits himself to no concrete statement, only to a psychological effect which he brings alive by entering his own narrative (*putem*). *Infectum* may have suggested *nigrescunt* to Valerius Flaccus, though there is no necessity for that supposition; but it certainly inspired Statius' *infecere diem*, and this fusion of details from various sources is a most striking characteristic of post-Virgilian epic.

The prestige of Lucan is very clear in the pages of his successors; but there was one respect in which they could not emulate him, and here his preeminence was a function of his intellectual strength. There are relatively few *sententiae* in later writers of the type that, combining wit and point, give memorable expression to an idea or point of view that genuinely engages the intellect. Lucan constantly improves on predecessors in this field.[32] Cicero wrote in a letter to Atticus (8. 7. 2) on Caesar's advance against Rome and Pompey's retreat: *quem fugiam habeo: quem sequar non habeo.* Lucan makes Pompey, in a boastful apostrophe to Caesar, say (2. 575): *heu demens! non te fugiunt, me cuncta sequuntur* ('O you madman! The world is not running away from you: they are all following me'). Labienus composed[33] the neat paradox against Caesar: *necesse est multos timeat quem multi timent*, and Seneca used it in *Oedipus* (705–6): *qui sceptra duro saevus imperio regit | timet timentes*, where the introduction is overexplanatory. Lucan twice used the idea in quite different ways and with exemplary elegance: (4. 185) *usque adeone times quem tu facis ipse timendum?* ('Do you really dread him whom you yourself make dreadful?') and (6. 666) *quis timor, ignavi, metuentes cernere manes?* ('What fear, cowards, is there in setting eyes on the fearful spirits of the dead?'). Lucan appreciated the younger Seneca, his uncle, and used his ideas (to improve on them). For instance, Seneca says (*de ira* 1. 13. 4) *non aliquoties. . .mortis timor etiam inertissimos excitavit in proelium?* ('Has not fear of death sometimes spurred to battle even the most cowardly?'). Lucan's improvement was (7. 104–5) *multos in summa pericula misit | venturi timor ipse mali* ('the very fear of danger to come has thrust many into the worst dangers').

Seneca was equally generous in supplying Martial with material both from his philosophical works (with which Martial must have had little sympathy) and especially from his epigrams;

32. In what follows I rely heavily on the work of Bonner (1966).
33. See Macrobius *Sat.* 2. 7. 4–5.

in every case Martial can be seen to have improved the point. A famous example is the epigram on the grave of Pompey, a theme which goes back at least to Propertius. Seneca's epigram is (*Anth. Lat.* 402):

> Pompeius totum victor lustraverat orbem,
>   at rursus toto victus in orbe iacet.
> membra pater Libyco posuit male tecta sepulchro;
>   filius Hispana est vix adopertus humo;
> Sexte, Asiam sortite tenes. divisa ruina est:
>   uno non potuit tanta iacere solo.

Pompey traversed the whole world as its conqueror, but in his turn conquered throughout the whole world, he lies dead. The father laid his bones ill-covered in a Libyan tomb; his son was scarcely covered in his Spanish grave; Sextus, Fate assigned you Asia for yours. The destruction has been shared out: it was so great that it could not lie in one country.

Martial then wrote (5. 74):

> Pompeios iuvenes Asia atque Europa, sed ipsum
>   terra tegit Libyes, si tamen ulla tegit.
> quid mirum toto si spargitur orbe? iacere
>   uno non poterat tanta ruina loco.

The young Pompeys Asia and Europe cover, the father the land of Libya—if it covers him at all. What wonder that the ruin is scattered over the whole world? It was too huge for one place to contain.

Martial has not only shortened and sharpened the composition; he has also simplified it. The first couplet of Seneca's epigram uses the word *Pompeius* in an extended sense of 'the name of Pompey' since the same name also covered the great man's sons; and the repeated idea of 'the whole world' is intended to mean that the victories of father and sons covered the whole world. Martial omitted that concept as unnecessary and clumsy. So did Lucan in one rendering of the epigram. Erichtho, the witch, prophesies and warns Sextus (6. 817–18):

> Europam, miseri, Libyamque Asiamque timete:
> distribuit tumulos vestris Fortuna triumphis.

Poor creatures, feel fear of Europe and Libya and Asia: Fate has distributed your graves among your triumphs.

This is excellent: it gets everything essential in his uncle's epigram, and Martial, challenging the uncle, has certainly not improved on the nephew. But Lucan came back to the theme after the death of Pompey (8. 796–99):

> cur obicis Magno tumulum manesque vagantis
> includis? situs est qua terra extrema refuso
> pendet in Oceano; Romanum nomen et omne
> imperium Magno tumuli est modus.

Why do you force a tomb on Magnus and hem in his roving spirit? He is buried where the ends of the world hang over the circling Ocean: the name of Rome and the whole of the Empire forms the limit to Magnus' tomb.

The idea of 'his tomb is the whole world' was derived easily from an ambiguity inherent in the second line of Seneca's epigram: *at rursus toto victus in orbe iacet*, where *toto victus in orbe* can belong closely together; but Lucan explored the possibility of taking the phrase also with *iacet* to create a fine rhetorical picture. Martial was the professional epigrammatist who, like the Greek epigrammatists, used the same material again and again (often imitating and improving on Greek epigrams),[34] varying sometimes the form, sometimes the treatment, often both. But the point of his challenge, whether directed towards a predecessor or towards himself, is always clear. Lucan was a freer, more imaginative spirit.

Juvenal, too, took thematic material from his predecessors— from the *Silvae* of Statius but also on a large scale from Martial,[35] and he accommodated it to the different tone and structure of continuous hexametric poetry. He also repeated closely related themes of his own, varying the treatment according to the con-

34. See, in general, Weinreich (1928) *passim* (Index s.v. 'Anthologia Palatina'), and on Martial's use of themes from Lucillios see Barwick (1959), 34.

35. On this, see, for example, Weinreich (1928), 166–70 and Anderson (1970).

text. An obvious example is the homosexual theme in *Satires* 2 and 9, but the same interest can also be seen in the parade of unlovely women in *Satire* 6. He also, like Lucan, took and improved *sententiae* from earlier authors. For instance, Cestius Pius is reported by the elder Seneca (*suas*. 1. 5) to have coined the phrase about Alexander: *orbis illum suus non capit* ('the world that he has captured does not contain him');[36] Juvenal adapted this as (10. 168) *unus Pellaeo iuveni non sufficit orbis* ('one world is not big enough for the young man from Pella'), which is more suggestive in what it does not say. He had a rich source of material in Lucan, who, for example, makes Curio say to Caesar (1. 290–91) *partiri non potes orbem: / solus habere potes* ('you cannot share the world: you can only own it alone'); Juvenal adapted this to a bitter hit at Greeks (3. 121–22) *qui gentis vitio numquam partitur amicum: / solus habet* ('who, with the vice of his race, never shares a friend: he keeps him for himself').

Even Tacitus was interested in refurbishing the *sententiae* of predecessors. No direct source is extant on any scale for Tacitus, but Plutarch's *Life of Otho* and Tacitus' account of the period in *Histories* 1 and 2 are close enough to show common dependance on one particular source, probably Cluvius Rufus.[37] When Tacitus, with characteristic wit, says of Otho (1. 81. 1) *cum timeret Otho, timebatur* ('when Otho was frightened, he was frightening'), Plutarch, at much greater length, makes a similar point[38]—'fearing for the men, he was himself fearful to them'— but Tacitus has greatly increased the bite and point. The epigram is related to the paradox of Labienus (developed by Seneca and Lucan),[39] which Tacitus polished even more brightly in (*Hist*. 2. 76. 4): *satis clarus est apud timentem quisquis timetur* ('a man who is feared is famous enough—to those who fear him'). Of a donative made shortly before Otho's death Tacitus says

36. On the diverse forms given to this idea, see Mayor on Juvenal 10. 168.
37. See especially Mommsen (1870); also Syme (1958), 177 ff. and 199 f., and Townend (1964).
38. *Life of Otho* 3.
39. See p. 207 above.

(2. 48. 1): *pecunias distribuit parce nec ut periturus* ('he distributed money like a miser, not like a man who was soon going to die'); again Plutarch, at much greater length, says:[40] 'In a generous mood he distributed money, to one more, to another less, not like a man thrifty for what belonged to another, but carefully keeping account with due and proper moderation'. Here Tacitus has got to the point and contrast, which no doubt Cluvius Rufus had been pleased to note, with devastating wit and speed.

Tacitus himself put into Aper's mouth[41] an explanation of what is happening in all these writers: 'Now our young men, still in training, follow orators about for their own advancement, wanting not only to listen but also to take away with them anything striking and worth memorizing; they pass that on in turn and often transmit it in writing to the colonies and provinces, especially if an idea has flashed out in a sharp and witty *sententia*; or if a passage has been polished with some recherché poetic touch'. The habit is clear too in the pages of the elder Seneca. *Sententiae* were endlessly collected, memorized, improved, passed on from orator to orator, from writer to writer.[42] A good *sententia*, like a good passage of poetry or prose, was a challenge to do better with the same material.

Repetition of thematic material was common at all periods of Greek literature, and Romans were always ready to use Greek material in the same way; in the late Republic and Augustan age they added earlier Roman poets to the legitimate quarries for material.[43] What was new in the writers of the early Empire has two aspects: first, the degree of repetition was enormously increased—to the extent that previously used material actually seems to have been preferable; second, the motive was new, and it can be diagnosed, for instance, from a whole series of descriptions of the death of Cicero that were collected by the elder

40. *Life of Otho* 17.
41. *Dialogus* 20. 4.
42. Seneca (*Epp.* 108. 6–7) describes notebooks brought to record memorable sayings.
43. See Williams (1968), 252 ff.

Seneca[44]—pleasure was taken in variation for its own sake. The Greek epigrammatists show how exciting was the exercise of ingenuity in word coinage and phrase making and in elaborating the interplay of vocabulary and ideas. The desire to vary was an inspiration in itself; and with that came the added pleasure of challenging a predecessor, for if writers of the early Empire knew one technique and found pleasure in it, it was that of engaging in competition. Seneca caught the attitude well in a letter to Lucilius (79. 4–6): 'What can I offer you not to describe Aetna in your poem? not to touch this topic which seems obligatory to all poets? The fact that Virgil had fully treated it[45] was no deterrent to Ovid;[46] and even both of them were no deterrent to Cornelius Severus.[47] Besides, the topic was a success in all of them, and I do not view predecessors as laying claim to material, but simply as opening it up. Yet it makes a lot of difference whether you take up material that is exhausted or merely well-prepared. The latter grows daily, and previous inventions are no obstacle to new inventions. Besides, the situation of the last author is best: he finds the words ready waiting—put in a different order they acquire a new appearance. And he is not laying violent hands on them as another's property, for by then they are common property'.

Two conclusions can be drawn immediately from this way of viewing the process of literary composition. First, interest came to be concentrated on style and treatment. The point is perfectly expressed in a judgement of Montanus Votienus, reported by the elder Seneca (*contr. 9 praef.* 1): 'The man who composes a declamation writes not to win but to please. So he searches out all the enticements he can: close reasoning, because it is boring and least susceptible of ornamentation he leaves out; with epigrams (*sententiae*) and expansions of themes he is happy to charm his audience. For he wants to have himself approved, not his case'.[48] The ideas were secondary to the way in which they

44. *contr.* 7. 2; *suas.* 6 and 7.   45. *Aeneid* 3. 570 ff.
46. *Metamorphoses* 15. 340 ff.   47. In his lost epic *Bellum Siculum.*
48. Cf. Quintilian 8. 3. 11.

could be handled. Generally, in these writers there is a distinct sense that the pressure of ideas was low; and even the few who really have something of their own to say rarely give the impression of being in a hurry to move on from one idea to another: the method is to linger over each point, treating each separately and exhaustively, and connectedness as such was not of first importance.

Second, and as a consequence of the first conclusion, there developed the capacity to treat any material that came to hand (improvisation was a favourite occupation)[49] and give it its appropriate *color*, without applying any other criteria to the material; hence the otherwise incredible lengths to which even good poets like Lucan or Statius could take the praises of the emperor. The idea did not matter as a thing in itself, but only the treatment to which it could be subjected, and the expansions and variations that could be introduced. The truth or falsity of the inventions was not a relevant issue. It is this attitude which explains the otherwise surprising fact that Seneca could write abject flattery of Claudius in the dialogue *ad Polybium* and a few years later treat the same monarch, now dead, with vicious satire in the *Apocolocyntosis*.[50]

2. Brevity and expansiveness

The challenge, then, could come not only from a predecessor but also from the material itself. No one has more letters addressed to him by Pliny than Tacitus, and in one of those letters (1. 20) he treats this topic: 'I am constantly having arguments with a man of great learning and experience. He admires nothing in legal oratory as much as brevity. . .'. Pliny's counter-

49. See p. 195 above.
50. Momigliano (1961), 74–79, achieved consistency between the *ad Polybium* and the *Apocolocyntosis* only by arguing that the former was deeply ironic. But this is no more than one striking example of contradictory opinions constantly expressed by Seneca: see, for example, Oltramare (1926), 254–57. The needs of the context governed choice of ideas, opinions, and tone.

ing view is (4): 'Like all good things, a good book is all the better if it is a long one; and statues, busts, pictures, the bodies of human beings and of many animals, trees too, provided they are well-proportioned, can be seen to gain from being on an ample scale. The same applies to speeches; and as books they gain in appearance and impressiveness by being large'. It is a very long letter and embodies its message in its own form. At the end, Pliny invites Tacitus' views—even in a short letter. The point of view expressed here recalls the vulgarity and lack of taste, the luxury in general, and the wealth without object that characterized much of the life of the period and that form the target of Martial's and Juvenal's satire no less than the object of Statius' extravagant praises in the *Silvae*. This would be unfair to Pliny, but the ideal of amplification for its own sake is a general characteristic of literature in the early Empire. It was closely linked to the instinct to concentrate on each idea and explore it to the full.

A ludicrous example of this is provided by Q. Haterius, no common declaimer but a senator who held the consulship in 5 B.C. The elder Seneca praises him[51] as the only Roman who brought to Latin the facility of Greek, and continues: 'His speed of speech was so great as to be a fault. So the deified Augustus excellently remarked: "Haterius needs a brake"—to such an extent did he give the impression not of running but of careering downhill. He was as full of ideas as of words. As often as you wished and for as long as you wished he would say the same thing, each time with change of figures and developments, so that he could be controlled but not exhausted. But he could not control himself. He used to have a freedman as control, and he used to proceed according as his freedman either spurred him on or reined him in. The man used to tell him to make a transition when he had spoken on one topic long enough: he would make the transition. The man would bid him dwell on the same topic: he used to dwell on it. His talent was in his own control, its application in another's'.

51. *contr.* 4. *pr.* 7–8.

The picture is splendidly satiric, but its message can be exemplified in great contemporary poets like Ovid, who loved to expand an idea by repeating it in different forms. In fact, Ovid was the inventor of a feature that became important in Roman literature—the list, not only as a multiplication of mythological *exempla*, but as a simple enumeration: for instance, in *Metamorphoses* 10. 86–105 a bare hill becomes covered with trees because Orpheus comes to it; the poet works no less than twenty-seven different trees into about seventeen lines. And nothing is more exuberant than Ovid's expansion of the love song of the Cyclops to his Galatea,[52] with twenty lines of comparatives to express first her incomparable beauty, then her incomparable unkindness (with her speed in flight the only quality he would wish absent); twenty-eight lines then list his possessions, and a final thirty his own personal qualities. Ovid always does this with wit and lightness of touch (even self-mockery), and infects the reader with the sense of self-conscious bravura. The technique, however, became a distinct stylistic feature of later epic and was naturally indulged with great seriousness by a poet like Statius, whether he was taking pleasure in interminable catalogues of forces or in the types of trees cut down to make a funeral pyre.

Such expansiveness and the concomitant concentration on the single idea inevitably led to lack of interest in the strict coherence and movement of ideas and in the organization of the whole. Haterius again serves as a warning:[53] 'He thought that it was important to structure a speech, if you were to put that question to him; but if you just listened to him, he did not hold that opinion. His own impetus was what dictated the order of ideas; he did not direct himself according to the rules of declamation'. Ironically, the younger Seneca, who is pictured as listening to these words of his father, was an outstanding example of the fault: the organization of his essays, his *dialogi*, suffers from the desire to explore each idea from as many points of view as possible rather than to move forward; this does not mean

52. *Met.* 13. 789–869.   53. *contr.* 4. *pr.* 9.

that Seneca gives the sense of being slow—quite the reverse—but he is relatively uninterested in weighing the place of any one idea in the strategy of the whole. Persius, too, is one of the most difficult of Latin poets because, on the one hand, he elevates Horace's linguistic brevity into a major stylistic principle, while, on the other, he tends to expand an idea by multiplication at the expense of the main drift of his argument—a tendency made the more productive of obscurity since he uses Horace's *sermo* style as a license for lack of connection in the argument. He has the habit, for instance, of adding an unexpected detail to a context simply because it suits a particular opportunity for expansion that has suddenly caught his eye: thus at 1. 22 the man who has been addressed since line 15 turns out to be *vetulus* because that gives Persius a new theme for abuse; or at 1. 36–40 the poet, whose poems were being recited from line 30, turns out to be dead because Persius wants the ironic picture of his grave (and not—as would have made the idea relevant— because his point is that fame only comes after death).

Something of the same can be seen in Juvenal, who is often hard to follow because he crowds in so many examples of a particular idea that his line of thought is imperceptibly altered. This fault is found in all writers of the early Empire: for instance, when Lucan describes the remarriage of Marcia and Cato (2. 350–71), the ceremony fills twenty-two lines, of which two are introductory; then two lines and the final line describe the rites they observed, while the rites which they did not observe occupy the intervening seventeen lines. Juvenal is particularly given to a method of turning aside to irrelevant details by means of parenthesis, as in 1. 42–44 or 1. 73–76 (a few lines later he bombastically expands the idea of 'the beginning of the world' into a four-line skit on Deucalion and Pyrrha that has no relevance to the context). Such parentheses are often very hard for the reader to recognize.[54] Sometimes expansion gets

54. For the way in which the speaking voice may have been relied on by the writer to make clear such parentheses and transitions, see sect. 3 below.

totally out of hand, as in the treatment of the *sportula* (1. 95–134), which has only a random and tenuous connection with the advertised theme of (88) *avaritia*. But occasionally, especially in later satires, this tendency of thought to deviate in expansions is mastered and made into an interesting and positive stylistic device by which the writer's mind drifts away on a tangential course and is then suddenly jerked back: the effect is something like that of a simile in epic. For instance, in *Satire* 13 he consoles a friend who is enraged because he has been cheated. His consolation at one point (120 ff.) consists of the disjunction: '(a) if the crime against you is unique, then rage and weep', but '(b) if you can see that and worse happening often, then calm yourself'. But between the two limbs of the argument, the idea of weeping over financial loss leads Juvenal off into a splendid picture, truly satiric, of the mourning lavished on money when it passes away from one. However, even in the early *Satire* 3 (254 ff.) we see this device: Umbricius lists the dangers of the city, ending with the picture of a man crushed to pulp under an overturned wagon and its enormous load; he then slides away into a detailed portrait of the family making all the normal preparations for the man's homecoming while he sits on the bank of the Styx without a coin to offer the ferryman. Then Umbricius swings back instantly to the night perils of the city. To question, on the basis of this, whether Juvenal believed in traditional religious ideas is irrelevant (he displays the opposite opinion at 2. 149–52 when it suited him); the value of the *locus* lies in its satiric pathos as well as in its function as an irrelevant expansion marking a major transition in the satire.

Truth or falsity are as irrelevant here as, for instance, in Lucan 7. 567–70, where Caesar, urging on his troops, is compared to Bellona or to Mars urging the Bistones against Athene. The problem is more acute at 7. 144–50, where the troops preparing their weapons before Pharsalia are compared to Mars, Neptune, Apollo, Athene, and Juppiter, each preparing their special weapons before the battle with the Giants; this is conventional Greek epicizing. Juvenal used the inspiration of this passage to better effect in constructing the fraudulent trustee's oath (13. 78–83). At 9. 359–60, in the middle of a foolish and repetitive mythological digression on lake Tritonis and the Hesperides, Lucan actually reproves anyone who levels such a criticism: 'Mean is the man who despoils aged antiquity of its fame and measures poets by the standard of truth' (*invidus, annoso qui famam derogat aevo, | qui vates ad vera vocat*). Yet this is the poet who can turn the conventional epic simile into a moving and relevant vision. For instance, Cornelia burns Pompey's possessions on a funeral pyre on the African shore, and others, following her example, remember their own dead at Pharsalia (9. 179–85):

> accipit omnis
> exemplum pietas, et toto litore busta
> surgunt Thessalicis reddentia manibus ignem.
> sic, ubi depastis summittere gramina campis
> et renovare parans hibernas Apulus herbas
> igne fovet terras, simul et Garganus et arva
> Volturis et calidi lucent buceta Matini.

All, in loving devotion, follow her lead, and along the whole shore pyres are built to render flame to those dead in Thessaly; as when an Apulian farmer, to make grass grow on the cropped plains and renew the fodder for winter, nurtures the soil with flame: then mount Garganus and the fields of Voltur and the cattle pastures of warm Matinus glow with light.

The mourning for the Roman dead is echoed in the Italian names of places where the burning stubble lights the night, as far from the African coast as that coast was from Thessaly. It was in this sphere, the sphere of the characteristically Classical concept of appropriateness (τὸ πρέπον, *decorum*), that most violence was done by writers of the early Empire; but it would perhaps be fairer to say that they redefined the criteria of its application in their own terms, and that those terms were not those of the great Classical writers.

Expansiveness in the treatment of material has no necessary link with redundance and verbosity: the repetition and expansion of ideas could be, and frequently was, executed with verbal economy and point, especially, of course, by writers like Persius and Juvenal and Lucan, but even by less taut writers like Seneca and Statius. In fact, the instinct to expand was accompanied by an instinct towards brevity of expression that took two forms: the first was expressed in the love of the epigram or *sententia*; the second, in the desire to make every word work for its place in each phrase. The interest in epigram concentrated on the matter as much as on the manner. The *sententia* ranged from a grandiose generalized reflection to a sharp pointed comment on a particular situation;[55] the intention was to achieve surprise by neatness and brevity. The younger Seneca was an outstanding practitioner both in his essays and in his tragedies; *sententiae* are so frequent that Quintilian clearly had him in mind[56] when he issued a stern warning on a dangerous fault (8. 5. 14): 'Today rhetors want every passage, every sentence to strike the ear by its close. And they think it disgraceful and pretty well illegal to take breath at any point that is not designed for applause. Hence tiny degenerate and irrelevant little sentences everywhere, for the number of good epigrams [*sententiae*] in the world can by no means equal the number of period-endings [*clausulae*]'. Quintilian had been talking about a favourite use of the *sententia* to close a paragraph or section of a work. In a special application of this type, Martial developed, as no one before him had developed, the form of verse epigram that reaches its climax in a *sententia*.[57] There is a slow buildup, then the unexpected and absolutely conclusive climax; for example, 3. 27:

> numquam me revocas, venias cum saepe vocatus:
> ignosco, nullum si modo, Galle, vocas.
> invitas alios? vitium est utriusque. 'quod?' inquis?
> et mihi cor non est, et tibi, Galle, pudor.

---

55. Quintilian 8. 5; see Bonner (1966), 260–61.
56. See Quintilian's specific criticism of him in 10. 1. 125–31, esp. 129 ff.
57. See on this Barwick (1959), though, in the interest of his thesis, he does not sufficiently recognize how far writers like Catullus and even Horace had moved towards the structure found in Martial.

You never invite me back, however often you come here on my invitation. I forgive you, Gallus, provided you invite no one else either. You do invite others? There is vice in both of us. What vice? you ask me? I have no sense, and you, Gallus, no decency.

Here the conclusive *sententia* is particular; but it is often of the other, generalizing type; for instance, 8. 12:

> uxorem quare locupletem ducere nolim
> quaeritis? uxori nubere nolo meae.
> inferior matrona suo sit, Prisce, marito:
> non aliter fiunt femina virque pares.

So you all want to know why I don't marry a rich wife? I've no desire to be my own wife's bride. A married woman, Priscus, ought to be inferior to her husband: that's the only way a man and a woman can be equal.[58]

Martial's type of epigram, though it has a close relationship to satire and shares the same material, requires a cool tone and a poker face; consequently, major emotional effects of anger or deep sorrow are inappropriate. Juvenal constantly uses the same technique as Martial, but, because of the larger scale of his composition, he can use it to sustain and express strong, even violent, emotions like anger.[59] There is an excellent example of this in his first satire (48–50):

> quid enim salvis infamia nummis?
> exul ab octava Marius bibit et fruitur dis
> iratis: at tu victrix, provincia, ploras.

What matter loss of reputation if the cash is safe? The fraudulent governor in exile starts drinking an hour before the cocktail hour and enjoys the disapproval of heaven: it is the province that is in trouble—and after winning the case.

The list of reasons for getting out of Rome reaches a climactic anticlimax, worthy of Martial in its unexpectedness but without losing the shrill note of indignation (3. 6–9): 'fires, collapse of buildings, and a thousand perils in the crime-ridden city and

58. A variation of the epigram (Seneca *contr.* 1. 6. 5) *omnes uxores divites servitutem exigunt.*
59. See especially Anderson (1970).

poets reciting their poems in the month of August'. This indignation is Juvenal's own and is designed to lead up to, and be
taken over by, the sustained anger of Umbricius. Juvenal, in
fact, uses the terminal *sententia* with such regularity that it is
one important way of marking transitions of thought. Juvenal
clearly uses this technique together with expansiveness, but even
Martial does that in his longer poems (his longest are in his
earlier books);[60] such poems achieve their length by lists and
simple expansion of detail.

But Tacitus, though he was also certainly capable of the most
extended thematic expansion (for instance, in the army mutinies
in *Annals* 1), was the most elegant and witty exponent of the
terminal *sententia*, partly because brevity and pregnancy were
his most stringent stylistic criteria, but partly too because his
tone normally purports to be cool and impersonal so that the
sententia achieves maximum surprise. It is a splendid moment
when, the *equites* Falernius and Rubrius having been accused
of disrespect to the memory of Augustus, the paragraph (*Annals*
1. 73) climaxes in the dry written comment of Tiberius: *deorum
iniurias dis curae* ('gods must be left to take note of injuries
done to gods'). That Tacitus too enjoyed the effect can be seen
from his cool, casual opening: *haud pigebit referre*. He, under-
standably, expanded on the murder of Agrippina (14. 4–8), but
ends a vital chapter on her psychology with the words (12. 64. 3)
filio dare imperium, tolerare imperitantem nequibat ('she could
give her son the crown, but could not bear his wearing it').
Speeches in Tacitus are usually good examples of expansion in
the sense used above, and these are often brilliantly punctuated
by *sententiae*. In A.D. 70, when the senate felt excited at the possibility of getting revenge on the *delatores*, Curtius Montanus
attacked the notorious Regulus. Tacitus reports his accusation
(*Hist.* 4. 42) that Regulus not only rewarded the murderer of
Piso Licinianus but had actually bitten the dead man's face (a

60. 1. 49; 3. 58; 3. 82. The two largest are 1. 49 (42 lines) and 3. 58 (51
lines). Then, just over or just under 30 lines in length are 3. 82; 4. 64; 5. 78;
6. 64; 8. 33; 10. 30 and 48; 11. 18; 12. 18 and 57.

story that perhaps inspired Statius to the cannibalism of Tydeus); then he reports the rest of his speech, ending with the epigram *optimus est post malum principem dies primus* ('when a bad emperor goes, the first day is the best'). The climax is perfectly concealed, and is prepared by praise of Vespasian at the same time as there is a call for vengeance on *delatores*, which itself reaches a climax with *diutius durant exempla quam mores* ('example lasts longer than character').

The epic poets found another use for *sententiae* in opening a topic or excusing a digression. In book 1 Lucan introduces a totally original form of the traditional catalogue of forces: it is a catalogue in reverse, and lists all the dangerous tribes that are being left unguarded by Caesar's withdrawal of Roman forces to invade Italy (396–465). In the course of it he comes to the Druids and pauses, quite unnecessarily, to digress on their religious beliefs; this he motivates by the striking *sententia* (452–53) *solis nosse deos et caeli numina vobis | aut solis nescire datum* ('alone you have been allowed to know about the gods and deities of the heavens, or alone not to know'). After that, no reader can fail to want to hear more. The technique is similar when Statius recounts the story of Dymas and Hopleus (*Thebaid* 10. 347–448), which he deliberately modelled on Virgil's Nisus and Euryalus (whom he actually names in the epilogue, 445–48). In the course of the story comes the *sententia* (384–85) *invida fata piis et fors ingentibus ausis | rara comes* ('Fate is grudging to loyalty and Luck seldom accompanies bold deeds'). The *sententia* is, typically, a variation on one of Seneca's (*Hercules Furens* 524–25): *o Fortuna viris invida fortibus, | quam non aequa bonis praemia dividis* ('O Fortune, how grudging you are to the brave, and how unfairly you distribute rewards to the good'); that *sententia* likewise functions to open a great choral passage. Statius has come to the main part of his story, and the *sententia* both marks the transition and foreshadows the disaster in its gloomy, impressive tones.

The second stylistic feature which can be identified as the product of an instinct towards brevity resulted from a concentration on manner and expression rather than on content. This was the basically excellent desire to make every word work for its place in a sentence, but the desire was satisfied not by pruning or generally restricting the expenditure of words; it showed itself in the creation of locutions which were surprising either in the significance of the words employed or in their syntax or both. The instinct was perfectly expressed by Persius in words put into the mouth of Cornutus (5. 14): *verba togae sequeris iunctura callidus acri* ('you select the words of ordinary life, cleverly inventing striking combinations').[61] Persius himself provides many examples of the technique: for instance, 1. 18, *patranti fractus ocello*; 1. 35, *tenero subplantat verba palato*; or 1. 90–91, *nec nocte paratum plorabit*. In the first, all three words work in the same direction of sexual degeneracy; in the second, it is the metaphor of 'tripping up' in the verb which is astonishing; and in the third, the syntax of *nocte paratum* and the demand for the complete visualization of the semantic field of the two words create an instant problem for the reader. What is common to all three phrases is the unexpectedness of the combination and the consequent demand on the reader to decipher. Persius was overambitious in this, and his phrases degenerate into mere riddles, far surpassing in interest the comparative vacuity of the ideas expressed.

The greatness of Lucan and his more mature view of what poetry was about appears in the extent to which, by pregnancy no less than unexpectedness of phrase, he forces a reader (or listener) to think. At the beginning of book 7 he foresees the death of Pompey, and that people in Rome will weep despite their fear of Caesar—but they will weep at the same time as they offer thanks for Caesar's victory. Then, with a characteristic shift of the time scale, he looks back from Nero's reign (43–44):

> o miseri quorum gemitus edere dolorem,
> qui te non pleno pariter planxere theatro.

I pity you: groans had to eat up your grief, and you could not crowd the theatre and mourn [Pompey] all together.

61. Based, as usual, on Horace (*AP* 47–48).

Editors usually decide that *edere* is corrupt, and Housman tried emendation—to no purpose: Lucan boldly reversed Ovid's description of Hecuba's grief when she saw Polydorus' body in the sea (*Met.* 13. 539–40): *et pariter vocem lacrimasque introrsus obortas | devorat ipse dolor* ('her grief actually swallowed both her voice and the tears that welled up within'). She kept silent while the other women screamed. Lucan's point, however, is that Romans did mourn, but each one to himself, and, instead of indulging the luxury of national lamentation, mere individual groans had to consume their grief. As is common in Lucan, the point here resides in the antithesis, and the astonishing phrase expresses the physical pain of deprivation. Often in Lucan it is the precise meaning of one word that needs to be found, and characteristically that word may have a very wide semantic field: for instance (4. 479–80), *nec gloria leti | inferior, iuvenes, admoto occurrere fato* ('nor does it lessen the glory of death, men, to go and meet a fate that has come close'). Vulteius is talking of suicide, and means that the glory of suicide is not lessened by the fact that death (in battle) is imminent anyway (and one is therefore not willingly foregoing years of possible life). All depends on catching the precise significance of *admoto*, which conveys not just the idea of closeness, but also the sense of something quite outside one's control.

Sometimes there is a play on words, as when Vulteius and his men commit mutual suicide (557–58): *minimumque in morte virorum | mors virtutis habet*. Here *mors* has two senses: the first is 'death', but the second is 'the act of dying', and *virorum* has the special sense of 'heroes' by association with *virtus*. So the phrase means 'and in the death of [those] heroes the act of dying involved the least courage' (courage being needed to kill their friends). In 6. 296–98, a concrete image suggested a highly metaphorical one and supplies the clue to a reader:

> Caesaris ut miles glomerato pulvere victus
> ante aciem caeci trepidus sub nube timoris
> hostibus occurrit fugiens.

Caesar's soldiers, conquered by the billowing dust before the battle and shivering under a cloud of blind terror, ran into the enemy as they fled.

Here 'the cloud' of fear is prefigured in the clouds of dust— the physical and the psychological are parallel and mutually supporting. The nearest predecessor to the image was Ovid's (*ex Ponto* 2. 1. 5) *pulsa curarum nube* ('dispelling the clouds of anxiety'), where the weather image is clear, and is then taken up with *serenum* ('clear sky'). Statius characteristically carried the image a stage further than Lucan when he described Polynices' brooding as (2. 321–22) *talem sub pectore nubem / consilii volvens*, where the single word *nubem* conveys the anxiety that accompanied the feverish mental planning of a return (his predecessors had to add the genitive of a noun signifying anxiety or fear, but Statius, as is common with all these writers, could rely on knowledge of the work of predecessors).[62]

In fact, it is particularly characteristic of Statius to push to a further extreme a bold locution used by a predecessor. Valerius Flaccus told of the last years of Phrixus (5. 224–25): *Scythica senior iam Solis in urbe / fata laborati Phrixus compleverat aevi* ('Phrixus, now grown old in the city of the Sun, had completed the lot of a life of toil'). In *Thebaid* 1. 336–46 Statius has a description of night and sleep that shows some of the quality

62. An outstanding example of this can be seen in Juvenal 3. 186–89, where the client is forced to attend the dedication of the beard of the master's favourite slave: *plena domus libis venalibus: 'accipe, et istud / fermentum tibi habe'. praestare tributa clientes / cogimur et cultis augere peculia servis.* 'The house is full of cakes for sale' (sold by the slaves of the house on behalf of the master); the poor client says: 'Take the money, and keep that [the cake] as a yeast for yourself'. Then Juvenal comments: 'We clients are compelled to pay tribute money *and* to increase the savings of sleek slaves'. The interpretation depends on remembering the famous passage in Petronius (76) where Trimalchio describes how he became rich: there was a disaster, but Fortunata sold her clothes and jewelry—'that was the yeast of my savings' *(hoc fuit peculii mei fermentum)*. With this in mind, Juvenal could write simply *fermentum tibi habe*, and only explain it in his comment *augere peculia*, which picks up *istud fermentum tibi habe* just as *praestare tributa* picks up *accipe*.

of *Silvae* 5. 4. Sleep is pictured (341) as *grata laboratae referens oblivia vitae* ('bringing back welcome oblivion to a life of toil'). It is much bolder to describe what men forget in sleep as *laborata vita* than to view a man's life as a whole at its end as *fata laborati aevi*. But Valerius Flaccus supplied Statius with much linguistic inspiration. He had a unique gift for the brief surprising phrase that says far more than appears at first sight. In general, he tends to skate over horrors, and slide into a rather abstract analysis, as in the very restrained description of the women of Lemnos slaughtering their husbands (2. 220–41), or the end of the fight with Amycus (4. 303–14); and this technique of allusive description works extremely well when he has to describe the freeing of Prometheus by Hercules (5. 154–76). It also works well in a traditional set piece, the beginning of a battle, whose elements came down through Homer and Virgil and Lucan and others. Valerius is very brief (6. 182–88):

> illi ubi consertis iunxere frementia telis
> agmina virque virum galeis adflavit adactis,
> continuo hinc obitus perfractaque caedibus arma
> corporaque, alternus cruor alternaeque ruinae;   185
> volvit ager galeas et thorax egerit imbres
> sanguineos; hinc barbarici glomerantur ovatus,
> hinc gemitus, mixtaeque virum cum pulvere vitae.

When they joined the shouting lines with close-set steel and man breathed on man with helmets forced together,[63] immediately then come deaths, weapons and bodies are broken in the bloodshed, on both sides there is blood, and on both collapses (185); the plain rolls helmets, and breastplates spout showers of blood. Here barbarian cries of triumph swarm, here groans, and the lives of men are mingled with the dust.

Here he remembered Lucan in *consertis . . . telis*[64] and Virgil in *virque virum*,[65] but the rest of the details are his own, with the characteristic surprises of *adflavit*, the transitive uses of *vol-*

63. For the obsessive interest in faces inside helmets, see p. 205 above.
64. *Bellum Civile* 7. 520.
65. *Aeneid* 10. 361 *haeret pede pes densusque viro vir*. Also *Aen.* 11. 631–35, which was influential in the treatment of the topic.

vit and *egerit*, *glomerantur* of the noises rather than of the men who make them, and, finally, the pathos (and surprise) of *vitae* for *cadavera*. Lucan used Virgil (*Aen.* 10. 359–61) for his description of the beginning of the battle at Pharsalia,[66] and Statius used Virgil[67] and Valerius Flaccus and—by far the most extensively—Lucan,[68] for his battle description in *Thebaid* 8. 395–427. The only detail from Valerius is the characteristic variation and expansion (400–401): *pariter suspiria fumant, / admotaeque nitent aliena in casside cristae* ('on both sides the groanings steam,[69] and crests clashing together shine over helmets not their own'); Statius has also pushed the idea much further.[70]

Valerius Flaccus' brevity goes with novelty of phrase: for instance, 1. 207 *totusque dei* ('possessed by the god': cf. 1. 414 *plena ... rege maris* 'pregnant by Neptune'); 1. 706 *nube nova linquente domos*, of Daedalus and his son ('a strange cloud rising above the houses'); 2. 430 *spumea subsequitur fugientis semita clavi* ('the foaming track of the rudder follows the fleeing men': cf. 3. 32 *leni canebant aequora sulco*, of a ship's wake at night, 'the seas were white with a quiet furrow'); 3. 65–66 *iniqui / nube meri*, of a mind 'clouded with excess wine'; 5.108 *et magnae pelago tremit umbra Sinopes*, of a city seen from far out at sea, 'and the shadow of huge Sinope trembles over the sea' (cf. 2. 6 *fretis summas aequatum Pelion ornos / mergunt*, of the mountain sinking below the horizon, 'they sink Pelion with the ash trees on its peak made equal with the sea'); as Styrus is drowned Valerius says (8. 368) *et tandem virgine cessit* 'and finally surrendered all claim to the maiden [Medea]'.

Statius often lacks the delicacy and neatness of Valerius Flaccus in brief, surprising locutions (they often defy translation), but his aim was primarily at novelty of combination. He can

66. 7. 485–95, with 514–520 inserted between 488 and 489: see Housman ad loc.

67. Shown in a number of details, but especially in the repetitious similes 407–11 and 423–27 based on *Aeneid* 10. 356–58.

68. Details from Lucan in 398, 412, 419–20, 421.

69. See note 63 above.

70. For another example see p. 225 above.

achieve this with very ordinary words: 1. 493 *obtutu gelida ora premit* ('he holds his face frozen in its gaze'), of Adrastus as he sees the oracle fulfilled; 2. 133 *sic excitus ira | ductor in absentem consumit proelia fratrem* 'so moved by anger the leader consumes [= uses up in advance] battles against his absent brother' (cf. 10. 563 *consumpsit ventura timor*); 2. 341–42 *necdum post flammea toti | intepuere tori*, said by his new bride to Polynices (who wants to be off to Thebes): 'nor yet since our wedding has our whole bed grown warm' (they have not had time to make love enough); 3. 362–63 *ipse ego fessus | quinquaginta illis heroum immanibus umbris* 'I, tired by those huge shades of fifty heroes' (that is, tired by the slaughter of fifty heroes); 3. 625–26 *nimiusque Phoebus* 'the compelling influence of Apollo'; 4. 82 *debitus hospes* 'a guest owed (by Fate)'—that is, predicted, foreordained; 4. 532 *poenarum lucra* 'gains from crime'; 6. 268–69 *series antiqua parentum | . . . miris in vultum animata figuris* 'ancient line of ancestors. . .wonderfully portrayed in living likenesses'; 7. 112–23 *bonus omnia credi | auctor* 'a counsellor to be trusted in everything'; 7. 702 *avertit Morti contermina Virtus* 'Bravery, near neighbour to Death, distracts him'; 8. 116–17 *nec deprecor umbram | accipere* 'and I do not refuse to receive the shade' (that is, become a ghost among the dead: cf. 10. 204 *solos infecerat umbra iugales*—also of Amphiaraus—'shade had only infected his chariot team'); 9. 228–29 *stupet hospita belli | unda viros claraque armorum incenditur umbra* 'the water, a refuge from war, is terrified and set on fire by the bright shadow [i.e., reflection] of the armour'; 9. 254–55 *et stamine primo | ablatum tellure mori* 'and in his earliest life thread death on land was taken from him' (that is, he was doomed to drown); 10. 238 *infelix virtus* 'courage born of disaster'; 10. 275–76 *et galeis inclusa relinquit | murmura*, of killing sleeping men, 'he leaves their [death] sobs shut up within their helmets'; 10. 300–301 *somnique et mortis anhelitus una | volvitur* 'the gasps of sleep and death issue together' (that is, the death gasp merges with the final snore); 10. 504 *falso gurges cantatus olori* 'the river made to resound to the false swan' (i.e., Juppiter); 12. 692–94 *sed pulvere crasso. . .Tyrios iuga perdere montes | aspicit* 'he sees the peaks of the Tyrian mountains blotted out by dense dust'.

The reader is very often aware of Statius' competitiveness, of the challenges issued to his predecessors. For instance, where Roman poets from Ovid (*Met.* 2. 221) had been content, following Sophocles *Antigone* 1126 ὑπὲρ διλόφου πέτρας, to call Parnassus *biceps*, Statius (*Theb.* 1. 628) calls it *bivertex*. At *Thebaid* 2. 9 he recalls Lucan's (1. 4) *cognatasque acies* ('battle lines of kindred') but writes *cognatis ictibus* ('kindred sword thrusts') for Oedipus' murder of his father. At 2. 76–77 he wrote *anhelum | proflabant sub luce deum* of drunken men ('they snored out the panting god in the light of day'), recalling Virgil's (*Aeneid* 9. 326) *toto proflabat pectore somnum* of someone deeply asleep— 'he snored out sleep with all his chest' (= with deep breathing); 2. 223–24 *foribus tum inmissa superbis | unda fremit vulgi* ('then a tidal wave of the mob roars flooding through the royal gates') carries further and makes more complete the image in Virgil *Georgics* 2. 461–62 *si non ingentem foribus domus alta superbis | mane salutantum totis vomit aedibus undam* ('if the towering house does not from its regal gates each morning vomit out a wave of clients from every room').[71] At 6. 872 *riget arta cutis durisque laborum | castigata toris* ('his skin is tight and rigid and schooled in hardship by hard muscles'), and even more at 9. 687–88 *colla sedent nodis et castigata iubarum | libertas*, describing a horse ('his neck lies flat in knots and the controlled luxuriance of his mane', that is, his flowing mane is carefully knotted close to his neck)—in both of these passages Statius recalls Ovid's remarkable phrase about Corinna's breasts (*Amores* 1. 5. 21) *quam castigato planus sub pectore venter!* ('how flat her belly below her well-schooled bosom').

There are two further stylistic characteristics of all these writers that can be seen in many of the passages quoted above. One is the interest in avoiding concreteness of expression in favour

71. Juvenal uses the image (3. 244) of the crowd that impedes the progress of the wretched walker in a Roman street.

of abstractness; since this can be regarded also as preferring the general to the particular, it is therefore a product of the same instinct that also found expression in gnomic *sententiae*. The result is often a most striking and condensed expression. When Lucan has finished the story of the mass suicide of Vulteius and his men, he reflects on it with a deep admiration which climaxes in these words (4. 580–81): *mors, utinam pavidos vitae subducere nolles, | sed virtus te sola daret* ('Death, would that you would refuse to rescue cowards from life, but that bravery alone had you in its gift')—a splendid paradox. Valerius Flaccus, in the battle description quoted above, says (6. 200) *mixta perit virtus* ('brave men perish, mingled in the mass'). Even more astonishing is his comparison of Jason's yoking the bulls and the Lapith subduing the first horse (7. 604–6):

> non secus a medio quam si telluris hiatu
> terga recentis equi primumque invasit habenis
> murmur et in summa Lapithes apparuit Ossa.

Just as when a Lapith invaded the back of a horse fresh from the midst of a gaping hole in the earth and (invaded) its first neighing with reins and appeared on the top of Ossa.

The zeugma of *invasit* pales before *murmur* for 'the neighing mouth'. Statius describes a landslide as (7. 746) *desilit horrendus campo timor* ('a fearful terror leaps down on the plain'); or the enemy asleep as (10. 214) *bellum iacet* ('war lies on the ground'); or a tiger leaping on its prey as (12. 172) *illa fames* ('that appetite'—that is, that ravening beast).[72]

The other characteristic stands in strong contrast with the practice of Augustan poets. With them words are often allowed

---

72. Cf. Juvenal 2. 119–20 *ingens cena sedet* 'a crowd sits down to dinner'; or 3. 16 *mendicat silva* 'the wood is full of beggars'. When Juvenal wrote (as I have no doubt he did) in 1. 144 *hinc subitae mortes atque intestata senectus*, he was experimenting with such abstract locutions: cf., for example, Adaeus *Anth. Pal.* 7. 51. 3 Ἅιδης καὶ γῆρας (of the manner of an old man's dying), or Crinagoras *Anth. Pal.* 9. 439. 3–4 ἀτυμβεύτου θανάτοιο / λείψανον (of a skull: 'a relic of unburied death'). Greek poets led the way in such experiments.

to suggest more than they precisely express: words are given such freedom that they are liberated from the tyranny of a context that demands a single sense on a single occasion, and they are allowed the full range of their associative potentialities.[73] Pretty well the opposite is true of the post-Virgilian epic poets or of Tacitus: key words are used in a single precise significance which is totally determined by the context; the literary interest comes from the demand on reader or audience to find the precise sense of the key word. This is the gap that the audience was left to close, and it was deliberately widened by using words of wide semantic field as key words, and even by artificially widening their field (for instance, by the very common practice of using simple verbs in the place of compound verbs). In that way locutions could be made to seem more oracular and significant than they really were, and the gap between expression and sense was the vehicle of the relevant aesthetic pleasure.

The stylistic devices analyzed in this section belong not to a literature of meditation and reflection, but to a literature of immediate impact: the aim was to stun, astonish, thrill, puzzle, impress with each relevant emotion an audience that was trained to respond to subtleties and attuned to recognize the stimuli. It was this training that encouraged writers to the invention of locutions that puzzled by various devices, some of which were discussed above; others are easily identified, such as periphrasis,[74] or the use of strange names for peoples, derived from the intricate background of myth or geography. A vast increase of mythological erudition was required to read Statius, for example, or Silius Italicus, both of whom delight in this latter device. Quintilian fully recognized the deliberation of this obscurity and condemned it;[75] but he was training barristers for real cases (or so he hoped) and valued clarity above all else.[76] His views were irrelevant to audiences who collected to experience the

73. See, for instance, Williams (1968), 768.
74. See, for instance, Kroll (1924), 266–67.
75. 8. 2. 12–21.
76. 8. 2. 22.

aesthetic pleasures of these very obscurities. The process of producing obscurity hardened, during the period beginning with Ovid's *Metamorphoses*, into a series of rhetorical techniques, and rhetoric achieved a new definition that was anathema to Quintilian. To the immediacy of trained and expectant response in the audience these writers also equally directed the use of figures like hyperbole and paradox, and the whole range of emotional effects that they commanded. They had redefined the function of literature, and Persius' first satire was a protest against the redefinition, to which, however, he was himself nonetheless fully committed.

3. *Genre and personality*

This new conception of the function of literature affected also the writer's attitude to the relationship between material and style. In Greek literature down to the end of the fifth century, subject matter and style had both been determined by genre.[77] But that relationship broke down in Hellenistic literature so that subject matter was no longer strictly differentiated by genre, though, to a large extent, style was. Such was the situation also in Rome up to the time of Augustus, and it can be seen, for instance, in the difference between the *Eclogues* and the *Aeneid*, or between Horace's *Satires* or *Epistles* and his *Odes*: in the case of each writer there is a certain community of subject matter possible between the different works, but these works are sharply distinguished from one another stylistically.

The process went further in the following period: while subject matter virtually ceased to be a differentia of genre by Augustan times, style also ceased to be a differentia of genre in the early Empire. In his *Aeneid*, Virgil made two entries (apart from conventional appeals to Muses and gods for inspiration)[78] in his own person: one after the deaths of Nisus and Euryalus

77. On this see especially Kroll (1924), chap. 9, 'Die Kreuzung der Gattungen', and Rossi (1971).
78. 1.1 ff; 6. 264–67; 7. 37–45; 9. 525–28.

(9. 446–49) and the other before the death of Lausus (10. 791–93). Ovid did not make lengthy personal entrances in *Metamorphoses*, except in the opening invocation and the unusual final σφραγίς. Lucan, however, makes extensive and highly personal entrances into his epic, and those increase in extent and boldness after the battle of Pharsalia. At 7. 209–13, he considers the possibility that his poem will contribute to the fame of Pharsalia, as he pictures future readers reliving the events as though they were still to come and still favouring Pompey. At 7. 768, where even later writers would use the generalizing second person singular, Lucan speculates in his own person (*putem*).[79] At 7. 803–24, he addresses Caesar and gives him advice. At 8. 842–45, Lucan expresses the extraordinary wish that Rome would request him to exhume and rebury Pompey in Italy.[80] During his account of the African campaign, Lucan stops in the middle of Cato's march to give his own assessment of Cato (9. 593–604), even expressing a personal preference to lead such a march rather than enjoy three triumphs. At 9. 680, he expresses his own view of Medea's poison (*rear*). But later in the same book, he again addresses Caesar (980–86):

> o sacer et magnus vatum labor! omnia fato
> eripis et populis donas mortalibus aevum.
> invidia sacrae, Caesar, ne tangere famae;
> nam, si quid Latiis fas est promittere Musis,
> quantum Zmyrnaei durabunt vatis honores,
> venturi me teque legent; Pharsalia nostra
> vivet, et a nullo tenebris damnabimur aevo.

O great and sacred task of poets! You rescue everything from death, and give life to mortal peoples. Be not touched by jealousy of that sacred fame, Caesar; for if the Muses of Latium may promise anything, then, as long as the memory of the bard of Smyrna

79. See p. 206 above.
80. Lucan seems not to have known the detail reported by Plutarch (*Pompey* 80) that Pompey's remains (τὰ λείψανα), perhaps meaning 'ashes', were given to Cornelia and buried by her on his Alban estate. Cf. 7. 411, where he asserts that Pharsalia does not occur in the Roman calendar—it did.

shall last, future generations shall read me and about you: our Pharsalia shall live, and no lapse of time shall condemn us to oblivion.

What is so extraordinary here is the way in which Lucan joins his hated hero to confer immortality on him and share it with him, calling Pharsalia, as it appears in the epic, a joint effort, waged by Caesar, told by Lucan.

This account of the *Bellum Civile* has not included innumerable authorial interventions by way of explanation, exclamation, and intensification. To some extent, Lucan might be thought to be in a unique position since he was historian as well as epic poet, and history naturally allowed authorial intervention and use of the first person singular. But what Lucan does goes far beyond anything to be found in any Roman or Greek historian; for he thrusts his personality on the audience. It has been suggested that the explanation lies in Lucan's combining of the two genres of epic and didactic.[81] But that is only to restate the problem in different terms. Why did Lucan want to alter the epic tradition in this way? Besides, later Latin epic poets, like Valerius Flaccus and Statius, make use of authorial interventions on Lucan's pattern. Valerius confines this to his account of the women of Lemnos, where he wonders if he can do justice to Hypsipyle and make her fame last as long as the Roman Empire (2. 242–46, closely based on Lucan 9. 980–86). Earlier (2. 216–19), he had expressed horror at the story he was about to tell, and wished that someone would stop him.

Statius frequently indulges in authorial comment which is delivered in his own person, though he does not use the first person singular. Thus he indignantly asks about the power of Fama (2. 212–13), or intersperses comment with narrative (2. 482–95), or turns aside, with an apostrophe (a favourite device of authorial comment in Statius), to reflect on bravery in the face of the tyrant (3. 99–113, and, again, 216–17). At 3. 551–65, he turns completely aside to speculate with the audience (553 *feras*) on the origin of the craving to know the future; this reads like a

81. For example, Dams (1970), 56–62, 220 ff.

passage of Juvenal (that is, it is closer to the genre of satire).[82] Before his account of the Lemnians' murder of their husbands, he makes his narrator (Hypsipyle) hesitate before the horrors (5. 34–37, like Valerius).[83] Authorial pathos, again introduced by apostrophe, reflects on the infant's death (5. 534–37), and, later, on Hypsipyle's future (5. 710–14). At 6. 934–37 and 938–46 he ends the book with foreboding authorial comment on, and interpretation of, omens. At 8. 162 there is an extraordinary appeal to the reader or audience: *quae tibi tunc facies postquam permissa gemendi / copia?* ('What do you think their faces looked like when opportunity for grief was given?'). This is a far more surprising address than the use of the generalizing second person singular (as in 9. 218 *audisse accensumque putes*—'you would think he had heard and was inflamed'), which is of a type that is quite common in Ovid's *Metamorphoses*.[84] At 10. 445–48, Statius not only imitates Virgil's apostrophe on the death of Nisus and Euryalus, but actually refers to it, and declares himself an inferior to Virgil. At 10. 827–36, Statius appeals to the Muses for help with the story of Capaneus, but also reflects on the task in a self-conscious literary way, whetting the audience's appetite. At 11. 648–60, Statius indulges a very Lucanian authorial reflection on tyranny. Finally, just before the final σφραγίς (which is an imitation of Ovid's), Statius ends the *Thebaid* by more self-conscious literary laments on his own lack of power to take the story any further; this is a highly emotional passage, and it neatly gets around the problem (virtually insoluble) of finding a convincingly conclusive ending.

These poets altered the epic conventions by removing some of its traditional restraints. It would be true to say that the epic now behaved more like didactic poetry, but the reason for this is what matters. The epic poet no longer felt it appropriate for him to adopt a remote and impersonal stance: he felt in close

82. But the material is largely taken from Lucan's wish that god had not made it possible to foretell the future—2. 1–15.
83. Cf. 5. 218–19.
84. E.g., *Met.* 6. 23.

touch with his audience, able to share his feelings with them,
or declare his own personal opinion. As a result, a number of
passages of Lucan read more like satire than epic: for instance,
the reflections on the moral state of Rome (1. 158–82) or the surprising excursus on thirst and avarice after the battle of Ilerda
(4. 363–81). Petronius was hitting shrewdly at his target when
he had Eumolpus recite a *de bello civili* in which satiric elements
are prominent.[85] But the reason for this is not that Lucan assimilated the genres of epic and satire; it was that, indulging in
personal reflection, he could not but sound like a satirist on certain topics. There are passages in the other epic poets that recall
other genres: for instance, Valerius Flaccus reports Orpheus'
song about Io; this is composed in a form and style strongly suggestive of bucolic.[86] Exactly the same can be said of the passage
(7. 162–211) where Silius Italicus turns aside from his theme (as
Hannibal provides the opportunity by entering Campania) to
tell the story of Falernus. It is also notable that Statius is particularly partial to a type of word order that Virgil virtually invented for bucolic poetry:[87] again and again Statius uses the pattern (3. 207) *immeritos patriae tot culmina cives*, which Virgil
only used in a very simplified form in the *Georgics* and avoided
in the *Aeneid*. Valerius Flaccus uses it occasionally,[88] and it is
even used by Juvenal.[89]

Not only do these features all point to the fact that in general
genre distinctions had broken down, but they also indicate that
the controlling impulse in the epic poets' use of the new freedom
was the novel intimacy between poet and audience; subordinate
factors were the desire for variety and variation, and the poet's

85. *Sat.* 118–24.
86. *Argonautica* 4. 344–421.
87. Williams (1968), 317–18 and 726–28.
88. E.g., 6. 94 *veterumque viris hortamina laudes*, 138 *turiferos felicia
regna Sabaeos*. Even Silius uses it: e.g., 1. 27 *Agamemnoniam gratissima
tecta Mycenen*; 1. 322 *hydro imbutas bis noxia tela sagittas*.
89. E.g., 7. 118 *virides scalarum gloria palmae*, 120 *veteres Maurorum
epimenia bulbi*; 11. 194–95 *similisque triumpho | praeda caballorum prae-
tor*; 13. 157 *custos Gallicus urbis*; (cf. 187–89 *felix. . .omnes prima docens
rectum sapientia*).

desire to exercise his powers over the widest possible poetic resources. But, basically, what sounds like bucolic or like satire or like didactic poetry is to be interpreted as the poet's using what means he can for inserting his own personality into his epic in pathos or comment. This was certainly the reason for the enormous increase in the use of apostrophe[90] by poets from Ovid onwards. Apostrophe had been a feature of neoteric style, but its use was infrequent and restrained in Virgil's *Aeneid*. Ovid, however, used it for a whole range of effects from humour[91] to pathos. The figure has often been judged to be a mere metrical device, but the inadequacy of this view is shown by Lucan's use of it, which far exceeds that of any other poet. The effectiveness of apostrophe is shown clearly, for instance, at the beginning of the passage 5. 722–815, which, in style and subject matter, is more reminiscent of love elegy than epic, and is far removed from Virgil's treatment of the love theme in *Aeneid* 4. The subject is the love and parting of Pompey and Cornelia, and Lucan works himself into the necessary emotional change of tone by apostrophes at the outset to the two lovers. Lucan uses apostrophe with more variety and genuine emotional impulse than the other epic poets, with whom it tends to broaden into a technique, but the motive is the same: the figure enabled the poet to inject his own personality into the narrative by joining his subject in immediate confrontation.

For this reason, speakers in epic are also allowed to use apostrophe, as, for instance, Vulteius in his speech exulting in the prospect of suicide (4. 476–520); not only is the speaker exhibiting his own emotion, but the poet is also impersonating the speaker. Hence Seneca in his tragedies uses apostrophe on the same scale as Lucan; for he is really writing speeches for himself—he is the omnipresent actor in all parts of all his plays. Quintilian makes an observation which has the widest possible application to the

90. See Quintilian 9. 2. 38–39 and 3. 24–27; but Quintilian is unhelpful on apostrophe. Endt (1905) gives a detailed, but essentially unenlightening, analysis.

91. E.g., *Met.* 10. 44.

whole of this period when he says:[92] 'It is indeed of the greatest importance for declaimers to consider what best suits each character, for they very seldom act as advocates in their own *controversiae*; they generally act the parts of sons or parents or rich men or old men or of harsh or kindly people or of misers or finally of superstitious, cowardly, or satiric persons. The result is that comic actors probably do not have to assume more roles on the stage than declaimers do in their performances'. The most useful way to view the new relationship between writer and audience is to see the poet as the actor of his poetry. The effect was far-reaching and twofold. First, the writer now saw an important part of his function as the presentation of his own personality to the audience. Second, he was no longer just the mediator of ideas to his audience, for his own emotional reaction to the ideas became an essential element in his subject matter. For there is a distinction to be made between the writer's putting the reader in immediate contact with a concrete situation and his allowing the situation first to generate emotion within himself so that he focusses the audience's attention on his own emotion. Put another way, it is the distinction, on the one hand, between the writer's energetically confronting ideas that naturally arouse his feelings, but only as a by-product of the intellectual vigour, and, on the other hand, the writer's searching for ideas that will excite interesting sensations in him vividly enough for him to communicate them to an audience. The former is characteristic of the main Classical tradition; the latter is the way of the early Empire, though, in some ways, it can be viewed as a continuation of the style, for instance, of Catullus 64.[93] The second effect followed from the first, but was more variable, being more true of some writers than of others.

Apostrophe was not admitted in historical writing, and Velleius Paterculus, as he commits apostrophe, apologizes[94]—it is

92. 3. 8. 51.
93. On the part played by the personality of the poet in the composition of Catullus 64, see Williams (1968), 226–29 and 699–705.
94. 2. 66. 3.

Antony's fault that he strays outside decorum: *cogit enim ex-cedere propositi formam operis erumpens animo ac pectore indignatio* ('indignation, bursting from my heart and soul, compels me to stray outside the stylistic norm of my chosen work'). When Tacitus broke into apostrophe to Agricola (45. 3), he was directly imitating a famous passage of Cicero,[95] and he did not do it again. But it is odd how often Tacitus deliberately enters his own work.

In general, Tacitus took Sallust as his model; but it is notable in Sallust that after half a dozen emphatic personal entrances in the *Catiline*[96] (excluding the prooemium and narrative devices that do no more than represent footnotes in modern works), there is only one in the *Jugurtha* (95), where Sallust gives his own view of Sulla. The trend to impersonality seems to have continued in the *Histories*. The opposite is the case with Tacitus. Apart from uses of the first person singular that are no more than equivalent to footnotes, there is only one major personal entrance in the *Histories*; it is at 2. 37–38, where Tacitus takes the opportunity (provided by his reporting the view of earlier writers that the soldiers really wanted peace) to trace the degeneracy of the present age to an instinctive love of power.[97] There are one or two minor entrances: at 3. 25 and 3. 51 two parallel pathetic stories of death in civil war are given personal introductions. In the *Annals*, however, there are a whole series of emphatic personal entrances, and there is a further difference between the personal entrances in the *Annals* and those in the earlier works; in the *Annals* Tacitus tends to use the first person plural where he used the singular before.[98] At 2. 88 Tacitus uses a report that poison was forbidden as a weapon against Arminius to praise Tiberius explicitly in his own person—the unusual circumstances warranting a personal entrance, which he then uses

95. *de oratore* 3. 12.
96. In 6, 7, 14, 36, 48, and 53.
97. Here Tacitus carefully refutes a widespread view by presenting an analysis of his own that is intended to be exemplary for the special terms in which (in Tacitus' view) the period ought to be explained.
98. See Wölfflin (1933), 25–26.

further to pronounce a laudatory obituary on Arminius, with
a dismissive comment on Greek writers who do not know of him:
*Graecorum annalibus ignotus qui sua tantum mirantur, Ro-
manis haud perinde celebris dum vetera extollimus recentium
incuriosi* ('unknown to self-admiring Greek historians, and not
well known to Romans since we extol the past at the expense of
the present'). At 3. 18. 4, when the name of Claudius is first written into the senate's records, the author presents himself as a
wry and brooding cynic: 'The more I reflect on events both recent and long past, the more I become aware of the mockery in
human affairs pervading all our concerns. You see, rumour, ex-
pectation, and obsequiousness backed every possible candidate
for the position of emperor, except the very one who was destined to be emperor and whom Fortune was keeping under
wraps'. The self-dramatizing emotionality of this is remarkable,
but the same quality can be seen in his reflection on the function of his history (3. 65. 1–2), or in the extraordinary pessimism
of his low assessment of his subject matter (4. 32–33). In 4. 71. 1–2,
he whets the audience's appetite by confessing his eagerness to
anticipate and tell immediately of certain deaths, but he carefully restrains himself. At 6. 22, he indulges in a lengthy and
emotional reflection on Fate and Necessity and the part they
play in human affairs. At 16. 16, there is an emotional defence,
allowing due place to satiety and cynicism, of his recounting the
series of ignoble deaths, combined with reflection on *ira illa
numinum in res Romanas*. All of these (and other) entrances
serve to present the historian to his audience as a discernible
personality—deeply brooding, pessimistic, with a sense of doom
spiced by a cynical view of human nature. The entrances body
out the voice that is constantly heard in pithy comment on events
and characters. Nothing could be further from the technique of
the mature Sallust, but then that is equally true of Tacitus' capacity for melodramatic exploitation of the irrational (such as
the suggestion that the gods provided a suitable night to expose
the murder of Agrippina,[99] or that Nero had offended the gods),[100]

99. *Annals* 14. 5. 1.   100. *Annals* 14. 22. 4.

or his expansive and emotional dwelling on scenes of horror (like the scenes at the last stand of the Vitellians in the streets of Rome).[101] The historian seized opportunities to affect his audience.

In fact, the very style of Tacitus can be viewed as a vehicle carefully designed, with all its Sallustian features, to convey the author's assumed personality to the audience; the consistency of the work strikes home as a consistency of viewpoint and personality. And there is no reason whatever to doubt that Tacitus recited his historical works to an audience, and that their impact in those circumstances was a primary consideration in their composition.[102] It is significant that in the one work where Tacitus explicitly withdrew his own person behind those of his friends and superiors he chose a modified form of Ciceronian prose as the vehicle. That choice was not a passive, genre-dictated acceptance of convention, as is usually asserted by those who do not doubt the work as Tacitus'; it was a style which, while giving no hint of the author's personality, could yet be used in a modest way, by restrained variations, to characterize the protagonists in the *Dialogus*. The picture of Tacitus meekly submissive to convention has always been implausible: he used convention to his own ends.

Various ways of analyzing the different prose styles of the early Empire have been applied. The *tria genera dicendi* can do no more than categorize writers more or less roughly, and the real function of the distinction was theoretical.[103] Still less useful is the supposed distinction between Atticism and Asianism. It is clear from Quintilian's discussion of it[104] that the distinction was obsolete and belonged to long-dead literary history; but he does make the very important point that the difference represented by the two labels, Attic and Asianic, should be referred to differences in audiences. Characteristic of the literature of the

101. *Hist.* 3. 82–85.
102. On recitation of history, see Pliny *Epp.* 1. 13. 3; 7. 17. 3; 9. 27. 1.
103. See Quintilian 12. 10 (esp. 58 ff.); Quadlbauer (1958).
104. 12. 10. 16; see Austin (1954) ad loc.

early Empire was a breakdown of the old basic distinction between poetry and prose; poetry came to be regarded as prose in
metre, and prose claimed a right to the whole spectrum of linguistic resources. There were limits imposed by considerations
of *decorum*, and orators, for instance, would hesitate to use
archaisms that would, however, be acceptable in epic or history—
though in both cases choice was virtually limited to archaisms
which had been sanctioned by Virgil on the one hand and by
Sallust on the other. Writers could be found at any time who
advocated Atticism—theoretically at least; but basically all were
calculating how best to make an immediate impact on a sophisticated audience. Tacitus characterized the aim in the hostile
words of Messalla:[105] 'You cannot call it an orator's, indeed not
even a man's, style that most barristers of our time use, so that,
by self-indulgence in vocabulary, triviality in ideas, and licentiousness in structure, they express tones suited to actors'. That is
certainly hostile, but it is basically true: writers composed with a
view to acting their works before an audience, and each constructed an idiosyncratic style, best suited, in his view, to convey
a sense of his individual personality to the audience. It is that
which explains the close similarity between Pliny's style in his
Letters and in his *Panegyric*,[106] and, no doubt, if his other
speeches had been preserved they would show the same style.
Pliny had created a verbal personality for himself. Much of
Quintilian's hostility to Seneca[107] can be put down to Seneca's
success in creating the most idiosyncratic style for himself, a
style that does not vary from his *Dialogues* to his *Epistles*, and can
even be seen appearing in metrical garb in the tragedies; it is
a grossly self-indulgent, self-admiring style, but it not only excellently conveys the sense of a character watching himself speak,
it is the effective expression of a tangible personality.[108] To

105. *Dialogus* 26. 2.
106. See especially Durry (1938), 68–72.
107. 10. 1. 125 ff.
108. See especially A. D. Leeman (1963), chap. 11, and, e.g., H. Mac L.
Currie (1966), 78 f.

Seneca ideas were not recalcitrant matter to be wrestled with and transmitted, but triggers of emotion within himself; and it was these emotions that formed his primary subject matter.[109] The same demand on the writer to create an effective personality produced similar results in poetry. These can be seen clearly, for instance, in satire. As a genre it had been given stylistic and metrical differentiae by Horace. Both were abandoned by Persius and Juvenal. Where Horace, for example, wrote one line that ended with a monosyllable (which was not preceded by a monosyllable) in every ten lines of his *Satires*, Persius wrote less than one in a hundred, and Juvenal just over three in a hundred. Both writers assimilated their metrical technique to that of Ovid in his *Metamorphoses*, with a very occasional bow in the direction of satirical informality. The type of line which produces a clash of ictus and accent in the fifth foot occurs slightly more often in Persius (just over one and a half percent), but it is almost non-existent in Juvenal, apart from Greek words and proper names; yet, even in the second book of Horace's *Satires*, such lines exceed eight percent. The same applies to their styles: both occasionally indulge a vulgar word to show the distinguishing privilege of satire, but in general their style is not conversational; it is that of Roman epic poetry as it had been established by Virgil and Ovid. The creation of a personality that would make a distinct impact on their sort of audiences needed the full range of epic language and its grand tones, whatever type of poetry was being composed. The one exception was the epigrammatic poetry of Martial, in which there was no time to make a specifically lin-

---

109. See Seneca's own description of the way in which inspiration seized him and transported him stylistically: *de tranq. an.* 1. 14 and 17. 10–11. Guillemin (1954), 259 ff. analyzes Seneca's style as a revision of Cicero's, controlled by three factors: a substitution of parataxis for hypotaxis, use of *sublimitas*, and a new theory of imitation which she finds expressed also by Dionysius of Halicarnassus and pseudo-Longinus. This is, as always with M. Guillemin, an illuminating hypothesis, but it is open to objection on the ground of paying more heed to what Seneca says than to what he does (see Currie (1966), 76 and n. 6): cf. also Guillemin (1957). The possibility of direct influence by diatribe needs notice, but is somewhat exaggerated in the latter article, as also in Albertini (1923) and in Oltramare (1926).

guistic impact on an audience: his impact was made by the poker face and the sudden *sententia*.

For these reasons genre distinction virtually disappeared both in prose and poetry as did even the basic distinction between prose and poetry. Instead, a linguistic continuum was established that was nearly the same for all writers, with exceptions governed by *decorum*, such that, for instance, historians could use—indeed were obliged to use—archaisms, and satirists a certain modest range of low words. It was not the writer's aim to express ideas or concrete situations directly through a distinct linguistic personality; rather ideas and situations were allowed to generate emotions in the writer, and it was these emotions that became the object of his attention. The writer thus became an actor whose function it was to arouse in an audience the emotions that he worked up in himself. This may have been a new situation for Roman literature in the first century A.D., but it was one to which Greek writers had long become accustomed,[110] and that is why audiences at Rome received Greeks with such enthusiasm.

Some puzzling features of the literature of the early Empire become clear when literary activity is viewed as a relationship between a performing writer and an expectant audience—for instance, the incoherence and the sheer lack of clues to the connection of thought in Persius' satires, and the difficulty (indeed, sometimes, impossibility) of deciding who is speaking. Persius would have justified all this by appeal to the informality of Horatian *sermo*. But that has nothing of incoherence in it: it is poetry of reflection and meditation, not an address to an audience—the reader overhears Horace talking to himself. Among various reasons why Persius did not realize the difference is the fact that he wrote with an audience in mind and relied on his own modulations of tone of voice to mark the transitions. This principle applies to most of the literature of the period. A small indication of it is the frequency with which epic poets fail to make textually clear the subjects of sentences, often relying

110. See Zwierlein (1966), 127 ff.

on a pronoun, which is ambiguous to a reader, to refer to a subject that has not been mentioned for some time.[111] These are
characteristically places where a reciter's tonal inflection would
be sufficient indication to an audience of the intended subject.
A fairly exact analogy can be seen in the way in which Cicero
varies the object of his address in his speeches without warning,
and, equally without textual warning, shifts from a second-person
address to reference to the same individual in the third person.
These are places where the speaker would turn or gesture. The
same technique can be seen in Pliny's *Panegyric*.[112] The texts,
however, in which readers have to be most careful to visualize a
speaker and his movements and gestures are those of Plautus
and Terence.[113] What was new in the early Empire was that this
technique came to be used automatically in formal poetry.

This constant sense of the writer's voice, speaking the words,
varying his tone, and acting out the ideas will also explain the
very puzzling way in which Juvenal can turn aside into parentheses, which the ordinary reader picks up with difficulty—if at
all. For instance, Housman was not the first to diagnose a lacuna
between lines 131 and 132 of *Satire* 1, and his diagnosis is now
generally approved and assumed without question.[114] But the

---

111. For instance, Lucan: 6. 110 *cernit* (the subject, Caesar, is not stated);
6. 300 *ipse* is Pompey; 7. 460 ff. (no subject mentioned after a digression);
8. 610–12 (the subject, Pompey, is not stated). Valerius Flaccus: 1. 129
superaddit (change of subject without warning); 1. 348 *ille* is Jason; 3. 483
cessante viro must be Hercules; 4. 133–98 (Valerius Flaccus seems to have
invented the meeting with Dymas, but Dymas is only casually mentioned at
187); 4. 531 *ipse* is Phineus. Statius: 2. 451–52 (Tydeus is to be understood
as subject); 7. 468 *ille* must be Oedipus; 7. 818 *illum* is Amphiaraus, last
mentioned in 788 (but 815 *vati*); 9. 683 *illum* is to be identified from 570 ff.;
11. 9 *ille* is Capaneus. Silius Italicus: 1. 340 Hannibal is to be understood
as subject (not mentioned for 30 lines); 1. 508–9 the subject is changed
without warning.

112. E.g., 39. 4, and Durry (1938) ad loc.

113. For example, in *Eunuchus* 615–28 Terence has used various forms
of *ille* without explanation, making understanding difficult for the mere
reader.

114. Not, however, by Clausen in his OCT; he merely mentions Housman's suggestion in the *apparatus criticus*.

difficulty occurs towards the end of the great digression on the
sportula. The poet's eye has been caught by detail after detail
and, finally, by the well-to-do who come to collect the dole, rid-
ing in a line of *lecticae*, wives, even if sick or pregnant, accompanying their husbands. At that point he cannot resist the
anecdote of the fraudulent use of a sedan to claim for a non-
existent wife. This is a characteristic expansion by means of a
parenthesis (123–26). By now, even this poet senses that he should
be returning to his main theme, greed, and he intends to do
that by picking up (from 94–95) the dining habits of the rich.
But the exposition is firmly stuck in early morning (the time at
which Juvenal has imagined the *sportula* being collected). He
needs, therefore, to get to the evening, and so he races through
the rest of the day, with the clients accompanying the rich man
to the Forum, the law courts, the statues of the *triumphatores*—
at this point he once again cannot resist another scurrilous
parenthesis to add a completely irrelevant detail (the parenthesis
occupies two and a half lines: *inter quas. . .meiiere fas est*). Now
(132) he is at last where he needs to be: the tired clients, having
hopefully followed their lord home (that did not need stating
specifically), are dismissed unfed; and then the great man dines,
alone. The coherence of this very complex movement of ideas
only had the changing tone of the poet's delivery to make it clear.

4. *The cult of the episode*

The *Metamorphoses* of Ovid was a model of the greatest influence for at least a century in many ways, but especially as an
exemplary structure. It consists of a series of more or less dis-
connected episodes, which the poet, with great wit and ingenuity,
has welded into a (1. 4) *perpetuum carmen* in defiance of Callimachus. This was done in various ways.[115] First, most obviously,
there is the skilful linking of episodes so that one seems to lead
inevitably to the next. Second, collections of episodes are held
together by subject matter, or geography, or narrator (in book

115. A good analysis by Coleman (1971).

10, for instance, Orpheus narrates a series of stories), or by internal mythic relationship. Third, there is a sketchy chronological progression from Chaos to the Roman Empire and Augustus. Fourth, there is a double ring composition—not only the obvious one between the personal opening (1. 1–4) and the even more personal σφραγίς, but also between the series of references to Augustus in book 1 and the explicit appearance of Augustus in book 15. This is a new kind of poetry: a reader can take it up at any point, and, provided he is careful to identify the beginning of an episode, he can read without needing to know what has preceded—in fact, straight progress through the work is probably the worst way to treat it; its essential lack of unity breeds tedium. More important, perhaps, the poet could perform a suitable section from the work without irrelevant puzzling of his audience.

The work of the same name by Apuleius, about a century and a half later, shows the same type of episodic composition, again held together both by a ring composition between the transformation into an ass and the initiation into the cult of Isis and by themes such as that of *curiositas* that keep appearing in the main narrative[116] and also in various stories and descriptions loosely connected to it. In between the two *Metamorphoses*, all major works show the influence of this type of composition. Even on the basis of the small proportion that has survived, it is certain that Petronius' novel was of this episodic type, with similar devices used to hold it together. This type of composition was well recognized in rhetoric.[117]

Much more surprising is the epic of Lucan, for here was a subject with an obvious narrative unity—the same unity that the subject has in Caesar's own history of the civil war and that Livy, Lucan's main source, certainly had in at least the same degree. Yet again and again Lucan has broken up the clear unity by inserting alien episodes. Some of these are mere mythology, like (4. 581–660) the account of Antaeus, produced on the thin pretext of explaining the name, or (9. 348–67) the account of Tri-

116. See especially Wlosok (1969).   117. Quintilian 10. 1. 21.

tonis, or (9. 619–99) the mythical explanation of the origin of snakes in Libya. The description of the Delphic oracle and of its consultation by Appius (5. 65–236) is similar, but it also expresses Lucan's fascination with the numinous and mysterious, which was the cause of many digressions: 1. 584–695, the sacrifice of Aruns and the prophecies of Nigidius Figulus and the frenzied matron; 3. 399–452, the description of the Druidic grove and its felling by Caesar; and 6. 413–830, on Thessalian witchcraft and Sextus Pompeius' consultation of Erichtho. Some digressions are due to a fascination with horrific aspects of death, such as the deaths at the sea battle off Massilia (3. 583–751), or the variety of deaths by snakebite (9. 700–838). Some, again, are parades of knowledge, like the description of Thessaly (6. 333–412), or (10. 172–331) Achoreus' lecture on the causes of the Nile's flooding, or the extraordinary excursus (8. 331–453) on the Parthians and their sexual habits, motivated by a passing suggestion of Pompey's that the defeated might look for allies there. Others are deliberate expansions of unimportant incidents such as (4. 402–581) the suicide of Vulteius and his men, or (5. 476–677) Caesar's attempt to reach Italy by small boat (only inference tells the reader that he landed at the same place that he embarked), or Caesar's visit to Troy (9. 950–1003), or (10. 1–52) Caesar's thoughts at the tomb of Alexander.

There must have been at least two reasons for discarding a ready-made unity in favour of a deliberately contrived disunity, of such a kind that the major part of the epic is constructed from digressions. First, connectedness of plot—such that it formed a story with a linear progression from beginning, through middle, to end—must have been something to avoid rather than seek; and, as a corollary, there must have been a premium on episodic construction. It is easy to see—and understandable—that Lucan picked out a series of major conflicts leading to Pharsalia and omitted everything else. So he chose Caesar's march on Rome, the siege of Massilia, the Ilerda campaign, Curio's defeat in Africa, and Pompey's breaking out of Caesar's ring in Epirus. And it was natural that each should be worked up into a brilliant and self-contained episode. But that does not explain all the digressions, each itself a self-contained episode. The choice of episodic structure must have been for the benefit of the audience at public performances, desirable not only for the constantly changing variety of topic and style and tone, but, perhaps even more, for the possibility of beginning and leaving off at almost any point without loss.

Second, Lucan was also able to achieve his own kind of unity by this deliberate destruction of the historical plot. This can be seen in one of the most extraordinary digressions. Book 2 opens, after the author has deplored the existence of omens and the means of foretelling the future, with a series of lamenting figures that reaches a climax with an old man who can remember the civil war of Marius and Sulla; he then recounts this (68–232) in great detail (and is particularly lavish with bloody horrors). The relevance of the speech comes in its climax: 'What is going to happen this time will be much worse, since Caesar and Pompey already have as much as Marius and Sulla'. This note of foreboding fills the first half of the poem, constantly iterated in different ways. This is the function of the digression on prophecies in 1. 584–695, and the frenzied matron is introduced so that the vision of doom can be carried allusively beyond Pharsalia to Philippi. In fact, Lucan, by destroying the historical unity of plot, has created a more artistic and emotional unity: before Pharsalia, everything looks forward to it, and after Pharsalia, everything looks back to it. The historical perspective of the poem is based on the view that Pharsalia settled the destiny of Rome right up to the time at which the poem is being written.

A closely related, equally emotional, theme intertwines with this: that is Lucan's conception of Cato. He makes a memorable single-line entry in book 1 (128), and then a massive appearance in book 2 (234–391) with the consultation by Brutus, followed by the remarriage to Marcia—of no historical value at all but of the greatest importance in the emotional unity of this theme, stressing Cato's self-discipline and asceticism. The strange account of the marriage (350–80) has often been ridiculed since the ceremony occupies twenty lines, seventeen of which describe what they did not do; but this, apart from the general poetic interest in lists, reinforces the self-deprivation and single-mindedness of Cato, who is the standard by which every judgement is measured. Despite the fact that his next effective appearance is not till book 9, his presence is now continuously felt.

Such an emotional unity is most effective in holding the poem together over all the successive digressions; it also creates a general consistency of tone, such that, wherever one happens to begin reading, the foreboding sense of doom quickly takes hold. It is a poem as intellectually strong as it is emotionally, and, though Lucan is certainly self-indulgent, the sense of a mind that has energetically confronted the facts before succumbing to emotion is powerfully conveyed.

In the *Thebaid* Statius had a unified theme with a fairly simple linear movement. But, like Lucan, he deliberately broke this up in two ways. First, by digressions, of which the most astonishing is the introduction of Hypsipyle. This is almost a minor epic in itself, extending from 4. 646 to 7. 226, and it is given its own unity by ring composition: it opens with Bacchus in action (4. 646–723) and ends with Bacchus' pleas to Juppiter. Statius no doubt invented this particular mythical link that brought Hypsipyle to Nemea, and he motivates her entrance by an implausible invention: Bacchus blocks up all rivers to destroy the expedition, but leaves one free which is known to Hypsipyle. The drought was part of the tradition; the action of Bacchus was Statius' invention. The digression is connected internally to the main narrative by two themes: the pyre is regarded by the Argive army as (6. 87) *infausti. . .atra piacula belli*, and the games are used to foreshadow the fates of the seven heroes. There are also many minor digressions: for instance, on the prehistory of the necklace of Harmonia (2. 265–305); Amphiaraus is even allowed, in the course of a prayer to Juppiter, to explain how obscure is the origin of the custom of augury (3. 482–96), and this is followed by a long description (502–47) of fantastic bird behaviour;[118] there are long *ecphraseis* of a grove (4. 419–42), or of the house of Sleep (10. 84–117), or of καπνομάντεια (10. 598–615), or of the altar of Clementia in Athens (12. 481–511). By all of these—and many more (for instance, enormous catalogues of forces)—the straight line of the narrative is broken up; but it is also broken up in another way.

As with Lucan's, the epic is constructed as a series of episodes, in such a way that the proportion of attention given to any one episode in no way reflects its proportionate importance in the narrative as a whole. This can often produce an extremely effective scene, such as the splendid storm at night, during which Polynices and Tydeus both arrive at Argos (1. 336–446). But sometimes even the episodes lack coherence because Statius has concentrated overmuch on a particular and inessential element in the episode. At the beginning (46–196), there is an episode in which the exile of Polynices is prepared: it is made up of a prayer by Oedipus (56–87), then a description of Tisiphone and her journey (88–124), and a Lucanian analysis of dyarchy (125–96). The description of Tisiphone is far out of proportion, and since she is not needed anyway, she is dismissed as soon as she arrives at Thebes, with the brief (124) *adsuetaque infecit nube penates* ('and she infected the house with her usual cloud'). The following episode is similarly flawed (197–311). It is a traditional council of the gods. Statius describes the gods assembling and their terror of Juppiter (197–211): significantly, he uses to describe Juppiter the same features that he uses in *Silvae* 1. 1 to describe Domitian, and he makes the gods stand up when Juppiter enters, as *Silvae* 4. 2 shows was usual for Domitian. When Ovid painted the same scene (*Met.* 1. 163–252), he used the gods to punctuate Juppiter's speech with roars of applause and questions. But Statius completely forgets the other gods, and the council is pared down to a confrontation between Juppiter and

118. Cf. the list of omens 7. 404–23.

Juno. This basic lack of proportion pervades Statius' whole work and renders nugatory the laborious schemes devised to show its symmetrical structure.

But it is held together by the same means that Ovid and Lucan used. There is a ring composition between books 1 and 12 in two striking respects: first, the balance between the picture of Eteocles' tyranny and that of Creon; and, second, that between the night journey of Polynices in book 1 from Thebes and the night journey of his wife Argia in book 12 in the opposite direction. But it also has the emotional unity of Lucan's epic, created by the sense of foreboding doom which is kept alive by a whole series of passages right through the epic: for instance, Juppiter's speech (1. 214 ff.), the eagles (3. 530–47) that prefigure the fates of the seven in their own fates, in many prophecies and divinations like the necromancy of Tiresias (4. 406–645), the games that prefigure the deaths of the seven (6. 249–946) and that end with an authorial intervention to reveal the future of Adrastus by interpreting an omen, appeals to the Muse before the death of Hippomedon (9. 315–38) and before the death of Menoeceus (10. 628–31). There is constant anticipation of what is to come, not only up to the climax of horror in the brothers' duel, but right to the intervention of Theseus at the end. That unity is further maintained by a concentration that is nothing short of sentimental on the two daughters of Adrastus who marry Polynices and Tydeus. Their marriages are given as much attention as that of Marcia and Cato in the *Bellum Civile*, and the reader's thoughts are romantically concentrated on them by deliberately erotic passages. No less important, of course, is the figure of Oedipus, constantly present, constantly described. It is clear that Statius, just as deliberately as Lucan, destroyed the natural unity of linear narrative, but was equally careful to construct other means of unifying the work.

The natural unity was destroyed in favour of episodic composition, and this feature can be seen to be characteristic of all major writers of the period. Tacitus can be seen to break up the movement of the narrative by digressions, by collecting minor incidents and facts together, by speeches, and, most conspicuously, by designating certain episodes for expansive and dramatic treatment. But even Juvenal structures his longer satires, such as 3 or 6, into a series of episodes with clear breaks. This must have been in the interest of the audience. Pliny describes[119] how, at a reading that lasted two days, he recited a work consisting of short poems in different metres 'for that is how those of us who have small confidence in our abilities avoid the risk of boredom'. Tacitus apologizes (*Annals* 6. 38. 1) for putting together a campaign which extended over two summers: he did it 'to rest the mind from the tale of ills at home'. Not only was boredom a consideration, but there were clearly pauses in recitations. Some authors read out only specially selected passages: Cicero wrote to Atticus in 44 B.C.:[120] 'I have sent you my *De Gloria*. So you will keep it carefully as usual. But I should like selections to be marked for Salvius, when he has collected a good audience, to recite—at dinner, of course'. And Pliny's *Letters* give evidence of the same practice.[121] That would allow for easy breaks. But with a long work, the best way to allow for such inevitable interruptions—and at the same time make possible the selected reading of special passages—was to compose episodically. It is a notable feature especially of the epic poets that episodes stay within certain fairly precise limits of length: they may be as long as one hundred and eighty lines or as short as sixty, but they are generally about one hundred and twenty lines; that might represent something like half an hour's recitation. This would have allowed for pauses at will, but it would also have ensured frequent changes of mood and topic; and, finally, it would have permitted the author to start at any point without unnecessarily puzzling his audience, or obliging him to give lengthy and boring introductory explanations.[122]

119. *Epp.* 8. 21.
120. *ad Att.* 16. 2. 5.
121. For example, *Epp.* 4. 14. 6; 8. 21. 4.
122. Pliny disliked *praefationes* unless they were essential (*Epp.* 4. 5. 3; 4. 14. 8; 5. 12. 3; 8. 21. 3), and his experience was extensive.

5. Ready-made poetic ideas

The distinction was made above between a writer's mind actively engaging a concrete situation in such a way that emotion supervened as a by-product and the deliberate excitation by a writer in his own mind of an emotion that he intended should become the object of his attention. Writers of the early Empire were particularly interested in two different types of subject matter, and their treatment of these can be recognized as an outstanding characteristic of the period as a whole. They may be designated as ready-made poetic ideas in virtue of their already possessing, before they come into the poet's mind, certain structural features that were automatically accessible to modes of treatment basic to all writing of the period. These ideas fell into two distinct, almost opposite, categories.

The first belonged to an area that can be characterized as comprising the melodramatic, the miraculous, the mysterious, and the horrifying; it covered topics like astrology, magic, witchcraft, ghosts, superstition, cruelty and violence. The distinguishing feature of such subjects is that they are of their nature already charged with an emotional excitement of their own. The concept of a sacred grove (especially connected with human sacrifice) already contains the capacity to excite awe in listeners who are trained to respond and who share the same outlook as the poet; he has only to concentrate on a simple expansion of details, and the emotional impact on trained minds will grow in proportion to the expansion. It was argued in the previous lecture that an interest in these areas was a characteristic of the real life of the time. It can now be seen that they also had a particular literary appeal, which was separate from, though reinforced by, the real-life interest.

Horrible wounds, the result of cruelty and violence, excite a readily available horror, and the exploitation of this goes back to Ovid. Here poetic ingenuity and imagination were effectively displayed, for instance, in the scene where Pyramus commits suicide (Met. 4. 115–24):

velamina Thisbes
tollit et ad pactae secum fert arboris umbram,
utque dedit notae lacrimas, dedit oscula vesti:
'accipe nunc' inquit 'nostri quoque sanguinis haustus!'
quoque erat accinctus demisit in ilia ferrum,
nec mora, ferventi moriens e vulnere traxit   120
et iacuit resupinus humo. cruor emicat alte,
non aliter quam cum vitiato fistula plumbo
scinditur et tenui stridente foramine longas
eiaculatur aquas atque ictibus aera rumpit.
arborei fetus aspergine caedis in atram   125
vertuntur faciem, madefactaque sanguine radix
purpureo tingit pendentia mora colore.

He picked up Thisbe's veil and carried it to the shade of the tree
where they were to meet; and, after lavishing tears and then lavishing kisses on that so well known garment, he said: 'Now take
great gulps of my blood too!' He plunged the sword, which he was
wearing, into his side, and instantly, as he died, tore it from the hot
wound (120) and fell back on the ground. His blood shot high in
the air, very much as when a pipe bursts because the lead has been
flawed, and through the narrow hissing crack a high jet of water
is flung up and it pulses on the air. The leaves of the tree were
sprayed with his blood and turned a dark colour (125); and its
roots, saturated with blood, tinged the pendent berries a dark red.

Here the poet needed to do nothing but let the details, focussed by the surprise of the splendidly realistic simile, speak for
him. The excitement of the horror is increased by the poet's air
of clinical detachment as he carefully runs the details of the whole
scene through his mind. A slightly contrasting technique can
be seen in the poet's visualization of the silencing of Philomela
(*Met.* 6. 549–60):

talibus ira feri postquam commota tyranni
nec minor hac metus est, causa stimulatus utraque,   550
quo fuit accinctus, vagina liberat ensem
adreptamque coma flexis post terga lacertis
vincla pati cogit. iugulum Philomela parabat
spemque suae mortis viso conceperat ense.
ille indignantem et nomen patris usque vocantem   555
luctantemque loqui comprensam forcipe linguam

abstulit ense fero; radix micat ultima linguae,
ipsa iacet terraeque tremens inmurmurat atrae,
utque salire solet mutilatae cauda colubrae,
palpitat et moriens dominae vestigia quaerit.

The anger of the cruel tyrant was aroused by her words and no
less his fear: goaded by both emotions (550), he freed from its
sheath the sword that he wore. He seized her by her hair, twisted
her arms behind her back, and forced manacles on her. When she
saw the sword, she was filled with hopes of death, and presented
her throat. But, as her tongue reviled him and kept calling her
father's name (555), he grasped it with forceps and, as it struggled
to speak, sliced it off with his cruel sword. The stump of her tongue
flickered in her throat, while the tongue itself lay wriggling and
muttering to the black earth; and, as the tail of a snake writhes
after it has been chopped off, it fluttered, and, as it died, tried to
reach its mistress's feet.

Ovid modifies his detachment from this sadistic scene in two
ways: he enters the scene at the beginning with adjectival support for the tortured girl and abuse of the cruel tyrant; at the
end it is he who interprets the pathos of the dying tongue's desire. But the physical details of the horror are enhanced by detached and appreciative observation. There is a pleasure in the
horror, and the poet leaves nothing to the imagination: he ex-
hausts the possibilities of the scene, where Virgil understates
and focusses horror in pity for the sufferer—for instance, in the
death of two identical twins (*Aeneid* 10. 390–96):

vos etiam, gemini, Rutulis cecidistis in arvis,
Daucia, Laride Thymberque, simillima proles,
indiscreta suis gratusque parentibus error;
at nunc dura dedit vobis discrimina Pallas.
nam tibi, Thymbre, caput Evandrius abstulit ensis;
te decisa suum, Laride, dextera quaerit
semianimesque micant digiti ferrumque retractant.

You too fell on Rutulian fields, twin Larides and Thymber, identical offspring of Daucus, indistinguishable to your own parents
and source of happy error. But now Pallas gave you harsh distinctions. For with Evander's sword he cut off your head, Thymber;

and your right hand, Larides, chopped off, tried to find its owner,
and your still-living fingers twitched and kept grasping the sword.

Ovid's detail of the severed tongue was appreciated by Lucan,
who used it as one of the many tortures applied to M. Marius
Gratidianus (2. 173–90). But, as was characteristic of later writers, he indulged hyperbole, and while using Ovid's word (182)
palpitat, he added *et muto vacuum ferit aera motu* ('and beat
the empty air with its dumb movement')—the words suggest
a boxer failing to land punches rather than a tongue failing to
articulate because deprived of all its associated apparatus. Silius
Italicus was taken with the idea of a man subjected to many tortures, and he imitated the passage in the torturing of Tagus'
slave (1. 169–81): he was tortured in every conceivable way, his
limbs grew to accommodate the tortures, all his blood was spilled,
his limbs melted away but the bones still smoked—and he mocked
his torturers. The tendency can be seen in the later use of a
detail from Ovid—the idea that pressure of blood expels an in-
trusive weapon (*Met.* 13. 391–94):

> dixit, et in pectus tum demum vulnera passum,
> qua patuit ferro, letalem condidit ensem;
> nec valuere manus infixum educere telum,
> expulit ipse cruor, rubefactaque sanguine tellus. . . .

He spoke, and, where it was vulnerable, buried the deadly sword
in his breast that only then at last suffered a wound; his hands
had not the strength to draw out the imprisoned weapon. His blood
itself expelled it, and the earth was reddened. . . .

Lucan relates, as the first of twelve carefully arranged deaths
in the sea battle, the following of Catus (3. 587–91):

> terga simul pariter missis et pectora telis
> transigitur: medio concurrit corpore ferrum,
> et stetit incertus, flueret quo volnere, sanguis,
> donec utrasque simul largus cruror expulit hastas
> divisitque animam sparsitque in volnera letum.

He was transfixed equally in his back and in his breast by weapons fired simultaneously: the steel clashed in the middle of his

chest, and the blood was halted, uncertain from which wound to flow, until, in a flood, it expelled both spears at the same time and, dividing his soul, distributed his death between both wounds.[123]

Valerius Flaccus is brief (3. 105–7):

> subit ilia cuspis
> Olenii: dedit ille sonum compressaque mandens
> aequora purpuream singultibus expulit hastam.

The Olenian's spear entered his groin: he groaned and, biting the ground that he fell on, expelled the dark red spear with his sobs.

Earlier than Lucan or Valerius, Seneca had used the motif in tragedy. After making Iocasta debate for nine lines which part of her body to pierce and, finally, having her decide on her womb, he has the chorus explain (*Oedipus* 1040–41):

> iacet perempta. vulneri immoritur manus
> ferrumque secum nimius eiecit cruor.

She lies slain. Her hand dies upon the wound, and a torrent of blood has shot the sword out with itself.

Statius combined this motif with that of a severed tongue (2. 624–28):

> dum clamat, subit ore cavo Teumesia cornus,
> nec prohibent fauces; atque illi voce repleta
> intercepta natat prorupto in sanguine lingua.
> stabat adhuc donec transmissa morte per artus
> labitur immorsaque cadens obmutuit hasta.

As he shouts, the Teumesian shaft enters his open mouth, and his throat did not halt it; and his tongue, cut off as it was in full voice, swam forth on a torrent of blood. He stood awhile, till death was dispersed through his limbs; he fell and, falling, was silent as his teeth bit the spear.

Statius goes on, in imitation of Virgil's lines on the twins, to describe a twin brother transfixed by a spear which also goes through the fallen twin; they die kissing and embracing. Later

123. This final detail was, no doubt, a deliberate challenge to Virgil's (*Aen.* 10. 487) *una eademque via sanguis animusque sequuntur.*

he describes the death of a man who has been drinking wine and now lies asleep on the ground (10. 320–23):

> madida ora redundant,
> accensusque mero sopor aestuat. ecce! iacentis
> Inachius vates iugulum fodit, expulit ingens
> vina cruor fractumque perit in sanguine murmur.

His mouth overflows with liquor, and his sleep, inflamed with wine, is turbulent. See! the Inachian seer pierced his gullet, and a flood of blood expelled the wine, and his death cry was broken and perished in the tide.

Another variation of Statius is this (9. 130–2):

> faucibus ille cavis hastam non ore receptam
> miratur moriens, pariterque et murmure plenus
> sanguis et expulsi salierunt cuspide dentes.

As he dies, he is astonished to have received the spear in his hollow throat, not his mouth; and simultaneously there shot forth both blood filled with his death cry and teeth knocked out by the spear.

Statius goes the furthest in sheer amplification, using adjectives to gloat over the incredible details of otherwise revolting horror. In two passages (7. 760–70 and 10. 476–79), he describes chariot wheels and horses' hooves careering over dead and dying bodies, the wheels slowed by the blood and the horses' legs entangled in entrails. Ovid's strength lay in the clinical detachment and the restraint that refused amplification. For a moment he makes the scene, however incredible, strike home by its own force. Later writers failed to grasp the innate strength of realism. They exuberantly improved on reality, allowing their own emotions to become entangled in the concrete details and their itch for novelty to wallow in fantasy—to such an extent that when Lucan illustrated the horrible detail of a spear sticking in Scaeva's eye with a strikingly realistic simile of a bear whirling around to try and catch the spear that sticks in her (6. 220–23), Housman was moved to explain[124] that the poet had seen what he

124. Note to 220–223.

describes in the amphitheatre. Valerius Flaccus is more successful: abandoning Ovidian precision and realism, he used his gift
for allusive language to suggest rather than describe horror—
and exerts a more genuine sense of horror as a consequence. The
least successful was Silius Italicus, who was not prevented by
his lack of a strong visual imagination from trying to outshine
his predecessors in details of horror. He writes words that try
to be horrible, but the ideas are imperfectly realized and the
result collapses into silliness. For instance (1. 400–2):

> et ferit alte
> insurgens gladio cristatae cassidis aera
> perque ipsum tegimen crepitantia dissipat ossa.

And rising high, he strikes with his sword the bronze of the
crested helmet and scatters the bones rattling through the very
covering.

Everything is said, but characteristically the weak imprecision
of *tegimen* (which presumably just repeats *aera*), together with
the unnecessary emphasis of *ipsum*, spoils the horrible idea of
the noise made by the bones (not a good word) spilling from the
split bronze.[125] Silius Italicus lacked metrical dexterity,[126] but
what is most disturbing in a reading of his epic is a constant in-
felicity and clumsiness in the choice of words. His general falli-
bility of judgement is shown by the way in which Cannae is as
thickly infested with horrific deaths as any other part of the narrative that gave him the least encouragement. By contrast, Lucan
admirably concentrated his horrors in preliminary and subsequent incidents, but for Pharsalia the horrors are confined to a

125. The model was probably the Homeric (cf. *Iliad* 11. 97) adaptation
by Virgil in *Aen.* 10. 416 *ossaque dispersit cerebro permixta cruento*, where
ossa fits the idea of the head shattered by a rock; Silius took it over without
visualizing his different context.
126. This could be illustrated in many ways: for example, all these poets,
but particularly Statius, make effective use of the overrun of a sentence
from one line to another by just one dactylic word (which is consequently
followed by a strong sense pause); the pattern is extremely infrequent in
Silius Italicus.

brief, generalizing list with no names (7. 617–31). The disaster
bears more heavily on the reader for his unusual reticence.

A similar fantasizing over other areas of the horrible or the
mystifying could be illustrated in much the same way in all these
poets. The truth of what they said was of no concern; what mattered was more and novel detail. Even Tacitus can be seen to
have indulged such fantasies to some degree. His description
(*Annals* 1. 61–62) of the site of Varus' disaster when it was visited
by Germanicus uses incredible details of horror and mystery in
a desire to work up an aura of awe. He allowed the suggestion
that Piso or Plancina might have poisoned Germanicus to stand,
against his own judgement, and so (2. 69–73) indulged much
melodrama over supposed details of magic and witchcraft. Even
passages where he allows two opinions to stand (one of which
is quite unworthy—notoriously, for instance, in his gratuitous
suggestion that Agricola may have been poisoned on Domitian's
orders) should be regarded as an aspect of the writer's yearning
for mystery at all costs and for the emotion that is associated with
it. More obvious examples of his subduing belief to fantasy are
statements that the gods hate the Roman people (*Histories* 1. 3. 2,
non esse curae deis securitatem nostram, esse ultionem 'the gods
are concerned not for our safety, but that we are punished'), or
that the gods provided a fine night to reveal the murder of Agrippina (*Annals* 14. 5. 1), or his own speculations on Fate and Fortune (*Annals* 6. 22).[127] The writer need not indulge such fancies
often to infuse disproportionate areas of his work with a sense of
hidden and mysterious forces, repugnant to the intellect but
gratifying to the sensation-craving soul.

The other material that may be designated as providing ready-
made poetic ideas belongs to an area which seems at an opposite
extreme, in that it carries no emotional overcharge. In fact, a
scale could be constructed to illustrate the interaction of subject
matter and treatment such that pure emotion lay at one extreme
and absence of emotion at the other. It would be roughly ac-

127. Other examples of allusive *fatum* are in *Annals* 1. 55. 3; 3. 30. 4; 4. 1.
2 (*deum ira*); 13. 12. 2.

curate to say that writers of the early Empire move between both extremes without dwelling on the broad central area, which was the real concern of the mainstream of Classical writers. One area of the unemotional material is that in which mere cleverness is at a premium, as in word play. This was one of the most widespread vices of the age, indulged by all writers, even at solemn moments, as when Lucan plays on two senses of *mors* or of *libertas*;[128] but the most constant practitioner was Seneca,[129] though his father condemned the practice as 'the most abject and vulgar bad taste'[130] and Quintilian gave very limited approval.[131] Another area comprises the playing with ideas for their own sake, where the idea is not of the slightest significance to the writer. A good example of that is *Bellum Civile* 1. 412–19, where Lucan adduces three possible reasons for the tidal rise and fall on the Dutch coast (a question completely irrelevant to the catalogue of places abandoned by Caesar's troops); he then calmly remarks (417–19): 'You find out, whom the working of the universe concerns: but for me remain hidden, as the gods wished, whatever you are that cause such constant movements'. Nevertheless, at a later point (9. 303–18), he will gladly devote sixteen lines to various explanations of the origin of the Syrtes. Statius takes this sort of play to more absurd lengths. At *Thebaid* 7. 426–29, a river floods either because of a rainbow or mountain clouds or because it wanted to stop the army. At 7. 809–16, the earth opened for Amphiaraus either because winds broke out of it, or hidden waters ate it away, or the fabric of the heaven leaned that way, or Neptune moved the whole sea, or, finally, because it was a tribute to Amphiaraus or a threat to the brothers. At 10. 831–36, there are multiple speculations on the reason for Capaneus' action. All of this is connected with the widespread phenomenon of an interest taken in pedantry or

128. See p. 224 above, and *Bellum Civile* 3. 145–47.
129. A good collection of material is in Summers' introduction to his selection from the *Epistles*, pp. lxxxii–xc.
130. *suas.* 7. 11.
131. 9. 3. 71.

mere information for its own sake,[132] without regard for its relevance.

But the most important area of unemotional material comprised personifications, which, in this period, became so extended that they qualify for the name of allegories. Many personifications are simply neat linguistic gestures that epitomize complex situations, as when Horace says (*Odes* 3. 1. 40) *post equitem sedet atra Cura*, or Dido says (*Aeneid* 4. 27) *ante, Pudor, quam te violo aut tua iura resolvo*. Others are emblematic: this applies particularly to the concept of attendants on a deity. So, in imitation of Homer, Virgil at one time (*Aeneid* 9. 717–19) makes *Fuga* and *Timor* the attendants of Mars; at another time (12. 335–36), *Formido, Irae* and *Insidiae*. But this technique lent itself to expansion. Virgil lists as hanging about the door of the underworld (*Aeneid* 6. 274–80) *Luctus, Curae, Morbi, Senectus, Metus, Fames, Egestas, Letum, Labos, Sopor, mala mentis Gaudia,*[133] *Bellum* and *Discordia*; if *Invidia* is added from *Georgics* 3. 37, that covers almost all the personifications used by later poets. Ovid has a nice picture of the Sun-God (*Met.* 2. 25–30) surrounded by *Dies, Mensis, Annus, Saecula, Horae, Ver, Aestas, Autumnus* and *Hiems*; and *Fama* is accompanied by (*Met.* 12. 59–61) *Credulitas, Error, Laetitia, Timores, Seditio,* and *Susurri*. But the greatest change in this period was made by concentrating this expansive ingenuity on single personifications.

Virgil only did this twice, both times following traditional patterns (*Fama* in *Aeneid* 4. 173–88 and *Dirae* in 12. 845–68—the latter really being a sort of divine intervention by Juppiter). Ovid took the decisive step[134] in a great series of ingenious expansions in *Metamorphoses*: *Invidia* (2. 760–82), *Fames* (8. 788–813), *Somnus* (11. 592–615—also Morpheus 633–49), and *Fama* (12. 39–63). When Virgil described *Fama*, he simply encoded in

132. See p. 191 above.
133. Oddly transformed by Valerius Flaccus (6. 178) into *mala Leti Gaudia*.
134. He had already shown interest in the technique: cf. Elegia in *Amores* 3. 1.

his description, very lightly disguised, the activities of gossip mongers. But Ovid described her home and created a picture of delightful fantasy belonging to another world, with the distance between the disguise and the corresponding reality in the concrete world vastly increased. He used this technique for all his personifications. This technique ('The house of. . .') has a quality of fairy tale and gives free rein to the imagination, without any need for the slightest verisimilitude as such; the ingenuity of the disguise was what mattered. In Ovid it also admitted humour, both in the exuberant joy of amplification and also in the Ovidian touch of making the goddess who visits *Somnus* hurry away since she begins to feel sleepy, while the visitor to *Fames* begins to feel hungry.

Valerius Flaccus has his own description of *Fama* (2. 116–22), which owes something to Virgil and nothing to Ovid; and he has other, but modest, applications of this type of material. Silius Italicus, too, has a number of uninteresting pictures, for instance, of *Fama* (6. 552–54) or *Somnus* (10. 340–56), but they are just traditional and Virgilian. Lucan personifies *Fortuna* throughout his epic, but only to treat her as a deity to be addressed, harangued, abused; he has no extended personifications, probably because, in spite of *Fortuna*'s ultimate responsibility for everything, his human actors are shown to be immediately motivated by their own personal emotions, concretely apprehended, and responsible for their actions. It was Statius who responded fully to the inspiration of Ovid, and in doing so he adapted traditional deities to this process. The extensive description of Bacchus returning from war (4. 652–63) is cast as an allegorical scene of Drunkenness and his attendants; and the house of Mars (7. 40–63) is pure Ovidian expansion. But his greatest triumph is the house of Sleep (10. 84–117), followed by a long account of Iris' waking of Sleep and his obedient response (118–55). Unlike Ovid, however, Statius has not allowed the faintest trace of humour to intrude on his description of *Somnus* doing the one thing he is designed not to do—wake up. There are many more extended personifications in Statius. The role of *Pietas* (11. 457–96) is characteristic, and shows Statius at the opposite extreme from Lucan. The constant appearances of Tisiphone, Megaera, *Pietas, Luctus, Pavor* and the rest, show Statius always concerned to explain motivation by reference to another world, one corresponding to the old divine machinery, but differing in that it is a world almost completely composed of allegorical figures who provide a sort of shorthand for dealing with psychological explanation. These abstractions love and fight and make alliances among themselves, and these movements and emotions determine what happens among men below.

In this sense personifications provided poetic raw material, capable of infinite manipulation and ingenious expansion. Their use is to be seen at its best in Statius' finest poem, to Sleep (*Silvae* 5. 4). There Statius avoids lapsing into a fulsome self-pity by objectifying sleep as a relationship between the whole world and a beneficent deity; in his case the relationship is imperfect, and he can pray to the god. The emotion of the poem is strictly controlled by this device; but the poem's power comes from the real agony of the poet which finds admirably indirect expression. In impersonal epic, the effect of the device is quite different, being purely intellectual and neutral emotionally.

Personification is of two closely related types: when a man is the object of envy or rumour, fellow human beings are converted by personification into an inhuman or superhuman force that is the emblem of their actions; when he is subject to fear or hunger or lust, personification confronts him with a force outside himself which is the emblem of the things going on inside him. In both cases, men become helpless victims of arbitrary forces, and their situation is objectified by identifying it as a relationship between themselves and the external force. If, in this relationship, the victim is emphasized, the personification becomes a neat linguistic gesture of impersonal generalization.[135] If, however, the force or emotion is emphasized, then the device tends to become a self-generating conceit, treated for

135. As, for instance, in Horace *Odes* 3. 1. 37–38 *sed Timor et Minae / scandunt eodem quo dominus.*

its own sake. The latter is what happened widely in literature of the early Empire. Such allegories leave nothing unsaid, in the sense that the poet has fully articulated every possibility inherent in the relation between the reality and the disguise, and consequently they carry no emotional overcharge. Their value lay in their providing a basic pattern which, by a process of encipherment, could be used to cover a whole range of human activities and sensations, with the audience's pleasure in deciphering being in direct proportion to the poet's ingenuity in the encoding. They provided a stimulus on the level of a puzzle for both writer and audience, and a relief from the intensity of emotion that was otherwise maintained near the level of a scream.

6. *Rhetoric*

The age of the early Empire has traditionally been the Age of Rhetoric, and the pervasive influence of rhetoric has been used to explain the changed or decadent nature of the literature. Implausibly,[136] for rhetoric has always had the humble but admirable purpose of organizing the skill of effectively expressing ideas. Rhetoric was not at fault, but the ends to which it was used. For—to oversimplify—literary communication involves a relationship between three elements: (1) the ideas, (2) the speaker or writer, and (3) the audience. If emphasis is concentrated on the first element, the result is density, brevity, and (often) obscurity. The opponent in Pliny's letter quoted above[137] was emphasizing the relationship between the first two elements, and that was essentially the extreme Atticist position. There was something which had to be expressed; whether or not it got effectively across to the third element was not the point. Cicero's way of refuting this position in the *Brutus* was to place an implausible emphasis on the importance of the third element in the judgement of oratory; at times, he actually asserts that the

136. See the excellent remarks of Hermann Fränkel (1945), 5–7, 167–69.
137. See beginning of sect. 2 above.

audience is the best judge of oratory.[138] But by this exaggeration
he was only concerned to right the balance against Atticist neglect of the audience.

The whole movement of literature in the early Empire was
in the direction of emphasizing the relationship between the
second and the third elements. Since oratory was no longer concerned to persuade, the aim was to move, and the 'moving' was
to be of the oddly stationary type that issued in no action, but
only the illusion of action by way of emotional participation in
an imaginary scene. But the other end of the spectrum was also
drawn into service since pleasure could also be won from complete absence of emotion in the virtuoso display of verbal tricks.
Consequently, the first element was relatively disregarded so
long as it could provide an adequate supply of emotional excitement to charge the relationship between speaker or writer and
the audience. And, as far as titillating the mind was concerned,
an adequate technique could make use of any material. The
growing popularity in the period of impromptu performances
(often on subjects suggested at random by the audience) reflects
the shift of emphasis to the relationship between the second and
third elements—and this was not only in prose, since Statius'
Silvae, for instance, contains many poems written to order on
the spur of the moment.[139] Here ancient rhetorical theory was
encouraging. The words that to us suggest imaginative creation,
εὕρεσις or *inventio*, had nothing to do with that. The 'discovery'
involved was the discovery of what needed to be said on a given
topic or of the treatment appropriate to that topic. The assumption was that in a given piece of material the things that need
to be said in dealing with it were somehow latent and inherent
in it; a poet had some licence to make things up, but that was
not at all necessary and was not to be exercised too often.

The poet, then, became assimilated to the orator, and, since

138. See especially *Brutus* 181–200.
139. The interest in this type of composition and its different criteria
are expressed by Statius in his prefatory letters (esp. 1, 2, and 4). Martial
also clearly composed extempore epigrams (e.g., 9. 89).

the function of both was to entertain an audience, particularly by generating emotion that would move them, measurement of the emotion so generated became a measure of the quality of a composition. That put a premium on sensationalism and melodrama. It also meant that the audience or reader needed to feel in a privileged position; he had to feel that he was being addressed, that he was being operated on actively by the writer. Consequently, reflective poetry virtually disappeared. In Augustan poetry the reader, as it were, accidentally overhears or eavesdrops on the poet. In the satires of Juvenal or the tragedies of Seneca, the poet seems to be speaking at the top of his voice all the time. The opposite of this is the private conversational style of Horace, infinitely varied in tone, but always with the sense of a private, not a public, occasion. Juvenal and Seneca are always busily operating on a sophisticated audience that is ready with instant and well-trained response to the coded signals that were the commonly agreed prescriptions supplied by rhetorical theory.

Two far-reaching observations can be made on this situation. First, a distinction was made above between emotion that is presented for its own sake and emotion that emerges as a by-product of the energetic analysis of a situation handled in concrete detail. In the former the emphasis is transferred to the end that the poet has in view: as when Persius[140] justifies the use of grandiose epic language to Cornutus (who has recommended the simple earnest style) by asserting that he was really speaking sincerely but that he wished to convey his gratitude to Cornutus with due weight in epic language—that is, he wanted to move Cornutus in a particular way. What is lost in these circumstances may be termed the pleasure of intellectual assent, the pleasure of following a cogent organization of ideas and responding with appropriate emotions at each stage. For the writer is engaged in attempting a more or less direct excitation of an audience in response to a series of more or less agreed signals which are independent—or as independent as form can ever be from con-

140. *Sat.* 5. 19–29.

tent—of the ideas they purport to express. To put it another way: the sources of power and energy which this literature possesses can be discovered by simple analysis of its language and style.[141] It does not mean more than it says, for then an opportunity would have been lost. Such an analysis will obviously not suffice for Virgil; but it is not completely adequate for Ovid, nor for Lucan, nor for Tacitus, nor even for Juvenal. These writers all, to some extent, bring their minds to bear on material that resists, that needs intellectual domination, and they become emotionally involved in that struggle. Juvenal, for instance, is not just satirically entertaining: his anger in early satires is certainly the cloak of a *persona*, chosen for its usefulness in self-generating emotion; but he also succeeds in arousing (as, for instance, Seneca often does not, though dealing with the same material) intellectual curiosity and excitement—subject matter and emotion converge to demand intellectual assent. But of most literature of the early Empire that is simply untrue. There is a gross disproportion between the energy of utterance and the weight of the ideas it is required to bear. Pliny's *Panegyric* is a perfect example, and it makes the point clearly that it was the shift of emphasis to the end or effect aimed at that so easily accommodated the whole ideology of emperor worship to the process of literary composition.

Second, a tension was inevitably created between the technique of composition, which was totally prescribed by rhetorical theory, and the uncomfortable need to find material on which to practise it—the need, in fact, for inspiration. The result was that the condition of the latter was assimilated to the former, in such a way that recognized sources of material came to be established and were subject to ordering by rules that placed reliance on themes which, by their nature, contained the capacity to move and excite, or else to tease and titillate the mind.

141. Quintilian 10. 1 17–19 has some perceptive remarks on the differences in the critical judgement applied by the listener on the one hand and by the reader on the other. For Horace on the same topic, see *Epp.* 2. 1. 214 ff.

Hence the use of the same material again and again, hence *imitatio* and *aemulatio*, and hence what have been called above 'ready-made poetic ideas'. The paradoxical situation that the urge for originality was concentrated on the technique of expression (which was totally prescribed by rhetorical theory) came to be accepted as the norm. Hence came the itch, characteristic of most literature of the early Empire, to leave nothing to the imagination: to anticipate and express everything that could be conjured out of a given idea. For the exhaustion of all such possibilities, rhetorical rules were devised and constantly enlarged. What was lost by this was the sort of humility which admits that everything cannot be known, let alone said. That is a creative humility, and it is the basis of the capacity to mean more than actually seems to be said. It was a characteristic of the great Augustans; the instinct to exhaust every possibility was first displayed by Ovid.

The gulf that grew between the Augustan age and that of the early Empire was partly the result of nonliterary causes which will be examined in the next lecture. But it may have been increased by the fact that the ancient world had no adequate technique for literary history.[142] Much of the poetry of the great Augustans was inadequately understood and positively misunderstood from a period not very long after it was written: the fact is written large in the ancient commentaries that have survived and in later imitations of them. Later readers (and writers) seem not to have possessed the criteria for judging and appreciating it. One difficulty must have been that literary history was assimilated to the history of oratory, with devastating results. First, it meant that all later writers were condemned to a sense of inferiority by the theory of decline from Cicero—a sense which can have been little mitigated by the sort of allusive encouragement found in Tacitus' *Dialogus*. Second, literary history requires value judgements based on a proper understanding of the relationship of author and genre to the historical environment

142. On the importance of literary history for the writer's grasp of tradition, see especially Wellek (1941) and Lipking (1970), esp. 328 ff.

as well as to predecessors and successors. But the history of oratory had two methods of procedure: the one by 'canons' or lists
of the great, the other by survey in an antiquarian fashion (which
could be well done by Cicero, who had the advantage of seeing
everything leading up to himself). Later poets were consequently unable to place themselves critically in relation to the great
Augustans; their only way of attempting that was by *imitatio*
and *aemulatio*. The concept of 'development' had never been
defined in such a way as to apply to anything except the emer-
gence of an art form from its primitive analogue, a type of investigation that had been taken to its limits by Aristotle. Quintilian's catalogue of writers in book 10 is a stark example of how
inevitably a sense of the contemporaneity of all writers filled
the vacuum created by the lack of a proper literary history. Para-
doxically the Augustans breathed down the necks of all later
writers, but were to them only an inert quarry for material; and
the only way of treating them was to use their ideas again and
again, with an increasingly oppressive sense of their infinite
superiority. Freedom and independence were impossible without an adequate critical viewpoint.

But freedom and independence have also wider bases, and
these were deeply undermined during the early Empire, not
only by the censorship that was, to some extent, imposed by
every emperor to the time of Trajan, but also by social factors
and by changes both social and political that affected the relationship between literature and society. The further problem
now needs to be faced: why, after the political situation of the
writer apparently changed so dramatically for the better under
Trajan, did Roman literature run out so soon into the sands of
the archaizing movement? These problems, together with the
basic question of whether the early Empire should really be
treated as one coherent and unified period, will be considered
in the following lecture.

VI

Literature and Society

LITERATURE stands in a dual relationship with the process of history: on the one hand, there is a component that penetrates literature which is derived from the particular features of a period; on the other, literature, as one of the arts, shares in the vicissitudes of the society that produces it. Flattery of the emperor is an obvious example of the former; the disappearance of political oratory, of the latter. But it is less obvious phenomena that are the concern of this lecture—in particular, that whole range of variables which may condition both the position and the outlook of writers as well as the valuation which society places on the activity of writing. The period of the early Roman Empire treated here was not long by some reckonings, but the social and political conditions of the Roman people went through a series of swift, even traumatic, changes, and that elusive ghost, the spirit or atmosphere of the age, went through at least three quite different phases during that period. It is the purpose of this lecture to trace the interaction of literature and society in those years, at the same time drawing into the argument what appear to be the conclusions of the five earlier lectures.

1. *The senate and the emperor*

The ideal of Augustus was something like Mommsen's theory of a dyarchy: it was an ideal of cooperation between a senate largely composed of the remains of the great aristocratic families and the emperor who originated policy. But Augustus was compelled into increasing isolation and autocracy. Tiberius started with a modesty and deference towards the senate which Tacitus took to be evidence of duplicity and dissimulation. A depressing historical pattern comes into view: as each emperor declines into tyranny and dies or is slaughtered, the next comes forward with the old ideal of cooperation, only to be forced into isolation in his turn. It was with cynical reflection on that fact that Tacitus put into Curtius Montanus' mouth the words *optimus est post malum principem dies primus*.[1] Tiberius, Gaius, Claudius most of all, Nero once again, Vespasian, even Domitian—it was true of all of them: a bad emperor was always succeeded by a good one. And each time the principate ended up looking more like a conventional Hellenistic monarchy. Gaius saw the logic of the situation: the senate had to be destroyed. He deliberately set out to create a monarchy of the Oriental type, with worship of himself as a god, in association with his family (he deified his sister Drusilla); he went so far in attacking the senate as to deprive it of its hollow right to elect magistrates. Claudius, however, conceived the different approach of building up a secretariat independent of the senate. But nothing worked.

Cooperation was in principle impossible for two converging reasons, both of which go back to the shape given to the principate by Augustus: first, the senate, in the last analysis, had no power, since the army was under direct control of the emperor; second, Augustus had created a hereditary monarchy, and the hereditary principle had to be maintained within the Julio-Claudian family—not always by the will of its members. When Gaius was murdered, the senate made ineffectual movements in the direction of re-establishing the Republican form of government, but it was the elite Pretorian guard that dragged Claudius out of hiding and forced him onto the throne. The hereditary principle had been left in good hands. But the truth was that the senate had only vague aspirations and no real plans for re-

1. *Hist.* 4. 42. 6.

establishing the Republic. This was demonstrated for the last time after the murder of Nero. There was then no hereditary principle to be maintained: the opportunity was perfect. Army commanders in A.D. 68 and the succession of short-lived emperors in A.D. 69 alike displayed a most satisfying respect for senatorial legality—they were, after all, senators themselves.[2] But when Vespasian came to power, he too was caught by the inexorable logic of the situation: his first priority had to be to secure constitutional safeguards for himself. In consequence, the senate, which had eagerly seized the opportunity to put on trial the *delatores* who had operated so successfully against it under Nero, was compelled to abandon the cases.[3]

Particularly significant was the attack of Helvidius Priscus on Eprius Marcellus, for Vespasian found that the only way to deal with the intransigent Stoic doctrinaire was to exile him and then have him killed.[4] In fact, Vespasian's judgement was accurate: this was pretty well the last act of senatorial opposition, for, if one thing had emerged with unpleasant clarity from the year A.D. 68–69, it was that the alternative to an emperor was not Republican government, but civil war (which was how the whole thing had started). Resuscitation of the Republic could only serve to revive the dilemma of the Republic: Caesar or civil war, Augustus or civil war. Senatorial opposition was, however, given artificial respiration by Flavian assertion of a new hereditary principle, and Vespasian seems to have asserted this from an early stage, for Cassius Dio[5] reports his leaving the senate in A.D. 70, after an attack by Helvidius Priscus, in tears and saying: 'My son shall be my successor, or no one'. That spur to opposition was aided by the obliging self-portrait of a Nero presented by Domitian. But after Domitian's slaughter, the astute Nerva established the new principle of adoption well in advance of any

2. See, for example, Suetonius *Galba* 10. 1.
3. See Tacitus *Hist.* 4. 1–11 and 38 ff.
4. Tacitus *Hist.* 4. 6–8 and 43; Suetonius *Vesp.* 15. See chap. I, sect. 7 above.
5. 65. 12; Suetonius *Vesp.* 25.

question of succession, and mildly left the scene to the convincing Trajan. This was the point where the principate merged irretrievably into the Empire, and the principle of autocracy was finally accepted by the senate. Future emperors could be left to emerge from the ruling class by a convincing display of military ability.

2. Literature and the senate

This whole situation vitally affected literature in the period, because literature had become largely a product created by senators for consumption by senators. The earliest Roman poets had been of inferior social status. Senators only wrote speeches or technical handbooks or history to benefit the world with the fruits of their experience. That was changed when Lucilius invented a type of poetry that could respectably be written by senators.[6] The last century of the Republic shows writers largely from the senatorial class or from families of equivalent status. Acquaintance with Greek culture caused Romans to recognize literature as a status symbol. That recognition can be seen, for instance, in Strabo's dedication of his *History* and *Geography* to Roman senators, or in the constellation of great names among the addressees of epigrams in the *Garland of Philip*. The senatorial grip on literary production is illustrated by an unpleasing fact. Seneca, in his abjectly flattering essay from exile addressed to Polybius, the imperial secretary of Claudius, praised that worthy's literary activities; he mentions his translations of Homer into Latin and of Virgil into Greek, and also his Aesopean fables. The last work he describes (8.3) as *intemptatum Romanis ingeniis opus*. That was blatantly untrue. Phaedrus had written five books of such fables, and quite recently and notoriously. For the first two books had given such offence to Sejanus, who felt himself slandered, that he prosecuted Phaedrus and obtained some unknown penalty against him.[7] Seneca must have deliberately ig-

6. See chap. III, sect. 1.
7. The story emerges from the preface to the third book of Phaedrus *Fables*.

nored him because he was a freedman (of Augustus), and mention of so low a person as a literary predecessor would have taken the edge off his flattery of that grand freedman (of Claudius), Polybius.[8]

The composition of literature was a senatorial activity, or one closely controlled by the senate. Characteristically, however, writers, if senators ,were *novi homines*. The great aristocratic families had never shown much talent in that direction. It is something of an exception when Pliny writes enthusiastically to Vestricius Spurinna (5. 17) about his having heard Calpurnius Piso give a recitation of his poem in elegiac couplets on καταστερισμοί. His modesty and blushes particularly appealed to Pliny ('rare enough in the young, even rarer in the noble young'), who afterwards rewarded the young man 'kissing him often and long, which is the most stimulating encouragement'. Pliny prays for more such 'so that our nobility may have some distinction in their houses besides ancestral portraits'. But he was to be disappointed.

Senatorial control of literature operated through patronage. Whoever Calpurnius Siculus may have been, he was probably a freedman, and he expresses gratitude to a patron as he composes panegyric on Nero.[9] Patronage was needed, and it created prestige. Martial complains that patrons are far less generous than under Augustus,[10] but he is unfailingly favourable to the hated *delator*, M. Aquillius Regulus, even to the extent of joking with him (a humour which only conceals its flattery: 7. 16):

> aera domi non sunt: superest hoc, Regule, solum
> ut tua vendamus munera: numquid emis?

> I haven't a cent to my name: the only thing left me, Regulus, is to sell your presents: are you in the market?

8. He could have made a thin excuse from the fact that Phaedrus presented a more mixed and original work than a translation: see Oltramare (1926), 226 ff. The technique of Phaedrus may also have helped to create prejudice: see p. 309 below.

9. On the nature of this panegyric and the (comparative) originality of the *carmina Einsiedlensia*, see especially W. Schmid, (1953).

10. E.g., 1. 107; 8. 56; 11. 3.

Writers like Martial and Statius needed patronage, where most writers of the period, being senators or the equivalent, did not. The finances of writing and publishing are very obscure. The elder Pliny left his nephew one hundred and sixty volumes of notes. When the uncle had visited Spain,[11] the *iuridicus*, a famous orator called Larcius Licinus, offered 400,000 sesterces for the notebooks (fewer in number then).[12] However, this very considerable sum (the amount a man needed to qualify for the *equites*) was not being offered with a view to publication: Licinus shared the elder Pliny's interest in encyclopedic information (and supplied Pliny with some strange 'facts', which were recorded in the *Natural History*).[13] The period of the early Empire was a time when Roman culture spread all over the Roman world. Martial (7. 88) expresses delight at the news that his poems are being read in Vienne on the Rhone: 'every old man there and young man and boy reads me—and chaste brides in the presence of their respectable husbands'. He goes on to say that he is happier with this than if he were to hear that Egyptians and Spaniards were reading him—presumably because he felt that the cultural level of Gaul was considerably higher than that of Egypt or Spain (and about the latter he should certainly have known). He no doubt flattered himself humorously in his estimate of the proportion of the population that read him. Pliny (9. 11) hears from a friend that his books are being sold in Lyons: he is delighted that his popularity is as great abroad as in Rome, the more so because he did not even know that there was a bookseller in Lyons. But the financing of all this remains obscure. Martial elsewhere (11. 3) says that his books are being read in South Russia and in Britain, but that his purse knows nothing of that. Pirated editions were certainly not unknown: so there was profit to be had. For instance, some of Quintilian's speeches were transcribed in court in inaccurate versions and could be purchased at booksellers.[14] Martial tells readers (1. 2 and 113)

11. Early in the reign of Vespasian: see Syme (1969), 215 ff.
12. Pliny *Epp.* 3. 5. 17. 13. *NH* 19. 35; 31. 24.
14. *Inst. Orat.* 7. 2. 24.

where *de luxe* editions of his poems can be bought, and, when Lupercus asks to borrow a copy, Martial advises him (1. 117) to buy one instead; so too when Quintus asks for a present of his poems (4. 72). It seems likely that such purchases represented some profit to Martial; otherwise it is hard to make sense of his ironical recommendations. But patronage was clearly needed in addition, and thereby was created dependence on the senatorial class together with a useful theme for epigram.

But reading no less than writing required education, and that was extremely costly both in terms of the cost of tuition and of the 'opportunity cost' (leisure was needed). It also needed books, and they certainly seem to have been very expensive. The evidence of Libanius on fourth-century Antioch[15] shows that demand for books was relatively small, and that it was steadiest in circles that were interested in teaching and among the small minority of the upper class at whom especially orations and other sophistic performances were aimed. But John Chrysostom and Libanius both complain about the absence of good literature in such homes and indeed about the lack of desire for it.[16] In the fourth century, the Christians made some attempt at mass production of sacred texts, but two factors were against it: first, the tradition of oral presentation and memorization; second, the high costs of books. The level of demand that could have reduced costs failed to appear; for, in general, literature was regarded as public entertainment to be ingested through the ears not the eyes.

The division between the educated and the uneducated was unbridgeable. It is hard to find out what happened below the level of literate culture. What must have been a familiar scene appears from a letter of Pliny (2. 20), which opens *Assem para et accipe auream fabulam—fabulas immo* ('Have ready your penny and hear a first-rate story—stories rather'). It seems that a story-teller gathered a crowd, collected money in advance, and then told stories. Probably the same sort of scene is assumed in Quin-

15. See Norman (1960).   16. Norman (1960), p. 126.

tilian[17] when he speaks of fables 'which are best known by Aesop's name. They exercise an especial attraction on rude (rusticorum) and uneducated minds which listen in an unsophisticated way to fiction, and, when pleased, fall into easy acceptance of what gives them pleasure'. Lower-class people also came to listen to speeches in law courts, as appears from a sudden picture that emerges from a letter of Pliny (7. 17). He recollects the nervousness felt just before speaking (9): 'Is it not the moment when you rise to make your speech that you feel the severest loss of confidence, and you wish not just most things, but everything, in your speech changed? Especially so if the occasion is imposing and the audience varied; for one feels intimidated even by the sight of men in dirty working clothes'. Pliny is contrasting a real speech made in a real court with a private recitation of a speech before an invited audience; and he prefers the latter. An odd fact about the Latinity of the Bible illustrates differences in educational level.[18] When the time came that Christianity was advancing into the senatorial class, the sermo humilis of the Bible revolted educated pagans to whom it was vulgar and gross, awkward in syntax and vocabulary, and riddled with Hebraic constructions. But the text of the vetus Latina had by then acquired such authority with congregations and this had been so reinforced by memorization that, despite its provenance in the intellectual level of the first Latin-speaking Christians (Greek having been the language of Christianity to the third century), even Jerome's fresh translation could not make real use of the opportunity and was limited to superficial changes.

In all of these ways literature and the appreciation of literary culture was confined to a narrow section of the upper classes—Petronius gives a splendid picture of pretentious and unsuccessful aspiration in the character of his Trimalchio. Literature was primarily a senatorial activity, and increasingly so in the time of

17. 5. 11. 19.
18. See Auerbach (1965), chap. 1: Sermo humilis.

Trajan—it is extraordinary how many of Pliny's friends turn out to be hopeful poets.

3. The differing characters of the different periods

Three distinct periods come into question: the Julio-Claudian to the death of Nero in A.D. 68, the Flavian to the death of Domitian in A.D. 96, and the period of Trajan and Hadrian. A sense of their distinctness is vital to proper judgement of the literature of the early Empire.

The Julio-Claudian period.—This was a period of aristocratic monarchy and a society still led by aristocratic families. It was a witty society, with lively interesting women who had an occasionally ill-timed capacity for orgies on a large, even vulgar, scale. Much of the gaiety that characterized the circles in which Ovid moved survived the increasing disapproval of Augustus. And not only did Ovid himself in some sort survive Augustus, but the poetry of which he was the master continued to be written. In general, it combined fantasy themes and themes from Greek mythology with flattery of the emperor. But the impression is inescapable that imaginative literature had by now, very much under Ovid's influence, come to be regarded as a form of entertainment: it was deeply escapist.[19] Characteristic of the way fantasy and panegyric could be combined with a pretty frivolity are the *Eclogues* of Calpurnius Siculus (based on a quite mistaken interpretation of Virgil's *Eclogues*) and, somewhat more interesting, the *Einsiedeln Eclogues*.

But it was also in this period that there grew up the only genuine spiritual force in the first century and a half of the Empire: Republican idealism. What prevented its lapsing into nostalgic impotence was the fact that it found shape and expression in Stoic philosophy, with the martyrdom of Cato as the bridging element

19. With the loss of so high a proportion of the literature of this period, judgement must be based on scraps of information: for a thorough examination see Bardon (1956), vol. II, 123 ff.

between Greece and Rome. The men who were inspired by these ideals were no academic philosophers; they were senators first and Stoics second. This was true even of Seneca; for, like Cicero, he only wrote in the relatively peaceful intervals of a public career. But Stoicism broadened the base of their beliefs, gave them a theoretical framework, and elevated the technical details of Roman government to aspects of the human condition as such. When it was fused with Republican ideals, Stoicism offered two extreme positions: on the one hand, fanatical opposition, conspiracy, and martyrdom; on the other, complete withdrawal from any participation in the tainted process.[20] Seneca, together with a majority in the senate, took a midway course, holding that a system of cooperation on some level between emperor and senate had to be made to work within the established constitution. For he was no fanatical Republican; he recognized a distinction between ideals and reality, and by the time that senators had come to know and endure the later years of Tiberius, Gaius, and Claudius, he, with many others, looked back no further than the system as it had been operated by Augustus: that was the ideal— a compromise between the dead past and the unendurable present.[21] Nothing is more significant of Seneca's point of view than the fact that, in his *Apocolocyntosis*, the real attack on Claudius in heaven is put into the mouth of Augustus.

Besides the escapist literature, there was a literature inspired by the deeper seriousness that grew from the union of Stoicism and Republicanism. It sprang from basic ethical questions about the ways a man could behave under a tyranny, though it generally found less dangerous expression by skirting a direct confrontation with that problem and concentrating on a variety of practical moral questions. All of Seneca's best work confronts these safer problems, with the dangerous question always at the edge of his consciousness and often appearing only in the examples offered.

20. But withdrawal was dangerous if it were obvious, since that implied condemnation: see MacMullen (1966), 50–51, 78–79.
21. But Seneca was no admirer of Augustus as such: see the careful investigation by Jal (1957).

Lucan found himself forced more and more beyond control, as his epic progressed, into absolute moral condemnation of the Caesars.[22] The seriousness of Persius, however, was untinged by any sense of real political life, and his attack on the frivolous literature of escapism was the nearest he came to the real issues of his time. A remarkable antithesis to all this was the man who re-created the gaiety and wit and elegance of the Augustan age at its best for Nero, and then died under his persecution. That gaiety and irreverence informs all of Petronius' novel that survives, and his death, to the accompaniment of songs and verse and entertainment, was a considered riposte to melodramatic Stoic suicides.

The Flavians.—The short-lived emperors who succeeded Nero were not Julio-Claudians, but they did the best they could for themselves by proclaiming descent from Juppiter and Pasiphae,[23] or from Etruscan princes,[24] or from Faunus and the local goddess Vitellia.[25] No greater contrast could be imagined to these idiotic pretensions than the hard common sense of the provincial army commander Vespasian. The tone of society became high and moral, serious and earnest;[26] that in this Vespasian was also responding to a pre-existing longing in society may be seen not only from Seneca's description[27] of the way theatre audiences spontaneously applauded condemnation of vices like avarice, but also from Lucan's thoroughgoing admiration for Cato's asceticism.[28] That new tone comes alive in Pliny's straitlaced disapproval[29] of the gay old lady, Ummidia Quadratilla, who had been born about A.D. 26 and died about A.D. 105. She had flourished under Nero and had acquired a taste for unproductive pleasures: she kept a troupe of mime actors in her house, and she divided her attention between them and her dice games. Through Pliny's

22. See p. 165 above.   23. Suetonius *Galba* 2.
24. Suetonius *Otho* 1. 1.   25. Suetonius *Vitellius* 1.
26. Well characterized by Tacitus *Annals* 3. 55. 4–5.
27. *Epp.* 108. 8–12.
28. *Bellum Civile* 2. 326 ff., and 9 *passim*.
29. *Epp.* 7. 24.

evident disapproval only one word of praise escapes: she made a good will. But Pliny's real interest is in her grandson who 'in spite of his good looks, was, as a youth, untouched by scandal', and though 'he lived in her house, he was able to combine high moral standards with due deference to his self-indulgent grandmother'. She was a brave survivor from the gay life of half a century earlier into the puritanical self-esteem of a complacent age.

Tacitus several times draws the contrast in explicit terms and discusses the causes: for instance (3. 55. 2–5) 'Formerly rich and distinguished families of the nobility came to ruin through love of display. For even then[30] it was legal to woo the people, the provinces and client kings—and to be wooed; according as each man was conspicuous for wealth, house and trappings, so did reputation and clientships elevate him to higher distinction. But after executions and the reign of terror, when a great reputation spelt death, those who were left turned to more prudent ways. At the same time, new men from towns of Italy and even from provinces crowded into the senate, bringing with them a native frugality; and, although many of them came by luck or hard work to a wealthy old age, the former attitudes remained. But the outstanding cause of puritanical behaviour was Vespasian, himself the product of the old standards and way of life. So deference to the emperor and a zeal for emulation proved stronger than the fear of legal penalty. Except that there may be a cyclical movement in everything, so that as times change so also do morals. And yet, not everything was better in earlier times, but our age too has produced many examples of character and talent for posterity. I hope that these honourable contests with our ancestors may persist among us'. It is characteristic of Tacitus to allow the mysterious and implausible suggestion of hidden historical forces to stand beside his careful analysis of causes,[31] and to contradict it obliquely in the final two sentences.

The changed moral atmosphere of the Flavian period can be seen clearly but indirectly in the fact that when Juvenal wanted

30. He means in the time of Augustus.
31. See p. 183 above.

illustrations of vice and luxury (which he often did), he normally went back over the Flavian period to the late Julio-Claudian. He was writing under Trajan and Hadrian; so his reticence was not due to tact (as Domitian's council on the fish shows), but to lack of exciting material. It was an age of serious, high-minded, and irrelevant epic poets. It is notable how much less Valerius Flaccus, Statius, and Silius Italicus express Stoic attitudes than Lucan did, and, where Stoicism appears at all, it is in a vague, watery form.[32] In fact, in this period, philosophy no longer inspired literature: its function was practical—to formulate ideals of conduct. Tacitus expressed the attitude when he said of Agricola (4. 3): 'I recall his often saying that in his early youth he would have indulged too deep an interest in philosophy—beyond what was admissible in a Roman and a senator—had not his sensible mother restrained his fire and zeal'. Systematic philosophy was not for a Roman gentleman (Nero's mother stopped him from studying it as bad for rulers),[33] and Tacitus himself easily avoids the reproach of knowing too much philosophy in his philosophical observations in *Annals* and *Histories*. Vespasian banned philosophers (in A.D. 71), while he set up the first chair of rhetoric in Rome: that is the emblem of the age.

The one light note in literature came from Martial, and that was only at the expense of gross flattery. It was perhaps not so much that other writers were silenced as that the interest in, and scope for, literary expression of ideas, especially poetic ideas, were lacking. The force of the new emperor's example worked as well against speculation and imagination as it did against frivolity; while Domitian's encouragement proved too formidable.

Trajan and Hadrian.—A new accord between emperor and senate was monumentally expressed in Pliny's *Panegyric*. The senate accepted as inevitable the principle of a Roman version of Hellenistic monarchy. In the new atmosphere of harmony there was

32. On Stoicism in Silius Italicus, see, for instance, Edward L. Bassett in Wallach (1966), 258–73.
33. Suetonius *Nero* 52.

a sudden flowering of impressive, even great, literature, with
Pliny, Tacitus, Suetonius, and Juvenal. The extent to which this
new itch to write penetrated literate society can be seen from
Pliny's letters. Many senators are discovered writing poetry, both
serious and frivolous (including Pliny himself); prose works,
mostly of an improving nature, were also being written and recited. It was a society that took itself very seriously both at work
and play: the same men, who competently and with conscientious
pride sustained their part in the administration of the Empire,
spent their leisure in literary pursuits. These men had no doubts
of their value or their sense of values. Pliny is often optimistic.
A typical outburst is this, written in A.D. 97:[34] 'This year has
brought a splendid crop of poets: in the whole of April scarcely
a day passed without someone giving a recitation. I am delighted
that literature flourishes and that geniuses are appearing and displaying themselves—though people are slow about taking their
places in the audience. . .'. Juvenal might have been glad to explain why; yet he too was optimistic about the sort of literature
that he valued. But the most striking evidence comes from Tacitus. After the veiled optimism of his *Dialogus*, he had this to say
about P. Pomponius Secundus, consul suffectus in A.D. 44:[35]
'The *ornamenta triumphalia* were decreed to Pomponius—only a
minor addition to his distinction in the eyes of posterity, among
whom the glory of his poetry is supreme'. Tacitus can only be
endorsing the judgement of posterity in considering a Roman
triumph inferior to poetic merit. When Cornelius Nepos said
of Cato (1. 4) that his discovery of Ennius in Sardinia and his
bringing of the poet to Rome can be estimated as equivalent to
the most magnificent triumph from Sardinia, he was indulging a
pleasing hyperbole. That passage can be used to show the completely different nature of Tacitus' cool assessment. Two statements are implicitly made that would have been very strange in
A.D. 50: the first is that literary composition is a surer foundation
for fame than military achievement, and that times have so

34. *Epp.* 1. 13. 1.
35. *Annals* 12. 28. 2; cf. *Dialogus* 13. 3.

changed that this opinion is now widely held in the senatorial class; the second is that Tacitus himself not only shares the opinion, but regards the place of literature in society as firmly enough established to guarantee its future.

It is a peculiar irony that soon after that confidence and optimism had been so widely expressed, literature at Rome dwindled to the point of extinction. As a preliminary to approaching that problem, it will be useful to establish what were the factors of success in the literature of the earlyEmpire.

4. *Factors of success*

There seem to have been two major factors of literary success in the period. The first—not surprisingly—was a subject matter that was capable of engaging both the intellect and the emotions at the same time. Successful escapist literature could not easily emulate the achievement of Ovid, and it was bound to fail either intellectually or emotionally or both. Subject matter of the right sort was virtually confined to two sources. The more deeply spiritual subject matter, that touched all the wellsprings of action in the Julio-Claudian period, was Republican idealism, with its theoretical skeleton of Stoicism. But that had a limited life, hardly extending, as far as literature was concerned, beyond the death of Nero. The other source (not always distinct) lay in the realities of contemporary life and society and politics, with all the dangers attendant on the use of such material. The second factor of success was the creation of a style that was capable of expressing a personality.[36] The lack of such a distinctiveness of style will explain, as well as anything, the insipidity of a poet like Calpurnius Siculus.

Among the most successful writing of the period was that which purported to be the reflection of a more or less private personality. What the elaboration that was the great characteristic of the period most needed was energy and intellectual control; and the difficulty of achieving a positive attitude that succeeded in com-

36. See chap. V, sect. 3 above.

bining intellectual and emotional elements was least in those literary genres that depended on self-generated aggressive emotions like anger, contempt, or amusement. Horace found anger a useful means for starting a poetic career, as appears from what are probably the earliest of his *Epodes* and *Satires*. It seems likely that a similarly shrewd assessment led Juvenal to write his first two books of satires with a fine show of anger. That created a personality that was easy to sustain, and that personality served to impose a unity on widely scattered material. Juvenal achieved a wider range of tone in his later writing (when he had sufficient confidence to drop the simple pose of anger), but he continued to infect all his writing with a sustained sparkle of wit that proceeded from his extremely successful adaptation of the epigram to the process of continuous composition.

Pliny was, on the face of it, very different, but he shared a wide community of thematic material, drawn from real life, with Martial and Statius; in consequence, there was also a considerable thematic overlap with Juvenal. Pliny created a style that was carefully controlled to expose the character of a Roman senator and gentleman at its very best. Emotions are mainly in a low key —friendly, concerned, urbane; only occasionally do they rise to a restrained show of indignation or confess, in a coy revelation of embarrassment, an itch to write naughty verses. He gives an excellent imitation of a real person reacting to real things all round him—even if the reaction was carefully studied. To read his *Panegyric* beside the letters is to hear the same voice considerably raised, and to realize forcefully how deeply vitiated public rhetoric was by the lack of connexion with, indeed concern for, truth and reality.

Martial can share this success. He too used the material of real life (or the pretence of it); but the surprise element in his type of epigram needed the assumption of a personality yet again different to carry it off—cool and straight-faced; and that is what Martial's style expresses. There is nothing of the apparently crusading fire of Juvenal, for that was the *persona* of the grand satiric manner. With the same personality Martial can tell a dirty

story (worthy of the—now withdrawn—honour of Italian translation in the Loeb edition), or mock a vicious individual, or
grieve memorably over the death of a friend. Emotion in this
genre is the more successfully communicated the more strictly it
is held under control. With much the same range of material
Petronius wrote with elegance and grace, wittily getting inside
each of his characters in turn, and achieving in this way surprising and exciting changes in tone and point of view. Even less than
with Martial can the question be asked what Petronius really
thought himself. His own personality lies far behind the facade
of his writing: he impersonates his characters.

But it is difficult to resist the identification of Tacitus' Petronius with the author. Tacitus recognized an original and surprising
character who, deliberately flouting all the Roman ancestral virtues, could yet show himself an energetic consul and an efficient
provincial governor.[37] The identification is important in two
ways: first, his death, like his writings, was a calculated insult to
exemplary establishment figures like Seneca (and Lucan). The
suicide, as Tacitus describes it, was, as it were, an extension in
real life of his writing—especially in the insistence on making it
seem natural and everyday. Tacitus marks well the connexion
between life and literature, in a man for whom he felt as much
attraction as repulsion, with the memorable phrase *erudito
luxu*.[38] The second point is more significant, for it was not only
an insult but a well-calculated psychological blow at Nero. Tacitus reports (16. 19. 3):

> ne codicillis quidem, quod plerique pereuntium, Neronem aut
> Tigellinum aut quem alium potentium adulatus est, sed flagitia
> principis sub nominibus exoletorum feminarumque et novitatem
> cuiusque stupri perscripsit, atque obsignata misit Neroni. fregitque
> anulum ne mox usui esset ad facienda pericula.

> He did not, as most did on their deathbeds, flatter Nero or
> Tigellinus or any other of the powerful in his will; but he wrote
> out the disgraceful details of the emperor's behaviour, prefixing

37. *Annals* 16. 18. 3–4.   38. *Annals* 16. 18. 1.

the names of homosexual prostitutes and of women and the novelty of each sexual perversion; this he sealed [like a will] and sent to Nero. He then broke his signet ring to prevent its use to endanger others.[39]

It has often been remarked that if this is the novelist Petronius, it is strange that Tacitus refrains from mentioning his writing: hence either there were two separate men or such mention 'was alien to the dignity of history'.[40] But what did Tacitus imagine Petronius to be doing in his 'mock will'? It would seem boring and obvious for such a man to draw up a solemn list of the emperor's sexual eccentricities, with names attached; and it could well be a laborious and time-consuming procedure (of which Tacitus gives no hint). The small section of the novel that remains is rich in less normal forms of sexual behaviour. I suggest that Petronius caused the emperor the pain of realizing that the admired novel could be read as a *roman à clef*[41] in which the initiated could find all Nero's favourite and embarrassing activities carefully recorded, and with whom, if one put the right real names to characters. Petronius did not have time to do more than send two correlated lists of names—nor did he need to. He did not need to write out the *novitates stupri*, which would certainly have taken time. The emperor had only to be sent running for his copy of a favourite book. Petronius need not have designed the novel with that end in view for the mock will to cause the emperor pain and apprehension—and the desire for revenge (and silence) that Petronius foresaw when he broke his signet ring.

Two writers in the period derived subject matter and inspiration from a passionate devotion to Stoicism, and both expressed completely different personalities in widely differing styles. Persius, in a tortured striving for linguistic originality and surprise,

39. For the danger involved, see the description in *Annals* 16. 17. 4–6.
40. Syme (1958), 336, n. 5.
41. The concept of the *roman à clef* was an obsession of the period, which found its richest source in misconceptions of Virgil's *Eclogues* (to be traced in the ancient commentaries, the *Lives*, and, for instance, in references to Alexis by Martial—5. 16. 12; 6. 68. 6; 7. 29. 7; 8. 56. 12; 8. 73. 10); these were worked out in detail by Calpurnius Siculus.

comes across as an austere and unworldly preacher, always speaking at the top of his voice. Seneca, in staccato outpourings that alternate emotionalism with cleverness, with constant repetition of the same idea in different words, expresses the *persona* of an evangelical parent, conscious of an effortless superiority over his audience and demonstrating it in an agonized self-revelation. Neither writer expresses any real sense that the philosophy that inspires him had become the living embodiment of Republican idealism; in *Satire* 4 Persius actually addresses a young political careerist as if politics were still free at Rome. In fact, flattery in Seneca corresponds to doctrinaire withdrawal in Persius. Ultimately both writers indulged the stylistic vices of the period to the limit, and that, combined with poor intellectual organization, has lessened their impact. But what merits both writers display are due to a genuine concern with real problems in a real world.

Two important examples of success remain: Lucan and Tacitus. The former was passionately inspired by Republican ideals in a Stoic framework, and was gifted not only with an incredible linguistic ingenuity but also (as Housman once said unkindly of H. W. Garrod) with a strong desire to shine.[42] Tacitus was inspired by an intellectual passion to tear away the pretences from social and political man and expose the reality. Morbidly defensive against revealing any weakness or sentimentality (except where it suited), he displayed one feature unique in writers of the early Empire: he often said less than he meant and knew that it is a great strength in a writer to trust the reader's understanding. He is continually exciting to read because his intellect is continuously engaged; the interplay of fact and judgement, of pretence and revelation, constantly generates emotion from a normally impersonal text. With Tacitus the reader is always aware of being occupied with a mind, seldom with a man, except at those points where he chose deliberately to force his own personality on the reader; and those are probably the least successful passages. The sharpness of the style, which perfectly matched the

42. *M. Manilii Astronomicon: Liber Quintus*, 2nd ed., Cambridge, 1937, p. xxv.

author's intellectual qualities, suited a certain impersonality on his part. The curious fact is that the author chose increasingly (in conformity to a tendency of the age) to enter his own text as an individual personality.[43]

In spite of great technical abilities in practitioners, epic did not flourish: the vices of the age fed and multiplied on the fantasies of Greek mythology and on the inanities of the divine machinery—which Silius Italicus brought back into historical epic to show how sound Lucan's judgement had been. To say that these epics were pure escapism should not be to condemn them: there was much to escape from and there was need for innocent entertainment. But much of this writing reads like something designed to meet a consumer need rather than something that burned a hole in the poet's mind. The exception was Lucan. In him an ever-growing passion for Republicanism combined with a very personal style and an intellect capable of memorable epigram to carry the reader over the many digressions and fantasies, the repetitions and the artificialities, to see the unity derived from the writer's increasing hatred of Caesar and his shining romantic admiration of Cato. Lucan's personality intrudes more and more as he realizes less and less escapably the logical impossibility of compromise with any aspect of Caesarism. His imagination admittedly concentrated on the period immediately preceding the most sensitive period of Roman history; for the opening of the civil war between Pompey and Caesar was less dangerous to handle than the period that contained the murder of Caesar and the establishment of the primacy of Augustus—the period from which his relatives dissuaded even the future emperor Claudius.[44] Hatred of Julius Caesar (who gets a poor press even with Augustan writers) was a good deal less dangerous, and the period had the universally admired figure of Cato to recommend it. But Lucan, though he avoided the danger of touching on the real founder of the dynasty, presents a fascinating picture, since he found it more and more impossible to avoid seeing the founder and all his successors, right up to Nero, in the figure of Julius

43. See chap. V, sect. 3 above.   44. Suetonius *Claudius* 41. 2.

Caesar. Juvenal in his satire about Domitian's council on the great fish blandly omitted the figure of Nerva; Lucan's uncontrolled fire could admit no such easy solution.

5. Factors of decline

Why then did literary composition in Rome run out into the sand so soon after the establishment of the new political accord between senate and emperor? Some factors have been suggested in earlier lectures, and the most obvious and important of them may be listed as follows:

1. The tension between monarchical government and the Republican ideal of free speech (for relevant classes in society). Freedom of speech, in that limited sense, had already been threatened under the Republic, but under conditions that looked forward to the Empire. Cicero, for instance, had been compelled in the fifties in a humiliating way by the triumvirs to defend men designated by them; and when Cicero was writing the *de oratore* in 56/55 B.C. he reflected bitterly on earlier orators who, in civil wars, had been silenced and even killed.[45] Similarly, the elder Seneca seems to have dated the retreat of Truth from the beginning of the civil wars, perhaps inspired by Cicero. That was in his *Histories*, but the statement may be a comment by his son.[46] In either case it pushes back Roman writers' own diagnoses of the decline in freedom of speech to the Republic. But this must not mislead. The Republic was a time of freedom: one can contrast Cicero's use of declamation in Greek and Latin to speculate on the question of submission to a tyrant[47] with Dio Chrysostom's statement[48] that an orator should take his examples from ancient times. Seneca in *de beneficiis*[49] traces the increased vigilance exercised by Augustus and then by Tiberius over men's words and casual acts till it reached a climax of horror under Caligula.[50] Already during the earliest period of the Empire it had proved

45. *de oratore* 3. 1–4.   46. Frags. 98–99 Haase.
47. *ad Att.* 9. 4.   48. *orat.* 21. 11.
49. 3. 26–27.   50. *de ira* 3. 19.

virtually impossible to keep literature out of politics, and Ovid was the paradigm case.

2. The increasing admiration of the senatorial classes for Hellenic culture. Due to this fact, taste and literary interests took their standards and models from Greece; this was inevitably accompanied by an increasing sense of inferiority to Greek achievement in the great past.

3. The growth of a rhetorical ideal that laid emphasis on style and treatment rather than subject matter. This led easily to the complete exhaustion (through endless borrowing and imitation) of the great Roman Classical tradition, with its creative fusion of Greek and Roman elements; at that point this factor was clearly reinforced by the previous one.

4. The growth of irrationalism in a very general way in Roman life, leading to loss of intellectual nerve and energy, and an emphasis on emotion at the expense of reason (reinforced by the immediately preceding factor).

5. Republican ideals were the only genuine spiritual force in the early Empire, and they finally lost what little power remained in them with the new accord between emperor and senate.

These factors operated with different force at different times. The factors listed as 2, 3, and 4 were gaining ground fast under Trajan. But the factors 1 and 5 worked in an opposite direction to one another. Trajan honoured the Stoics whom Domitian had exiled, and he went some way towards punishing *delatores*.[51] But there was more. Titinius Capito got Trajan's permission to erect a statue to L. Junius Silanus Torquatus, who had been executed by Nero in the aftermath of the conspiracy of Piso in A.D. 66; and he himself had *imagines* of Brutus, Cassius, and Cato prominently displayed in his house.[52] Trajan himself had coins issued with the inscription LIBERTAS BRUTUS,[53] and under him there were written a spate of martyr biographies of the Neronian

51. Pliny *panegyricus* 35.
52. Pliny *Epp.* 1. 17.
53. Toynbee (1944), 45; but on the interpretation see MacMullen (1966), 23 and n. 37.

and Domitianic persecutions.[54] The danger of such subjects had obviously been judged by authority to have evaporated, and Trajan could actually signal the new accord by suggesting a sort of rebirth of the Republic that Brutus and Cato had known, a suggestion once again, as always, going back for its legitimation to the founder Augustus. So speech could not be freer,[55] but perhaps the topics had lost their power to inspire in proportion as they ceased to be perilous.

What then of Pliny and Tacitus and Juvenal? It is certainly significant that all three had been silenced under Domitian. The most explicit evidence comes from the autobiographical opening to Tacitus' life of his father-in-law, Agricola. Tacitus, in company with others, had been silenced for fifteen years by executions and burnings of books. The biography, Tacitus claims, will be a memorial to that servitude as well as a testimony to present felicity.[56] It may be conjectured that the repression had had something of the effect of a new injection of Republican idealism. This inspired Tacitus to a re-examination of the imperial system through its history, beginning, in his *Histories,* with the more recent Flavian period that commenced with the death of Nero. Tacitus was no Republican, but he had a highly critical eye for weaknesses in the system and their origin in the inevitable clash between emperor and senate; that led him to the contrast with the Republic and the origin of the principate. However, he did not treat that clash directly in the person of the founder (that might well still have been too sensitive), but only from the point where a successor clearly marked the downward trend towards

54. Pliny himself wrote *libri de Helvidii ultione* (*Epp.* 9. 13. 1); Gaius Fannius wrote *exitus occisorum aut relegatorum a Nerone* in at least three books (*Epp.* 5. 5. 3); and Titinius Capito wrote *exitus inlustrium virorum* (*Epp.* 8. 12. 4).

55. Pliny explains that a speech of thanks in the senate, which previously would have bored after a minute, now finds an audience for three days on end—due to the inspiration provided by the new freedom of speech (*Epp.* 3. 18. 6). In *Epp.* 8. 14. 3 he explains that he is ignorant of certain procedures in the senate because Freedom has only recently been restored.

56. *Agricola* 3. 3.

Nero. The analogy he saw between Domitian and Tiberius has often been observed. But there was another psychological impulse which affected Pliny no less than Tacitus. In the first chapter of his *Agricola*, Tacitus contrasts the Republican past, when the historical account of great merits was welcomed, with the present day:

> at nunc narraturo mihi vitam defuncti hominis venia opus fuit, quam non petissem incusaturus: tam saeva et infesta virtutibus tempora.

> But now as I undertake to write the biography of a dead man I have had to ask indulgence—which I would not have had to ask had I been attacking him: so harsh and hostile to merit is our age.[57]

Tacitus is not just saying that men give a readier hearing to invective than to eulogy;[58] he is suggesting, as he was to say explicitly in the *Annals*,[59] that men can feel hostility to accounts of merit because they see in them an implied criticism of themselves. What Tacitus meant here comes out more clearly in what follows, and especially in the words (2. 3) 'we have given outstanding proof of submissiveness; and, just as earlier times explored the extreme in licence, so we in servitude'. The contrast between the extremists in both directions under Domitian and those who, like Tacitus or Agricola or Pliny, achieved a working compromise with the tyrant fascinated both Tacitus and Pliny. A number of letters of Pliny[60] are especially revealing, and the epistolary form gave Pliny the opportunity of formulating his point of view (and reformulating it) in a personal way that was anecdotal rather than carefully analytical. Tacitus is similarly to be seen to some extent considering his own position in his portrait of life under Domitian.

57. This should not be interpreted as an assertion by Tacitus that he had to ask permission from Domitian, which is both in itself unlikely and would make the final generalization empty. Tacitus has found it necessary, even in good times, to ask pardon for the praise of outstanding merit.
58. As he does in *Hist.* 1. 1. 2.
59. 4. 33. 4.
60. Cf. *Epp.* 8. 14.

Pliny found his perfect literary form in the Republican free-dom and intimacy of Cicero's letters. All Pliny's instincts (like those of his teacher Quintilian) went to an admiration of Cicero as human being, orator, and politician (this was the point of view that Tacitus represented in his *Dialogus* in the character of Messalla). It is even possible to see Pliny reconstructing his rela-tions with Domitian on the pattern of Cicero's[61] with the tri-umvirs, and later with Caesar. The contrast between public and private life under Trajan and what it had been under Domitian is a powerful motif in Pliny's letters, even when not explicit.

Of Juvenal too little is known to be certain of anything except that his type of satire would have been impossible under Domi-tian. Since Martial only knew him as *facundus*,[62] he may have confined himself to the declamation schools. To that extent he may have been silenced; at least he must have felt the atmosphere of repression. Its lifting inspired him to a witty assault on the structure and character of his own society, including a whole satire devoted to Domitian himself. It is interesting that the age of Nero should so fascinate a man writing satire under Trajan; his explanation that it was the result of prudence on his part can only be partial, and it seems more likely that he too, like Tacitus and Pliny, could only find subject matter that inspired him from times of oppression, analogous to those of Domitian.

All of this literary activity, consequently, may be seen as an immediate (and temporary) result of the lifting of the Domitianic terror. There was great optimism expressed by all three writers about the future of literature at Rome. But perhaps unguarded moments show a different view. Pliny wrote to Cornelius Mini-cianus as he was about to attend a recitation by Titinius Capito, whom he praises for his generosity as a literary patron. In the course of this,[63] he says of Capito: 'he who restored and reformed literature itself when it was in decline'. This seems more a mo-ment of truth or of wishful thinking than the sort of inane flat-tery with which Statius praised Manlius Vopiscus in *Silvae* 1

61. Starting from *Epp.* 1. 5.   62. 7. 91. 1; cf. 7. 24 and 12. 18.
63. *Epp.* 8. 12. 1.

praef.: *qui praecipue vindicat a situ litteras iam paene fugientes* ('he who is especially reclaiming from decay a literature that is already almost in flight from our midst'). Then, again, Pliny says[64] of the great lawyer Titius Aristo, who has been ill: 'There is nobody more serious, more influential and more experienced in literature, so that not just an individual, but literature itself and all the liberal arts seem to be in utmost peril in that one man'. Pliny's rhetorical instinct was probably stronger than his perception, but doubts certainly seem to have lurked at the edges of his mind, even if the perimeter was firmly guarded. The sense of what Pliny says fits with Tacitus' gloomy comments[65] that it is easier to repress literature than to bring it alive again, that inactivity comes to be enjoyed, and that the writers oppressed by Domitian are now *senes* and have outlived themselves. The stimulus that came from the repression and its lifting was not only artificial, it was also temporary. The period contemporary with the literary works of all three was filled with facile composers, producing ephemeral effusions of all sorts to fill their own and their friends' leisure hours. The pressure of ideas dropped sharply with the removal of the one spiritual force that had proved capable of engaging intellect and emotion at the same time.

But there were other factors of decline.

6. Patronage

Juvenal bursts out with optimism at the beginning of *Satire* 7:

> et spes et ratio studiorum in Caesare tantum;
> solus enim tristes hac tempestate Camenas
> respexit, cum iam celebres notique poetae
> balneolum Gabiis, Romae conducere furnos
> temptarent, nec foedum alii nec turpe putarent
> praecones fieri, cum desertis Aganippes
> vallibus esuriens migraret in atria Clio.

All hope and prospect for literary studies depend completely on Caesar; for he alone has taken an interest in the dejected

---

64. *Epp.* 1. 22. 1.   65. *Agricola* 3. 1–2.

Muses at this period of time when celebrated and famous poets have to become bath attendants at Gabii or bakers in Rome, and still others of them see nothing disgraceful in becoming auction-eers, since starving Clio has had to desert the valleys of Helicon for the sale rooms.

With allowance made for exaggeration, the situation implied as the antecedent to the new happiness sounds like the less opti-mistic descriptions of Tacitus and Pliny. The Caesar meant by Juvenal is undoubtedly Hadrian, who became emperor in A.D. 117. He certainly patronized the arts as much as he practised them. But there is no sign that he helped any to literary success, except for Suetonius and Juvenal, both of whom were already well established. It seems likely that at least as much, and perhaps far more, of Hadrian's interest was devoted to Greek literary artists, a fact that Juvenal may not have realized when he wrote that eulogy—or he may have blandly opposed it by assuming the opposite to be true. But Hadrian's great model was Augustus, and it is worth looking briefly at the vicissitudes of imperial patronage over the whole period.

Augustus was on intimate terms with poets; and though in earlier times he managed literary patronage through Maecenas, it is clear that literary men, both poets and historians, Greek and Roman, were familiar and welcome figures about his court. That the break with Ovid left him mainly with Greeks seems likely,[66] for the Greek poets continued to produce and are found equally in the court of Tiberius. However, it looks as if the case of Ovid was not only paradigmatic and discouraging, but that it also convinced Tiberius of two things: first, that literature was of no interest except as entertainment and, second, that his adoptive father had been mistaken in the value he placed on literary sup-port. Tiberius had literary men about him, mainly Greeks, to amuse and entertain him. But the uninspired works of Velleius Paterculus and Valerius Maximus represent the sort of improving literature that would be worth his public support.

Roman poets—as distinct from Greek—had no support under

66. See p. 137 above.

Tiberius: one only has to look at the wretched uncertainties of Phaedrus, or of Ovid refurbishing the address of his *Fasti* not to Tiberius but to Germanicus (whereas Manilius had addressed his didactic poem to Augustus). However, Tiberius' curious literary interests did cause him to give patronage to Apollonides of Nicaea, who wrote a commentary on the *Silloi* of Timon and dedicated it to the emperor;[67] he also handed out, as Suetonius says in a particularly gossipy chapter (42), 200,000 sesterces to Asellius Sabinus for a dialogue between a truffle, a fig-pecker, an oyster, and a thrush. The situation was not better under Gaius; nor did it improve under Claudius—presumably because the pedantic weight of his erudition rejected poetic frivolity. If Seneca wrote his tragedies under Claudius, it was in exile. Everything changed suddenly with Nero:[68] the atmosphere of the early period of Augustus was recreated, and poets and prose writers alike started talking Golden Age imagery. To this period belong the flatteries of Calpurnius Siculus and of the *Einsiedeln Eclogues*, also Seneca's *Apocolocyntosis* and *de clementia*, and, most significantly, Lucan's address to Nero towards the opening of the *Bellum Civile*. There the important theme is peace, and it is handled with serene optimism. Lucan views the present as of such quality and promise that the civil wars could be regarded as a costly but necessary step on the way to a universal peace; the central Augustan theme of patriotism was abandoned in favour of this Stoic universalism. There was no incompatibility between Stoicism and monarchy as such, and Lucan may have been planning to take the line that Seneca took in *de clementia*. Nero revived the Augustan idea of the supreme importance of literature, and he went beyond Augustus in instituting festivals to mark that importance and assimilate literature into the national life. In this way, he also provided a framework in which literature could be controlled—no doubt he had benefitted from the sad spectacle of Augustus and the desperate attempts at repression. Petronius transferred the Golden Age to the amusing milieu of

67. Hillscher (1892), 387–88.
68. On the Neronian literary scene, see especially Momigliano (1944).

vulgarians in low society. Persius played the ill-natured Stoic
recreating Horace—in whom Stoics had only aroused laughter.
The accord could not last. The more successful the programme,
the more independent the poets became and the less conspicuous
the part played by the emperor. But it was, for a time, a remarkable revival, and it showed one thing clearly beyond all doubt—
that imperial patronage was essential. That it collapsed in bloodshed was due to the inevitable increase in the emperor's isolation
and in the tension between emperor and senate.

The increasing isolation, which had been discovered by Augustus, also meant that Augustus' solution (which he himself
had felt compelled to drop) of using a Maecenas was even less
possible. The case of Ovid is the paradigm for the whole period.
Emperors were compelled to be more watchful over literature
than eager to encourage it. Vespasian, again trying to be a new
Augustus as he founded a new dynasty, subvented the arts, but
he had little talent for recognizing talent and no adviser was at
hand. Besides, his interest was practical and educational: the
training of future administrators of the Empire was a primary
consideration.[69] One senses also under Vespasian a significant
increase in that militarization of the court that was to be complete
by the late third century.[70] The major problems were administrative and military; interest focussed more and more on the complex events in far-off provinces. Consequently, the people about
the court were mainly soldiers. The figures of Quintilian and
Saleius Bassus do little to offset an austere impression.[71]

69. See p. 140 above.
70. On the later stages of this, see MacMullen (1963), chap. 7.
71. It does not help much to add Statius' father: see Thiele (1916), 250.
Valerius Flaccus too should be added, for it seems certain that the prooemium of the *Argonautica* was addressed to a Vespasian who was still alive:
see especially Strand (1972), 7–38 (specifically on the dating of 23–38, but
that problem cannot be separated from problems of text and interpretation).
Lefèvre (1971) agrees on the question of dating, but tries to interpret (15)
ille as Domitian and the references to cult and temple as a metaphor for
poetry (cf. Virgil *Georgics* 3. 12 ff.): this is ingenious, but cannot be recon-
ciled with the immediately connected (16 *cum tu, genitor, lucebis. . .*) picture
of the deification of Vespasian to be carried out, actually, by Titus. The

Domitian, in contrast, was *Nero redivivus*. Martial complains about lack of patrons, but he is talking about Maecenases and Messallas.[72] (There could be no complaint against the emperor: Martial, bachelor though he was, received the *ius trium liberorum*.)[73] The result was another literary revival, encouraged again—and controlled—by poetic festivals, Greek no less than Latin. Writing did not always need patronage, at least in a financial sense: Silius Italicus was a man of wealth who felt the encouragement created by Domitian and his own love of Virgil sufficient to launch an epic. Like Lucan, he must have published the early books at an early stage, since, in Virgilian style, he depicts Venus anxiously consulting Juppiter about the perfidies of Carthage. Juppiter replies with a survey of Roman history that takes nine lines to reach the time of Vespasian; there are thirteen lines on Vespasian and Titus, then a climax of twenty-three lines heralds Domitian—conqueror, orator, poet, and future god.[74] Silius Italicus did not begin his epic before Domitian was emperor.[75] Vespasian, however, was living at the time Valerius Flaccus began his epic, but the prooemium is also designed as flattery of Domitian.[76] The centrepiece of all Statius' work is Domitian, and the emperor is also flattered inordinately by Quintilian.[77] But the accord was shattered again—not because writers found it impossible to avoid offence: nothing was easier for them,

---

whole passage suffers from Valerius' *breviloquentia*, but he must have intended (12) *proles tua* as Domitian, and (15) *ille* as Titus, taking up the immediately preceding mention of Titus. The suspicion occurs easily that poetic activity under Vespasian owed far more to the interest of Domitian than to that of his father, and the suspicion is confirmed by the manner in which Valerius refers to Domitian's poetic activity: see n. 76 below.

72. See sect. 2 above.

73. 2. 92—so he had received it by A.D. 86. He had previously been given the privilege by Titus—3. 95. 5; 9. 97. 5.

74. 3. 557–629.

75. On the dating of Silius see Wistrand (1956): he dates the praise of the Flavians to A.D. 83/84 (p. 58).

76. It is clear that, like Lucan and Silius Italicus, Valerius published some early books as a unit soon after they were written. This will have been before the death of Vespasian. See note 71 above.

77. See chap. IV, sect. 2 above.

since, unlike Neronian poets, they gave themselves to irrelevant topics. The accord broke where the reality was—in politics; and there literature only mattered if dead Stoics could be resurrected to inspire new conspiracies.[78]

Trajan's court reverted to the austere militarism of Vespasian's, and such interest in the arts as was displayed there proceeded from his wife. Pliny in his *Panegyric* (54) prophesied that Trajan's dismissive attitude to flattery and honours, so different from Domitian's, would have the opposite effect and that all sorts of honours would be proffered spontaneously and from the heart. In particular, he predicted, serious poetry and the eternal distinction of historical writing would laud his rule, in contrast to what he was pleased to call the brief and unworthy address now being presented (that is, the *Panegyric* itself). Pliny's prediction proved false, but it was perhaps with a similar zest to honour the new emperor that Tacitus, avowing that his own official career owed its beginnings to Vespasian and Titus and its further advancement to Domitian (a fact which he says he does not wish to deny), promised that, if he lived, he would write the history of the deified Nerva's reign and the imperial career of Trajan.[79] He did not do it—naturally; no more did he write of the reign of Augustus, as he promised in the *Annals*:[80] a likelier promise, if as dangerous, but death robbed him of any need to explain his failure.

This was the point at which literature found its only possible social basis: an innocent entertainment for the educated, with not the slightest importance. Revered Stoics could be resurrected with due admiration, or amatory verses composed, or any conceivable literary form could be given artificial respiration; it was all the same. The lesson of Augustus had at last been learned: literature is as important as it is allowed to be. Suppress it, and interest grows; allow anything to be written in an otherwise controlled society in which the controls are accepted, and

78. On martyrologies see Musurillo (1954), 236 ff.; Bardon (1956), 207–9.
79. *Hist.* 1. 1. 5.
80. 3. 24. 3.

nothing matters. Domitian's suppression inspired Pliny, Tacitus, and Juvenal, but there was nothing to inspire successors.

7. Public recitation

This whole tendency was promoted by the practice of public recitation. It had been a Greek custom to recite poetry in public. Some time after 39 B.C. the custom was introduced into Rome by C. Asinius Pollio[81]—another aspect of the influx of Hellenic culture in the period. Pollio recited his tragedies. Horace,[82] Virgil,[83] and Propertius[84] all seem to have avoided the temptation; all gave private readings to small groups of friends, but not as an entertainment in itself so much as to elicit criticism and comment. But all later poets recited their works publicly, and so did historians, orators, and philosophers.[85] In fact, all later writers ought to be viewed as having written their works with this form of live performance in mind as their immediate aim. There are many portraits of the occasion in Pliny's letters, and it is clear that this became a form of entertainment for the upper classes, exactly parallel to the declamations of rhetors and the epideictic speeches of sophists. From Epictetus[86] it appears that as many as a thousand people could be present, but Pliny's gatherings were more select and the audience individually invited.[87]

A number of results followed from this innovation, more or less directly. First, poetry became assimilated to the condition of prose: that is, in fact, the conception expressed by Aper in Tacitus' *Dialogus*, that poetry is a subsection of rhetoric.[88] Here lay the greatest contrast with the earlier Augustans. They wrote to be read, and could leave much to the imagination and under-

81. Seneca *contr.* 4 *pr.* 2.
82. *Sat.* 1. 4. 73–74.
83. Donatus *vita* 33.
84. Ovid *Tristia* 4. 10. 57–58.
85. See, for example, Pliny *Epp.* (poems) 3. 15; 4. 27; 5. 3 and 17; 7. 4. 7–10; 8. 21; 9. 22 and 34: (historians) 7. 12; 9. 27: (orators) 3. 18.
86. 3. 23. 19.
87. See especially *Epp.* 3. 18.
88. See chap. I, sect. 7 above.

standing of the reader. They could write with an allusiveness and subtlety that would be missed on a public reading. For this reason Virgil and Horace (and, one suspects, Propertius) were misunderstood from a time soon after they wrote. This can easily be traced in the interpretations of scholiasts and in the mistaken assumptions made by writers like Calpurnius Siculus and Martial. The degree of misunderstanding is at least of the same order as the misunderstanding of Elizabethan and Jacobean writers which can be traced in poets and critics of the Augustan age, like Samuel Johnson.[89] Earlier literature, including, presumably, Augustan poets as well as Greek poets, was read privately in houses on suitable occasions (as at dinner),[90] and slaves who could read well were particularly valued.[91] Virgil's *Eclogues* were used for stage performances,[92] and Tacitus records the popular enthusiasm for his verses;[93] but there is no record of other early Augustan poetry at any time receiving public recitation. It was not comprehensible on such an occasion.

The vital change was made by Ovid. He, of course, certainly understood his contemporaries and predecessors, but he had a different aim. He altered the whole process of poetic composition to make it an art form for public recitation rather than private reading. What was needed was a literature of immediate impact. The sort of poetry that grows by slow reading and careful rereading, that only by degrees reveals its full depths, was not only no longer of interest, it was impossible. So it came about that earlier literature was reserved for private reading, while the latest literature was heard at public performances that were like orchestral concerts. This placed a premium on novelty. Each performer naturally had to have something that he could claim was new, and over a long period this meant that poetry gave place to

89. On this, see, for instance, W. Jackson Bate, *The Burden of the Past and the English Poet*, Harvard University Press, 1970.

90. A good collection of material is found in Mayor's commentary to Juvenal, vol. I, 173ff.

91. See, for example, Pliny *Epp.* 5. 19.

92. Donatus *vita* 26; Servius on *Ecl.* 6. 11.

93. *Dialogus* 13.

prose. The most clear guarantee of novelty lay in extempore performance, like that of the great Euphrates or Isaeus, who came into the auditorium and then asked the audience for a subject.[94] There were, of course, extempore poetic compositions—a number of the poems in Statius' *Silvae* must have been extempore—but the practice clearly gave the preference to prose.[95]

A further result was the breaking down of stylistic distinctions between various genres, with the main emphasis now placed on the personality of the individual performer. Hence even the stylistic distinction between poetry and prose disappeared, and each writer created a style that would best carry his own personality, using all the linguistic resources that Latin provided. Juvenal did not imitate the private, informal style of Horace in his *Satires*, since that was quite unsuited to attaining the weight and impact needed for public performance. The sound of Juvenal, and so his rhetorical effect, is not very different from that of Ovid's *Metamorphoses* or of Lucan or of Statius. Persius was still close enough to Horace for a certain *aemulatio*, though it is at a far remove. Juvenal in his programmatic satire lays even more weight on Lucilius as his predecessor than on Horace: he was appealing to a tradition, not challenging an individual author, and he is really as far removed from Horace as he is from Lucilius.

One senses from the descriptions in Pliny's letters that prose performances and, even more, the epideictic declamations of great virtuosi like Isaeus or Euphrates were more entertaining and stimulating than poetry readings. So in the course of the second century A.D., poetry became a subject for antiquarian study by scholars in private or in small groups, like those depicted by Aulus Gellius in his *Attic Nights*. Literature as such became more and more just oratory, as society created more occasions for performances by the great virtuosi of the age—sophists and philosophers, some Roman but most of them Greek. At that point private reading came back into favour for certain types of literature that were more suited for private enjoyment. Hence, where-

94. On Euphrates see Pliny *Epp.* 1. 10, and on Isaeus, 2. 3.
95. See p. 267 above.

as Apuleius' other works envisage an audience, his novel, the
Metamorphoses, a number of times makes direct appeal to a
reader.[96] This fact seems to be reflected in the stylistic difference
between the *Metamorphoses* and Apuleius' other writings: it is
hard to imagine the involuted, ornamental, expansive sentences
of the *Metamorphoses* as capable of making an instantly intel-
ligible impact on an audience. Rather it is a style to be savoured
at leisure.

8. *The archaizing movement*

Roman literature after the age of Trajan (and except for sur-
vivors from that age such as Juvenal) ran out into the inanities
of the archaizing fad. Here it is more than usually difficult to
distinguish symptoms from causes, and, since the movement as
such lies beyond the scope of these lectures, only a preliminary
sketch will be attempted here.

In Greek the phenomenon can be traced back beyond the age
of Augustus, and indeed Roman taste and literary judgement reinforced the Greek instinct to turn back to the far past.[97] In
Greek this made sense, since the great masterpieces all lay back
beyond the Hellenistic period. However much Romans might
feel impressed by Alexandrian critical thinking and stylistic
standards, the fact was that no Roman shows any sign of being
dominated by them. As the only Greek poets who had self-
consciously examined what they were doing and expressed a
response to a crushing weight of tradition, the Alexandrians
were useful points of reference, sounding boards, for Roman
poets. But a poet like Propertius who could use Callimachus to
establish his own position, felt perfectly free to compose entirely
different poetry. That was positive and healthy, and it was com-
patible with total admiration for the great Greek past. But in
Greeks, the decision to ignore the existence of the Hellenistic
age quickly led to sterility in a number of ways. First, it led to

96. 1. 1. 16; 9. 30. 1; 10. 2. 12; 11. 23. 19.
97. See chap. III, sect. 3 above.

the artificial re-creation of a long past language and its pedantic maintenance against any tendency of living language to innovate. The barriers went up against new influences with dictionaries like the ten volumes of Pollux's *Onomasticon* and the grammatical works of Phrynichus.[98] Second, the remoteness of the great past and the decay of any living connexion with it that came about when poetry died at Alexandria meant that subject matter had to be taken from the far past too. So even Lucian often sets the scene of his dialogues in classical Athens, and in his satiric works his models were Plato and Old Comedy; he ventures no further forward than to use the third-century Cynic, Menippus of Gadara, as his mouthpiece. Alciphron's letters used fourth-century Athens as their scene, and the erotic novel of Chariton went back to the fifth century B.C. for its setting. Heliodorus used classical Delphi as the scene of his novel.[99] Third, rhetoric became definitive and prescriptive, for only by greater and greater refinement and definition of the rules could so artificial a form of composition be kept on the true road.

In Latin, however, the effect was far worse, since Romans had to turn back to a primitive and relatively unsophisticated literature. Such a literature could not offer subject matter; it could only influence style. The effect can be seen in a schematic contrast with writers of the early Empire. In writers such as Seneca or Statius it is a reasonable generalization to say that the focus of stylistic attention tended to narrow down from larger units of composition to concentration on the single phrase; this tendency was noted and criticized by Quintilian.[100] But in the writing and criticism of Fronto it is clear that the process had gone a stage further and that the focus had narrowed down further to concentration on the single word.[101] Only in that way could the primi-

98. See, for instance, Marache (1952), 105 ff.
99. See Bowie (1970), 3 ff.
100. In his criticism of Seneca, 10. 1. 130.
101. See generally Marache (1952), 70–76, 138 ff.; and Grube (1965), 320–22. Quintilian (8. *pr.* 31–32) already detected the tendency in his own day. Such concentration on the single word, particularly if it is strange and archaic, characterizes the literary criticism of Aulus Gellius.

tive vocabulary of early Roman writers be used with proper appreciation; for even an occasional archaic word, if properly placed and understood, could create atmosphere, while the lushness and luxuriance and high decibel level of the early writers could be imitated without insistent reproduction of their distasteful grammatical, syntactical, and morphological peculiarities.

Roman writers, especially poets, had always been archaizers. It was their way, learned from Greeks, of adapting to the solemnity of high poetry a language that had no specifically poetic diction;[102] and that process went right back to Livius Andronicus. Historiography, which needed an analogous solemnity and distance from the ordinary, used the same licence on a smaller scale;[103] hence the style of Sallust and of his great imitator Tacitus. That was a perfectly legitimate means of creating a style, and archaisms were only one ingredient among many. The taste for the archaic as such, however, was something different. It did not enter oratory in Rome until oratory began to cease being politically influential;[104] and when Tacitus makes Aper say[105] that Cicero shows signs of *antiquitas* in his earlier speeches, he is both exaggerating in the interest of his theory of relativity and applying the standards of his own time.

Tiberius seems to be an example of a man deliberately indulging a taste for archaism, and he incurred Augustus' criticism for it.[106] In this he seems to have shared the backward-looking ideals of Asinius Pollio, whom Aper condemns[107] for reproducing Accius and Pacuvius not only in his tragedies but also in his *ora-*

102. On the significance of this fact for Roman poetry, see Williams (1968), 743–50.

103. This is sometimes denied to Sallust's predecessors—wrongly: for just as Fronto and Apuleius created an archaizing style using few actual archaisms, so did the pre-Sallustian annalists; the effect of whole clauses, indeed of whole paragraphs (where possible), needs to be weighed.

104. See Marache (1952), 17 ff.

105. *Dialogus* 18. 1; 22. 3.

106. Suetonius *Aug.* 86.

107. *Dialogus* 21. 7. Aper may exaggerate here too, and Pollio cannot be assumed to have been an archaist like Fronto, but Marache (1952), 38–40, explains him away too easily.

tiones. The tendency was on the increase in the first century A.D. It is notable that Phaedrus in his *Fables* used a senarius based on that of Plautus and Terence, whereas Seneca in his tragedies deliberately imitated the Greek trimeter.[108] Seneca criticizes orators who 'take their words from an earlier age and speak the Twelve Tables'.[109] Persius seems to mock writers who are devoted to Accius and Pacuvius;[110] and those two tragedians became the conventional touchstone for an interest in archaizing.[111] By the time of Domitian, archaizing was a force to be reckoned with;[112] and both Martial (especially in 11. 90 where the attack is directly on an archaizing style, but also in 5. 10 and 8. 69 where a taste is criticized) and Quintilian[113] express their opposition to it. In fact, the way in which Quintilian has drawn up his canon of Greek and Roman literature in book 10 shows that part of his intention was to combat the new archaizing taste of his day.[114] Tacitus made Aper condemn archaizing in downright terms,[115]

108. Still observing, however, certain basic Roman features such as the Bentley-Luchs law governing the pattern of the last two feet; this law had an importance for the senarius analogous to that of the law concerning the pattern of the last two feet of the hexameter: for details see Strzelecki (1938) and (1963). But in the proportion of iambs, for instance, Seneca takes Greek technique as his model. On details of Phaedrus' technique, see Korzeniewski (1970).

109. *Epp.* 114. 13.

110. The lines (*Sat.* 1. 76–78) should not be read as a question, as Clausen does in his text (1956) and his OCT, relying on the arguments of K. F. Hermann. The double connective. . .-*que et*. . .in the second clause speaks strongly against taking the structure as a question. It is an emotional accusation, and the words should be given to Persius himself, who naturally condemns such nonsense.

111. Martial 11. 90; *Dialogus* 20. 5; 21. 7.

112. On M. Valerius Probus see Marache (1952), 62 ff.

113. 10. 1. 43 and 93. Marache (1952), 34 sees Martial as merely protesting, like Horace in *Epp.* 2. 1, against critics who prefer dead writers; but, whereas that may account for 5. 10 and 8. 69, it will not account for 11. 90, where deliberate archaism—not classicism—is in question.

114. For Quintilian see especially Marache (1952), 42 ff., who (rightly) distinguishes between the growing strength of the archaists and the decline of the long-outmoded Atticists—though he (wrongly) regards the former as unimportant for the growth of archaism in the second century.

115. *Dialogus* 23. 1–3.

and his own practice was simply in accord with his use of Sallust as a stylistic model. The most extensive evidence, however, comes from Pliny's letters, where a whole series of his friends can be seen turning back to primitive models: there is Vergilius Romanus writing *vetus comoedia* and *mimiambi*,[116] or Pompeius Saturninus imitating the rhetorical style of the Gracchi and even of Cato the censor;[117] Pliny tells of the latter reading out letters purporting to be from his wife (Pliny doubted it), which struck Pliny as being like Plautus and Terence in prose. We are, then, in immediate touch with Fronto and the attitude that, like the Greeks ignoring the Hellenistic age, regarded the great Classical period of Roman literature as exhausted and looked back over it to the second century B.C. It is no surprise then to find Hadrian preferring, on the one hand, Cato the censor to Cicero, Ennius to Virgil, and Coelius Antipater to Sallust and, on the other, 'more deeply devoted to Greek literature, and his mind so attuned to it that some actually called him *Graeculus*'.[118]

For the archaizing age was an age in which Greek culture completely dominated Roman (with very rare exceptions like Apuleius). Poetry had died in both cultures in favour of the scholarly study of early poets and other antiquarian pursuits. For poetry has dried up when it is represented by an effusion like that of Pankrates[119] urging Hadrian to name a certain lotus after Antinoos, asserting that the flower had sprung from the blood of a lion which the emperor, together with Antinoos, had killed near Alexandria. Old formulae are mechanically repeated according to most of the rules. It is notable that even the flatteries of such Greek poets, addressed to the emperor, are archaistic. For their forms of address to the emperor they went back to addresses to gods and kings in Homer, the Homeric hymns, and Pindar.[120] But the poets were not significant. The mark of the age was the great rhetors giving public performances in the cities of the Roman Empire, men like Dio Chrysostom or Aelius Aristides,

116. *Epp.* 6. 21.   117. *Epp.* 1. 16.
118. *vita Hadriani* 1. 5; 16. 2.   119. n. xv Heitsch.
120. See especially Opelt (1960).

to the fawning and tumult of admiring crowds. The despair of
Marcus Aurelius turning from rhetoric to philosophy is easy to
understand. In the first book of the *Meditations*, he lists the
blessings he has had from the gods, and among them is this (17.
4–5): 'that I did not make further progress in rhetoric and poetry
and those other studies in which I would probably have become
absorbed if I had seen myself proceeding easily along that road'.

Pliny, and others, must have foreseen something of the decliv-
ity on which they barely kept their feet, but he sounds optimistic,
sometimes despite what one senses was his better judgement. He
wrote on the subject of archaizing taste to Caninius Rufus (6.
21): 'I am among those who admire the ancients, without, however, as some do, despising the geniuses of our own times. And
it is simply not true that Nature, as if she were tired and exhausted, is now producing nothing worthy of praise'. The phrasing is like that of someone who hopes to convince himself no less
than his audience: and what is his evidence? It is that he lately
heard Vergilius Romanus reading to a select gathering a comedy
written so closely on the model of Old Comedy that it could at
some future time itself serve as a model of the literary form. It is
hard to imagine anything less encouraging. This is already the
world of Hadrian, admirer of Ennius above Virgil, *Graeculus*,
and *omnium curiositatum explorator*.[121]

Even more is it the world of Fronto and Aulus Gellius, who
carried the interest in archaic literature to its logical conclusion
by treating it as the ultimate model and exemplar. They were
doing no more than continue a trend that had been growing
throughout the first century A.D.; a previously existing taste for
the archaic was ready for them to build on. This is sometimes
denied, and Fronto is elevated into a great originating genius.[122]
But it was no accident that the taste for archaic literature was

121. Tertullian *Apol.* 5. 7.
122. This is the thesis of Marache (1952), who draws a sharp distinction
between a preference for dead writers (which is his characterization of
archaism in the first century A.D.) and the use of archaic writers as a model.
But the former lays the ground for the latter, and, in particular, he ignores
the important evidence in Pliny's *Letters*.

growing over the same period during which Greek culture was assuming a dominant position in Rome. The central importance of that fact is shown by Horace's *Epistle to Augustus*. There he took great trouble to demonstrate that the analogy of Greek literature, where excellence was attained at a very early period, had no relevance for Roman literature.[123] There were clearly already in Rome literary men who were using the critical attitudes of writers like Dionysius of Halicarnassus to support their own preference for the archaic literature of Rome, and some of them, no doubt, were doing no more than ape in Roman terms Greek habits of thought. In this way Greek culture not only overbore Romans by its own inherent power, but it actually encouraged Romans to destroy the strength of their own great Classical tradition by looking back over it, on the Greek analogy, to its primitive beginnings in the third and second centuries B.C. Those two factors in Roman literary decline gained strength from combination. It was in the atmosphere of despair created by the operation of these factors, and of the others discussed above, that Romans elaborated the various myths of decline (examined in the first lecture). Myths of decline are often the best means people have of achieving a spirit of resignation that will enable them to face a situation which causes them to feel despair but which they feel compelled to regard as inevitable. So it was with Romans in the period of the early Empire.

123. See Williams (1968), 71–76.

Select Bibliography

Albertini, E. *La Composition dans les Ouvrages philosophiques de Sénèque.* Paris 1923.

Albrecht, Michael von. *Silius Italicus: Freiheit und Gebundenheit Römischer Epik.* Amsterdam 1964.

———. 'Gleichnis und Innenwelt in Silius' Punica', *Hermes* 91 (1963) 352–75.

———. 'Claudia Quinta bei Silius Italicus und bei Ovid', *Der altsprachliche Unterricht* 11 (1968) 76–95.

Alexander, Paul J. 'Letters and Speeches of the Emperor Hadrian', *HSCP* 49 (1938) 141–77.

Alexander, W. H. 'The Professor's Deadly Vengeance', *Univ. of Toronto Quarterly* 4 (1934–35) 239–58.

Allen, Katharine. 'The Fasti of Ovid and the Augustan Propaganda', *AJP* 43 (1922) 250–66.

Anderson, William S. 'Imagery in Horace and Juvenal', *AJP* 81 (1960) 225–60.

———. 'Part versus Whole in Persius' Fifth Satire', *Philological Quarterly* 39 (1960) 66–81.

———. 'The programs of Juvenal's later books', *CP* 57 (1962) 145–60.

———. 'Multiple change in the *Metamorphoses*', *TAPA* 94 (1963) 1–27.

———. 'Talaria and Ovid *Met.* 10. 591', *TAPA* 97 (1966) 1–13.

———. '*Lascivia* vs. *ira*: Martial and Juvenal', *CSCA* 3 (1970) 1–34.

———. 'Recent work in Roman Satire (1962–68)', *CW* 63 (1970) 181–99, 217–22.

———. *Ovid's 'Metamorphoses' Books 6–10.* Univ. of Oklahoma Press 1972.

Auerbach, Erich. *Literary Language and its Public in Late Latin Antiquity and in the Middle Ages.* Bollingen Series LXXIV. 1965.

Austin, R. G. *Quintiliani Institutionis Oratoriae Liber XII.* Oxford 1954.

Avery, Mary M. *The Use of Direct Speech in Ovid's Metamorphoses*. Illinois 1937.

Aymard, Jacques. *Quelques Séries de Comparaisons chez Lucain*. Montpellier 1951.

Baldwin, Barry. 'Executions under Claudius: Seneca's *Ludus de Morte Claudii*', *Phoenix* 18 (1964) 39–48.

———. 'Rulers and Ruled at Rome: A.D. 14–192', *Ancient Society* 3 (1972) 149–63.

———. *Studies in Lucian*. Toronto 1973.

Bardon, H. *Les Empereurs et les Lettres Latines d'Auguste à Hadrien*. Paris 1940.

———. *La Littérature Latine Inconnue: II. L'Époque Impériale*. Paris 1956.

———. 'Le goût à l'époque des Flaviens', *Latomus* 21 (1962) 732–48.

Barwick, Karl. 'Der Dialogus de Oratoribus des Tacitus', *BVSA* 101 (1954) nr. 4.

———. 'Martial und die zeitgenössische Rhetorik', *BVSA* 104 (1959) 3–48.

Bassett, Edward L. 'Hercules and the Hero of the Punica', in *The Classical Tradition: Literary and Historical Studies in Honor of Harry Caplan*, edited by L. Wallach. New York 1966.

Beaujeu, Jean. 'Pline le Jeune 1955–1960', *Lustrum* 6 (1961) 272–312.

Beikircher, H. *Kommentar zur VI. Satire des A. Persius Flaccus. Wiener Studien*: Beiheft 1. 1969.

Benjamin, Anna S. 'The Altars of Hadrian in Athens and Hadrian's Panhellenic Program', *Hesperia* 32 (1963) 57–86.

Berlinger, Leo. 'Beiträge zur inoffiziellen Titulatur der römischen Kaiser.' Dissertation. Breslau 1935.

Bieler, L. 'Nachaugusteische nichtchristliche Dichter: II von Hadrian bis zum Ausgang des Altertums', *Lustrum* 2 (1957) 207–307.

Boissier, Gaston. *L'Opposition sous les Césars*. Paris 1875.

Bonner, Stanley F. *Roman Declamation in the Late Republic and Early Empire*. Liverpool 1949.

———. 'Lucan and the Declamation Schools', *AJP* 87 (1966) 257–89.

Booth, Wayne C. *A Rhetoric of Irony*. Chicago 1974.

Born, L. K. 'Animate Law in the Republic and the *Laws* of Cicero', *TAPA* 64 (1933) 128–37.

Bowersock, G. W. *Augustus and the Greek World*. Oxford 1965.

———. *Greek Sophists in the Roman Empire*. Oxford 1969.

———. 'A Date in the *Eighth Eclogue*', *HSCP* 75 (1971) 73–80.

Bowie, E. L. 'Greeks and their Past in the Second Sophistic', *Past and Present* 46 (1970) 3–41.

Bringman, Klaus. 'Aufbau und Absicht des taciteischen Dialogus de oratoribus', *MH* 27 (1970) 164–78.

Brisset, J. *Les Idées Politiques de Lucain*. Paris 1964.

Bruère, R. T. 'Lucan's Cornelia', *CP* 46 (1951) 221–36.

————. 'Tacitus and Pliny's *Panegyricus*', *CP* 49 (1954) 161–79.

————. 'Color Ovidianus in Silius *Punica* I–VII', in *Ovidiana*, edited by N. I. Herescu. Paris 1958, 475–99.

————. 'Color Ovidianus in Silius *Punica* VIII–XVII', *CP* 54 (1959) 228–45.

Brunt, P. A. and Moore, J. M. *Res Gestae Divi Augusti*. Oxford 1967.

Bücheler, F. 'Zur höfischen Poesie unter Nero', *RhM* 26 (1871) 235–40.

Buchheit, V. 'Statius' Geburtstagsgedicht zu Ehren Lucans (Silv. 2, 7)', *Hermes* 88 (1960) 231–49.

————. 'Mythos und Geschichte in Ovids Metamorphosen 1', *Hermes* 94 (1966) 80–108.

Büchner, K. 'Aufbau und Sinn von Senecas Schrift über die Clementia', *Hermes* 98 (1970) 203–23.

Burck, Erich. 'Die Schicksalsauffassung des Tacitus und Statius', in *Studies presented to D. M. Robinson*, St. Louis 1953, II. 693–706.

————. *Vom Römischen Manierismus*. Darmstadt 1971.

Butler, H. E. *Post-Augustan Poetry*. Oxford 1909.

Callebat, Louis. 'L'Archaïsme dans les *Métamorphoses* d'Apulée', *REL* 42 (1964) 346–61.

Cameron, A. 'Tacitus and the Date of Curiatius Maternus' Death', *CR* 17 (1967) 258–61.

Cancik, H. *Untersuchungen zur lyrischen Kunst des P. Papinius Statius*. Hildesheim 1965.

Canter, H. V. *Rhetorical Elements in the Tragedies of Seneca*. Illinois 1925.

Caplan, H. 'The Decay of Eloquence at Rome in the First Century', in *Studies in Speech and Drama in Honor of Alexander M. Drummond*, Ithaca 1944, 295–325.

Charlesworth, M. P. 'Providentia and Aeternitas', *HTS* 29 (1936) 107–32.

————. 'Flaviana', *JRS* 27 (1937) 54–62.

————. 'The Virtues of a Roman Emperor', *PBA* 23 (1937) 105–33.

————. 'The Refusal of Divine Honours', *PBSR* 15 (1939) 1–10.

————. 'Nero: Some Aspects', *JRS* 40 (1950) 69–76.

Cichorius, C. *Rom und Mytilene*. Leipzig 1888.

————. *Römische Studien*. Leipzig-Berlin 1922.

Ciulei, Georghe. 'Die xii Tafeln und die römische Gesandtschaft nach Griechenland', *ZSS: Röm. Abt.* 64 (1944) 350 ff.

Clark, D. L. 'Imitation: Theory and Practice in Roman Rhetoric', *Quarterly Journal of Speech* 27 (1951) 11–22.

Clarke, M. L. *Rhetoric at Rome*. London 1953.

————. 'Quintilian: A biographical sketch', *G&R* 14 (1967) 24–37.

Coccia, M. *I problemi del De Ira di Seneca alla luce dell' analisi stilistica*. Roma 1957.

Coffey, Michael. 'Seneca Tragedies: Report for the years 1922–1955', *Lustrum* 2 (1957) 113–303.

———. 'Seneca, Apocolocyntosis 1922–1958', *Lustrum* 6 (1961) 239–311.

———. 'Juvenal: Report for the years 1941–1961', *Lustrum* 8 (1963) 161–270.

Coleman, R. 'Structure and Intention in the *Metamorphoses*', *CQ* 21 (1971) 461–77.

Cook, A. B. *Zeus: A Study in Ancient Religion*. London 1914–1940.

Cousin, Jean. 'Quintilien 1935–1959', *Lustrum* 7 (1962) 289–343.

Cramer, F. H. *Astrology in Roman Law and Politics*. Philadelphia 1954.

Crook, J. *Consilium Principis*. Cambridge 1955.

Crosthwaite, R. E. (= Fantham, Elaine). 'Some Expressions of Politeness in Plautus and their Historical Background.' Dissertation for B.Litt. Oxford 1956.

Cupaivolo, Giovanni. 'Gli studi su Seneca nel triennio 1969–1971', *Bollettino di Studi Latini* 2 (1972) 278–317.

Currie, H. Mac L. 'The Younger Seneca's Style: Some Observations', *BICS* 13 (1966) 76–87.

Curtius, E. *European Literature and the Latin Middle Ages*. Trans. W. R. Trask. London 1953.

D'Agostino, Vittorio. 'Seneca Filosofo e Tragico negli anni 1953–1965: Saggio bibliografico', *Riv. Stud. Class.* 14 (1966) 61–81.

Dams, Peter. 'Dichtungskritik bei nachaugusteischer Dichtern.' Dissertation. Marburg/Lahn 1970.

Davies, C. 'Poetry in the "Circle" of Messalla', *G&R* 20 (1973) 25–35.

Debrunner, A., and Sherer, A. *Geschichte der griechische Sprache* II. Berlin 1969.

De Decker, Josué. *Juvenalis Declamans*. Gand 1913.

Degrassi, A. *Inscriptiones Italiae*: vol. XIII. *Fasti et Elogia*. Roma 1963.

De Lacy, P. 'Stoic views of poetry', *AJP* 69 (1948) 241–71.

den Boer, W. 'Religion and Literature in Hadrian's Policy' *Mnemosyne* 8 (1955) 123–44.

Dessen, Cynthia. *Iunctura Callidus Acri: A Study of Persius' Satires*. Illinois 1968.

de Zulueta, F. *The Institutes of Gaius*. Oxford 1946–1953.

Dill, Samuel. *Roman Society from Nero to Marcus Aurelius*. London 1911.

Dodds, E. R. *The Greeks and the Irrational*. California 1951.

Dölger, Fr. J. 'Gladiatorenblut und Martyrblut', *Vorträge der Bibliothek Warburg* 1 (1923–24) 196–214.

———. 'Antike Parallelen zum leidenden Dinocrates in der Passio Perpetuae', *Antike u. Christentum* 2 (1930) 1–40.

Due, Otto Steen. 'An Essay on Lucan', *Classica et Mediaevalia* 23 (1962) 68–132.

Durry, Marcel. *Pline le Jeune: Panégyrique de Trajan.* Paris 1938.

Eckardt, Liselotte. 'Exkurse und Ekphraseis bei Lucan.' Dissertation. Heidelberg 1936.

Endt, Johann. 'Der Gebrauch der Apostrophe bei den lateinischen Epikern', *WS* 27 (1905) 106–29.

Fahz, Ludovicus. 'De poetarum Romanorum doctrina magica.' Dissertation. Giessen 1904.

Faider, Paul. 'La Vie Littéraire à Rome sous le Regne de Neron: Le Rêve de Sénèque'. *LEC* 3 (1934) 3–16.

Farnell, L. R. *The Cults of the Greek States.* Oxford 1896–1909.

Festugière, P. *La Révélation d'Hermès Trismégiste*: I.*L'Astrologie et les Sciences Occultes.* 2d ed. Paris 1950.

Focke, Friedrich. 'Synkrisis', *Hermes* 58 (1923) 327–68.

Fraenkel, Eduard. 'Lucan als Mittler des antiken Pathos', *Vorträge der Bibliothek Warburg* 4 (1924) 229–257 (*Kleine Beiträge* II. 233–66).

———. *Aeschylus: Agamemnon.* Oxford 1950.

———. *Horace.* Oxford 1957.

———. *Elementi Plautini in Plauto.* Firenze 1960.

———. *Beobachtungen zu Aristophanes.* Roma 1962.

Fränkel, Hermann. *Ovid: A Poet between Two Worlds.* California 1945.

Frank, Tenney. 'Curiatius Maternus and his Tragedies', *AJP* 58 (1937) 225–29.

Fraser, P. M. 'Eratosthenes of Cyrene', *PBA* 55 (1971) 175–207.

Friedlaender, L. *Darstellungen aus der Sittengeschichte Roms.* 10th ed. (rev. G. Wissowa). Leipzig 1921–23.

Friedrich, Gustav. 'Zu Seneca und Martial', *Hermes* 45 (1910) 583–94.

Friedrich, W.-H. 'Untersuchungen zu Senecas dramatischer Technik.' Dissertation. Freiburg i, Br. 1933.

———. 'Cato, Caesar und Fortuna bei Lucan', *Hermes* 73 (1938) 391–423.

Fritz, K. von. 'Aufbau und Absicht des Dialogus de Oratoribus', *RhM* 81 (1932) 275–300.

Galinsky, G. Karl. 'The Cipus Episode in Ovid's *Metamorphoses* (15. 565–621)', *TAPA* 98 (1967) 181–91.

Garson, R. W. 'The Hylas Episode in Valerius Flaccus' *Argonautica CQ* 13 (1963) 260–67.

———. 'Some Critical Observations on Valerius Flaccus' *Argonautica*': I. *CQ* 14 (1964) 267–79; II. *CQ* 15 (1965) 104–120.

Getty, Robert J. 'The date of composition of the *Argonautica* of Valerius Flaccus', *CP* 31 (1936) 53–61.

———. 'The introduction to the *Argonautica* of Valerius Flaccus', *CP* 35 (1940) 259–73.

Goold, G. P. 'A Greek professional circle at Rome', *TAPA* 92 (1961) 168–92.

Gow, A. S. F. and Page, D. L. *The Greek Anthology: Hellenistic Epigrams.* Cambridge 1965.

———. *The Greek Anthology: The Garland of Philip.* Cambridge 1968.

Grimal, P. 'L'Éloge de Néron au début de la Pharsale', *REL* 38 (1960) 296–305.

Grube, G. M. A. *The Greek and Roman Critics.* London 1965.

Guillemin, A. 'L'Imitation dans les littératures antiques et en particulier dans la littérature Latine', *REL* 2 (1924) 35–57.

———. 'Sociétés de gens de lettres au temps de Pline', *REL* 5 (1927) 261–92.

———. 'La critique littéraire au Ier. siècle de l'empire', *REL* 6 (1928) 136–80.

———. *Pline et la Vie Littéraire de son Temps.* Paris 1929.

———. 'Le public et la vie littéraire à Rome au temps de la République', *REL* 12 (1934) 52–71, 329–43.

———. 'La culture du public Romain à l'Époque Imperiale', *REL* 15 (1937) 102–21.

———. *Le Public et la Vie Littéraire à Rome.* Paris 1937.

———. 'Le satirique Perse', *LEC* 7 (1938) 161–67.

———. 'L'inspiration Virgilienne dans la Pharsale', *REL* 29 (1951) 214–27.

———. 'Sénèque Directeur d'Ames I: L'Idéal', *REL* 30 (1952) 202–19.

———. 'Sénèque Directeur d'Ames II: Son Activité Pratique', *REL* 31 (1953) 215–34.

———. 'Sénèque Directeur d'Ames III: Les Théories Littéraires', *REL* 32 (1954) 250–74.

———. 'Sénèque Second Fondateur de la Prose Latine', *REL* 35 (1957) 265–84.

———. 'Ciceron et Quintilien', *REL* 37 (1959) 184–94.

Guite, Harold. 'Cicero's Attitude to the Greeks', *G&R* 9 (1962) 142–59.

Güngerich, R. 'Der *Dialogus* des Tacitus und Quintilians *Institutio Oratoria*', *CP* 46 (1951) 159–64.

———. Review of Barwick (1954) in *Gnomon* 27 (1955) 439–43.

———. 'Tacitus' Dialogus und der Panegyricus des Plinius', *Festschrift für B. Snell z. 60 Geburtstag*, edited by H. Erbse, München 1956, 145–52.

Haakanson, Lennart. *Statius' Silvae: Critical and Exegetical Remarks with some Notes on the Thebaid.* Lund 1969.

Hahn, Ludwig. *Rom und Romanismus im griechisch-römischen Osten.* Leipzig 1906.

———. *Zum Sprachenkampf im römischen Reich. Philologus*-Suppl. Bd. 10. 4 (1907) 677–718.

Hammer, J. *Prolegomena to an Edition of the Panegyricus Messallae.* New York 1925.

Hanslik, R. Article in P-W, vol 8A, cols. 131–157 on M. Valerius Messalla Corvinus.

————. 'Der Dichterkreis des Messalla', *Anzeiger der österreichische Akad. d. Wiss.: Phil.-Hist. Kl.* 89 (1953) 22–38.

————. 'Forschungsbericht: Plinius der Jüngere', *Anzeiger für die Altertumswissenschaft*, Wien 2 (1955) 1–18.

Hass-von Reitzenstein, U. 'Beiträge zur gattungsgeschichtlichen Interpretatin des Dialogus de oratoribus'. Dissertation. Köln 1970.

Hauser, Arnold. *Mannerism.* London 1965.

Häussler, R. 'Zum Umfang und Aufbau des Dialogus de oratoribus', *Philologus* 113 (1969) 24–67.

Heinen, Hubert. 'Zur Begründung des römischen Kaiserkultes', *Klio* 11 (1911) 129–77.

Heinze, Richard. *Vom Geist des Römertums.* 3rd ed., edited by E. Burck. Darmstadt 1960.

Heitsch, Ernst. *Die griechischen Dichterfragmente der römischen Kaiserzeit.* Göttingen: I (2nd. ed.) 1963; II 1964.

Helm, R. 'De P. Papinii Statii Thebaide'. Dissertation. Berlin 1892.

————. 'Nachaugusteische nichtchristliche Dichter: I. von Tiberius bis Trajan. 1925–1942', *Lustrum* 1 (1956) 121–318; 2 (1957) 187–206.

Henss, Dietrich. 'Die Imitationstechnik des Persius', *Philologus* 99 (1955) 277–94.

Herzog-Hauser, G. 'Kaiserkult', P-W Suppl. Bd. 4 cols. 806–53.

Hillscher, Alfredus. 'Hominum Litteratorum Graecorum ante Tiberii mortem in Urbe Roma Commoratorum historia critica', *Jahrb. f. class. Philol. Suppl. Bd.* 18 (1892) 355–444.

Holleaux, Maurice. 'Discours de Néron prononcé à Corinthe pour rendre aux Grecs la Liberté', *BCH* 12 (1888) 510–28.

Hollis, A. S. *Ovid Metamorphoses Book VIII.* Oxford 1970.

————. 'The *Ars Amatoria* and *Remedia Amoris*', in *Ovid*, edited by J. W. Binns. Greek and Latin Studies. London 1973, 84–115.

Hooper, R. 'A Stylistic Investigation into the Third and Fourth Books of the Corpus Tibullianum'. Ph.D. dissertation. Yale University 1975.

Howard, Donald R. 'Renaissance World-Alienation', in *The Darker Vision of the Renaissance*, edited by Robert S. Kinsman. California 1974, 47–76.

Jacobson, H. *Ovid's Heroides.* Princeton 1974.

Jal, P. 'Images d'Auguste chez Sénèque', *REL* 35 (1957) 242–64.

Jones, C. P. *Plutarch and Rome.* Oxford 1971.

Judeich, Walther. *Topographie von Athen.* Munich 1931.

Kennedy, George. 'An estimate of Quintilian', *AJP* 83 (1962) 130–46.

————. 'The rhetoric of advocacy in Greece and Rome', *AJP* 89 (1968) 419–36.

————. *Quintilian.* New York 1969.

————. *The Art of Rhetoric in the Roman World 300 B.C.-A.D. 300.* Princeton 1972.

Kenney, E. J. 'The First Satire of Juvenal', *PCPS* n.s. 8 (1962) 29–40.

———. 'The Poetry of Ovid's Exile', *PCPS* n.s. 11 (1965) 37–49.

Kirchner, J. *Imagines Inscriptionum Atticarum.* 2d ed. Berlin 1948.

Klauser, Theodor. 'Der Übergang der römischen Kirche von der griechischen zur lateinischen Liturgiesprache', in *Miscellanea Giovanni Mercati,* vol. I (*Studi e Testi* 121). Vatican 1946, 467–82.

Klingner, Friedrich. 'Beobachtungen über Sprache und Stil des Tacitus am Anfang des 13. Annalenbuches', *Hermes* 83 (1955) 187–200.

Klotz, Alfred. 'Klassizismus und Archaismus. Stilistisches zu Statius', *ALL* 15 (1906) 401–17.

Knoche, Ulrich. 'Senecas Atreus, ein Beispiel', *Die Antike* 17 (1941) 60–76.

Köhnken, Adolf. 'Das Problem der Ironie bei Tacitus', *MH* 30 (1973) 32–50.

Korzeniewski, D. 'Zur Verstechnik des Phaedrus', *Hermes* 98 (1970) 430–58.

Kraus, Walther. 'Die Briefpaare in Ovids Heroiden', *WS* 65 (1952) 54–77.

Kroll, Wilhelm. *Studien zum Verständnis der römischen Literatur.* Stuttgart 1924.

Kröner, Hans-Otto. 'Zu den künstlerischen Absichten des Valerius Flaccus', *Hermes* 96 (1969) 733–54.

Krumbholz, Gert. 'Der Erzählungsstil in der Thebais des Statius', *Glotta* 34 (1955) 93–139, 231–60.

Kruuse, Jens. 'L'Originalité artistique de Martial', *Classica et Mediaevalia* 4 (1941) 248–300.

Kunkel, W. *Introduction to Roman Legal and Constitutional History.* Oxford 1966.

Kytzler, Bernhard. 'Beobachtungen zum Prooemium der Thebais', *Hermes* 88 (1960) 331–54.

———. 'Gleichnisgruppen in der Thebais des Statius', *WS* 75 (1962) 141–60.

———. 'Der Bittgang der argivischen Frauen', *Der altsprachliche Unterricht* 2 (1968) 50–61.

———. 'Imitatio und Aemulatio in der Thebais des Statius', *Hermes* 97 (1969) 209–32.

Last, Hugh. 'The Social Policy of Augustus': Chapter XIV of *CAH,* vol. 10. Cambridge 1934.

Leeman, A. D. *Orationis Ratio: The Stylistic Theories and Practice of the Roman Orators, Historians and Philosophers.* Amsterdam 1963.

———. 'Das Todeserlebnis im Denken Senecas', *Gymnasium* 78 (1971) 322–33.

Lefèvre, Eckard. 'Schicksal und Selbstverschuldung in Senecas Agamemnon,' *Hermes* 94 (1966) 482–96.

———. 'Die Bedeutung des Paradoxen in der römischen Literatur der frühen Kaiserzeit', *Poetica* 3 (1970) 59–82.

———. 'Das Prooemium der Argonautica des Valerius Flaccus', *AAM* (1971) nr. 6, 1–70.

Legras, L. *Étude sur la Thébaide de Stace.* Paris 1905.

———. 'Les "Puniques" et la "Thébaide" ', *REA* 7 (1905) 131–46, 357–71.

———. 'Les dernières années de Stace', *REA* 9 (1907) 338–48; 10 (1908) 36–70.

Leo, Fr. Review of A. Gudeman, ed. Tacitus *Dialogus* (Boston 1894), *GGA* (1898) 169–88 (= *Ausgewählte Kleine Schriften*, Roma 1960, II. 277–98).

Lepper, F. A. 'Some reflections on the "Quinquennium Neronis" ', *JRS* 47 (1957) 95–103.

Lipking, Lawrence. *The Ordering of the Arts in Eighteenth Century England.* Princeton 1970.

Little, Douglas. 'The Speech of Pythagoras in Metamorphoses 15 and the Structure of the Metamorphoses', *Hermes* 98 (1970) 340–60.

Luck, G. 'Die Schrift vom Erhabenen und ihr Verfasser', *Arctos* 5 (1967) 97–113.

Lundström, Sven. *"Sprach's" bei Silius Italicus.* Lund 1971.

Lutz, Cora E. 'Musonius Rufus "The Roman Socrates" ', *YCS* 10 (1947) 3–147.

McAlindon, D. 'Senatorial Opposition to Claudius and Nero', *AJP* 77 (1956) 113–32.

McGann, M. J. *Studies in Horace's First Book of Epistles.* Collection Latomus C. Brussels 1969.

McKeon, Richard. 'Literary criticism and the concept of imitation in antiquity', *Modern Philology* 34 (1936) 1–35.

MacMullen, Ramsay. *Soldier and Civilian in the Later Roman Empire.* Harvard 1963.

———. *Enemies of the Roman Order.* Harvard 1966.

Marache, René. *La Critique Littéraire de Langue Latine et le Développement du Goût Archaïsant au IIe Siècle de notre Ère.* Rennes 1952.

———. *Mots Nouveaux et Mots Archaïques chez Fronton et Aulu-Gelle.* Rennes 1952.

———. 'La révolte d'Ovide exilé contre Auguste', in *Ovidiana*, edited by N. I. Herescu. Paris 1958, 412–19.

Mariotti, Scevola. 'La carriera poetica di Ovidio', *Belfagor: Rassegna di Varia Umanità*, Messina-Firenze 12 (1957) 609–35.

Marti, Berthe M. 'The Meaning of the *Pharsalia*', *AJP* 66 (1945) 352–76.

———. 'Cassius Scaeva and Lucan's *inventio*', *The Classical Tradition: Literary and Historical Studies in Honor of Harry Caplan*, edited by L. Wallach. New York 1966.

Martin, J. M. K. 'Persius: Poet of the Stoics', *G&R* 8 (1939) 172–82.

Marx, F. A. 'Tacitus und die Literatur der exitus illustrium virorum', *Philologus* 92 (1937) 83–103.

Mason, H. J. 'The Roman Government in Greek Sources', *Phoenix* 24 (1970) 150–59.

Mattingly, Harold. *Coins of the Roman Empire in the British Museum*, Vol. I: *Augustus to Vitellius*. London 1923.

Mendell, C. W. 'Martial and the satiric Epigram', *CP* 17 (1922) 1–20.

———. *Tacitus, the Man and his Work*. Yale 1957.

———. *Latin Poetry: The Age of Rhetoric and Satire*. New York 1967.

Merone, E. *Sulla Lingua di Valerio Flacco*. Napoli 1957.

Mesk, Josef. 'Die Überarbeitung des Plinianischen Panegyricus auf Traian', *WS* 32 (1910) 239–60.

———. 'Zur Quellenanalyse des Plinianischen Panegyricus', *WS* 33 (1911) 71–100.

Mette, J. 'Die römische Tragödie und die Neufunde zur griechischen Tragödie, 1945–1964', *Lustrum* 9 (1964) 5–211.

Miller, N. P. 'Tiberius speaks', *AJP* 89 (1968) 1–19.

Moisy, S. von. *Untersuchungen zur Erzählweise in Statius' Thebais*. Bonn 1971.

Momigliano, A. Review of B. Farrington, *Science and Politics in the Ancient World*. London 1939 in *JRS* 31 (1941), 149–57.

———. 'Literary chronology of the Neronian age', *CQ* 38 (1944) 96–100.

———. Review of Ch. Wirszubski (1950) in *JRS* 41 (1951) 146–53.

———. *Claudius: The Emperor and his Achievement*. New York 1961.

Mommsen, Th. 'Cornelius Tacitus und Cluvius Rufus', *Hermes* 4 (1870) 295–325 (= *Gesammelte Schriften* 7. 224–52).

———. *Römisches Staatsrecht*. Leipzig 1887.

Morford, M. P. O. *The Poet Lucan*. Oxford: Blackwell 1967.

Motto, Anna Lydia. 'Recent scholarship on Seneca's prose works, 1940–1957', *CW* 54 (1960–61) 13–18, 37–48, 70–71, 111–112.

———. *Guide to the Thought of Lucius Annaeus Seneca*. Amsterdam 1970.

———. 'Seneca's prose writings: A decade of scholarship, 1958–1968', *CW* 64 (1971) 141–58, 177–86, 191.

———. *Seneca*. New York 1972.

Mulder, H. M. *Publii Papinii Statii Thebaidos Liber Secundus*. Groningen 1954.

Murray, Oswyn. 'The "Quinquennium Neronis" and the Stoics', *Historia* 14 (1965) 41–61.

Nilsson, M. P. *Geschichte der griechischen Religion*. München: vol. I^2, 1955; II^2, 1961.

Nisbet, R. G. M., and Hubbard, Margaret. *A Commentary on Horace: Odes Book 1*. Oxford 1970.

Nock, A. D. *Conversion*. Oxford 1933.

———. *Essays on Religion and the Ancient World*, edited by Zeph Stewart. Oxford 1972.

Norden, E. *Die Antike Kunstprosa*. Berlin 1918.

———. *Aus altrömischen Priesterbüchern*. Lund 1939.

———. 'Die Genesiszitat in der Schrift vom Erhabenen', *Abh. deutsch. Akad. Wiss. Berlin (Klasse Spr.-Lit.)*. Berlin 1954, nr. 1.

Norman, A. F. 'The book-trade in fourth century Antioch', *JHS* 80 (1960) 122–26.

Obermeier, J. 'Der Sprachgebrauch des M. Annaeus Lucanus.' Dissertation. München 1886.

Oliver, James H. 'On the Hellenic policy of Augustus and Agrippa in 27 B.C.', *AJP* 93 (1972) 190–97.

Oltramare, André. *Les Origines de la Diatribe Romaine*. Geneva 1926.

Opelt, Ilona. 'Zum Kaiserkult in der griechischen Dichtung', *RhM* 103 (1960) 43–56.

Page, D. L. *Greek Literary Papyri*. Loeb Classical Library. 1942.

Palm, Jonas. *Rom, Römertum und Imperium in der griechischen Literatur der Kaiserzeit*. Lund 1959.

Parks, E. Patrick. *The Roman Rhetorical Schools as a Preparation for the Courts under the Early Empire*. Baltimore 1945.

Pfeiffer, R. *History of Classical Scholarship: From the Beginnings to the End of the Hellenistic Age*. Oxford 1968.

Pfligersdorffer, G. 'Lucan als Dichter des geistigen Widerstandes', *Hermes* 87 (1959) 344–77.

Pollitt, J. J. *The Ancient View of Greek Art*. New Haven 1974.

Pratt, N. T. 'The Stoic base of Senecan drama', *TAPA* 79 (1948) 1–11.

Preston, Keith. 'Martial and formal literary criticism', *CP* 15 (1920) 340–52.

Prinz, K. *Martial und die griechische Epigrammatik: I*. Wien and Leipzig 1911.

Quadlbauer, Franz. 'Die genera dicendi bis Plinius d.J.', *WS* 71 (1958) 55–111.

Radice, Betty. 'Pliny and the *Panegyricus*', *G&R* 15 (1968) 166–72.

Rahn, Helmut. 'Ovids elegische Epistel', *Antike und Abendland* 7 (1958) 105–20.

Rayment, Charles S. 'A current survey of ancient Rhetoric', *CW* 52 (1959) 75–91.

———. 'Ancient Rhetoric (1957–1963)', *CW* 57 (1964) 241–51.

Reardon, B. P. *Courants Littéraires Grecs des IIe et IIIe Siècles après J.-C.* Paris 1971.

Reckford, Kenneth J. 'Studies in Persius', *Hermes* 90 (1962) 476–504.

Regenbogen, O. 'Schmerz und Tod in den Tragödien Senecas', *Vorträge der Bibliothek Warburg VII*. Leipzig 1930, 167–218.

———. 'Seneca als Denker römischer Willenshaltung', *Antike* 12 (1936) 107–30.

Reuter, A. 'De Quintiliani Libro qui fuit De Causis Corruptae Eloquentiae.' Dissertation. Breslau 1887.

Rice Holmes, T. *The Architect of the Roman Empire: 27* B.C.-A.D. *14.* Oxford 1931.

Rist, J. *Stoic Philosophy.* Cambridge 1969.

Robert, L. *Gladiateurs dans L'Orient Grec.* Paris 1940.

————. *Hellenica: Recueil d'épigraphie, de numismatique et d'antiquités grecques.* Limoges 1940. (Reprint. Amsterdam 1972).

Rogers, R. S. 'Fulvia Paulina C. Sentii Saturnini', *AJP* 53 (1932) 252-56.

————. 'A Tacitean pattern in narrating treason-trials', *TAPA* 83 (1952) 279-311.

————. 'A group of Domitianic treason-trials', *CP* 55 (1960) 19-23.

Ronconi, Alessandro. 'Exitus illustrium virorum', *SIFC* 17 (1940) 3-32.

Rossi, L. E. 'I generi letterari e le loro leggi scritte e non scritte nelle letterature classiche', *BICS* 18 (1971) 69-94.

Rostovtzeff, M. *The Social and Economic History of the Roman Empire.* 2d ed., edited by P. M. Fraser. Oxford 1957.

Runchina, G. 'Tecnica drammatica e retorica nelle Tragedie di Seneca', *Annali delle Facoltá di Lettere-Filosofia e Magistero dell' Universitá di Cagliari* 28 (1960) 165-324.

Russell, D. A. *'Longinus' On the Sublime.* Oxford 1964.

————. *'Longinus' On Sublimity.* Oxford 1965.

————. 'On reading Plutarch's *Moralia*', *G&R* 15 (1968) 130-46.

————, and Winterbottom, M. *Ancient Literary Criticism.* Oxford 1972.

Rutz, Werner. 'Lucan 1943-1963', *Lustrum* 9 (1964) 243-340; 10 (1965) 246-59.

————. 'Lucans Pompeius', Der altsprachliche Unterricht 2 (1968) 5-22.

————, ed. *Lucan (Wege der Forschung 235).* Darmstadt 1970.

Ryberg, Inez Scott. 'Clupeus Virtutis', in *The Classical Tradition: Literary and Historical Studies in Honor of Harry Caplan,* edited by L. Wallach. New York 1966.

Sanford, Eva M. 'Nero and the East', *HSCP* 48 (1937) 75-103.

————. 'Contrasting views of the Roman Empire', *AJP* 58 (1937) 437-56.

Saunders, C. 'The nature of Rome's early appraisal of Greek Culture', *CP* 39 (1944) 209-17.

Sauter, F. *Der römische Kaiserkult bei Martial und Statius.* Stuttgart 1934.

Schetter, Willy. *Untersuchungen zur Epischen Kunst des Statius.* Wiesbaden 1960.

————. 'Die Einheit des Prooemium zum Thebais des Statius', *MH* 19 (1962) 204-17.

Schmid, Wolfgang. 'Panegyrik und Bukolik in der neronischen Epoche', *Bonner Jahrbücher* 153 (1953) 63-96.

Schotes, Hans-Albert. 'Stoische Physik, Psychologie und Theologie bei Lucan.' Dissertation. Bonn 1969.

Schulz, Fritz. *Principles of Roman Law.* Oxford 1936.

————. *History of Roman Legal Science*. Oxford 1953.

Schumann, Gerhard. 'Hellenistische und griechische Elemente in der Regierung Neros.' Dissertation. Leipzig 1930.

Scott, K. 'Plutarch and the Ruler Cult', *TAPA* 60 (1929) 117–35.

————. 'Emperor worship in Ovid', *TAPA* 61 (1930) 43–69.

————. 'Humor at the expense of the ruler cult', *CP* 27 (1932) 317–28.

————. 'The Elder and Younger Pliny on Emperor Worship', *TAPA* 63 (1932) 156–65.

————. 'Statius' adulation of Domitian', *AJP* 54 (1933) 247–59.

————. *The Imperial Cult under the Flavians*. Stuttgart-Berlin 1936.

Seager, Robin. *Tiberius*. London 1972.

Segal, C. P. 'ΤΨΟΣ and the problem of cultural decline in the *De Sublimitate*', *HSCP* 64 (1959) 121–45.

————. 'Myth and philosophy in the *Metamorphoses*: Ovid's Augustanism and the Augustan conclusion of Book XV', *AJP* 90 (1969) 257–92.

————. 'Ovid's *Metamorphoses*: Greek Myth in Augustan Rome', *Studies in Philology* 68 (1971) 371–94.

Seitz, Konrad. 'Der pathetische Erzählstil Lucans', *Hermes* 93 (1965) 204–32.

Shearman, John. *Mannerism*. London 1967.

Sherk, R. K. *Roman Documents from the Greek East*. Baltimore 1969.

Sherwin-White, A. N. *The Letters of Pliny: A Historical and Social Commentary*. Oxford 1966.

Stanton, G. R. 'Marcus Aurelius, Emperor and Philosopher', *Historia* 18 (1969) 570–87.

Starr, Chester G. 'Epictetus and the Tyrant', *CP* 44 (1949) 20–29.

————. *Civilization and the Caesars: The Intellectual Revolution in the Roman Empire*. Ithaca, New York 1954.

Steele, R. B. 'The Astronomica of Manilius', *AJP* 53 (1932) 320–43.

Steiner, G. *Language and Silence*. London 1969.

Strand, Johnny. *Notes on Valerius Flaccus' Argonautica*. Göteborg-Stockholm 1972.

Stroux, J. 'Vier Zeugnisse zur römischen Literaturgeschichte der Kaiserzeit', *Philologus* 86 (1931) 338–68.

————. 'Die stoische Beurteilung Alexanders des Grossen', *Philologus* 88 (1933) 222–40.

Strzelecki, Ladislaus. *De Senecae Trimetro Iambico Quaestiones Selectae*. Krakow 1938.

————. 'De rei metricae Annaeanae origine quaestiones', *Eos* 53 (1963) 157–70.

Sullivan, J. P. 'Petronius, Seneca, and Lucan: A Neronian Literary Feud?', *TAPA* 99 (1968) 453–67.

Süss, Wilhelm. 'Das Problem der lateinischen Bibelsprache', *Historische Vierteljahrschrift* 27 (1932) 1–39.

Sutherland, C. H. V. *Coinage in Roman Imperial Policy 31 B.C.-A.D. 68.* London 1951.

Syme, R. 'The *Argonautica* of Valerius Flaccus', *CQ* 23 (1929) 129–37.

———. *The Roman Revolution.* Oxford 1939.

———. *Tacitus.* Oxford 1958.

———. 'Livy and Augustus', *HSCP* 64 (1959) 27–87.

———. 'Pliny the Procurator', *HSCP* 73 (1969) 201–36.

Szelest, Hanna. 'Martials satirische Epigramme und Horaz', *Das Altertum* 9 (1963) 27–37.

Taylor, L. R. 'Tiberius' refusals of divine honors', *TAPA* 60 (1929) 87–101.

———. *The Divinity of the Roman Emperor.* A.P.A. Monographs 1931.

Thiele, Georg. 'Die Poesie unter Domitian', *Hermes* 51 (1916) 233–60.

Thomas, E. 'Some Reminiscences of Ovid in later literature', *Atti del Convegno Internazionale Ovidiano*: vol. 1. Roma 1959, 145–71.

Townend, G. B. 'Cluvius Rufus in the "Histories" of Tacitus', *AJP* 85 (1964) 337–77.

Toynbee, Jocelyn M. C. 'Dictators and philosophers in the first century A.D.', *G&R* 13 (1944) 43–58.

Travlos, John. *A Pictorial Dictionary of Ancient Athens.* London 1971.

Trillitzsch, Winfried. *Seneca im literarischen Urteil der Antike.* Amsterdam 1971.

Vahlen, J. *Ennianae Poesis Reliquiae*, 2d ed. Leipzig 1903.

Van Groningen, B. A. 'General literary tendencies in the second century A.D.', *Mnemosyne* 18 (1965) 41–56.

Vessey, David. 'Statius and Antimachus: a review of the evidence', *Philologus* 114 (1970) 118–43.

———. *Statius and the Thebaid.* Cambridge 1973.

Vollmer, Fr. *P. Papinii Statii Silvarum Libri.* Leipzig 1898.

Voss, B.-R. *Der Pointierte Stil des Tacitus.* Münster 1963.

Wallach, L., ed. *The Classical Tradition: Literary and Historical Studies in Honor of Harry Caplan.* New York 1966.

Walton, C. S. 'Oriental Senators in the service of Rome', *JRS* 19 (1929) 38–66.

Wanke, Christiane. *Seneca, Lucan, Corneille: Studien zum Manierismus der röm. Kaiserzeit und der französischen Klassik.* Heidelberg 1964.

Warmington, B. H. *Nero: Reality and Legend.* London 1969.

Watson, A. *The Law of the Ancient Romans.* Dallas 1970.

Weinreich, Otto. *Studien zu Martial.* Stuttgart 1928.

Weinstock, Stefan. *Divus Julius.* Oxford 1971.

Wellek, René. *The Rise of English Literary History.* North Carolina 1941.

Wheeler, Arthur L. 'Topics from the life of Ovid', *AJP* 46 (1925) 1–28.

Whitehorn, J. E. G. 'The Elder Seneca: A review of past work', *Prudentia* 1 (1969) 14–27.

Wilamowitz, U. von 'Asianismus und Atticismus', *Hermes* 35 (1900) 1–52.
————. *Griechische Lesebuch* I. Berlin 1903.
————. 'Griechische Literatur' in *Kultur der Gegenwart*³, Berlin 1908, 1 ff.
————. *Der Glaube der Hellenen*. Basel 1956.
Wilkinson, L. P. *Ovid Recalled*. Cambridge 1955.
————. 'The World of the Metamorphoses' in *Ovidiana*, edited by N. I. Herescu. Paris 1958, 231–44.
Williams, G. W. 'Some aspects of Roman marriage ceremonies and ideals', *JRS* 48 (1958) 16–29.
————. 'Poetry in the moral climate of Augustan Rome', *JRS* 52 (1962) 28–46.
————. *Tradition and Originality in Roman Poetry*. Oxford 1968.
————. *Horace. G&R: New Surveys in the Classics*, no. 6. Oxford 1972.
Winterbottom, M. 'Quintilian and the *Vir Bonus*', *JRS* 54 (1964) 90–97.
————. *The Elder Seneca: Declamations*. Loeb Classical Library 1974.
Wirszubski, Ch. *Libertas as a Political Idea at Rome during the Late Republic and Early Principate*. Cambridge 1950.
Wistrand, E. *Die Chronologie der Punica des Silius Italicus*. Göteborg-Stockholm 1956.
Wlosok, Antonie. 'Zur Einheit der Metamorphosen des Apuleius', *Philologus* 113 (1969) 68–84.
Wölfflin, Eduard. *Ausgewählte Schriften*. Leipzig 1933.
Woodside, M. St. A. 'Vespasian's patronage of education and the arts', *TAPA* 73 (1942) 123–29.
Zingerle, A. *Zu späteren lateinischen Dichtern*. Innsbruck: I, 1873; II. 1879.
Zwierlein, Otto. *Die Rezitationsdramen Senecas*. Meisenheim am Glan 1966.

Index of Passages Discussed

General Index

ventional epicizing in, 217–218; original use of epic device in, 218, 222;
surprising and pregnant locutions in,
223–225; word play in, 224, 262; enters his own narrative, 233–234, 291;
longs to exhume Pompey and re-bury
him in Italy, 233; asserts falsely Pharsalia not in Roman calendar, 233n;
introduces didactic and satiric elements into epic, 235, 236; subjects of
sentences unclear in, 245n; composes
in episodes, 247–250; unity of his
epic, 248–249; his pleasure in information for its own sake, 262–263; no
extended personifications in, 264; his
Stoicism, 282, 290, 299
Lucian, 18n, 19n; sets dialogues in remote past, 307
Lucilius, C., 103, 106–107, 110, 111, 113,
150, 196, 275
ludi maximi, 103
'Lygdamus', 67

Maecenas, 13, 56, 57, 59, 67, 298
Magic and the occult, interest in, 180–
181, 254
Magna Mater Idaea, cult of, 105
Manilius: ignores Hellenistic poets,
151n; addresses Augustus, 299
Manner rather than matter, concentration on, 212–213, 222–223, 266–270,
293, 307–308
Marcellus, C. Claudius (nephew of Augustus), 129, 130, 135
Marcus Aurelius, the Emperor, 311
Mars Ultor, temple of, 69, 70, 75, 76
Martial, 123, 130n, 148, 150, 284; his
flattery of Domitian, 166–168; his use
of climactic *sententia*, 219–220; his
tone cool (unlike Juvenal's), 220; complains about patrons, 276–277, 301;
flatters Regulus, 276; his poems sold
in Gaul, 277; his books read in South
Russia and Britain, 277; draws material from real life, 287–288; mis-
understands Augustan poets, 289, 304;
receives *ius trium liberorum*, 301; attacks archaizers, 309
Martyr biographies, 293–294, 302
meditatio mortis, life as a, 177
Meditation, literature of, 231, 268, 304
Meleager, 128, 194

Menippus of Gadara, 307
Misunderstanding of Augustan poets,
304
Montanus, Votienus, 212
Moral explanation of decline: optimism
of, 22–23, 31, 44; popularity of, 25;
Greek formulation of by Plato, Posei-
donius, Polybius and Dionysius of
Halicarnassus, 25n
Musical performance, Roman prejudice
against, 141
Musonius Rufus, C., 145, 176
Myron's cow, theme of Greek epigrams,
194
Mystery cults, Romans initiated in, 112,
122, 180
'Mythologizing' of martyr-tales by Sen-
eca, 179
Myths of decline, function of, 312

Naples, a Greek city, 121–122
Nero: conspiracy against, 12, 144–145,
288–289; literary renaissance under,
14, 24, 164–165, 299–300; devotion to
Greek culture, 140; degenerates into
tyrant, 155; flattered by Lucan, 161–
165; persecuted by his mother's ghost,
180; his torments in Hades, 180; and
Christians, 185; his early humanity,
185n; prohibits gladiatorial shows in
Greek East, 188
Nerva, the Emperor, 155, 160; estab-
lishes the principle of adoption, 274–
275
Nicias of Cos, 113
Nicolaus of Damascus, 122, 123, 191–
192
Nicostratus (Olympic victor of A.D. 36),
37–38
νόμος ἔμψυχος, 156, 158
Nostalgia of Greeks for the past, 18–
19, 120, 148, 150–151, 307
Numbers at recitations, 303

Obscurity, interest in deliberate, 231–
232
Oedipus in Seneca, 175
Otacilius Pitholaus, M., 114
Ovid: and Maternus, 50–51; his influence on later poets, 52, 243; his autobiography, 53–55; *Amores*, 55; *Heroides*, 55; *Ars Amatoria*, 55–56, 70–

Date Due

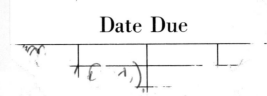